KORE
YAMAZAKI

FRAU
FAUST

1

contents

FRAU FAUST

CHAPTER 1:
THE MAN FROM the FAIRY TALE

3

CHAPTER 2:
WAITING IN the FOREST

47

CHAPTER 3:
THAT BELONGS to ME

85

THE INVISIBLE MUSEUM

125

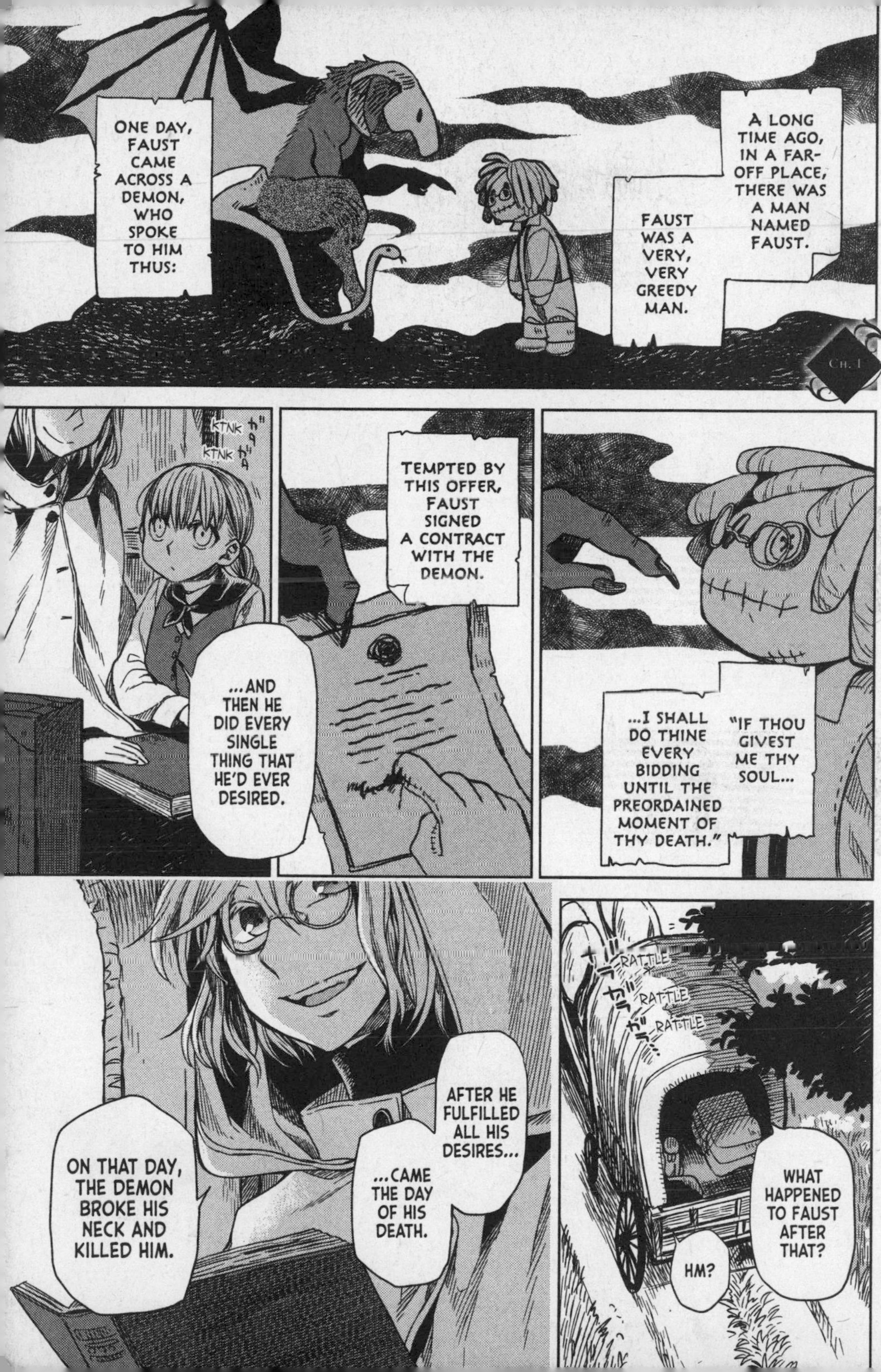
Ch. 1
A LONG TIME AGO, IN A FAR-OFF PLACE, THERE WAS A MAN NAMED FAUST.
FAUST WAS A VERY, VERY GREEDY MAN.
ONE DAY, FAUST CAME ACROSS A DEMON, WHO SPOKE TO HIM THUS:
"IF THOU GIVEST ME THY SOUL...
...I SHALL DO THINE EVERY BIDDING UNTIL THE PREORDAINED MOMENT OF THY DEATH."
TEMPTED BY THIS OFFER, FAUST SIGNED A CONTRACT WITH THE DEMON.
...AND THEN HE DID EVERY SINGLE THING THAT HE'D EVER DESIRED.
KTNK
KTNK
RATTLE
RATTLE
RATTLE
WHAT HAPPENED TO FAUST AFTER THAT?
HM?
AFTER HE FULFILLED ALL HIS DESIRES...
...CAME THE DAY OF HIS DEATH.
ON THAT DAY, THE DEMON BROKE HIS NECK AND KILLED HIM.

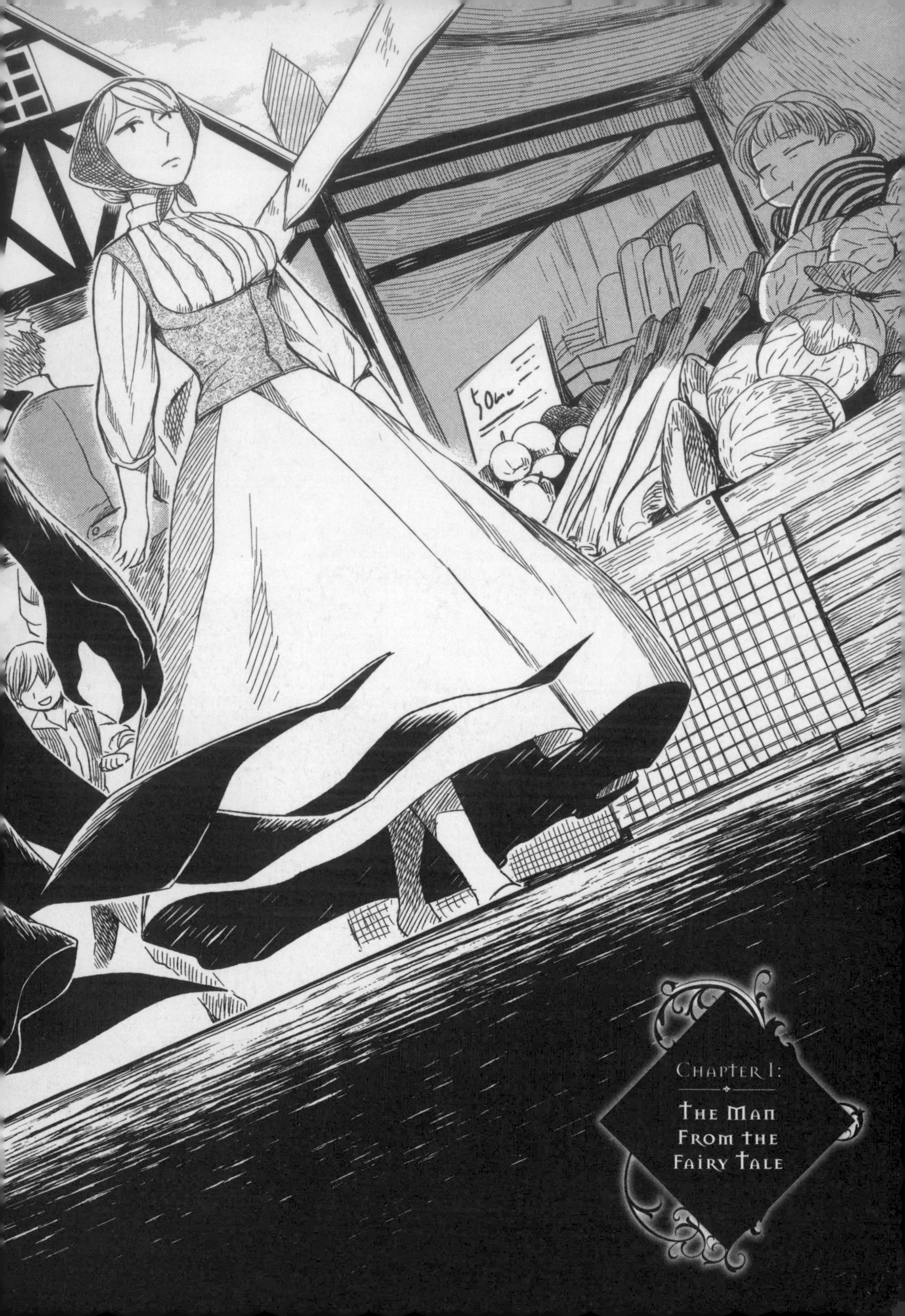
Chapter 1:
The Man From the Fairy Tale

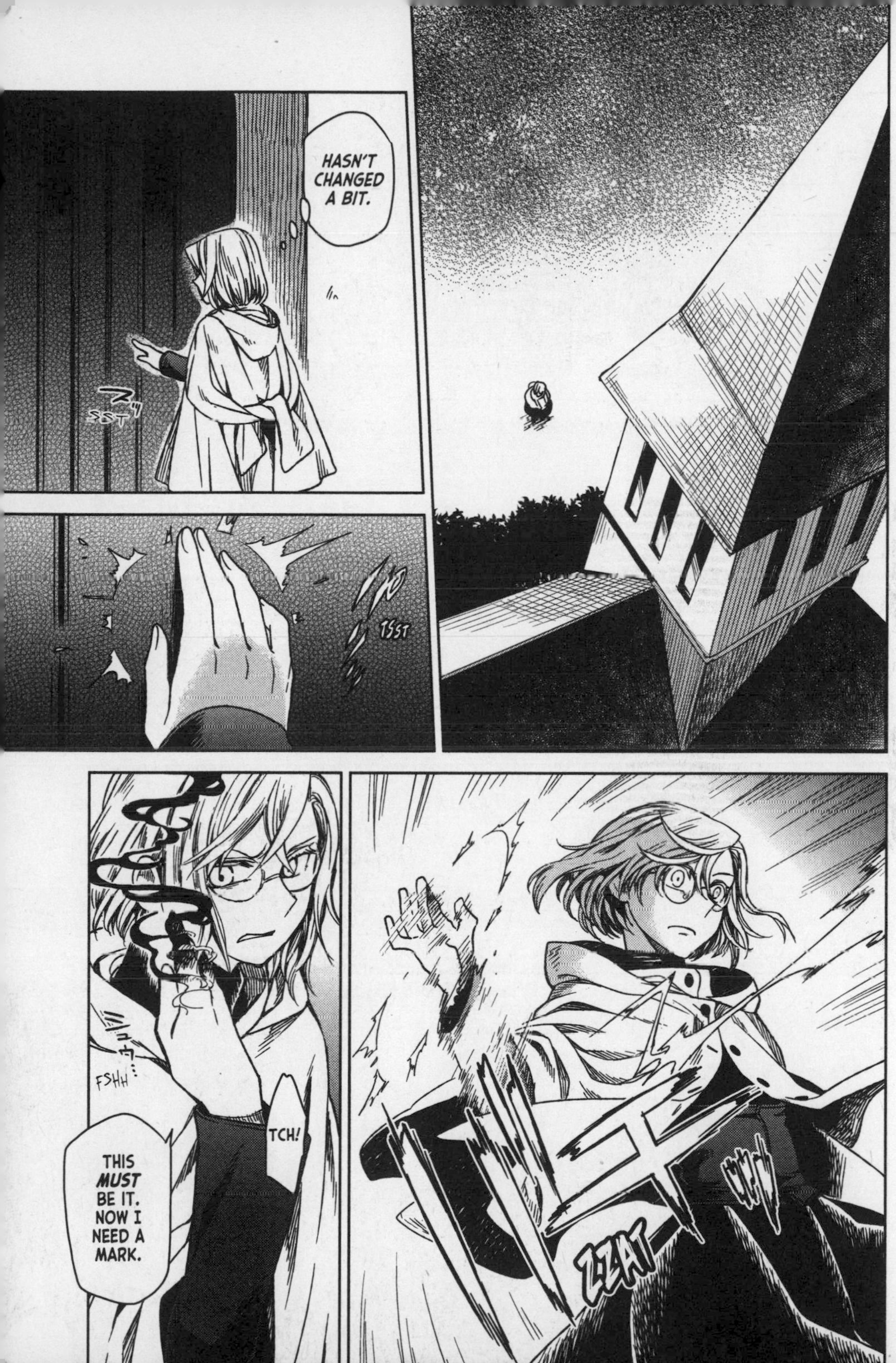
HASN'T CHANGED A BIT.
SST
TSST
ZZAT
FSHH
TCH!
THIS MUST BE IT. NOW I NEED A MARK.

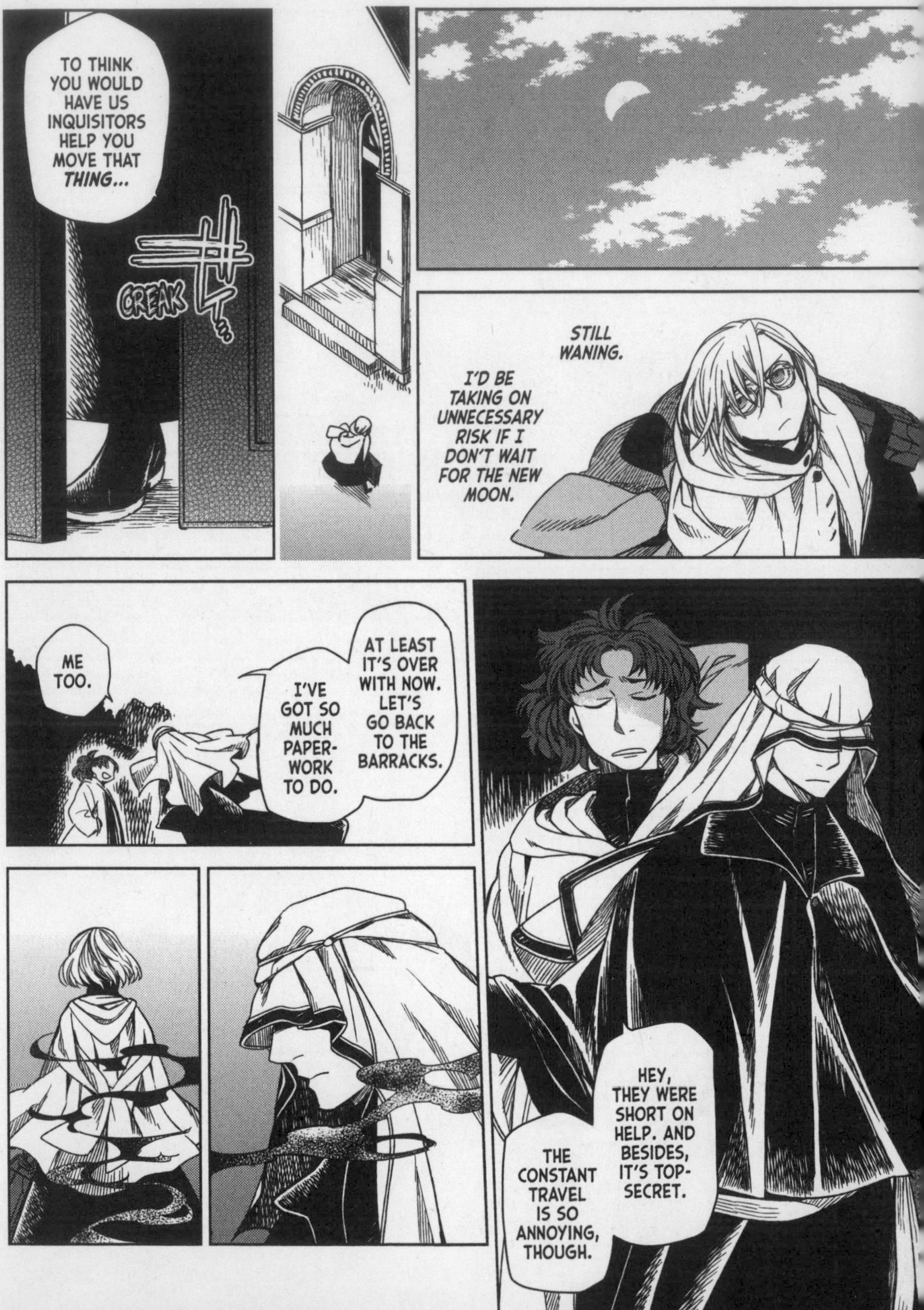
STILL WANING.
I'D BE TAKING ON UNNECESSARY RISK IF I DON'T WAIT FOR THE NEW MOON.
TO THINK YOU WOULD HAVE US INQUISITORS HELP YOU MOVE THAT THING...
CREAK
HEY, THEY WERE SHORT ON HELP. AND BESIDES, IT'S TOP-SECRET.
THE CONSTANT TRAVEL IS SO ANNOYING, THOUGH.
AT LEAST IT'S OVER WITH NOW. LET'S GO BACK TO THE BARRACKS.
I'VE GOT SO MUCH PAPER-WORK TO DO.
ME TOO.

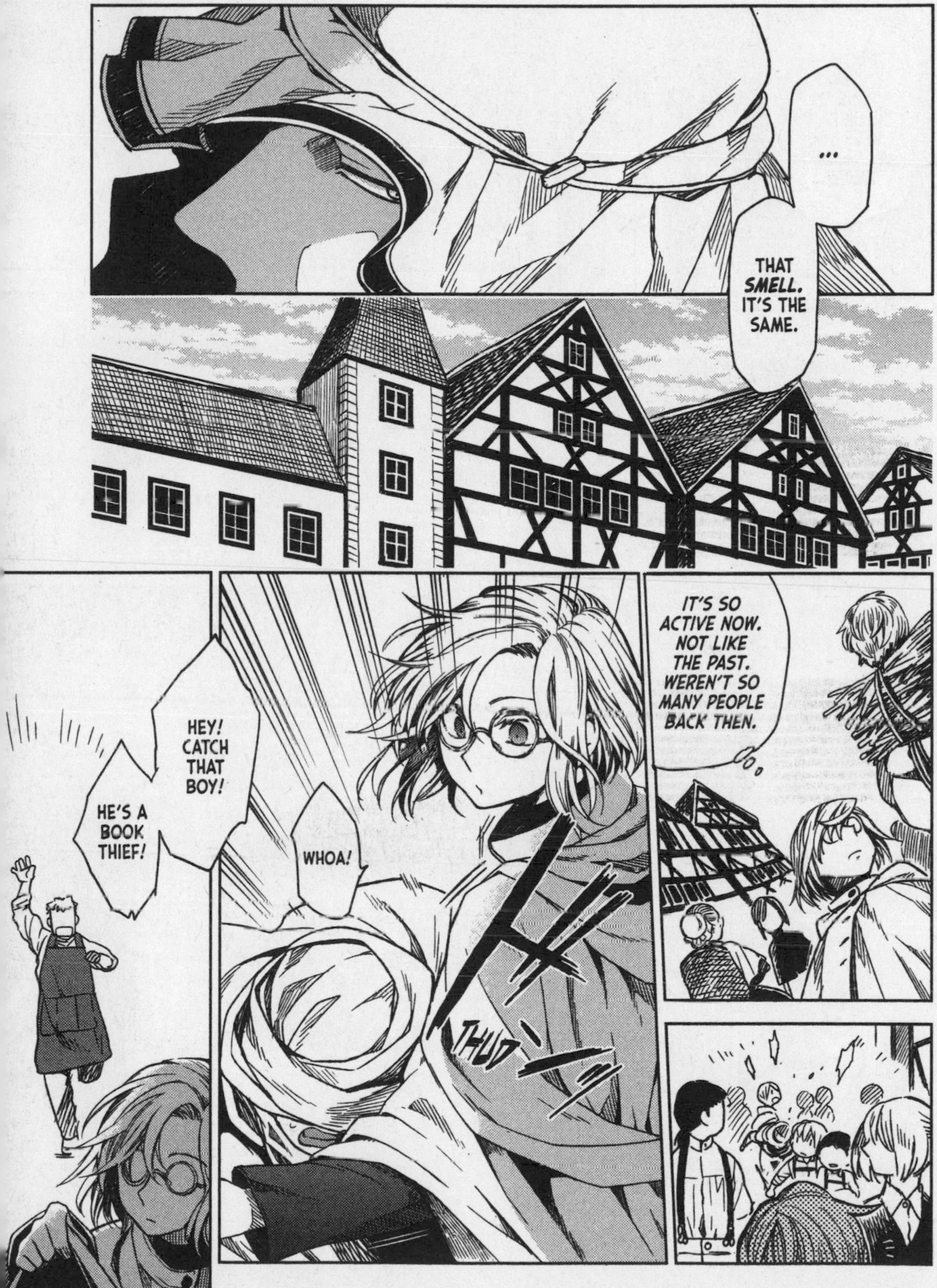
...
THAT SMELL. IT'S THE SAME.
IT'S SO ACTIVE NOW. NOT LIKE THE PAST. WEREN'T SO MANY PEOPLE BACK THEN.
WHOA!
THUD
HEY! CATCH THAT BOY!
HE'S A BOOK THIEF!

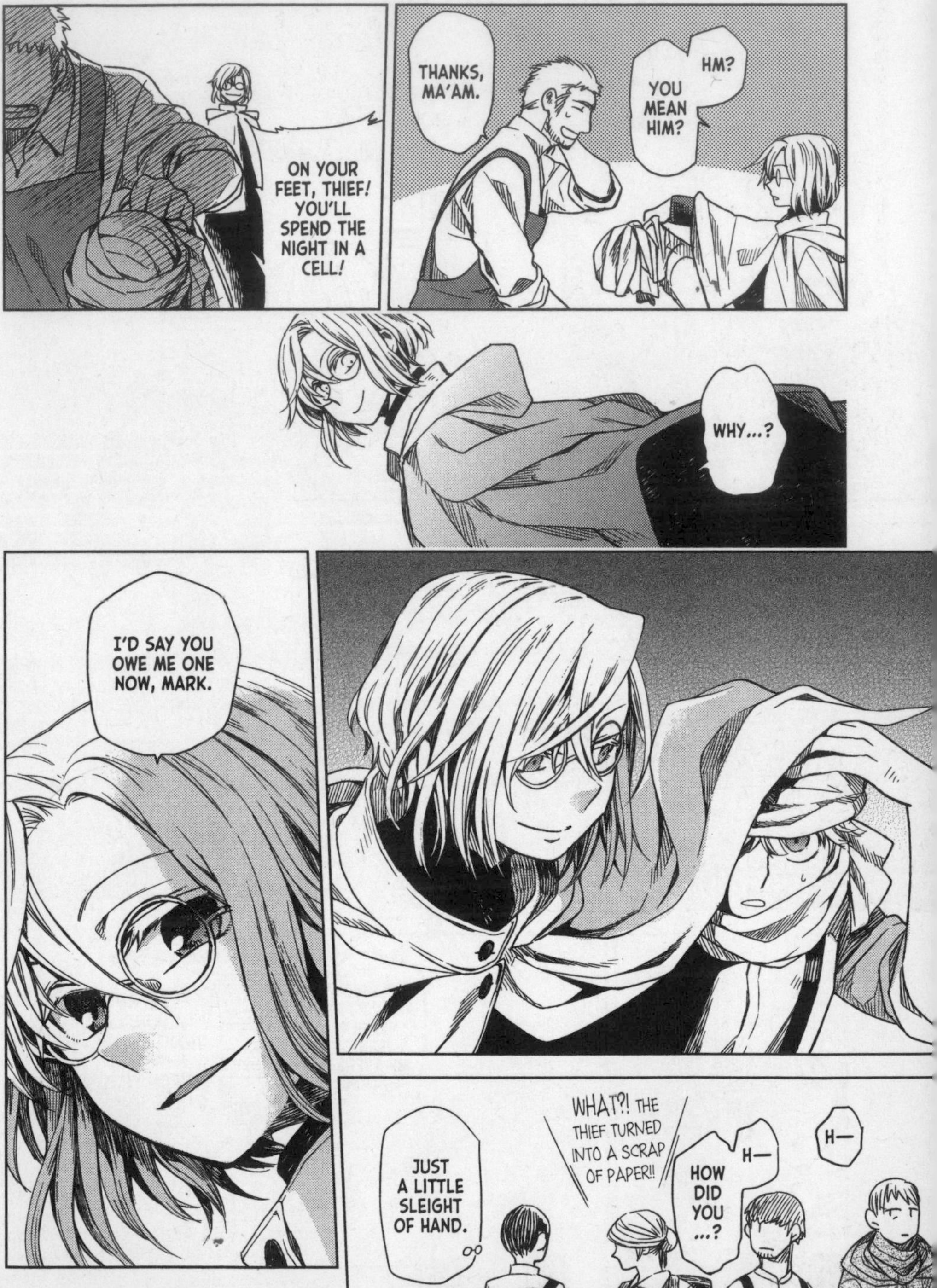
HM?
YOU MEAN HIM?
THANKS, MA'AM.
ON YOUR FEET, THIEF! YOU'LL SPEND THE NIGHT IN A CELL!
WHY...?
H—
H— HOW DID YOU ...?
WHAT?! THE THIEF TURNED INTO A SCRAP OF PAPER!!
JUST A LITTLE SLEIGHT OF HAND.
I'D SAY YOU OWE ME ONE NOW, MARK.

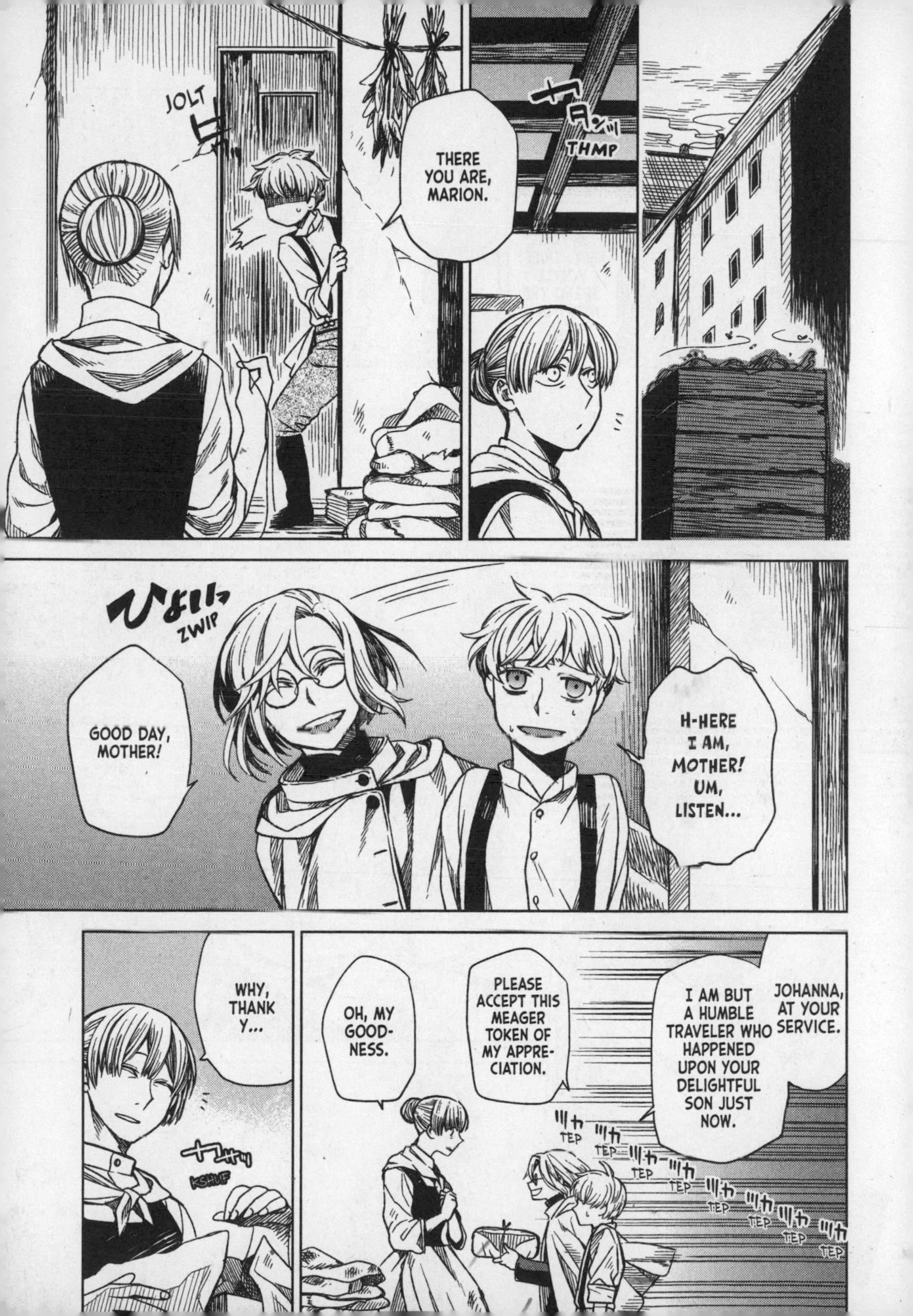
THMP
THERE YOU ARE, MARION.
JOLT
H-HERE I AM, MOTHER! UM, LISTEN...
ZWIP
GOOD DAY, MOTHER!
JOHANNA, AT YOUR SERVICE.
I AM BUT A HUMBLE TRAVELER WHO HAPPENED UPON YOUR DELIGHTFUL SON JUST NOW.
PLEASE ACCEPT THIS MEAGER TOKEN OF MY APPRE-CIATION.
OH, MY GOOD-NESS.
TEP TEP TEP TEP TEP TEP TEP TEP
WHY, THANK Y...
KSHUF

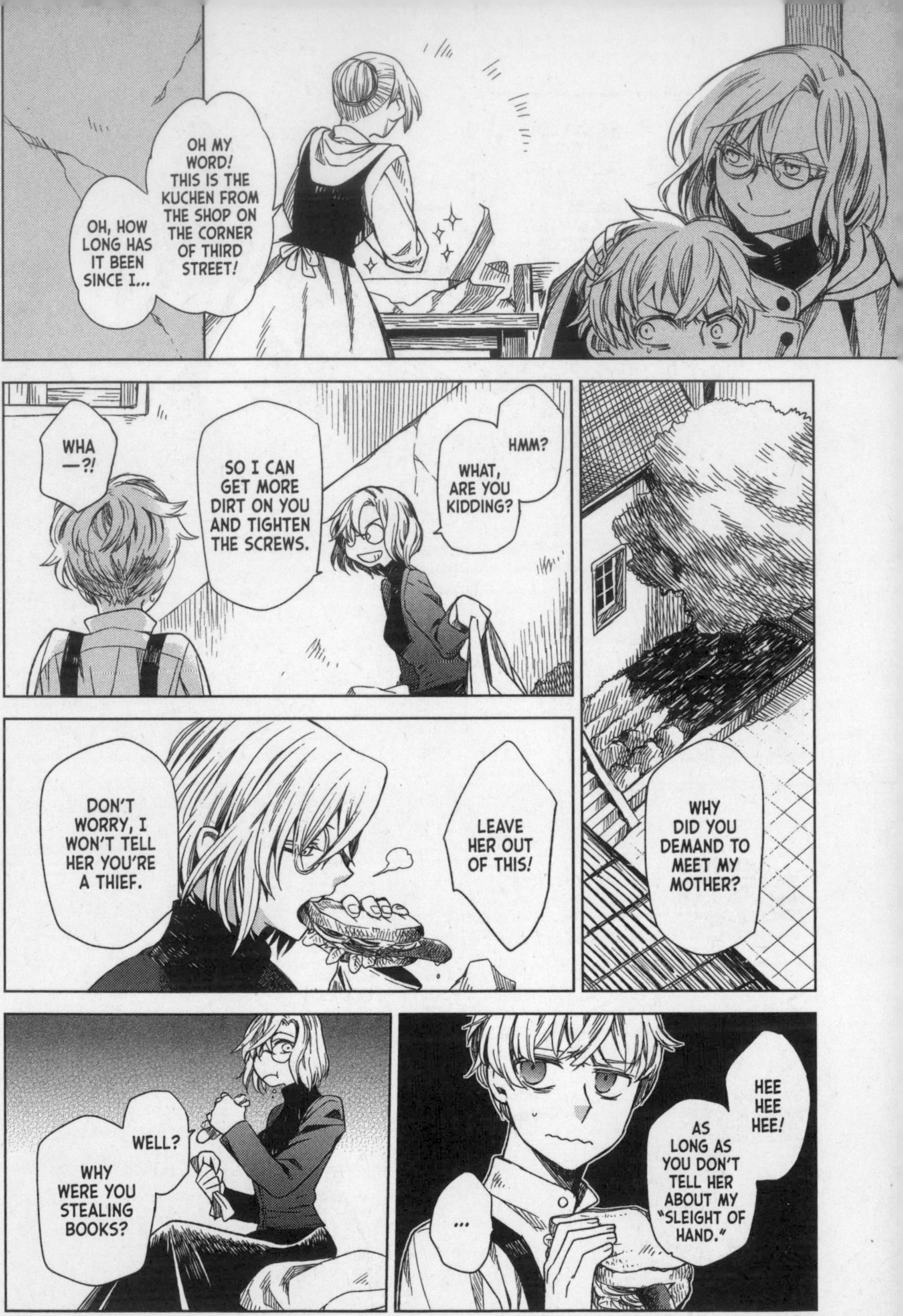
OH MY WORD! THIS IS THE KUCHEN FROM THE SHOP ON THE CORNER OF THIRD STREET!
OH, HOW LONG HAS IT BEEN SINCE I...
WHY DID YOU DEMAND TO MEET MY MOTHER?
HMM?
WHAT, ARE YOU KIDDING?
SO I CAN GET MORE DIRT ON YOU AND TIGHTEN THE SCREWS.
WHA—?!
LEAVE HER OUT OF THIS!
DON'T WORRY, I WON'T TELL HER YOU'RE A THIEF.
HEE HEE HEE!
AS LONG AS YOU DON'T TELL HER ABOUT MY "SLEIGHT OF HAND."
...
WELL?
WHY WERE YOU STEALING BOOKS?

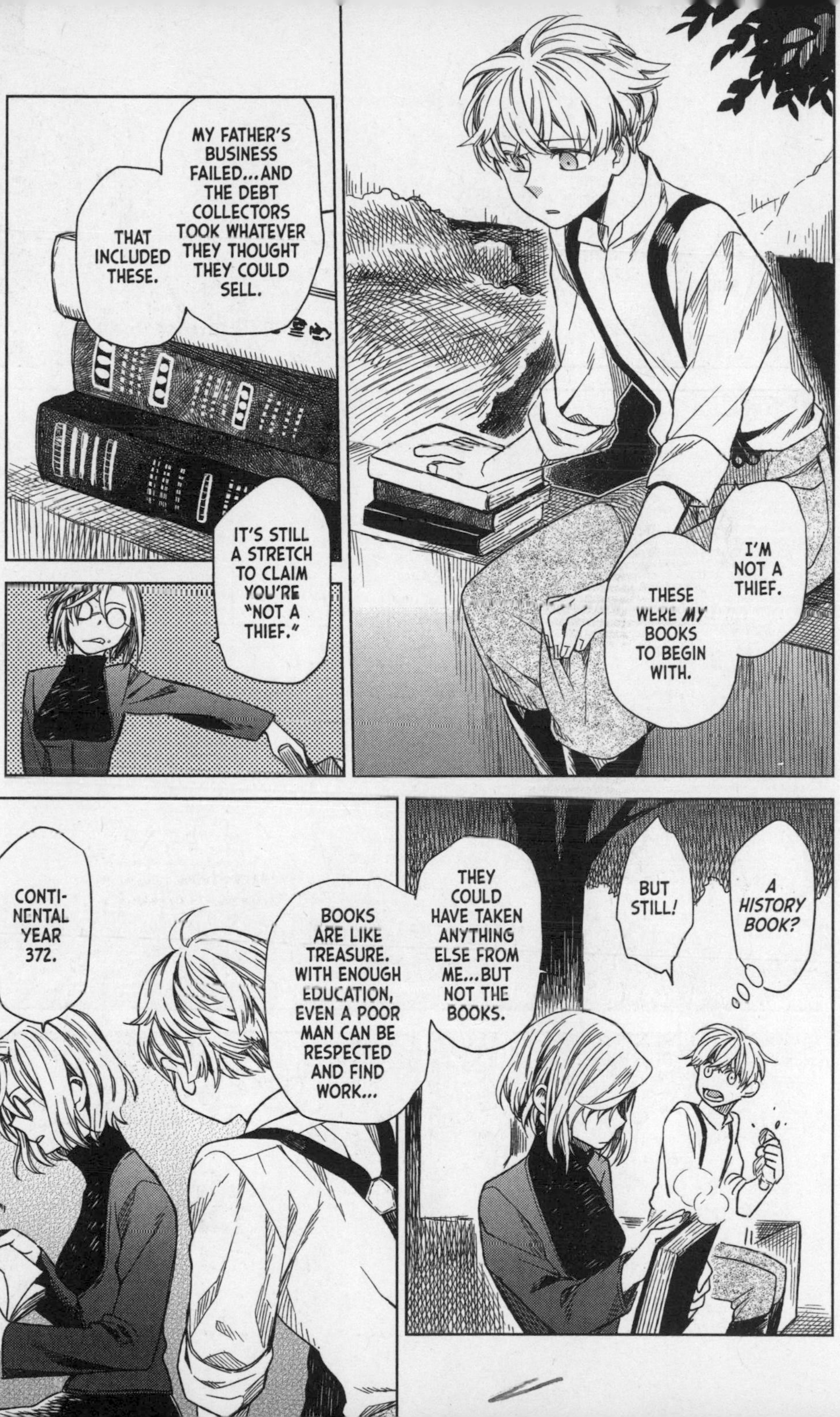
I'M NOT A THIEF.
THESE WERE *MY* BOOKS TO BEGIN WITH.
MY FATHER'S BUSINESS FAILED...AND THE DEBT COLLECTORS TOOK WHATEVER THEY THOUGHT THEY COULD SELL.
THAT INCLUDED THESE.
IT'S STILL A STRETCH TO CLAIM YOU'RE "NOT A THIEF."
A HISTORY BOOK?
BUT STILL!
THEY COULD HAVE TAKEN ANYTHING ELSE FROM ME...BUT NOT THE BOOKS.
BOOKS ARE LIKE TREASURE. WITH ENOUGH EDUCATION, EVEN A POOR MAN CAN BE RESPECTED AND FIND WORK...
CONTI-NENTAL YEAR 372.
FLIP

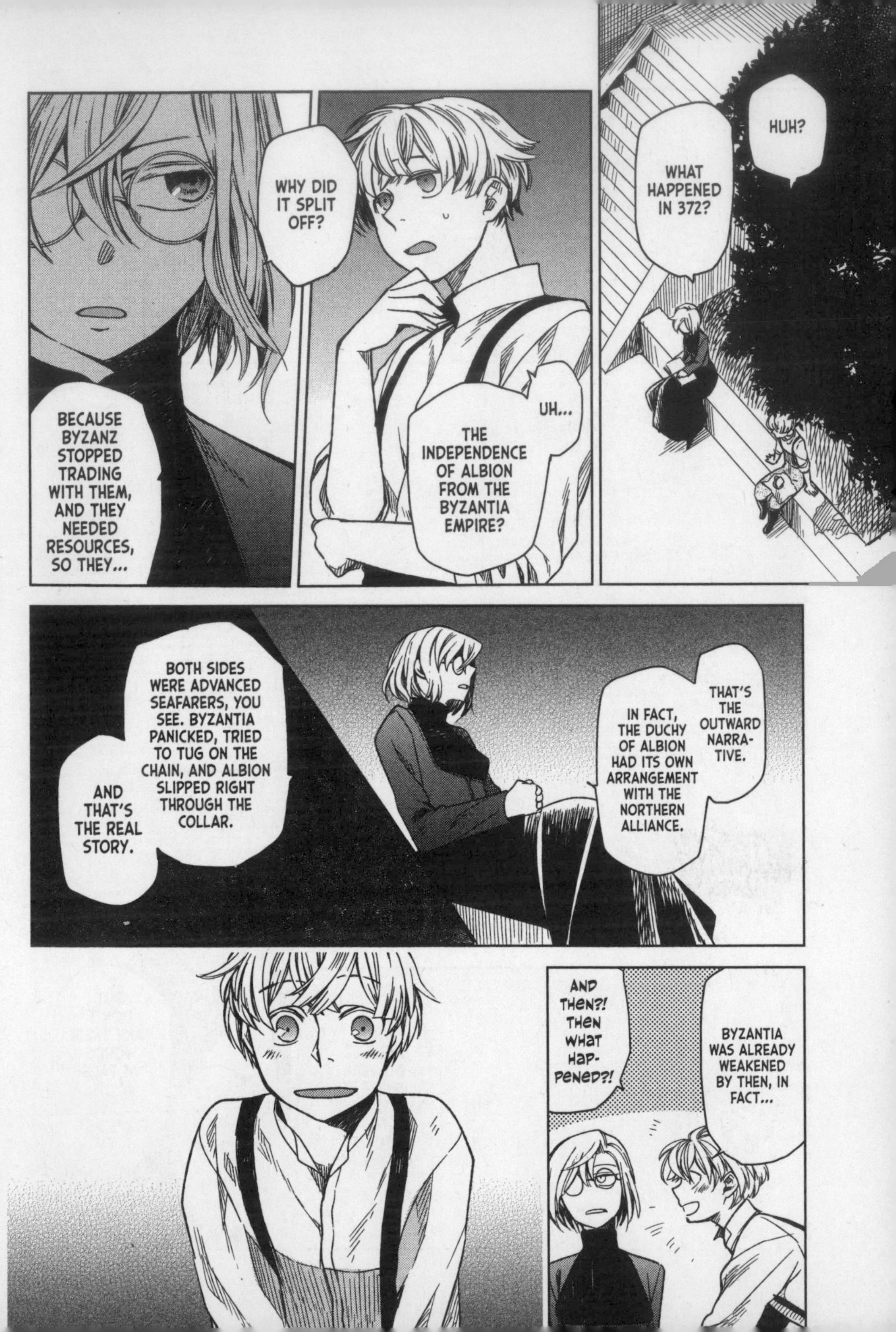
HUH?
WHAT HAPPENED IN 372?
UH...
THE INDEPENDENCE OF ALBION FROM THE BYZANTIA EMPIRE?
WHY DID IT SPLIT OFF?
BECAUSE BYZANZ STOPPED TRADING WITH THEM, AND THEY NEEDED RESOURCES, SO THEY...
THAT'S THE OUTWARD NARRA-TIVE.
IN FACT, THE DUCHY OF ALBION HAD ITS OWN ARRANGEMENT WITH THE NORTHERN ALLIANCE.
BOTH SIDES WERE ADVANCED SEAFARERS, YOU SEE. BYZANTIA PANICKED, TRIED TO TUG ON THE CHAIN, AND ALBION SLIPPED RIGHT THROUGH THE COLLAR.
AND THAT'S THE REAL STORY.
BYZANTIA WAS ALREADY WEAKENED BY THEN, IN FACT...
AND THEN?! THEN WHAT HAP-PENED?!

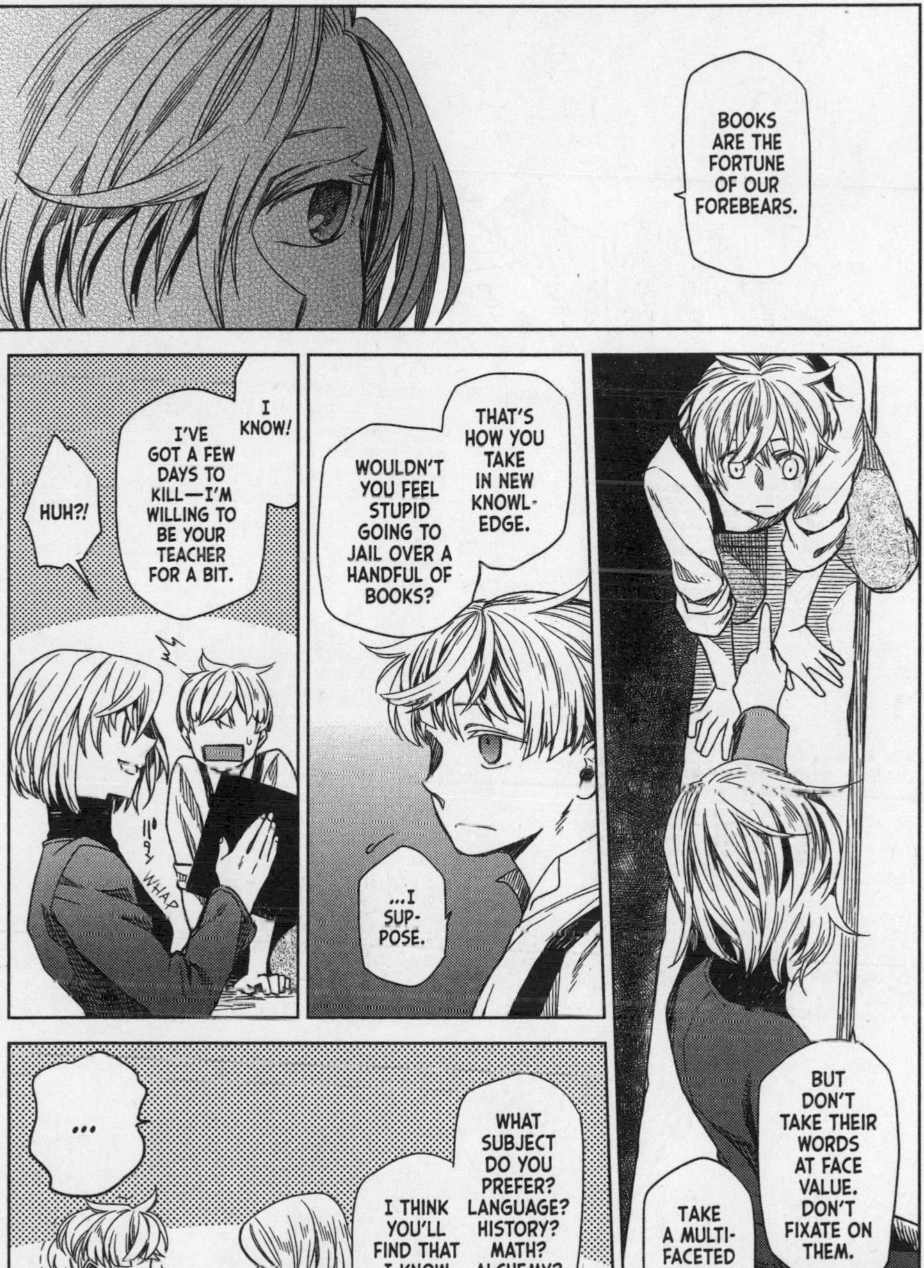
BOOKS ARE THE FORTUNE OF OUR FOREBEARS.
BUT DON'T TAKE THEIR WORDS AT FACE VALUE. DON'T FIXATE ON THEM.
TAKE A MULTI-FACETED VIEW OF THINGS.
THAT'S HOW YOU TAKE IN NEW KNOWL-EDGE.
WOULDN'T YOU FEEL STUPID GOING TO JAIL OVER A HANDFUL OF BOOKS?
...I SUP-POSE.
I KNOW!
I'VE GOT A FEW DAYS TO KILL—I'M WILLING TO BE YOUR TEACHER FOR A BIT.
HUH?!
WHAP
WHAT SUBJECT DO YOU PREFER? LANGUAGE? HISTORY? MATH? ALCHEMY?
I THINK YOU'LL FIND THAT I KNOW QUITE A BIT.
...

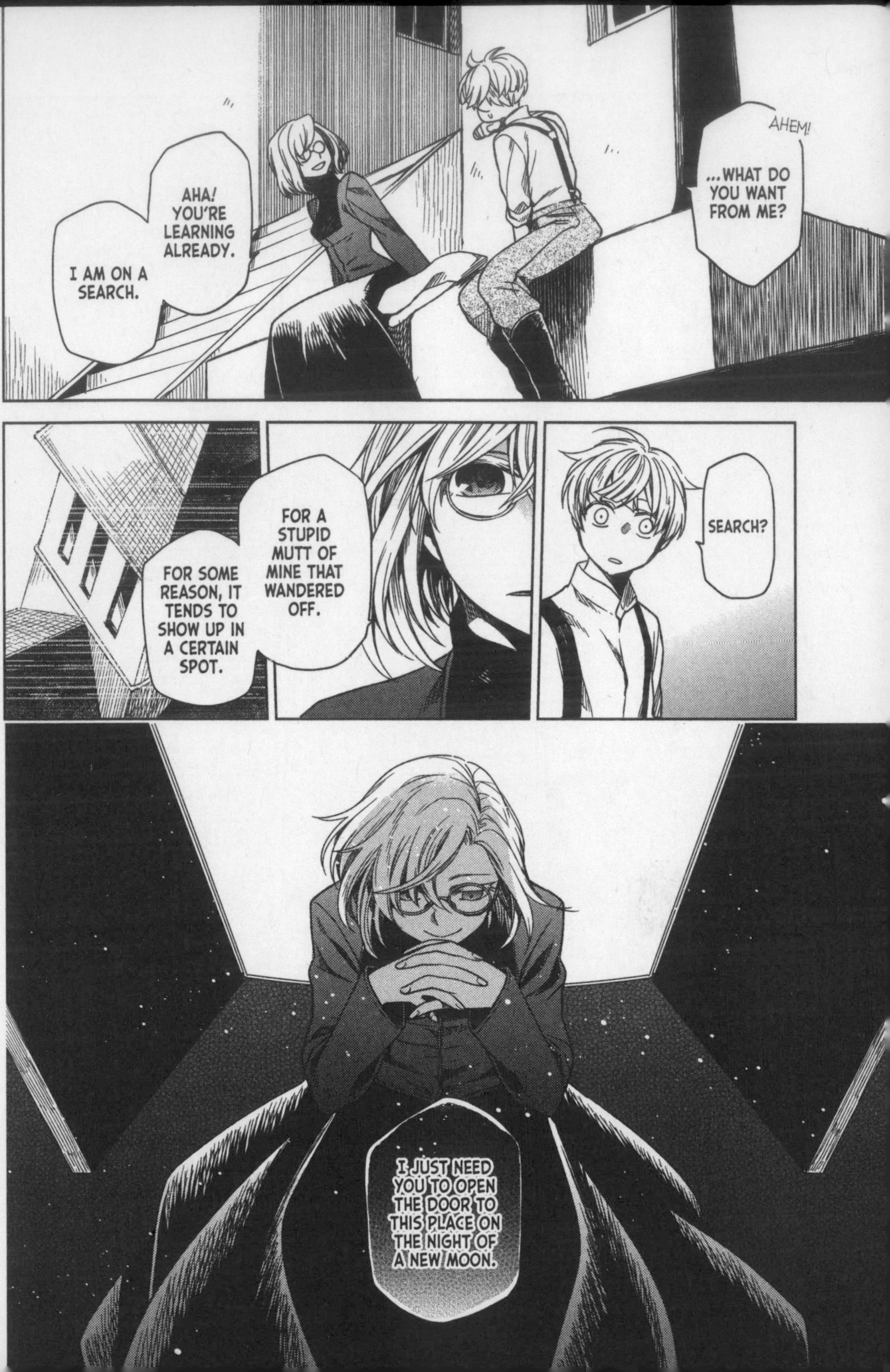
AHEM!
...WHAT DO YOU WANT FROM ME?
AHA! YOU'RE LEARNING ALREADY.
I AM ON A SEARCH.
SEARCH?
FOR A STUPID MUTT OF MINE THAT WANDERED OFF.
FOR SOME REASON, IT TENDS TO SHOW UP IN A CERTAIN SPOT.
I JUST NEED YOU TO OPEN THE DOOR TO THIS PLACE ON THE NIGHT OF A NEW MOON.

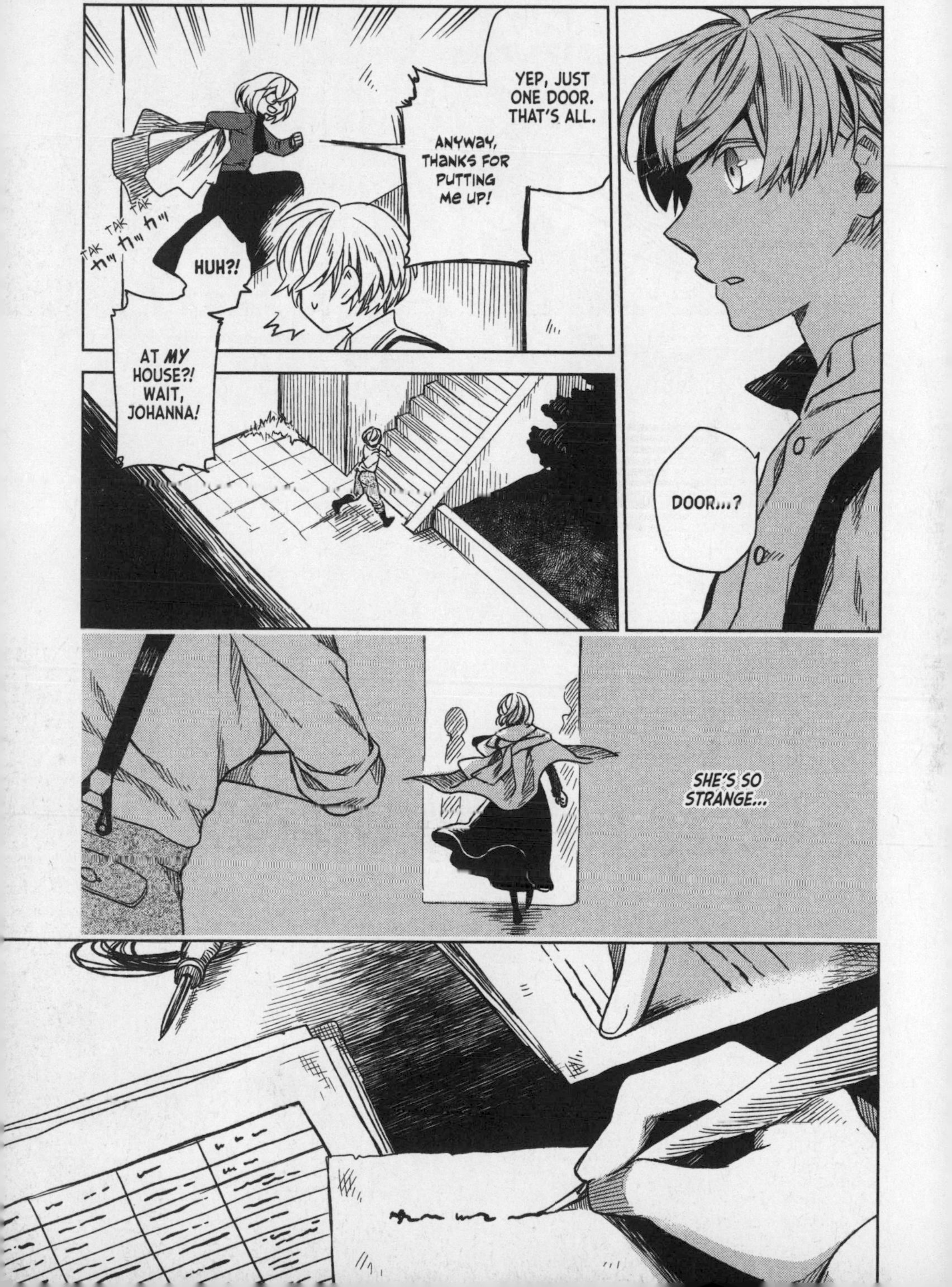
DOOR...?
YEP, JUST ONE DOOR. THAT'S ALL.
ANYWAY, THANKS FOR PUTTING ME UP!
TAK TAK TAK
カッ カッ カッ
HUH?!
AT MY HOUSE?! WAIT, JOHANNA!
SHE'S SO STRANGE...

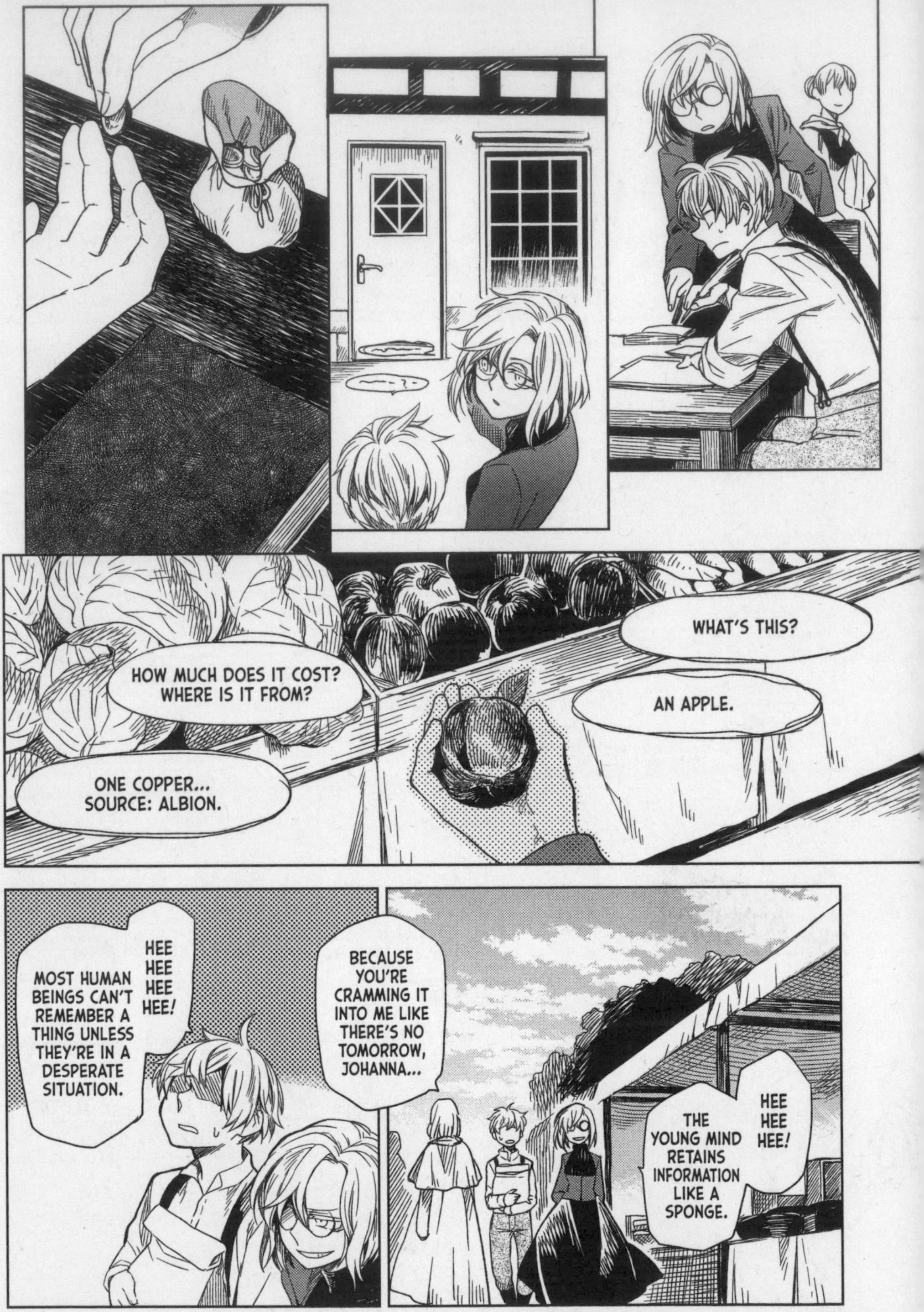
WHAT'S THIS?
AN APPLE.
HOW MUCH DOES IT COST? WHERE IS IT FROM?
ONE COPPER... SOURCE: ALBION.
HEE HEE HEE!
THE YOUNG MIND RETAINS INFORMATION LIKE A SPONGE.
BECAUSE YOU'RE CRAMMING IT INTO ME LIKE THERE'S NO TOMORROW, JOHANNA...
HEE HEE HEE HEE!
MOST HUMAN BEINGS CAN'T REMEMBER A THING UNLESS THEY'RE IN A DESPERATE SITUATION.

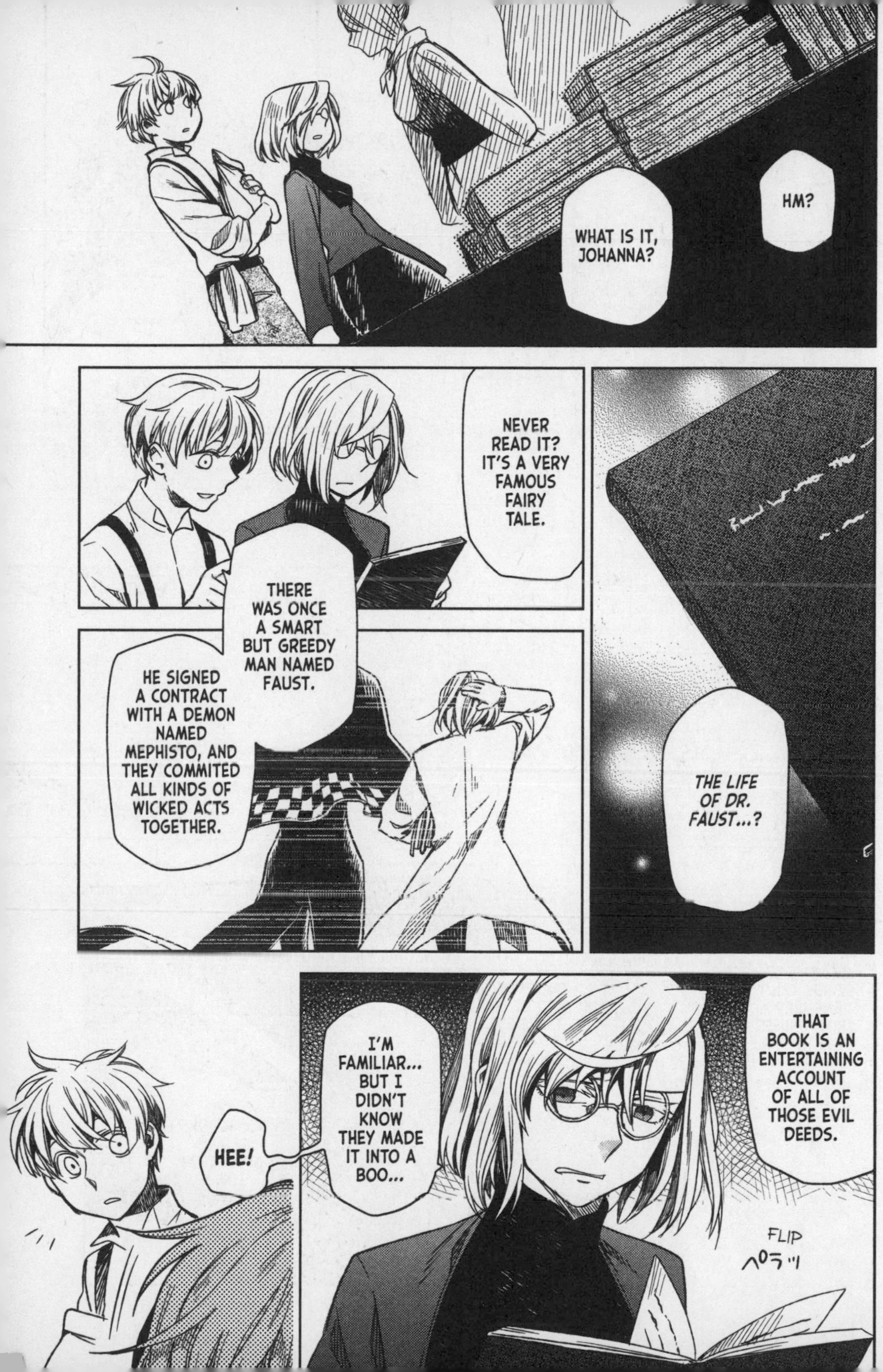
HM?
WHAT IS IT, JOHANNA?
THE LIFE OF DR. FAUST...?
NEVER READ IT? IT'S A VERY FAMOUS FAIRY TALE.
THERE WAS ONCE A SMART BUT GREEDY MAN NAMED FAUST.
HE SIGNED A CONTRACT WITH A DEMON NAMED MEPHISTO, AND THEY COMMITED ALL KINDS OF WICKED ACTS TOGETHER.
THAT BOOK IS AN ENTERTAINING ACCOUNT OF ALL OF THOSE EVIL DEEDS.
FLIP
ペラッ
I'M FAMILIAR... BUT I DIDN'T KNOW THEY MADE IT INTO A BOO...
HEE!

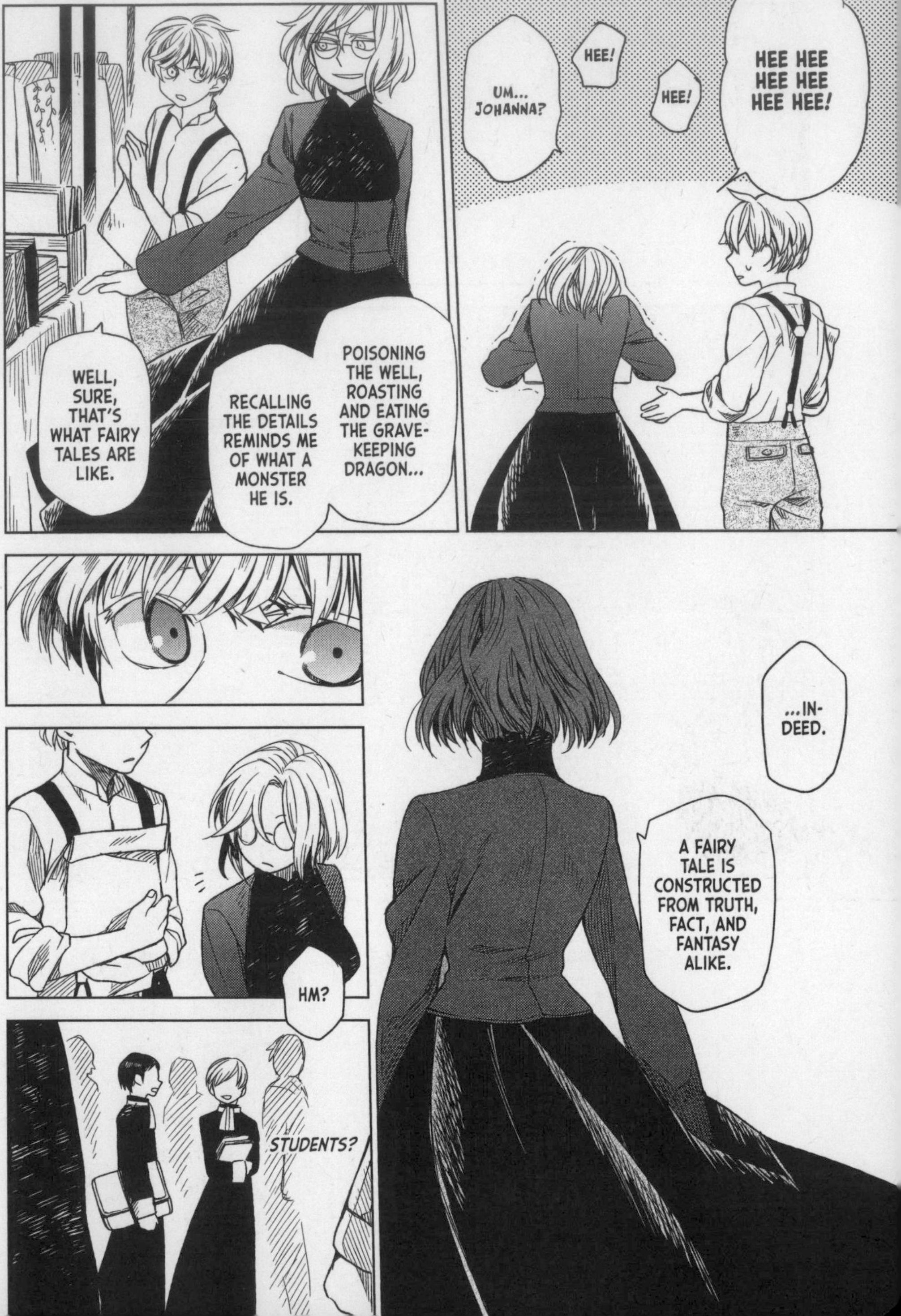
HEE HEE HEE HEE HEE HEE!
HEE!
HEE!
UM... JOHANNA?
POISONING THE WELL, ROASTING AND EATING THE GRAVE-KEEPING DRAGON...
RECALLING THE DETAILS REMINDS ME OF WHAT A MONSTER HE IS.
WELL, SURE, THAT'S WHAT FAIRY TALES ARE LIKE.
...IN-DEED.
A FAIRY TALE IS CONSTRUCTED FROM TRUTH, FACT, AND FANTASY ALIKE.
HM?
STUDENTS?

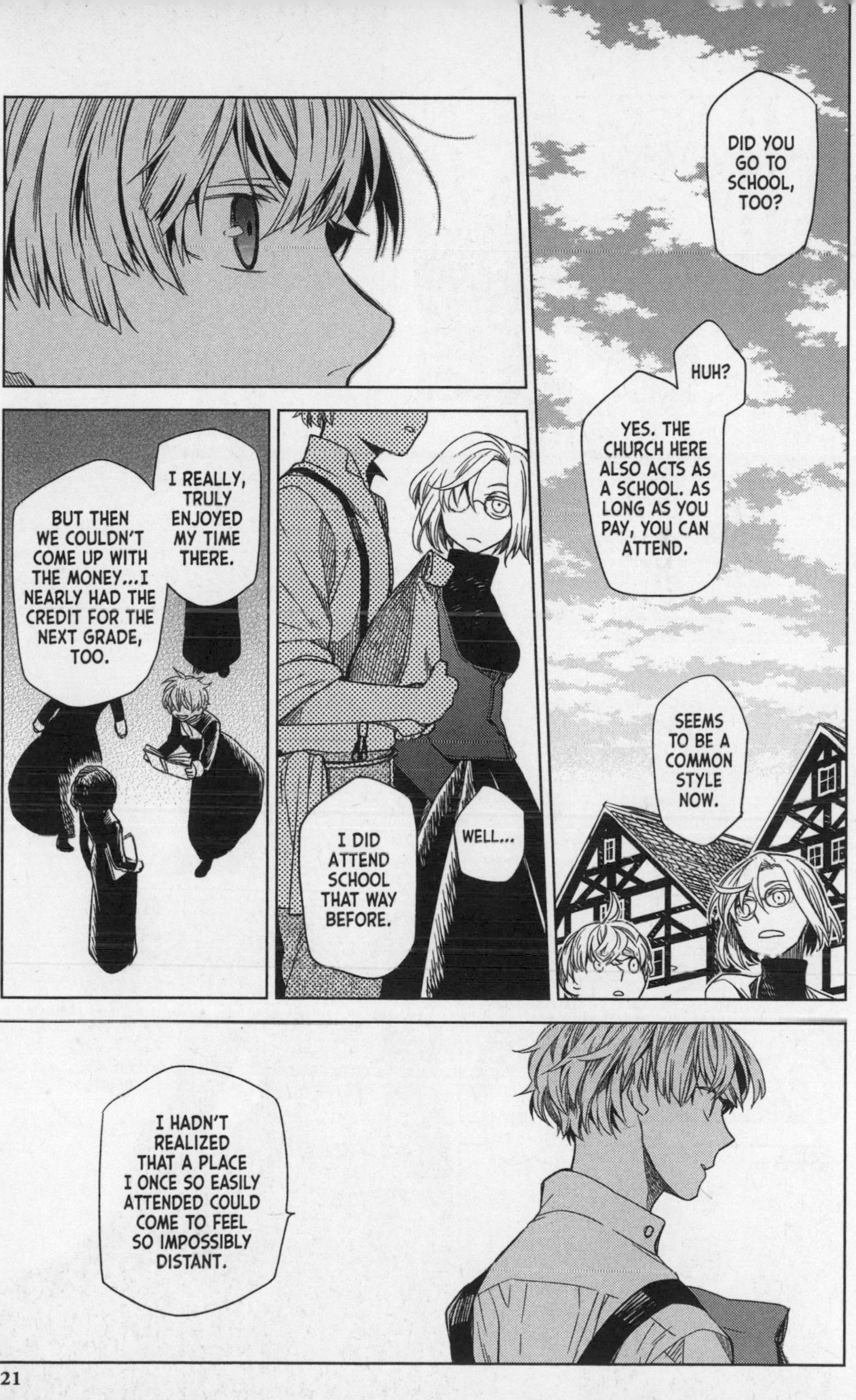
DID YOU GO TO SCHOOL, TOO?
HUH?
YES. THE CHURCH HERE ALSO ACTS AS A SCHOOL. AS LONG AS YOU PAY, YOU CAN ATTEND.
SEEMS TO BE A COMMON STYLE NOW.
WELL...
I DID ATTEND SCHOOL THAT WAY BEFORE.
I REALLY, TRULY ENJOYED MY TIME THERE.
BUT THEN WE COULDN'T COME UP WITH THE MONEY...I NEARLY HAD THE CREDIT FOR THE NEXT GRADE, TOO.
I HADN'T REALIZED THAT A PLACE I ONCE SO EASILY ATTENDED COULD COME TO FEEL SO IMPOSSIBLY DISTANT.

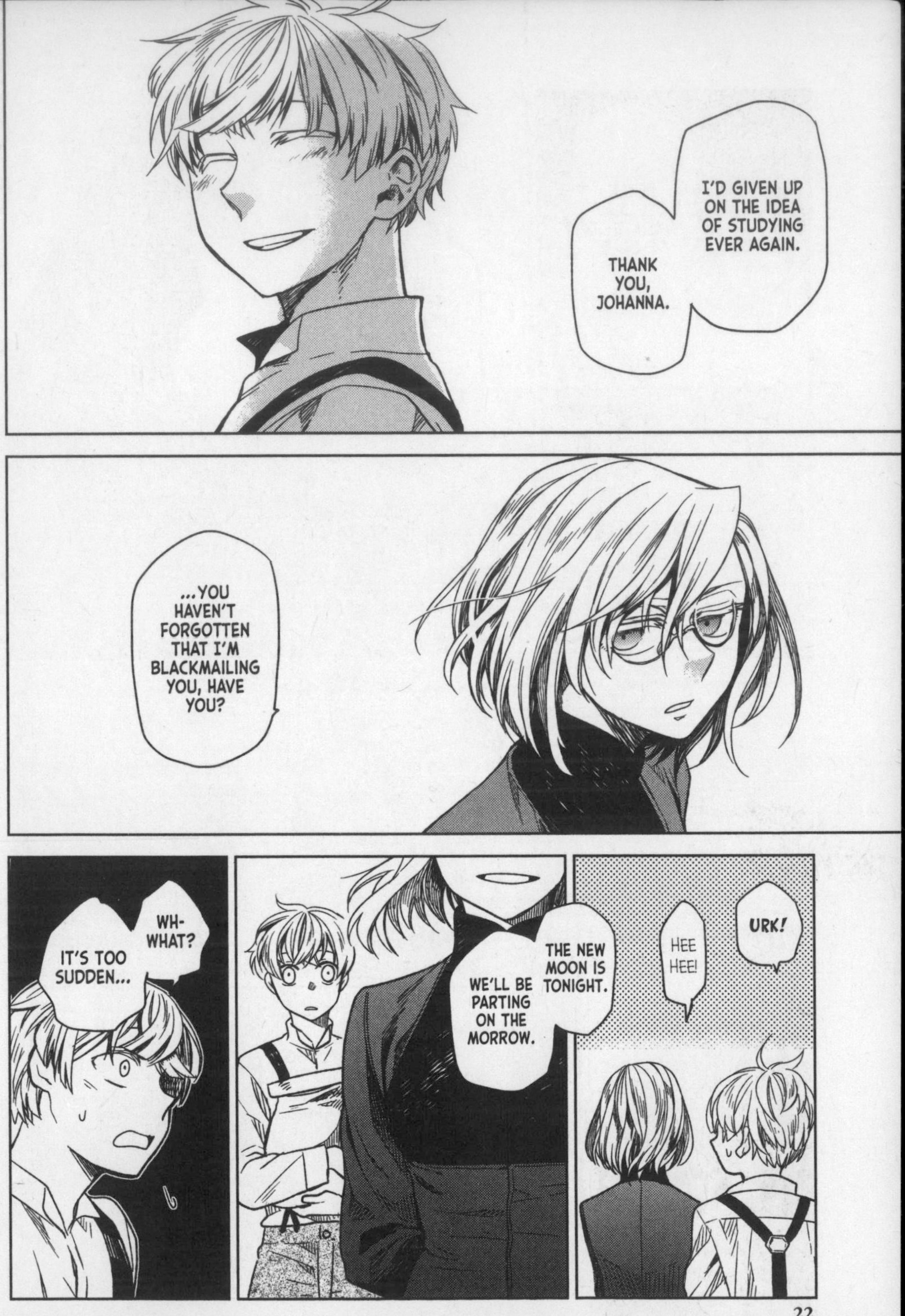
I'D GIVEN UP ON THE IDEA OF STUDYING EVER AGAIN.
THANK YOU, JOHANNA.
...YOU HAVEN'T FORGOTTEN THAT I'M BLACKMAILING YOU, HAVE YOU?
URK!
HEE HEE!
THE NEW MOON IS TONIGHT.
WE'LL BE PARTING ON THE MORROW.
WH-WHAT?
IT'S TOO SUDDEN...

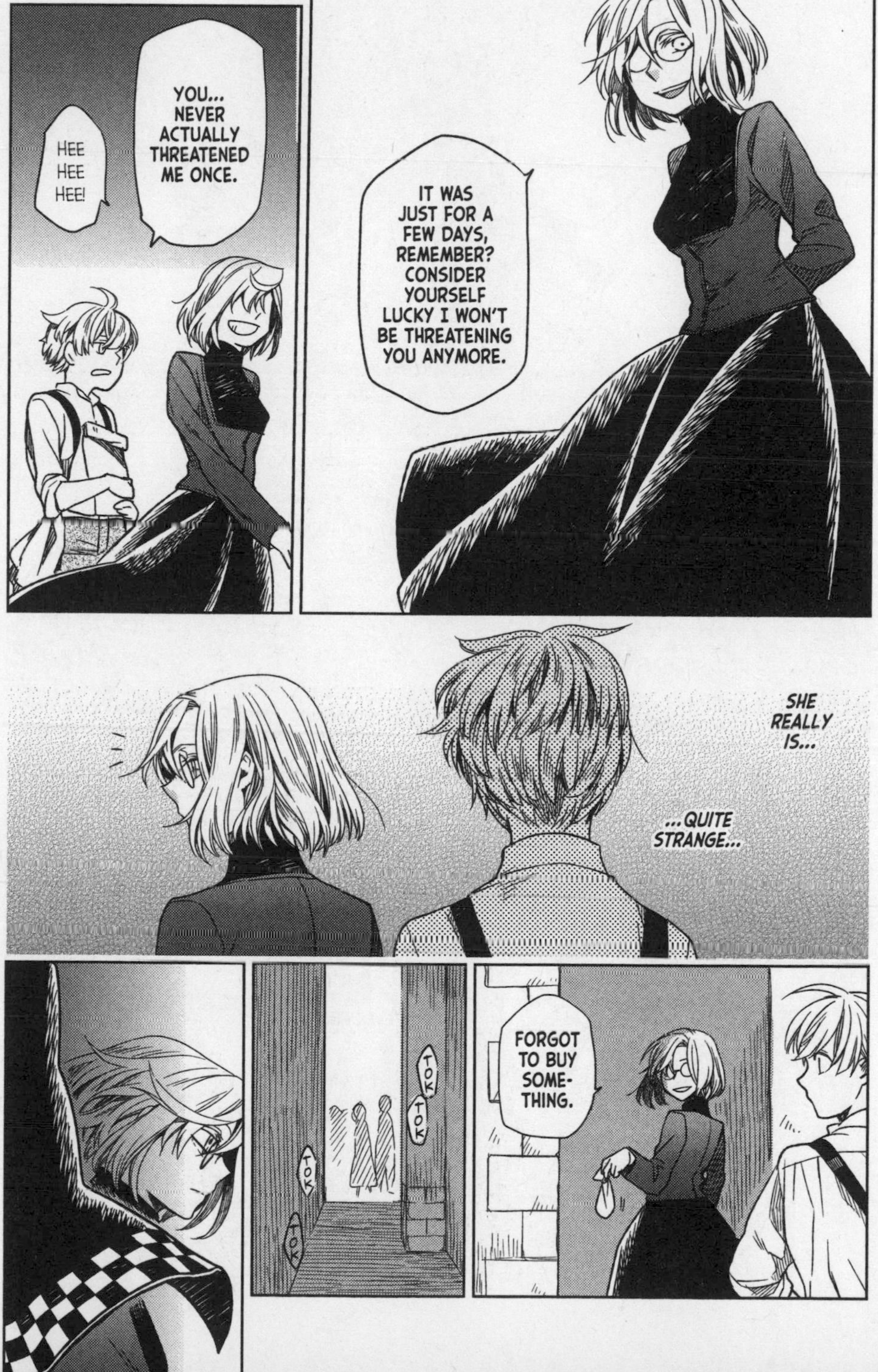
IT WAS JUST FOR A FEW DAYS, REMEMBER? CONSIDER YOURSELF LUCKY I WON'T BE THREATENING YOU ANYMORE.
YOU... NEVER ACTUALLY THREATENED ME ONCE.
HEE HEE HEE!
SHE REALLY IS...
...QUITE STRANGE...
FORGOT TO BUY SOME-THING.
TOK
TOK
TOK
TOK

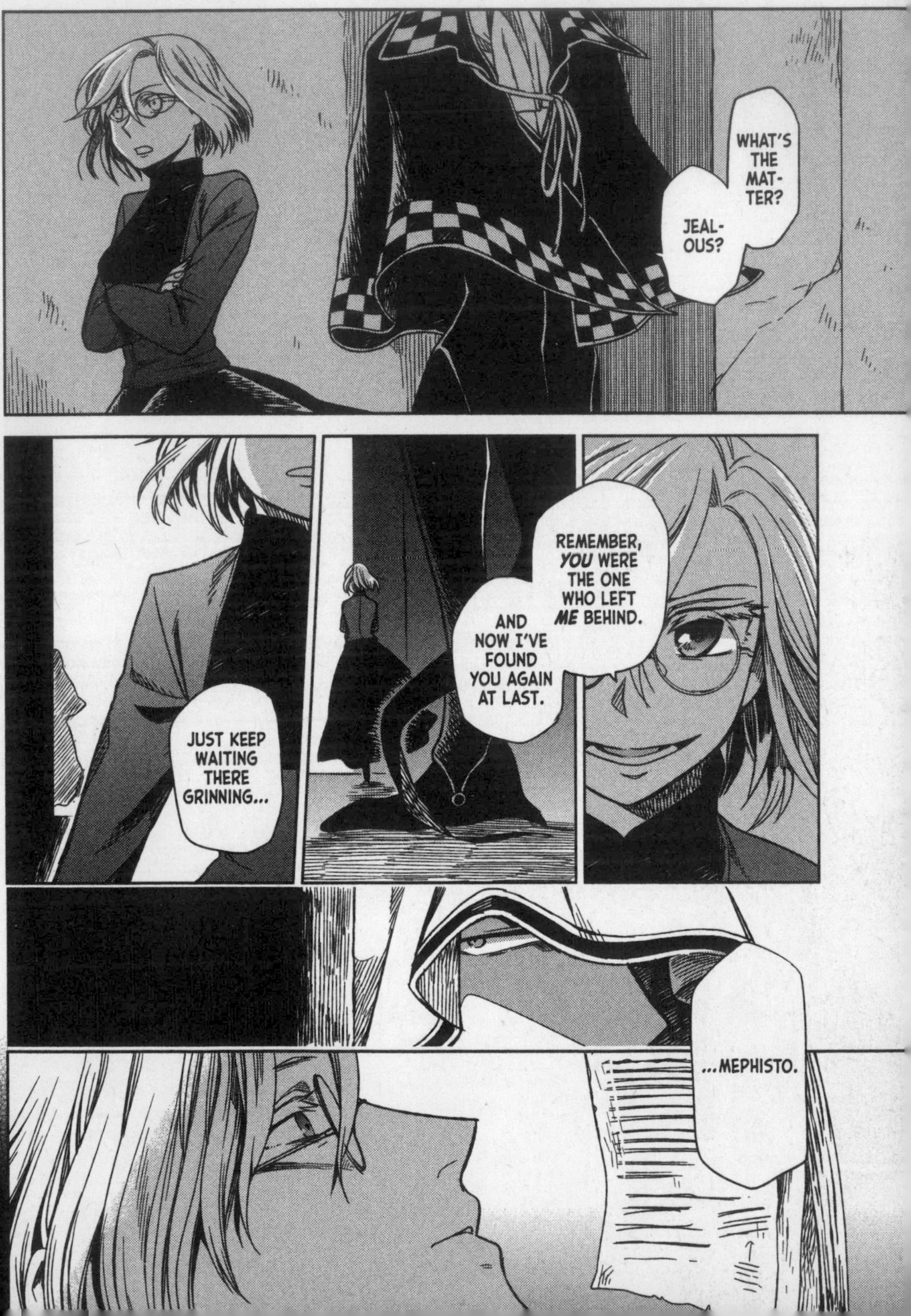
WHAT'S THE MAT-TER?
JEAL-OUS?
REMEMBER, *YOU* WERE THE ONE WHO LEFT *ME* BEHIND.
AND NOW I'VE FOUND YOU AGAIN AT LAST.
JUST KEEP WAITING THERE GRINNING...
...MEPHISTO.

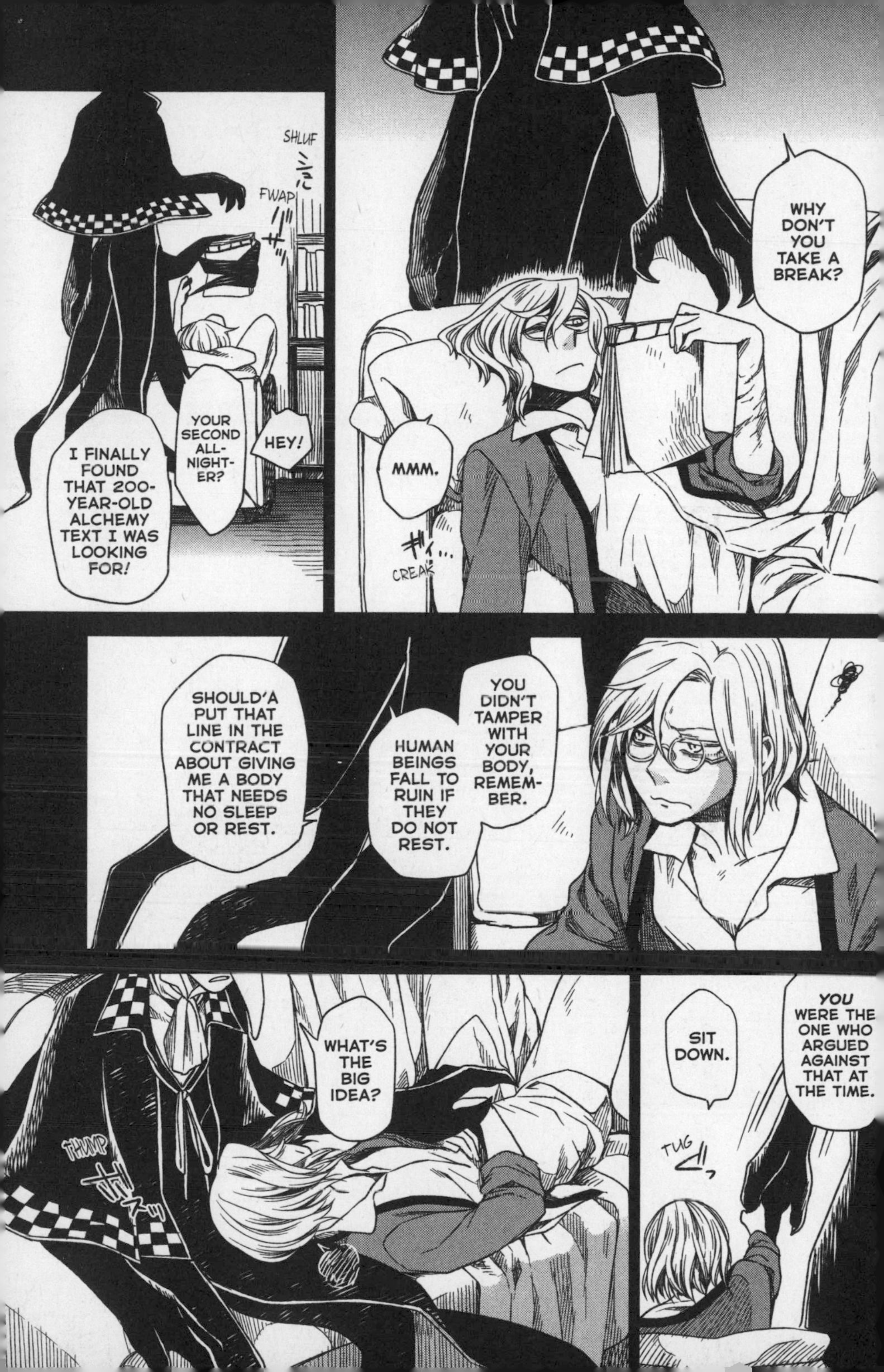
WHY DON'T YOU TAKE A BREAK?
MMM.
CREAK
SHLUF
FWAP
HEY!
YOUR SECOND ALL-NIGHTER?
I FINALLY FOUND THAT 200-YEAR-OLD ALCHEMY TEXT I WAS LOOKING FOR!
YOU DIDN'T TAMPER WITH YOUR BODY, REMEMBER.
HUMAN BEINGS FALL TO RUIN IF THEY DO NOT REST.
SHOULD'A PUT THAT LINE IN THE CONTRACT ABOUT GIVING ME A BODY THAT NEEDS NO SLEEP OR REST.
YOU WERE THE ONE WHO ARGUED AGAINST THAT AT THE TIME.
SIT DOWN.
TUG
WHAT'S THE BIG IDEA?
THUMP

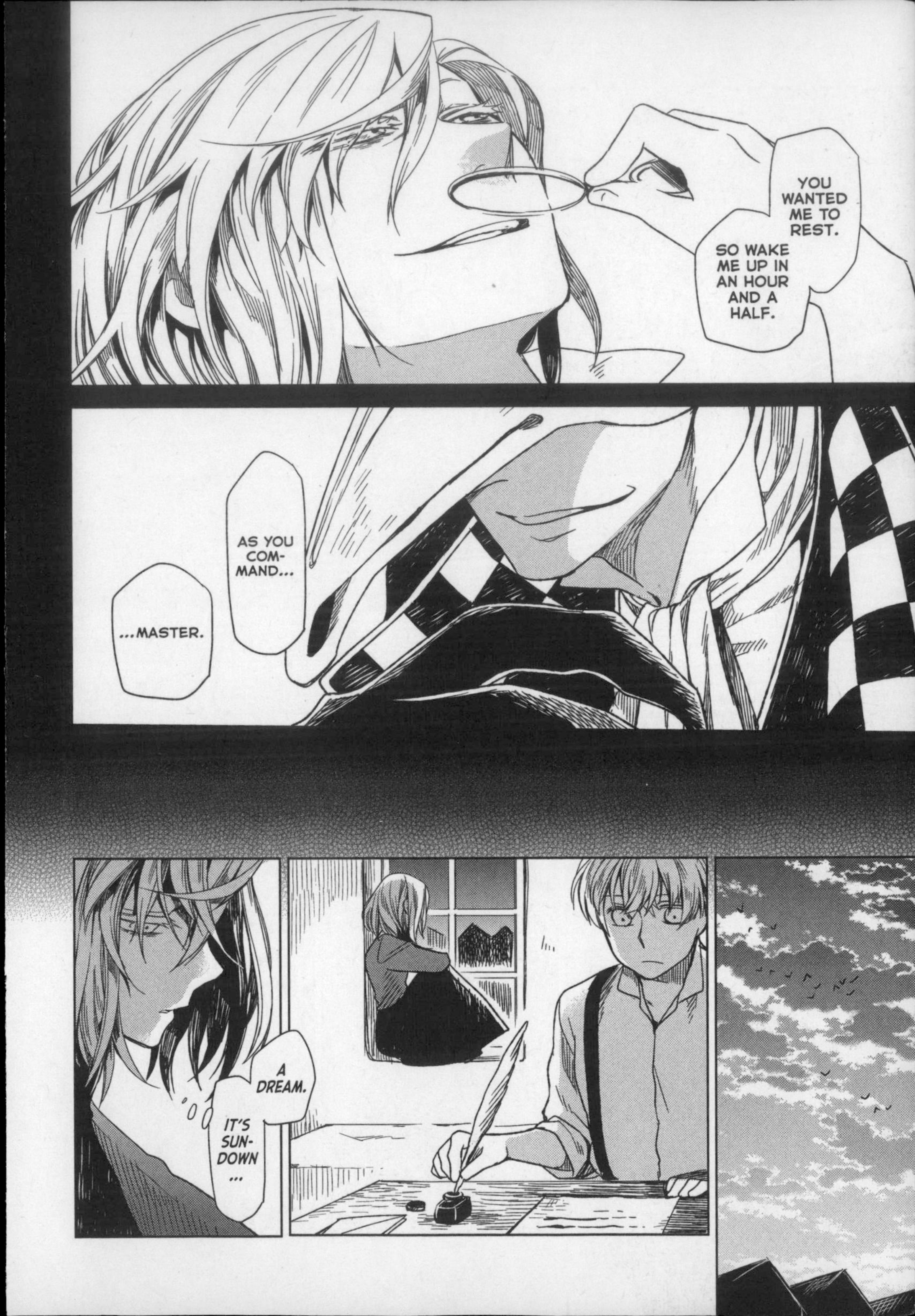
YOU WANTED ME TO REST.
SO WAKE ME UP IN AN HOUR AND A HALF.
AS YOU COM-MAND...
...MASTER.
A DREAM.
IT'S SUN-DOWN ...

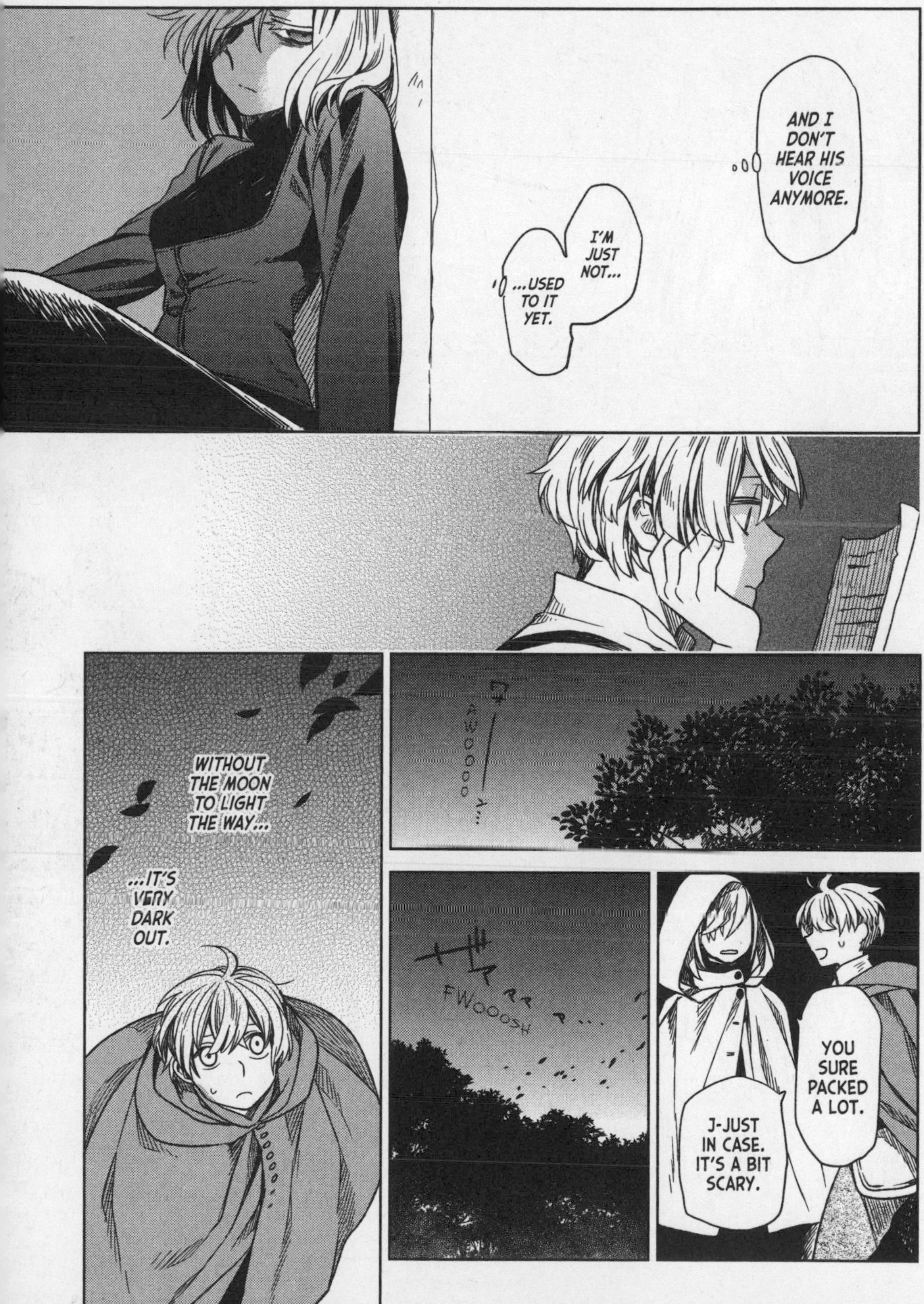
AND I DON'T HEAR HIS VOICE ANYMORE.
I'M JUST NOT...
...USED TO IT YET.
AWOOOOO
FWOOOSH
YOU SURE PACKED A LOT.
J-JUST IN CASE. IT'S A BIT SCARY.
WITHOUT THE MOON TO LIGHT THE WAY...
...IT'S VERY DARK OUT.

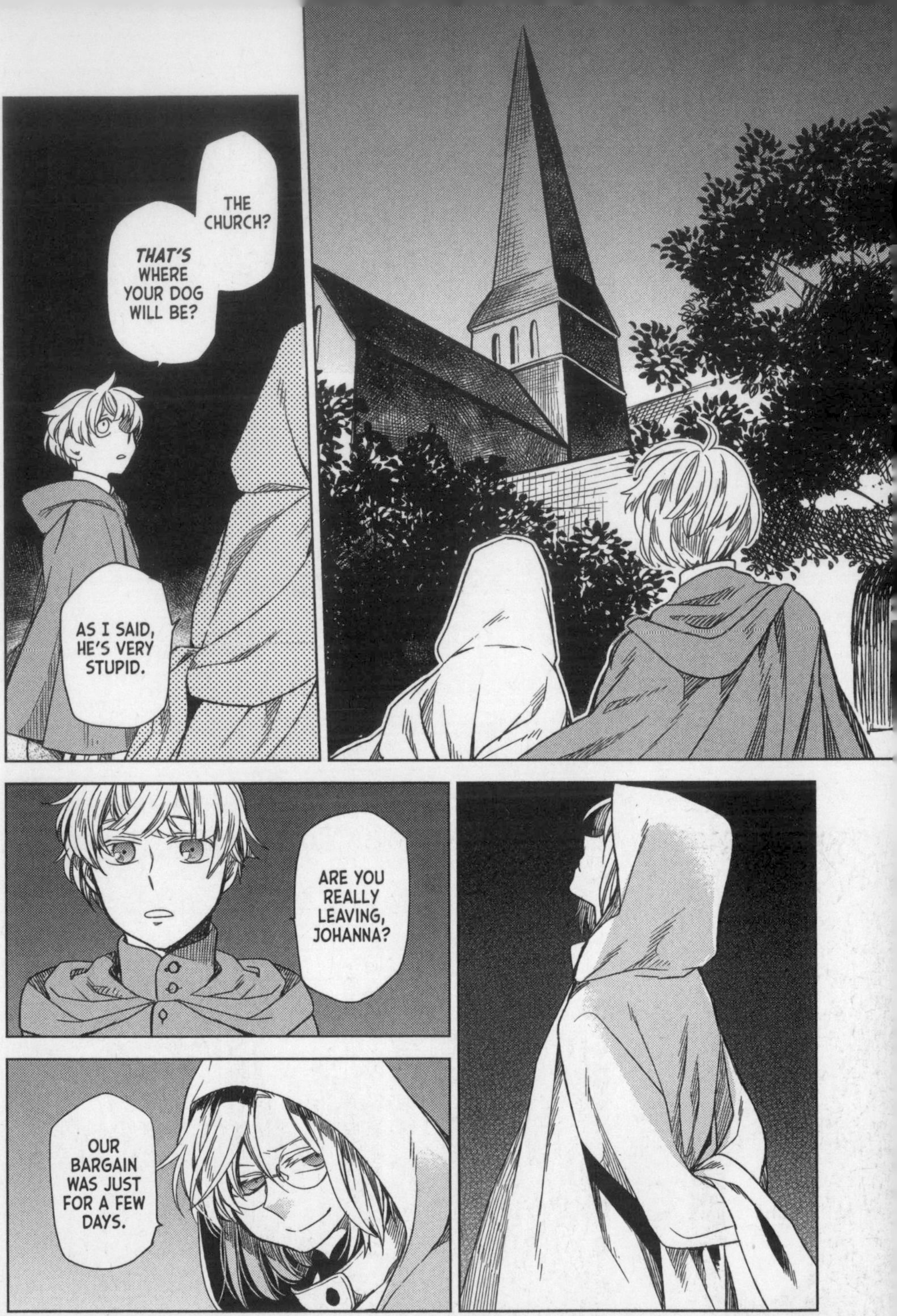
THE CHURCH?
THAT'S WHERE YOUR DOG WILL BE?
AS I SAID, HE'S VERY STUPID.
ARE YOU REALLY LEAVING, JOHANNA?
OUR BARGAIN WAS JUST FOR A FEW DAYS.

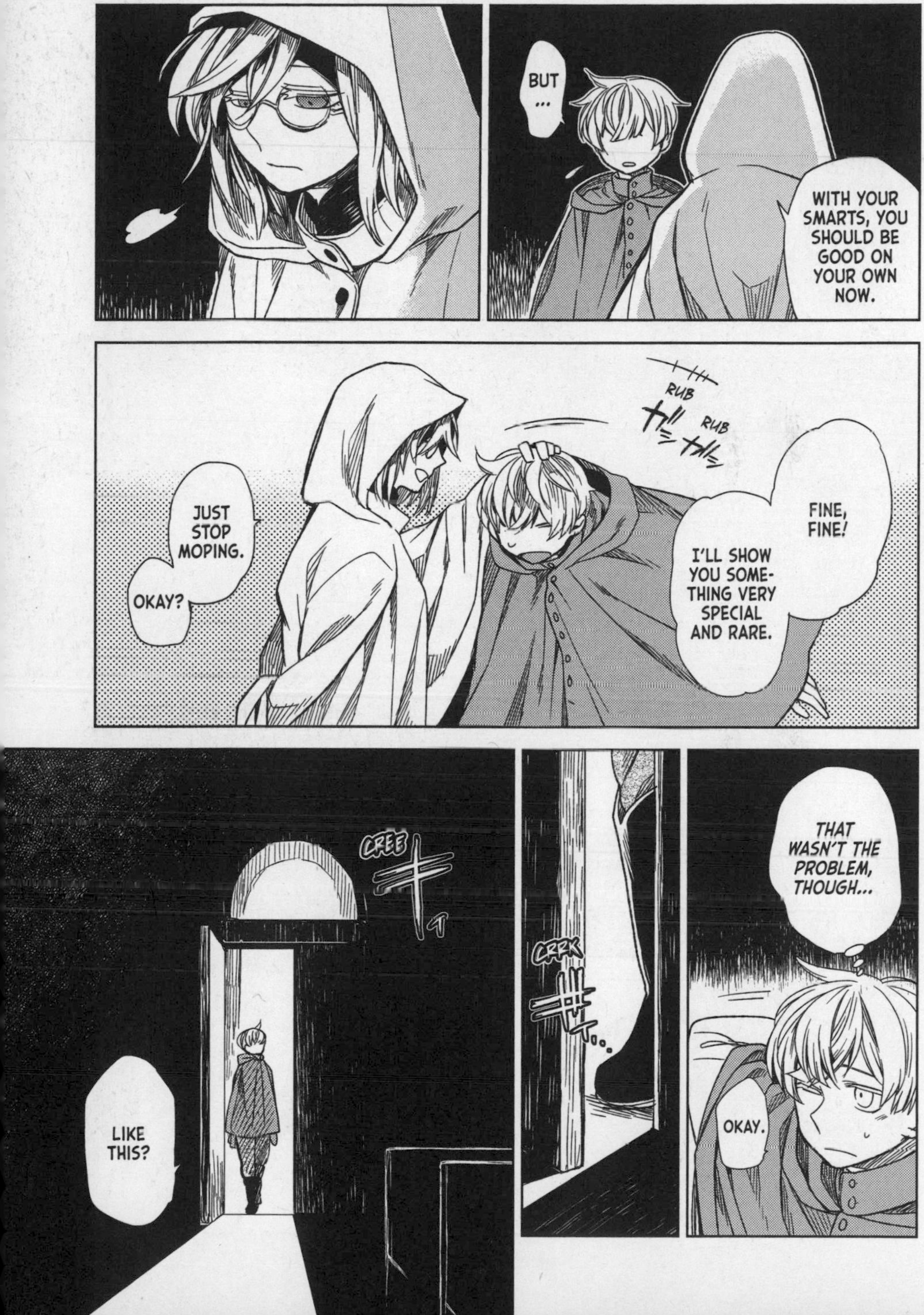

BUT ...
WITH YOUR SMARTS, YOU SHOULD BE GOOD ON YOUR OWN NOW.
RUB
RUB
FINE, FINE!
I'LL SHOW YOU SOME-THING VERY SPECIAL AND RARE.
JUST STOP MOPING.
OKAY?
THAT WASN'T THE PROBLEM, THOUGH...
OKAY.
CRRK
CREE
LIKE THIS?

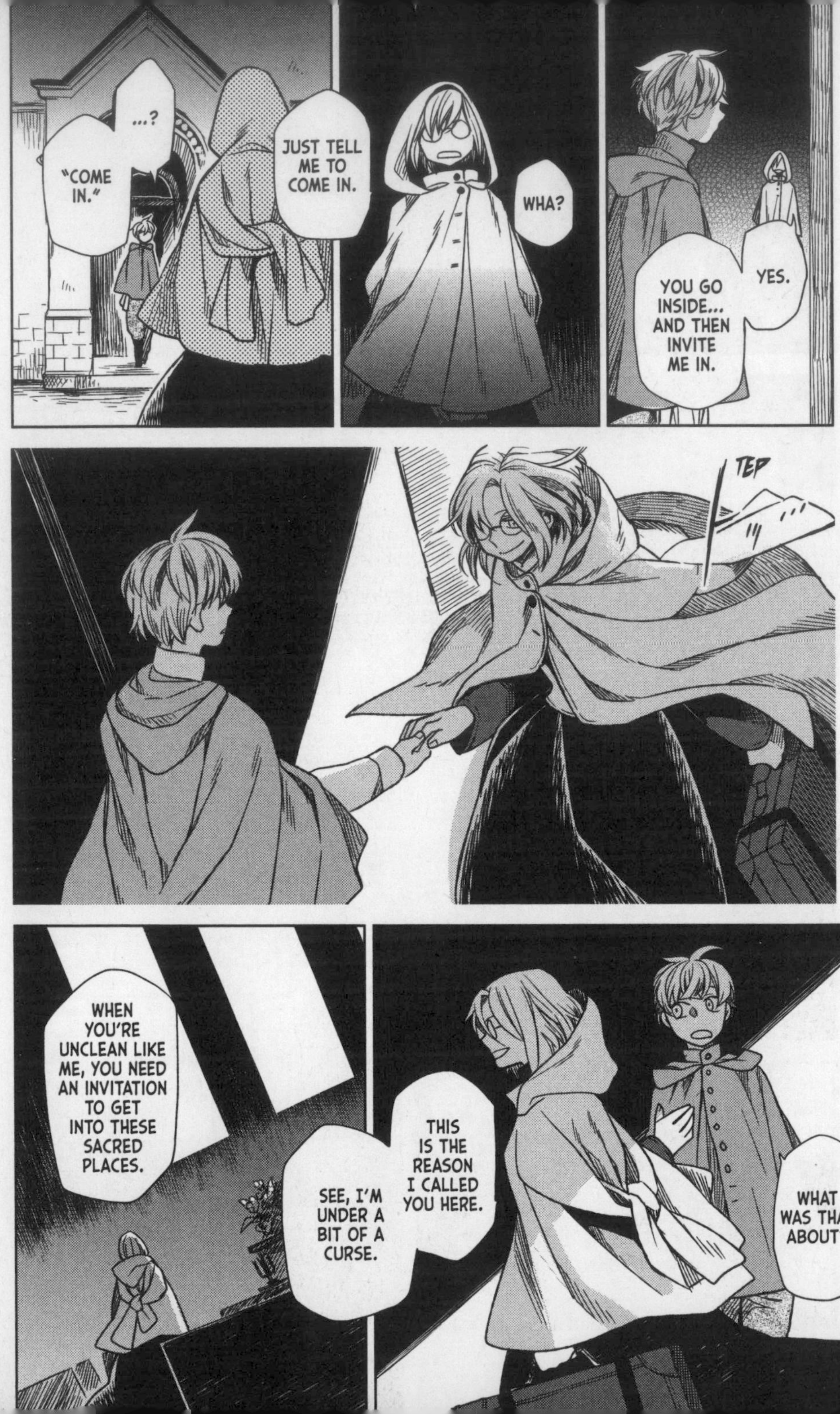
YES.
YOU GO INSIDE... AND THEN INVITE ME IN.
WHA?
JUST TELL ME TO COME IN.
...?
"COME IN."
TEP
WHAT WAS THAT ABOUT?
THIS IS THE REASON I CALLED YOU HERE.
SEE, I'M UNDER A BIT OF A CURSE.
WHEN YOU'RE UNCLEAN LIKE ME, YOU NEED AN INVITATION TO GET INTO THESE SACRED PLACES.

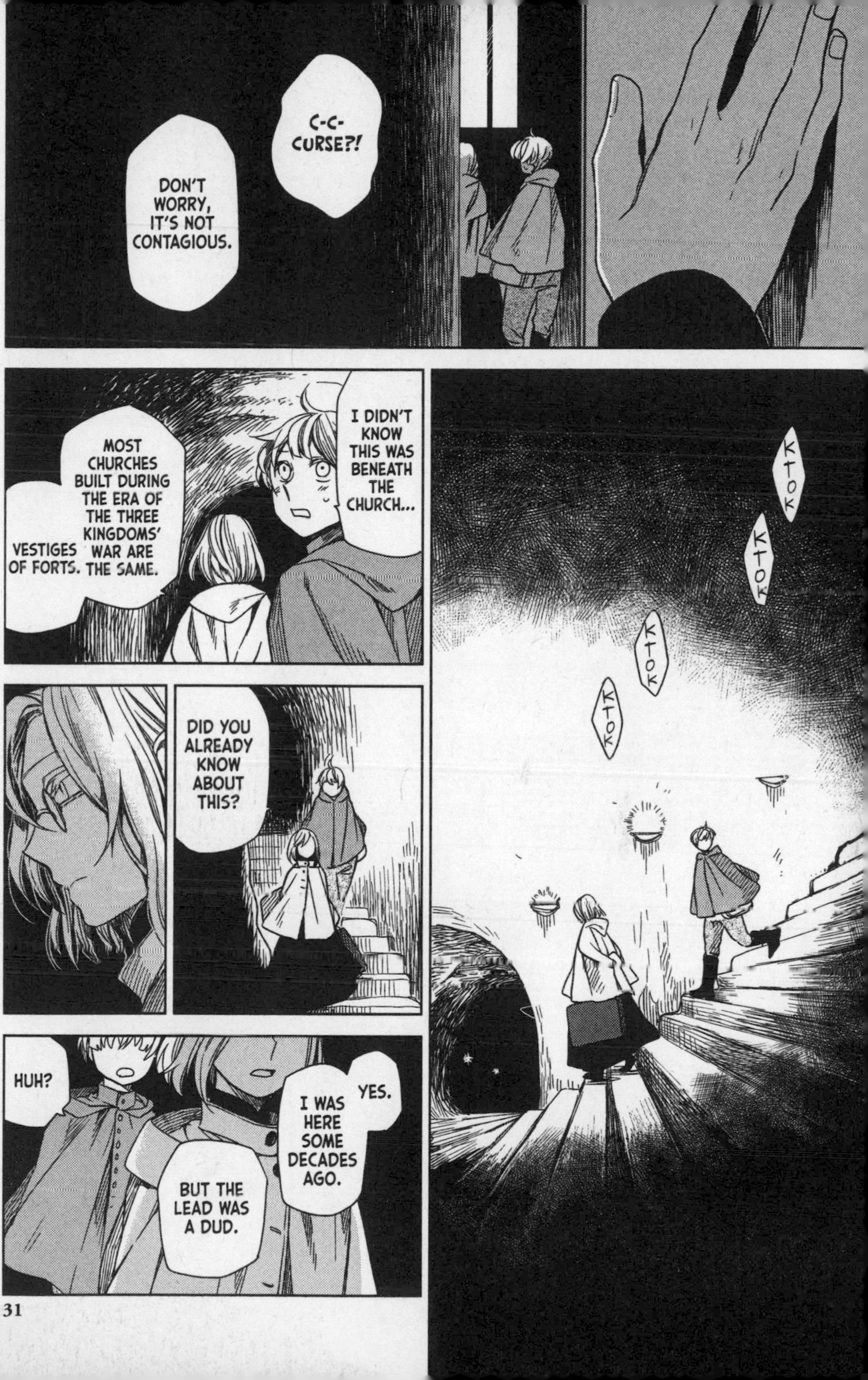
C-C-CURSE?!
DON'T WORRY, IT'S NOT CONTAGIOUS.
KTOK
KTOK
KTOK
KTOK
I DIDN'T KNOW THIS WAS BENEATH THE CHURCH...
MOST CHURCHES BUILT DURING THE ERA OF THE THREE KINGDOMS' WAR ARE THE SAME.
VESTIGES OF FORTS.
DID YOU ALREADY KNOW ABOUT THIS?
YES.
I WAS HERE SOME DECADES AGO.
BUT THE LEAD WAS A DUD.
HUH?

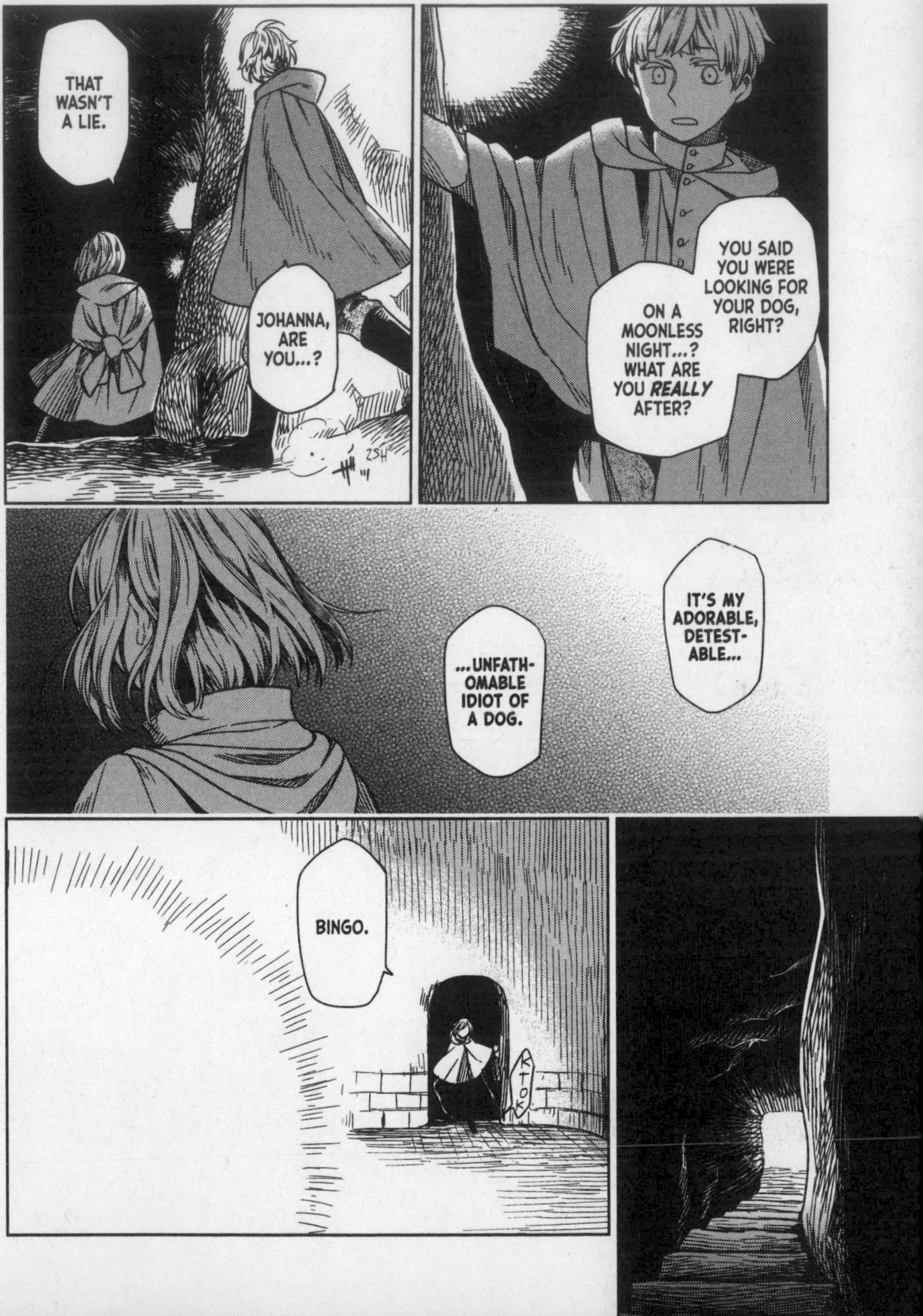
YOU SAID YOU WERE LOOKING FOR YOUR DOG, RIGHT?
ON A MOONLESS NIGHT...? WHAT ARE YOU *REALLY* AFTER?
THAT WASN'T A LIE.
JOHANNA, ARE YOU...?
ZSH
IT'S MY ADORABLE, DETEST-ABLE...
...UNFATH-OMABLE IDIOT OF A DOG.
BINGO.
KTOK

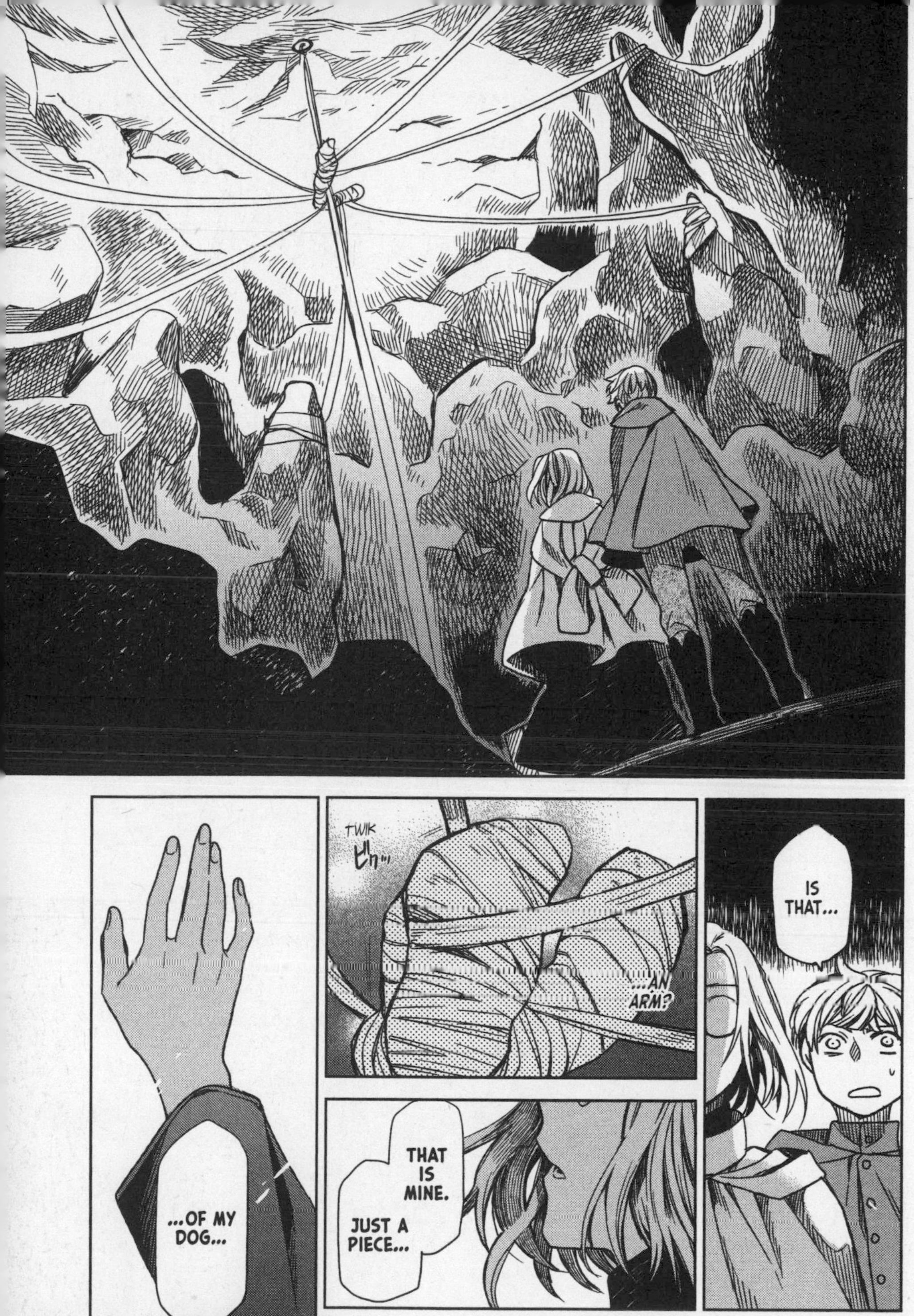
IS THAT...
T.WIK
ビクッ
...AN ARM?
THAT IS MINE.
JUST A PIECE...
...OF MY DOG...

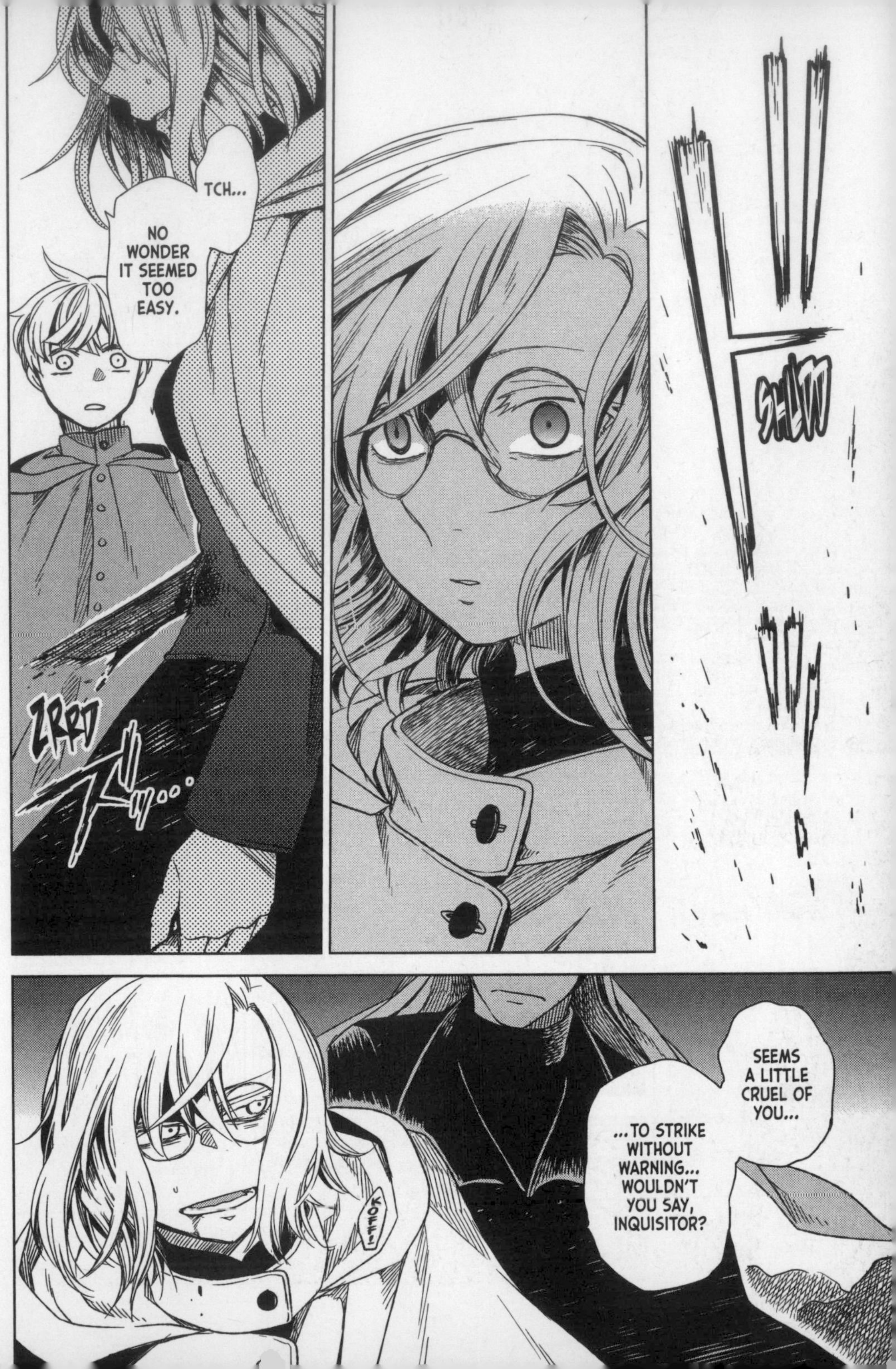
TCH...
NO WONDER IT SEEMED TOO EASY.
ZRRD
SEEMS A LITTLE CRUEL OF YOU...
...TO STRIKE WITHOUT WARNING... WOULDN'T YOU SAY, INQUISITOR?

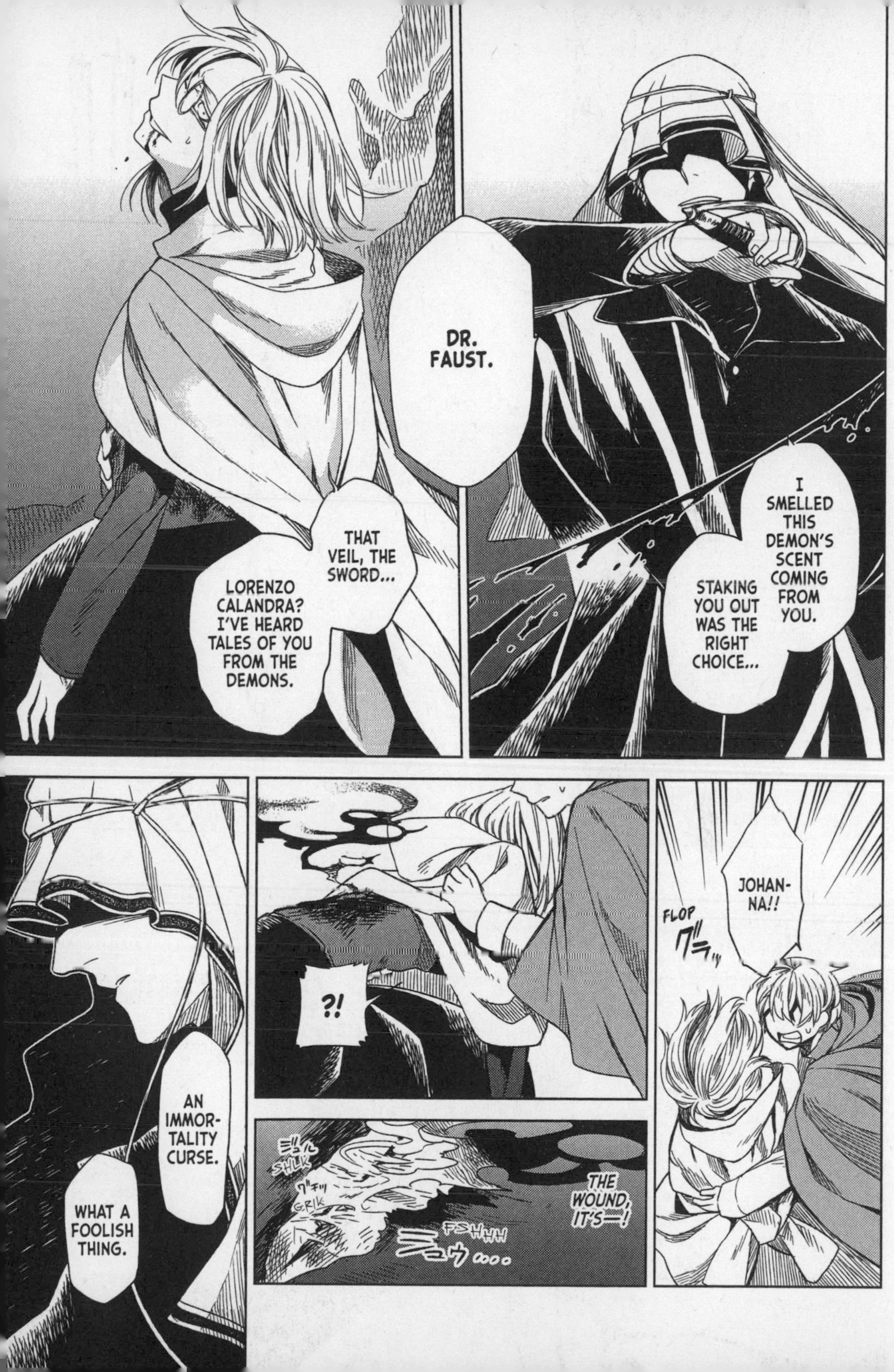
DR. FAUST.
I SMELLED THIS DEMON'S SCENT COMING FROM YOU.
STAKING YOU OUT WAS THE RIGHT CHOICE...
THAT VEIL, THE SWORD...
LORENZO CALANDRA? I'VE HEARD TALES OF YOU FROM THE DEMONS.
JOHAN-NA!!
FLOP
グラッ
?!
ジュル
SHLK
ブチッ
GRIK
THE WOUND, IT'S—!
FSHHH
シュウ…
AN IMMORTALITY CURSE.
WHAT A FOOLISH THING.

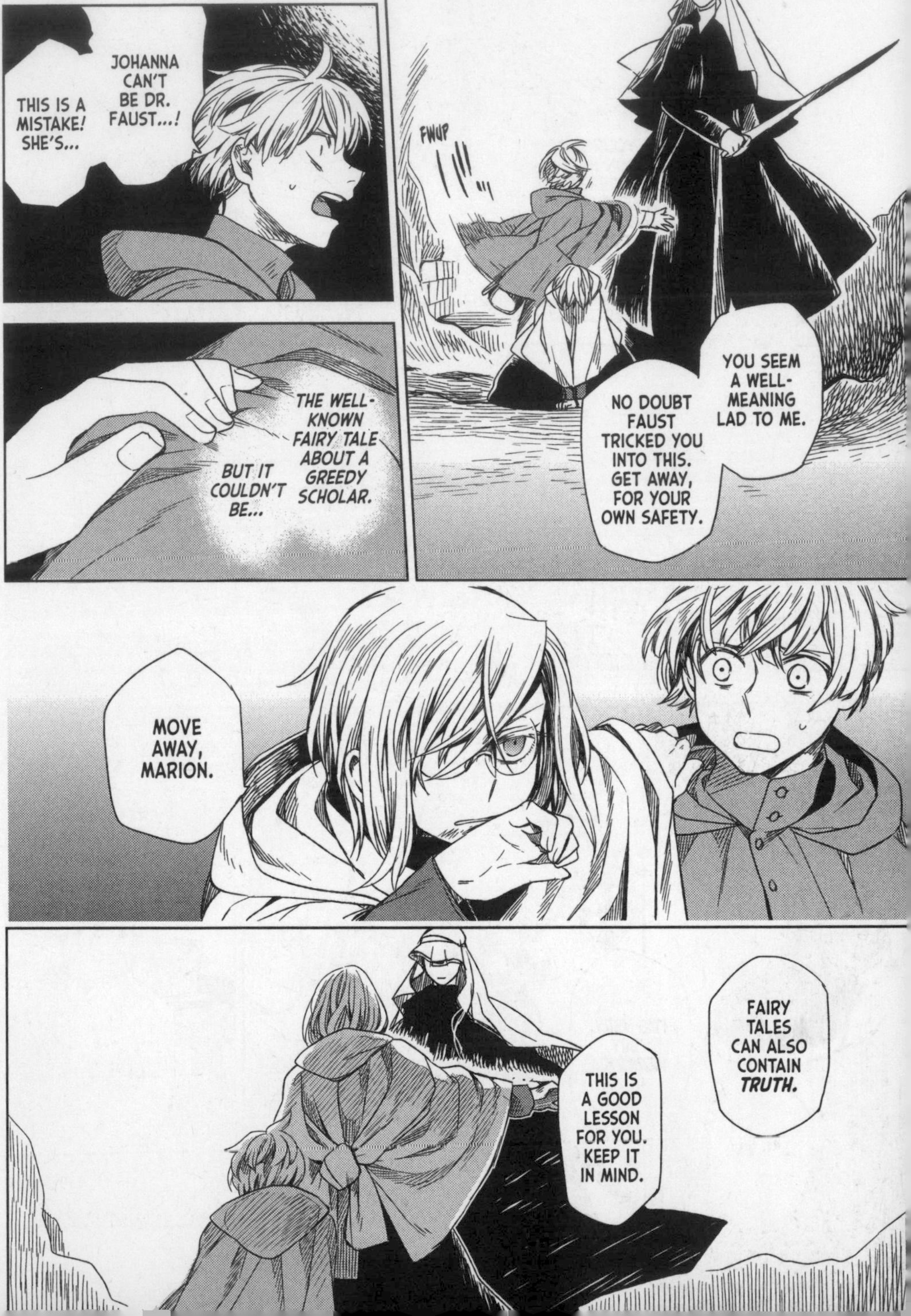
FWUP
YOU SEEM A WELL-MEANING LAD TO ME.
NO DOUBT FAUST TRICKED YOU INTO THIS. GET AWAY, FOR YOUR OWN SAFETY.
JOHANNA CAN'T BE DR. FAUST...!
THIS IS A MISTAKE! SHE'S...
THE WELL-KNOWN FAIRY TALE ABOUT A GREEDY SCHOLAR.
BUT IT COULDN'T BE...
MOVE AWAY, MARION.
FAIRY TALES CAN ALSO CONTAIN *TRUTH.*
THIS IS A GOOD LESSON FOR YOU. KEEP IT IN MIND.

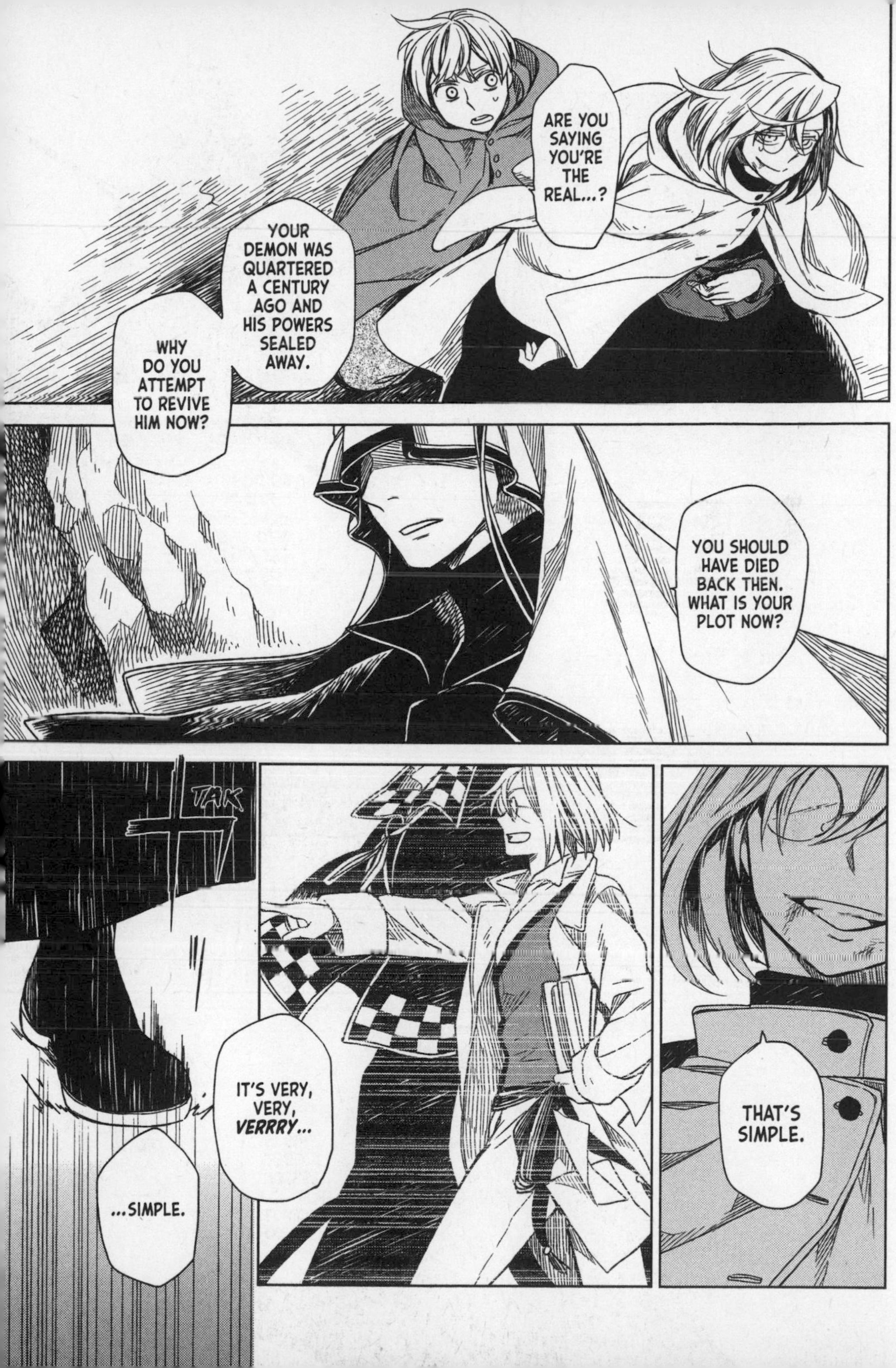
ARE YOU SAYING YOU'RE THE REAL...?
YOUR DEMON WAS QUARTERED A CENTURY AGO AND HIS POWERS SEALED AWAY.
WHY DO YOU ATTEMPT TO REVIVE HIM NOW?
YOU SHOULD HAVE DIED BACK THEN. WHAT IS YOUR PLOT NOW?
THAT'S SIMPLE.
IT'S VERY, VERY, *VERRRY*...
TAK
...SIMPLE.

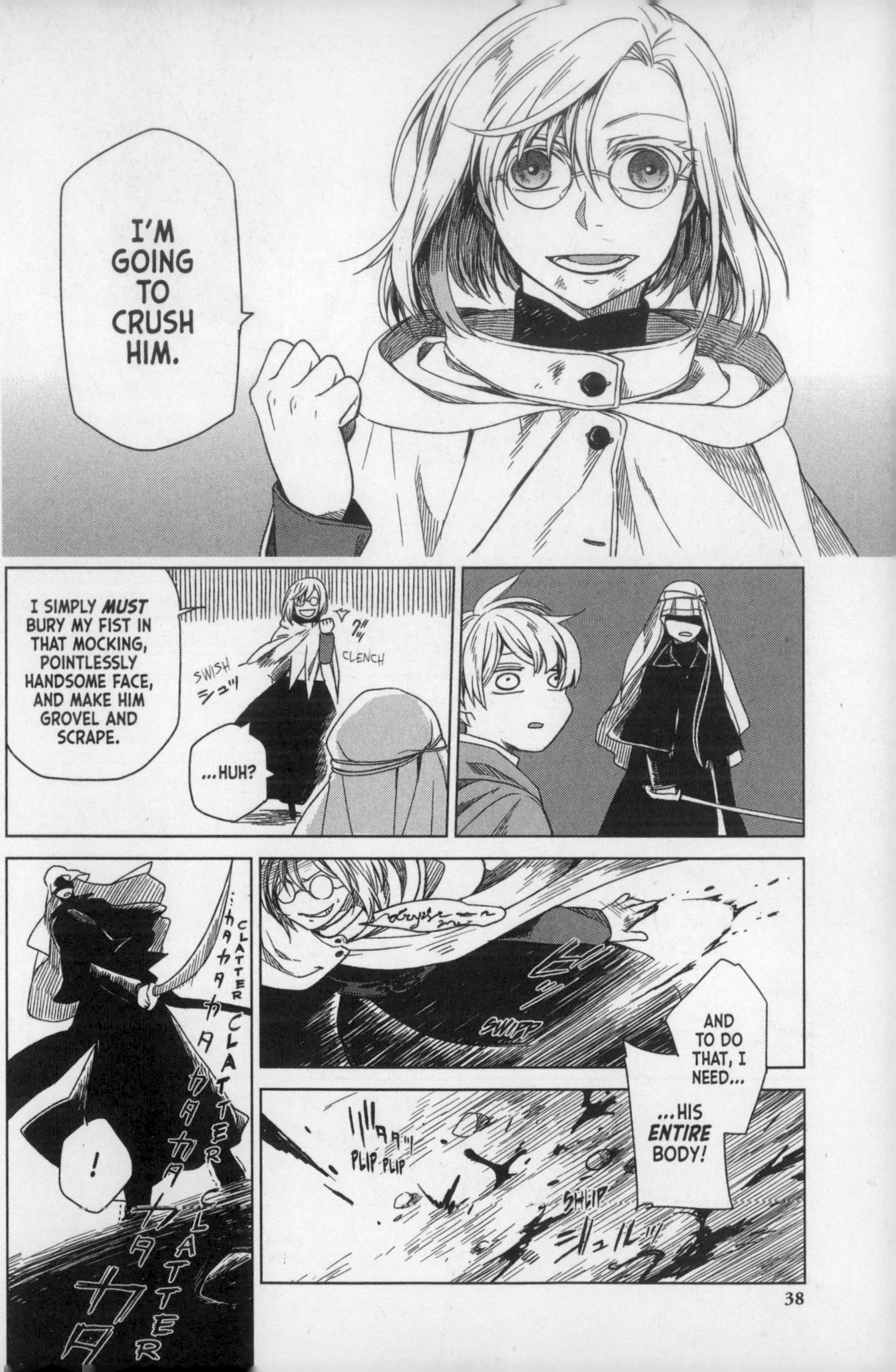
I'M GOING TO CRUSH HIM.
I SIMPLY *MUST* BURY MY FIST IN THAT MOCKING, POINTLESSLY HANDSOME FACE, AND MAKE HIM GROVEL AND SCRAPE.
CLENCH
SWISH
シュッ
...HUH?
SWIPP
AND TO DO THAT, I NEED...
...HIS *ENTIRE* BODY!
PLIP PLIP
SHLIP
シュルッ
CLATTER
CLATTER
CLATTER
CLATTER
!

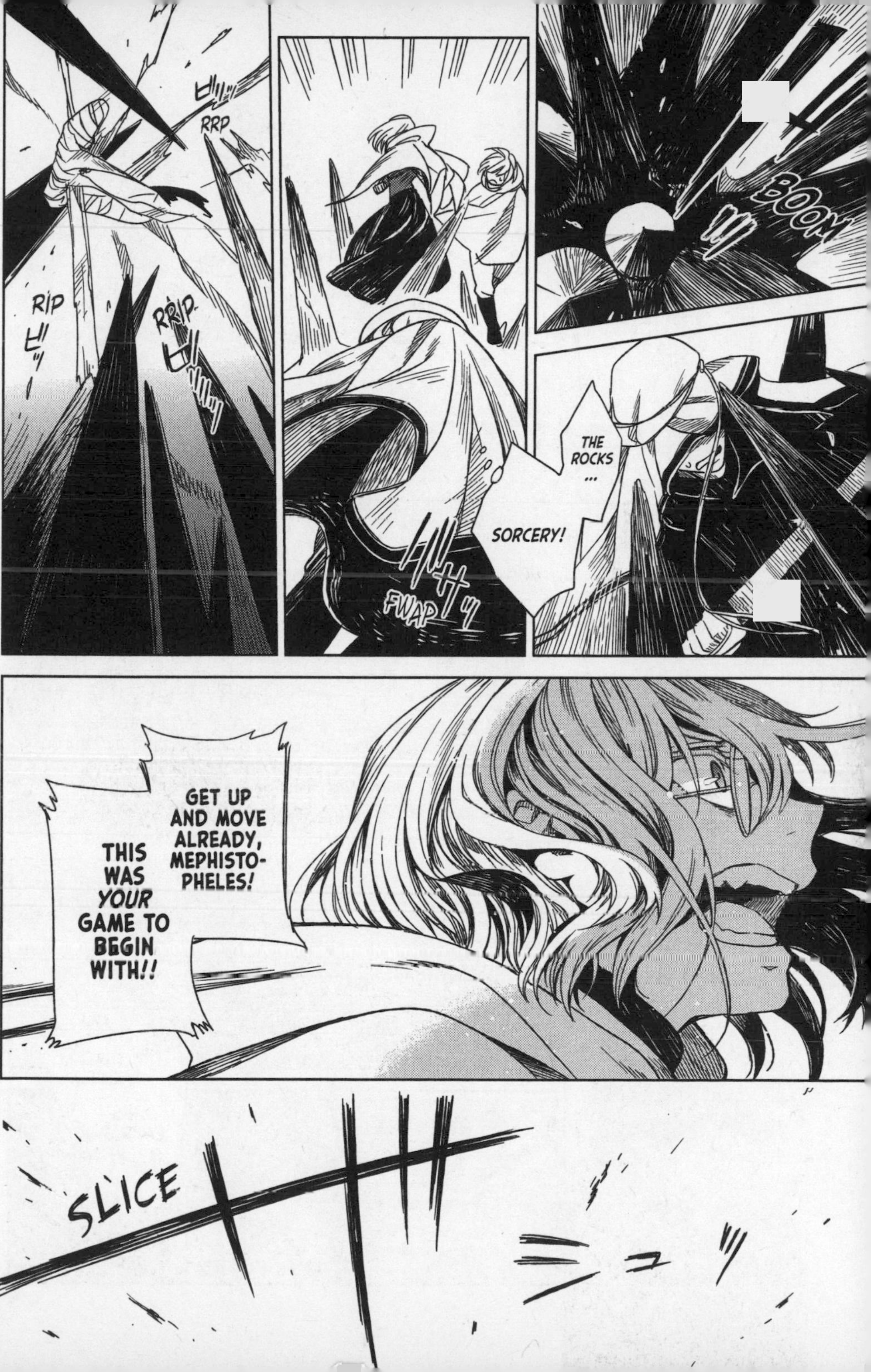
BOOM
THE ROCKS...
SORCERY!
FWAP
RRP
RRIP
RIP
GET UP AND MOVE ALREADY, MEPHISTOPHELES!
THIS WAS *YOUR* GAME TO BEGIN WITH!!
SLICE

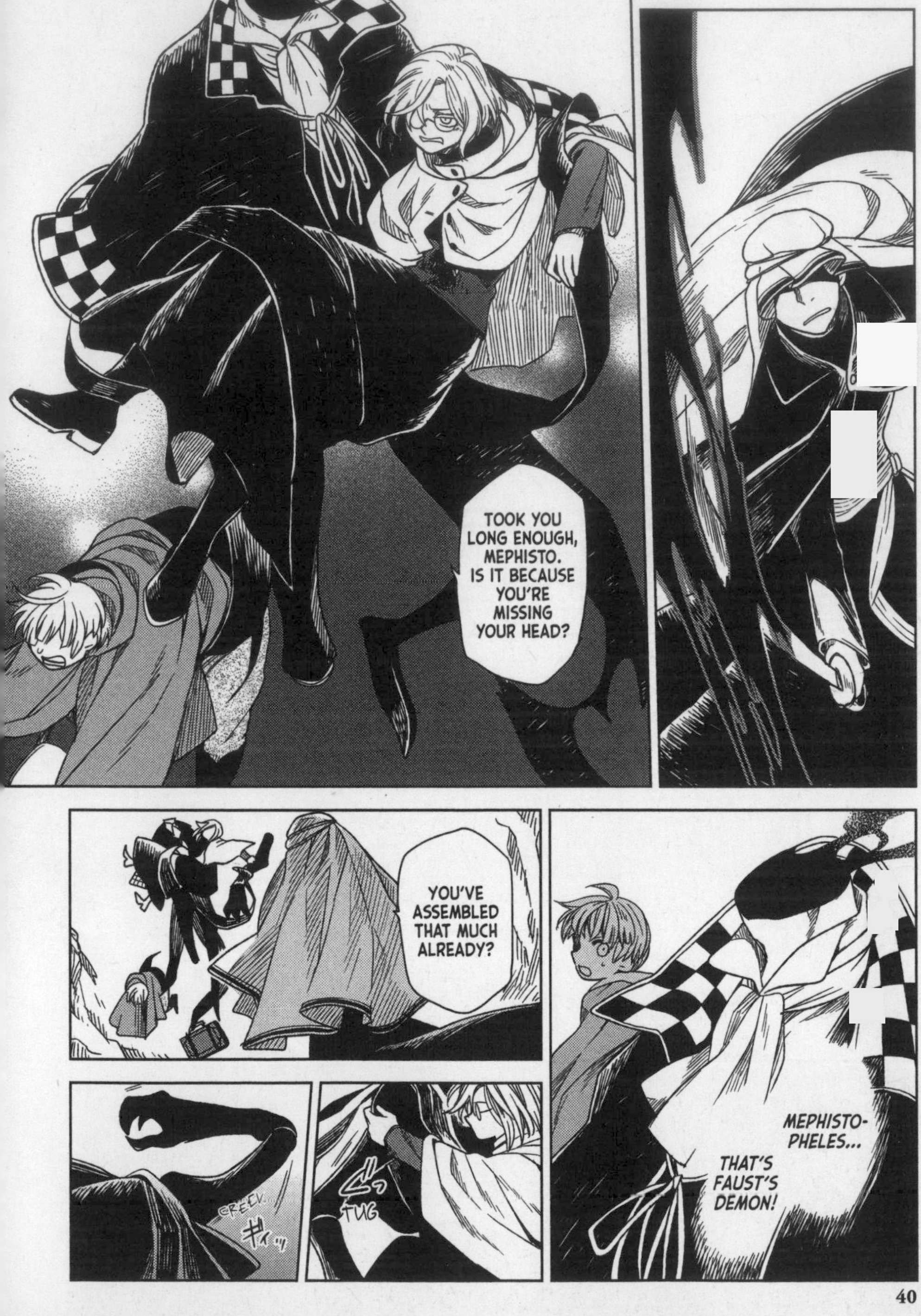
TOOK YOU LONG ENOUGH, MEPHISTO. IS IT BECAUSE YOU'RE MISSING YOUR HEAD?
MEPHISTO-PHELES...
THAT'S FAUST'S DEMON!
YOU'VE ASSEMBLED THAT MUCH ALREADY?
グッ
TUG
CREEV...
ギィッ

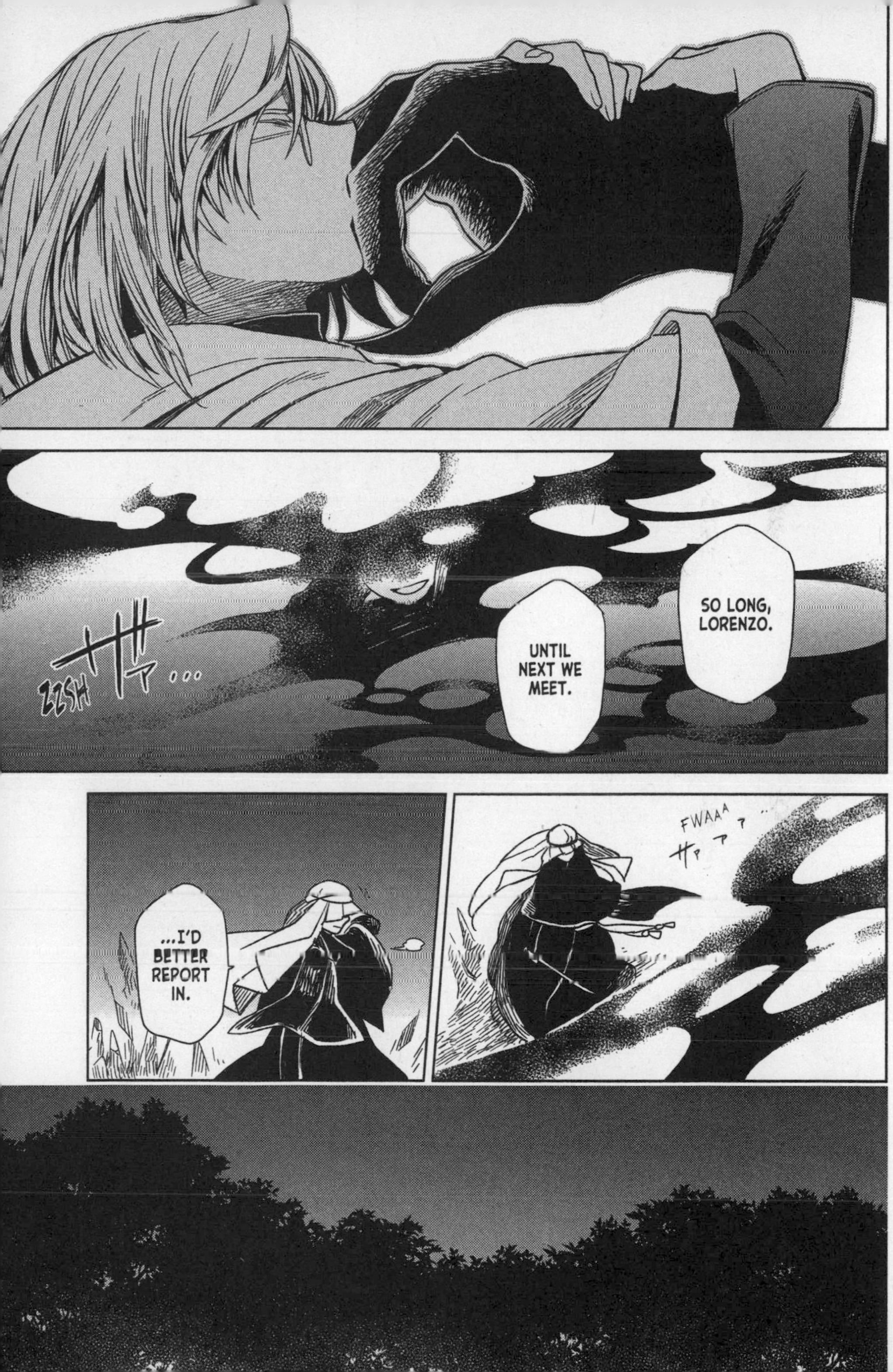
SO LONG, LORENZO.
UNTIL NEXT WE MEET.
ZZSH ...
FWAAA
...I'D BETTER REPORT IN.

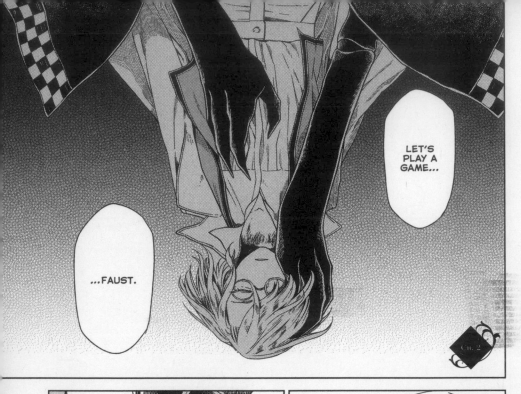

LET'S PLAY A GAME...

...FAUST.

IF YOU CAN CATCH ME, YOU WIN.

IF YOU COME TO A STOP, I WIN.

BUT THIS GAME WILL BE DIFFICULT FOR YOU AS A MORTAL.

SO I PROPOSE...

...A *HANDICAP* FOR YOU.

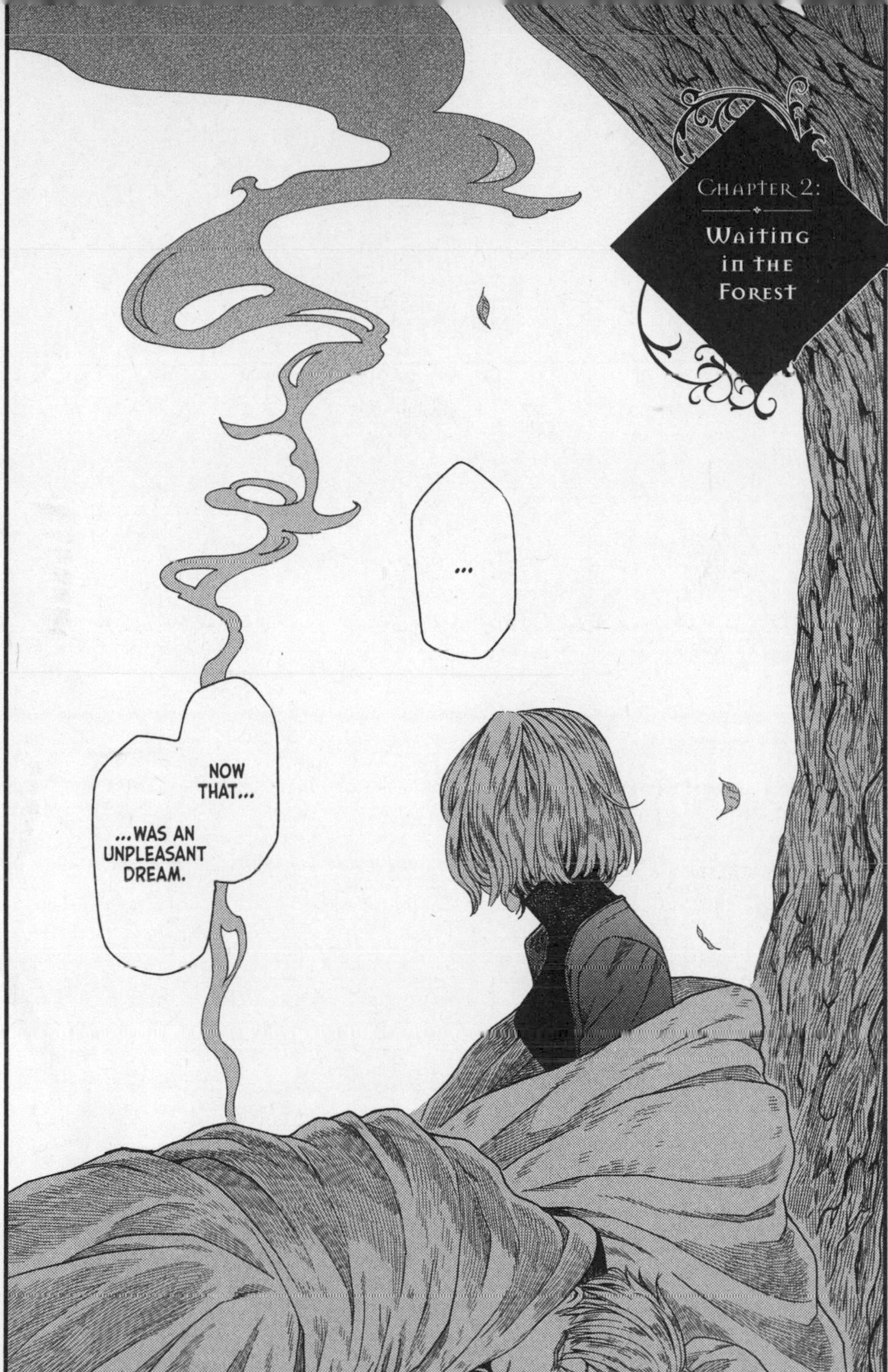
Chapter 2:
Waiting in the Forest
...
NOW THAT...
...WAS AN UNPLEASANT DREAM.

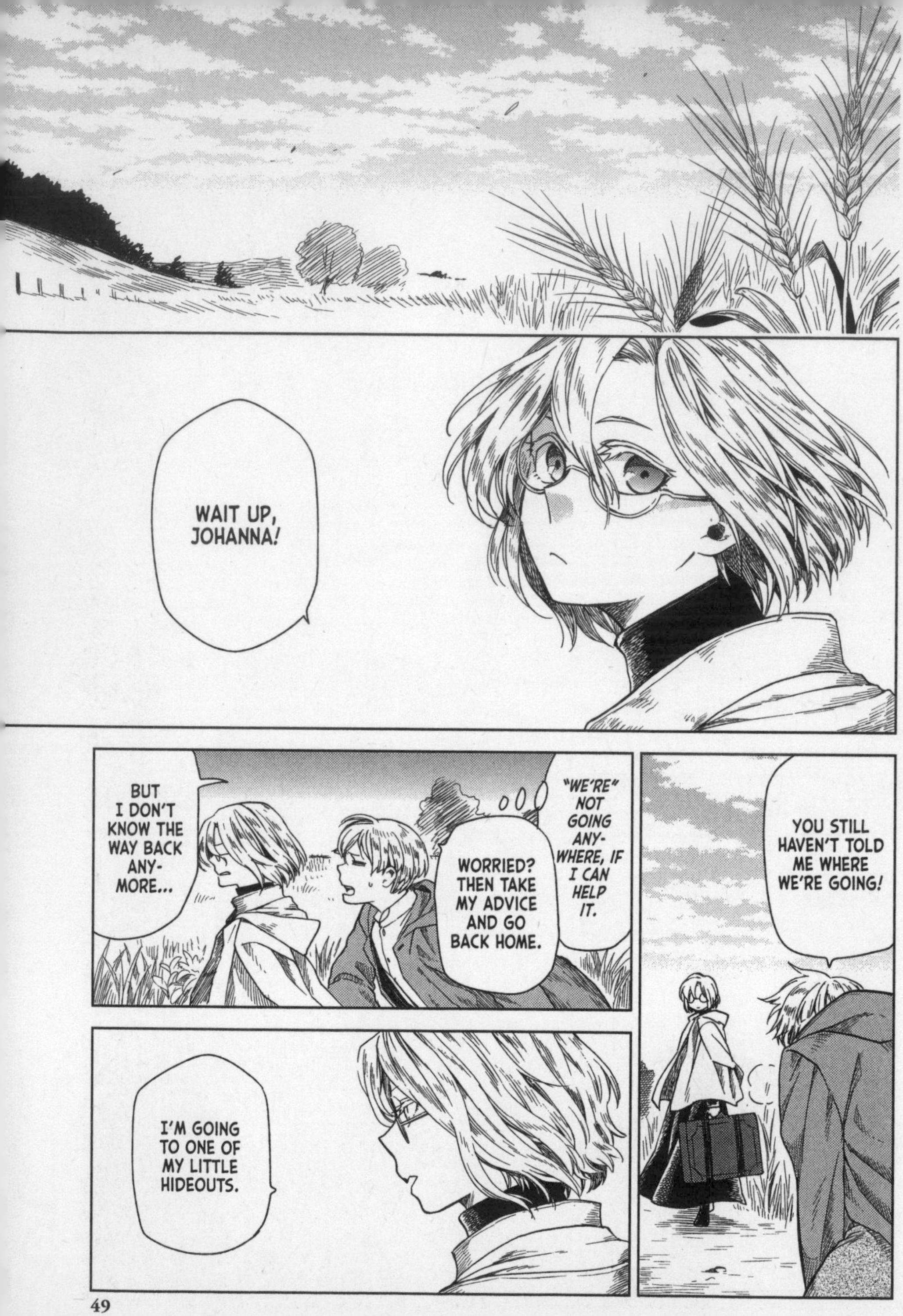
WAIT UP, JOHANNA!
YOU STILL HAVEN'T TOLD ME WHERE WE'RE GOING!
"WE'RE" NOT GOING ANY-WHERE, IF I CAN HELP IT.
WORRIED? THEN TAKE MY ADVICE AND GO BACK HOME.
BUT I DON'T KNOW THE WAY BACK ANY-MORE...
I'M GOING TO ONE OF MY LITTLE HIDEOUTS.

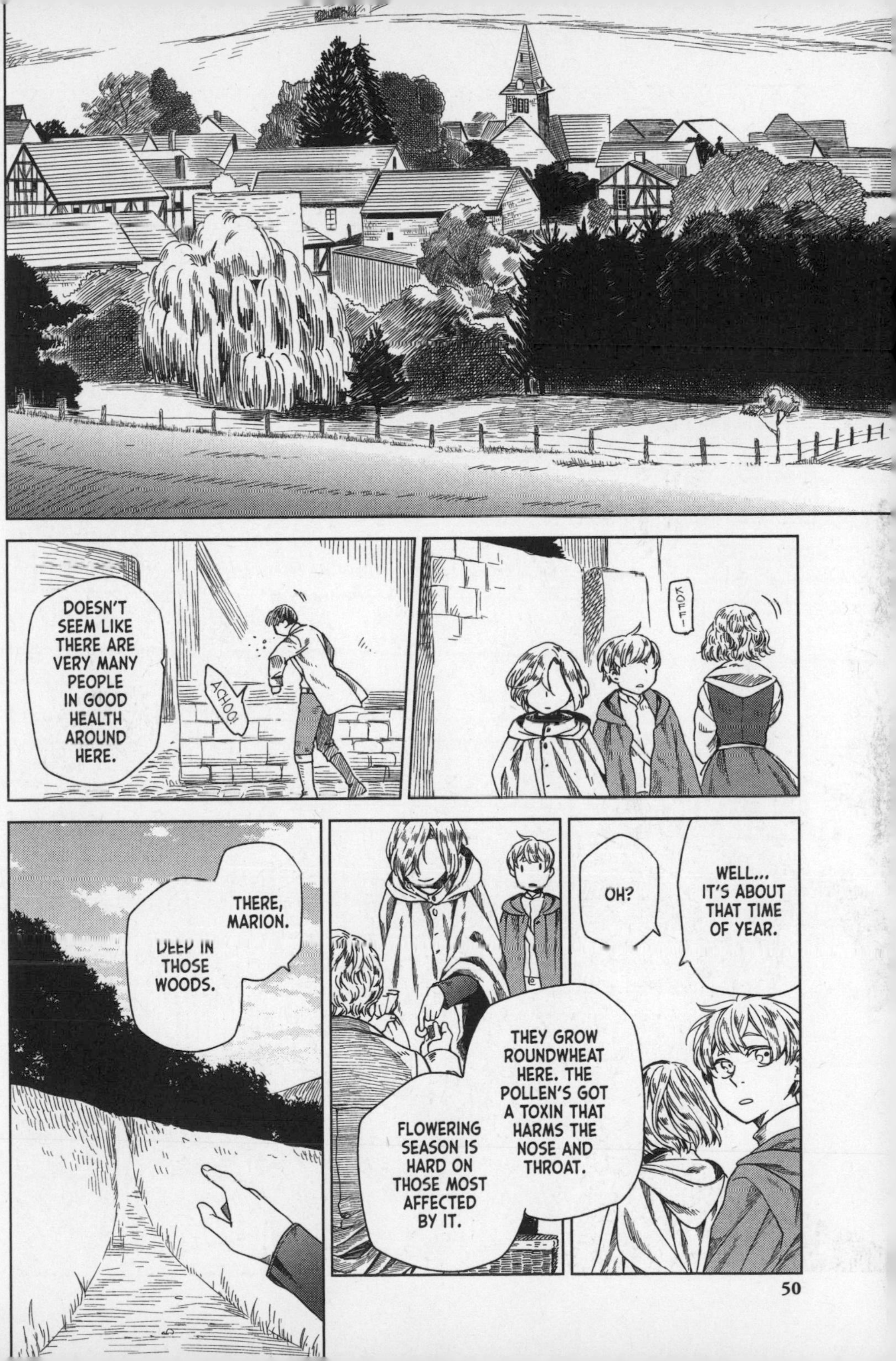
KOFF!
ACHOO!
DOESN'T SEEM LIKE THERE ARE VERY MANY PEOPLE IN GOOD HEALTH AROUND HERE.
WELL... IT'S ABOUT THAT TIME OF YEAR.
OH?
THEY GROW ROUNDWHEAT HERE. THE POLLEN'S GOT A TOXIN THAT HARMS THE NOSE AND THROAT.
FLOWERING SEASON IS HARD ON THOSE MOST AFFECTED BY IT.
THERE, MARION.
DEEP IN THOSE WOODS.

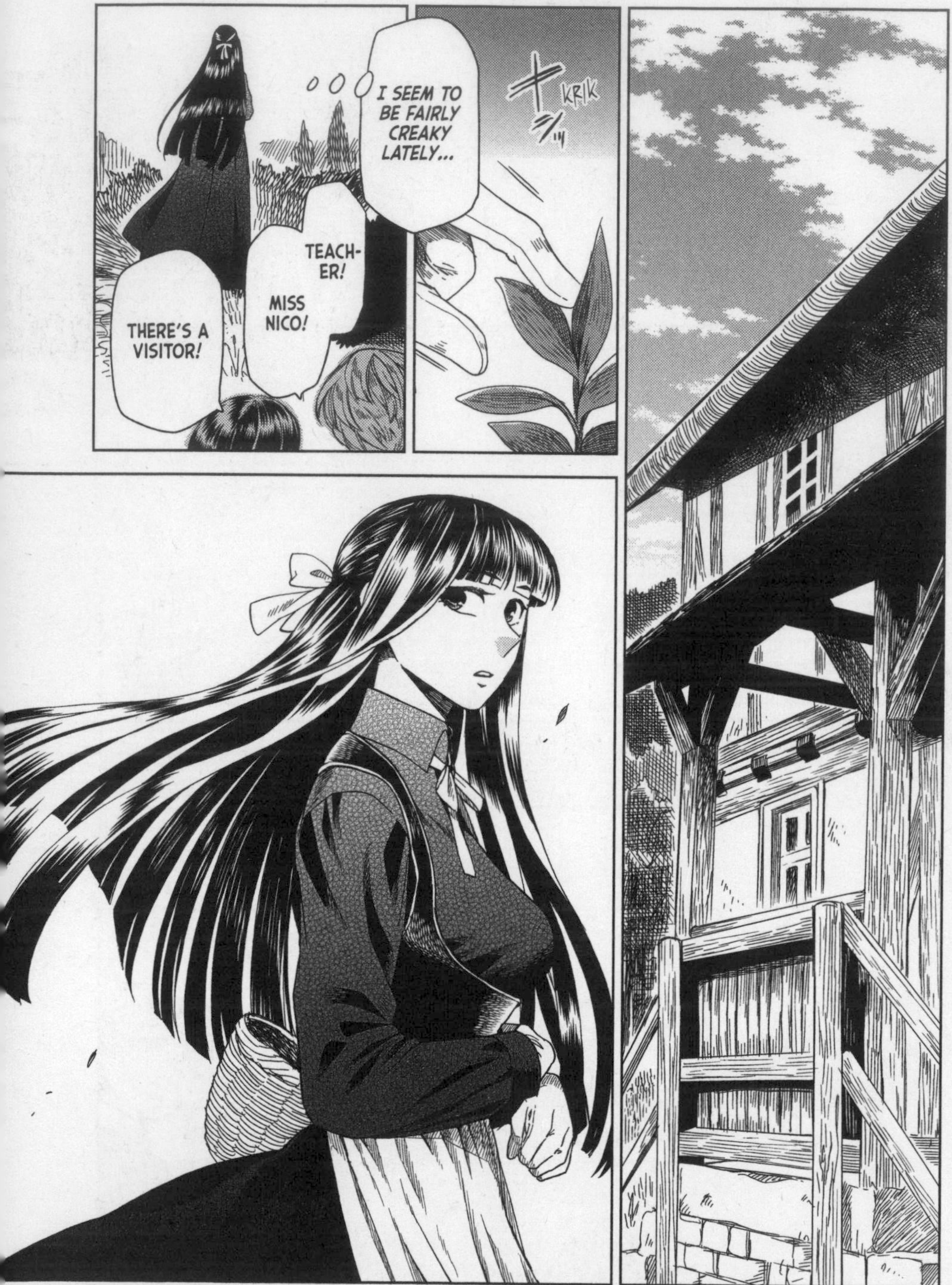
KRIK
I SEEM TO BE FAIRLY CREAKY LATELY...
TEACHER-ER!
MISS NICO!
THERE'S A VISITOR!

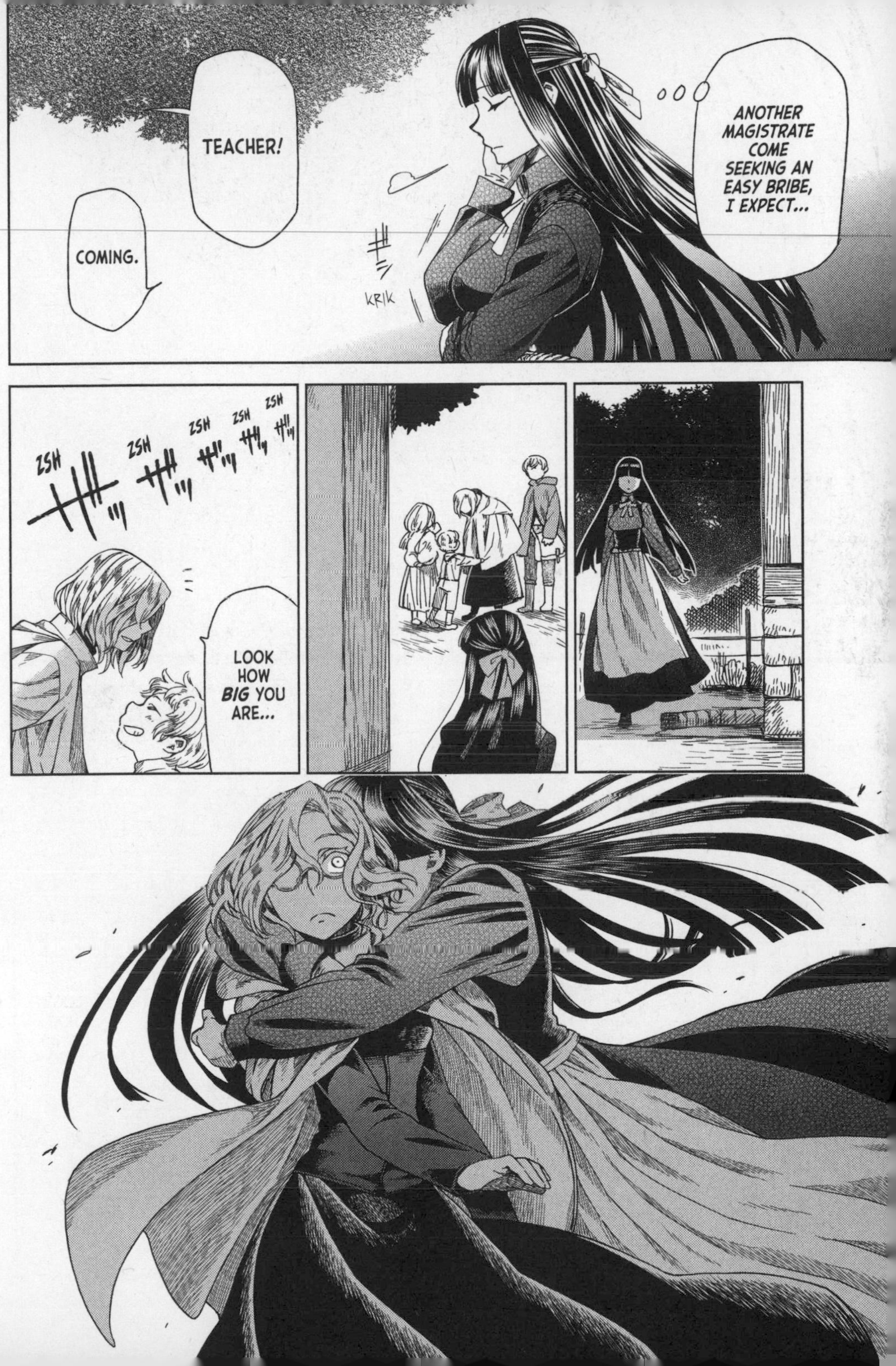
ANOTHER MAGISTRATE COME SEEKING AN EASY BRIBE, I EXPECT...
TEACHER!
COMING.
KRIK
ZSH ZSH ZSH ZSH ZSH
LOOK HOW *BIG* YOU ARE...

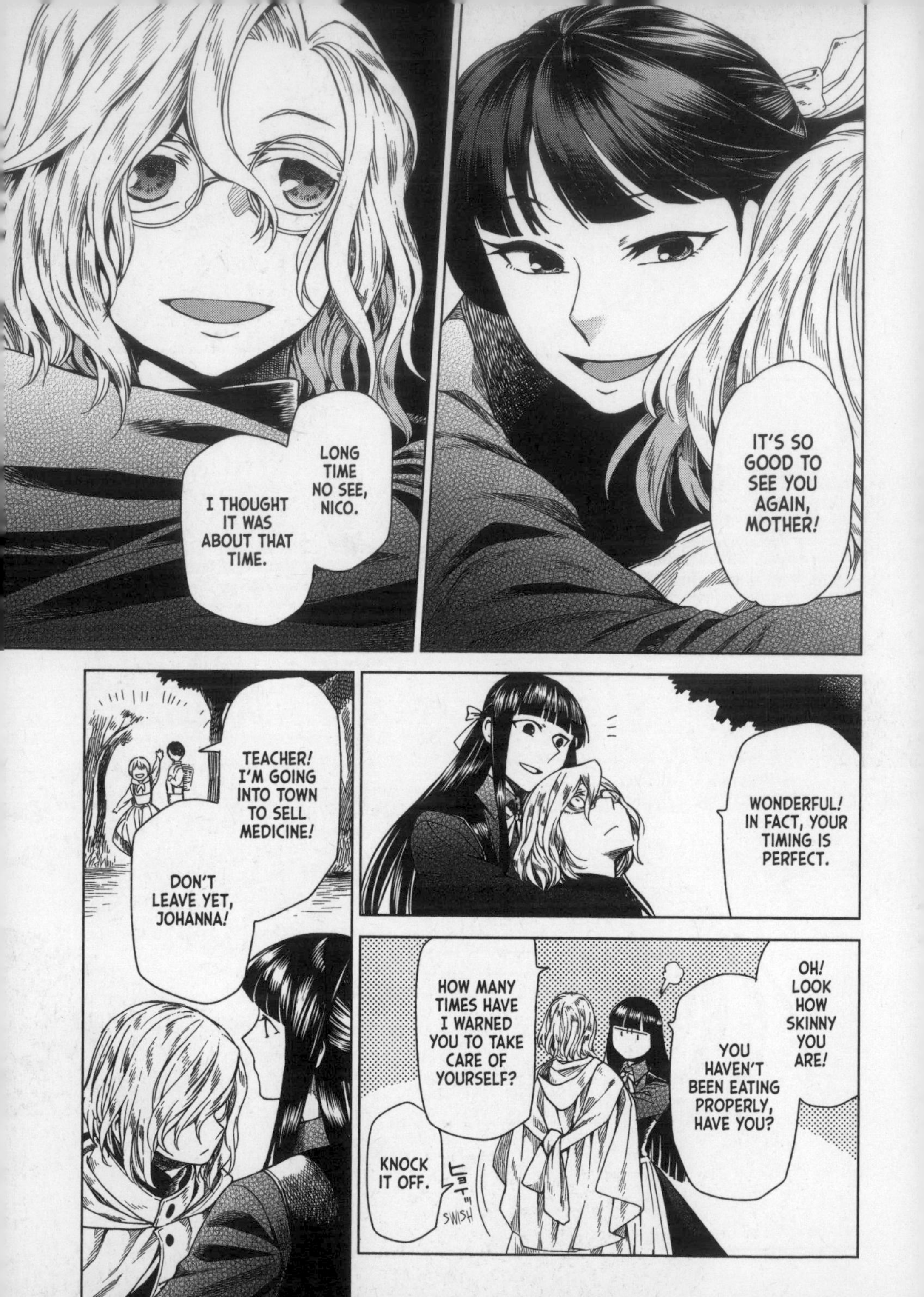
IT'S SO GOOD TO SEE YOU AGAIN, MOTHER!
LONG TIME NO SEE, NICO.
I THOUGHT IT WAS ABOUT THAT TIME.
WONDERFUL! IN FACT, YOUR TIMING IS PERFECT.
OH! LOOK HOW SKINNY YOU ARE!
YOU HAVEN'T BEEN EATING PROPERLY, HAVE YOU?
HOW MANY TIMES HAVE I WARNED YOU TO TAKE CARE OF YOURSELF?
KNOCK IT OFF.
SWISH
TEACHER! I'M GOING INTO TOWN TO SELL MEDICINE!
DON'T LEAVE YET, JOHANNA!

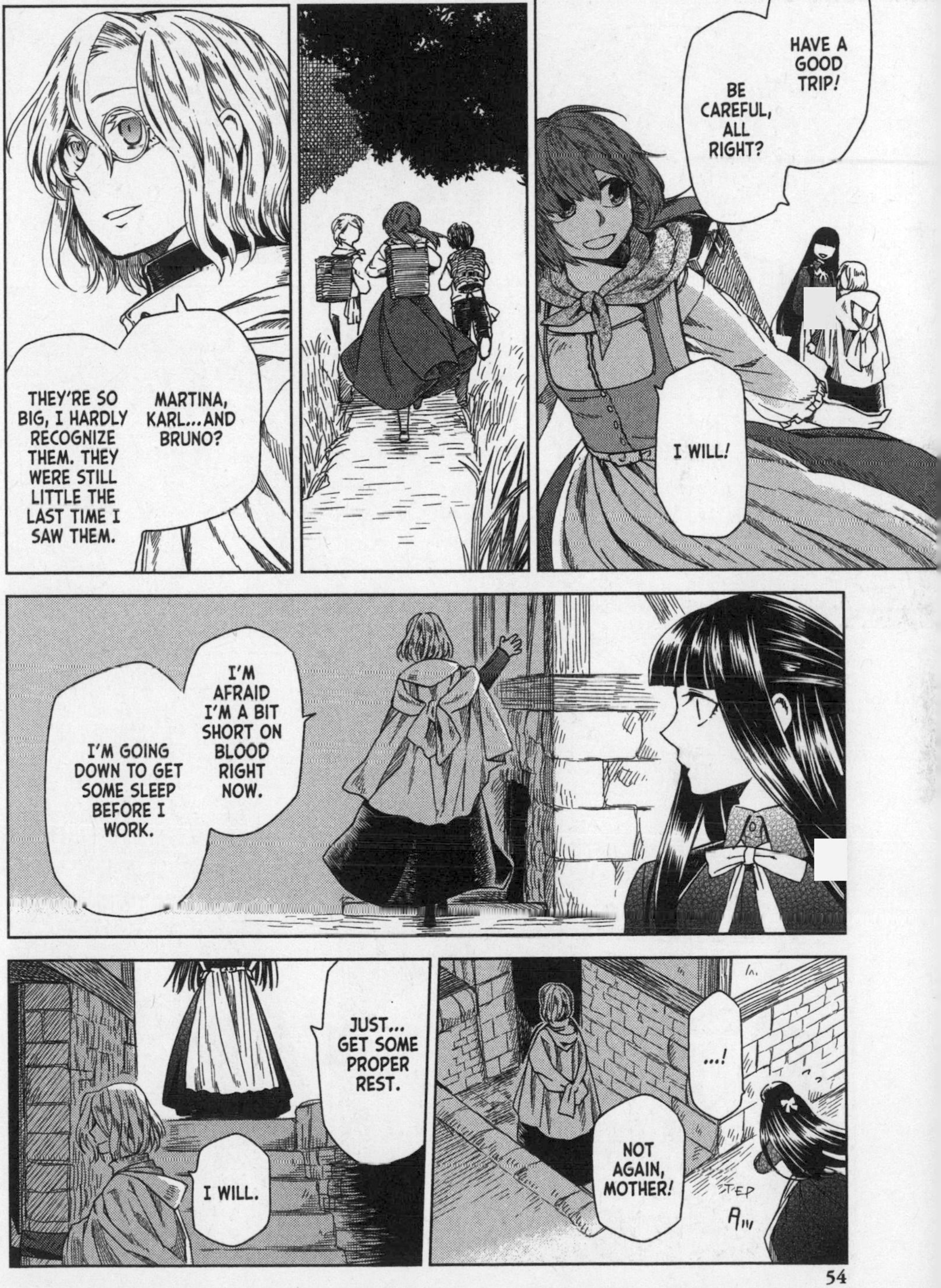
HAVE A GOOD TRIP!
BE CAREFUL, ALL RIGHT?
I WILL!
MARTINA, KARL...AND BRUNO?
THEY'RE SO BIG, I HARDLY RECOGNIZE THEM. THEY WERE STILL LITTLE THE LAST TIME I SAW THEM.
I'M AFRAID I'M A BIT SHORT ON BLOOD RIGHT NOW.
I'M GOING DOWN TO GET SOME SLEEP BEFORE I WORK.
...!
NOT AGAIN, MOTHER!
JUST... GET SOME PROPER REST.
I WILL.

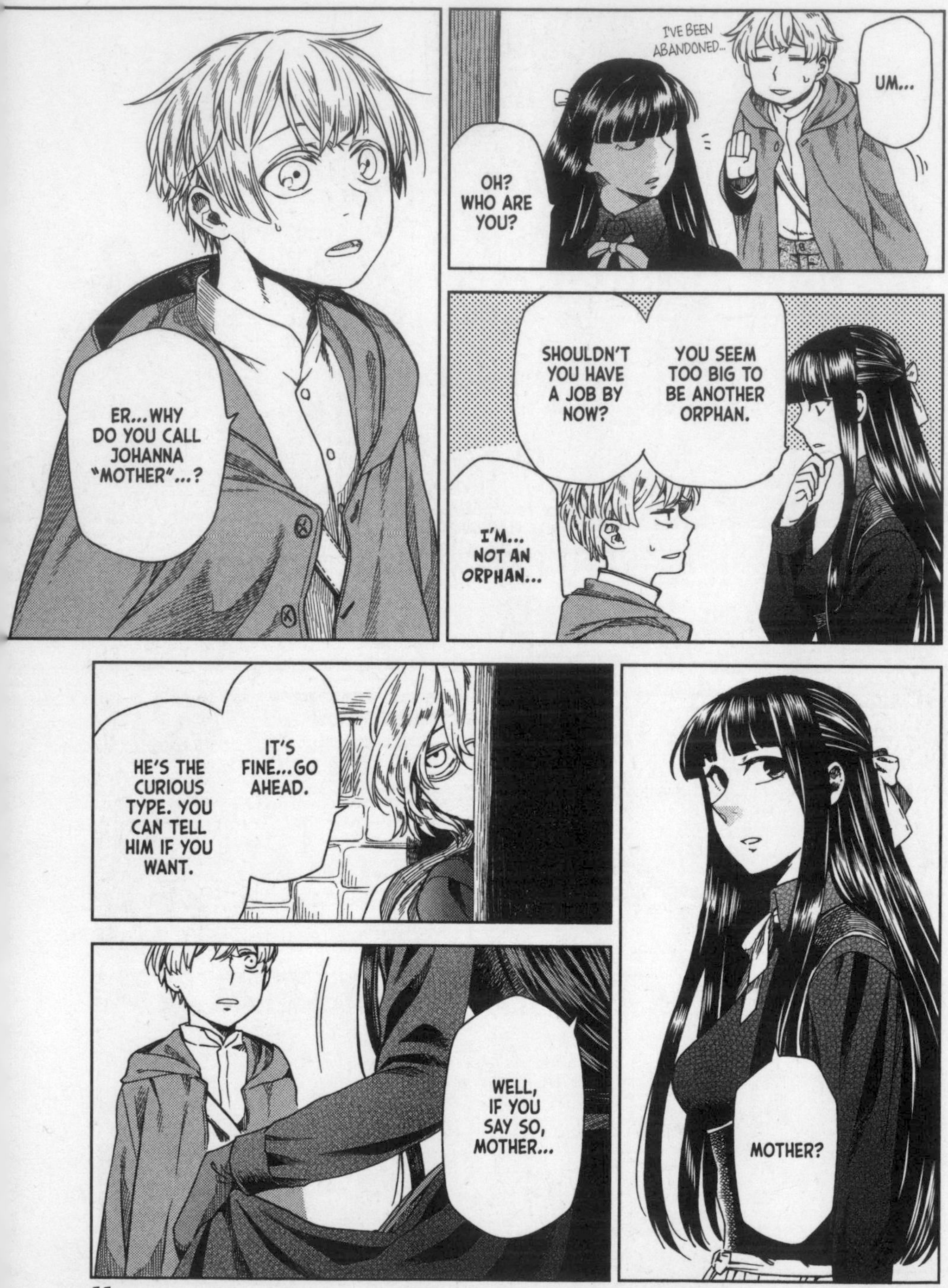
UM...
I'VE BEEN ABANDONED...
OH? WHO ARE YOU?
YOU SEEM TOO BIG TO BE ANOTHER ORPHAN.
SHOULDN'T YOU HAVE A JOB BY NOW?
I'M... NOT AN ORPHAN...
ER...WHY DO YOU CALL JOHANNA "MOTHER"...?
MOTHER?
IT'S FINE...GO AHEAD.
HE'S THE CURIOUS TYPE. YOU CAN TELL HIM IF YOU WANT.
WELL, IF YOU SAY SO, MOTHER...

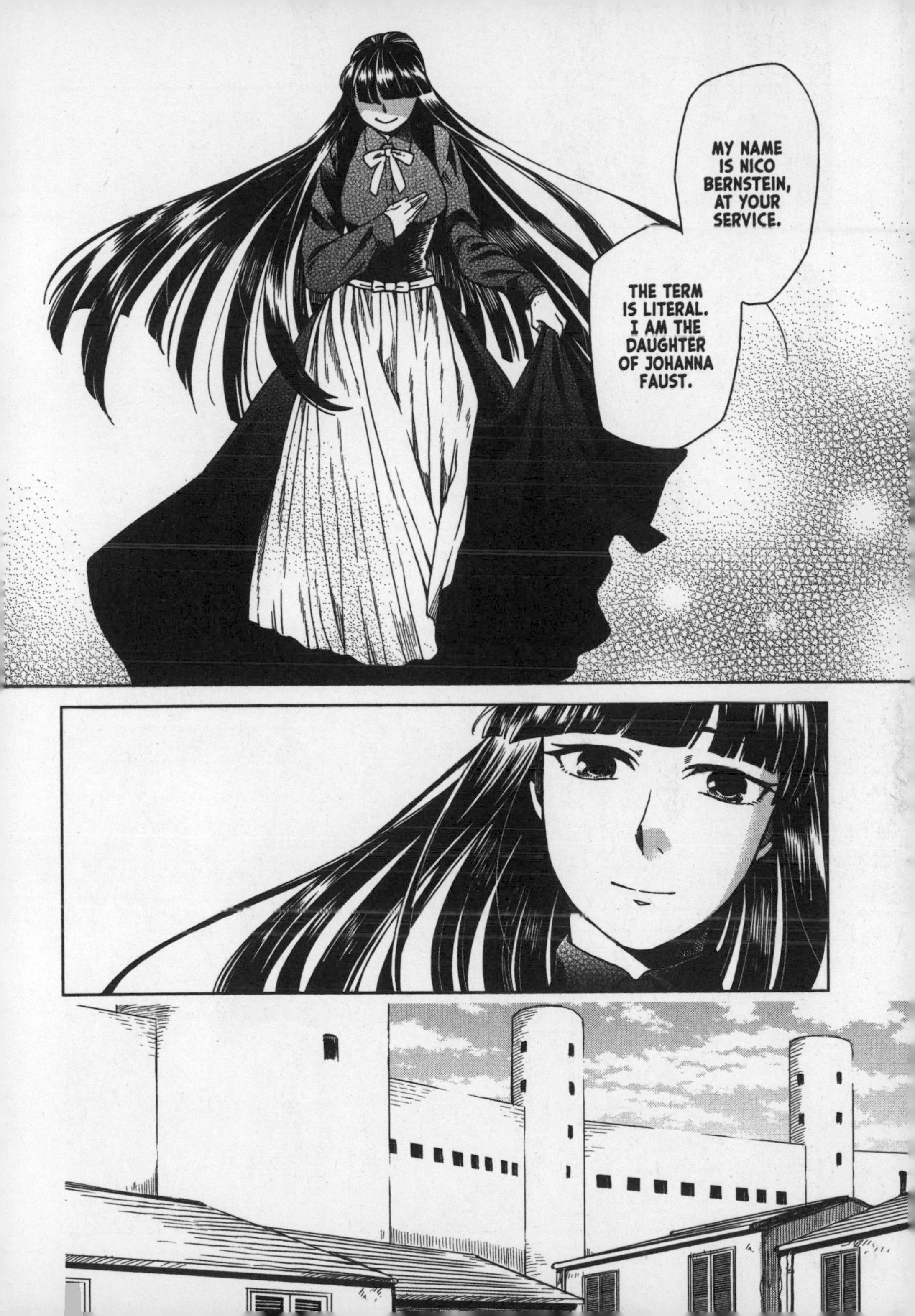
MY NAME IS NICO BERNSTEIN, AT YOUR SERVICE.
THE TERM IS LITERAL. I AM THE DAUGHTER OF JOHANNA FAUST.

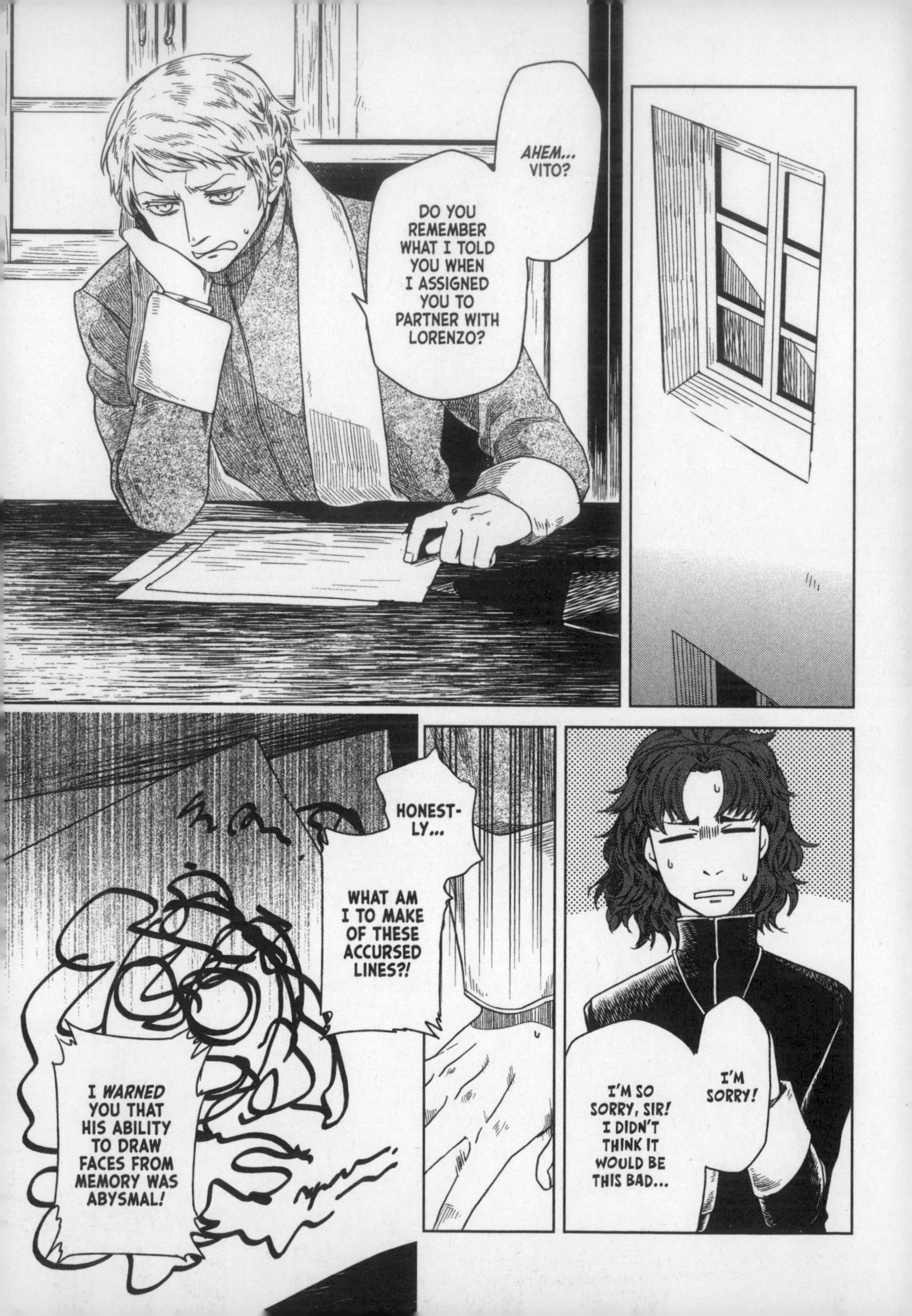
AHEM... VITO?
DO YOU REMEMBER WHAT I TOLD YOU WHEN I ASSIGNED YOU TO PARTNER WITH LORENZO?
I'M SORRY!
I'M SO SORRY, SIR! I DIDN'T THINK IT WOULD BE THIS BAD...
HONESTLY...
WHAT AM I TO MAKE OF THESE ACCURSED LINES?!
I WARNED YOU THAT HIS ABILITY TO DRAW FACES FROM MEMORY WAS ABYSMAL!

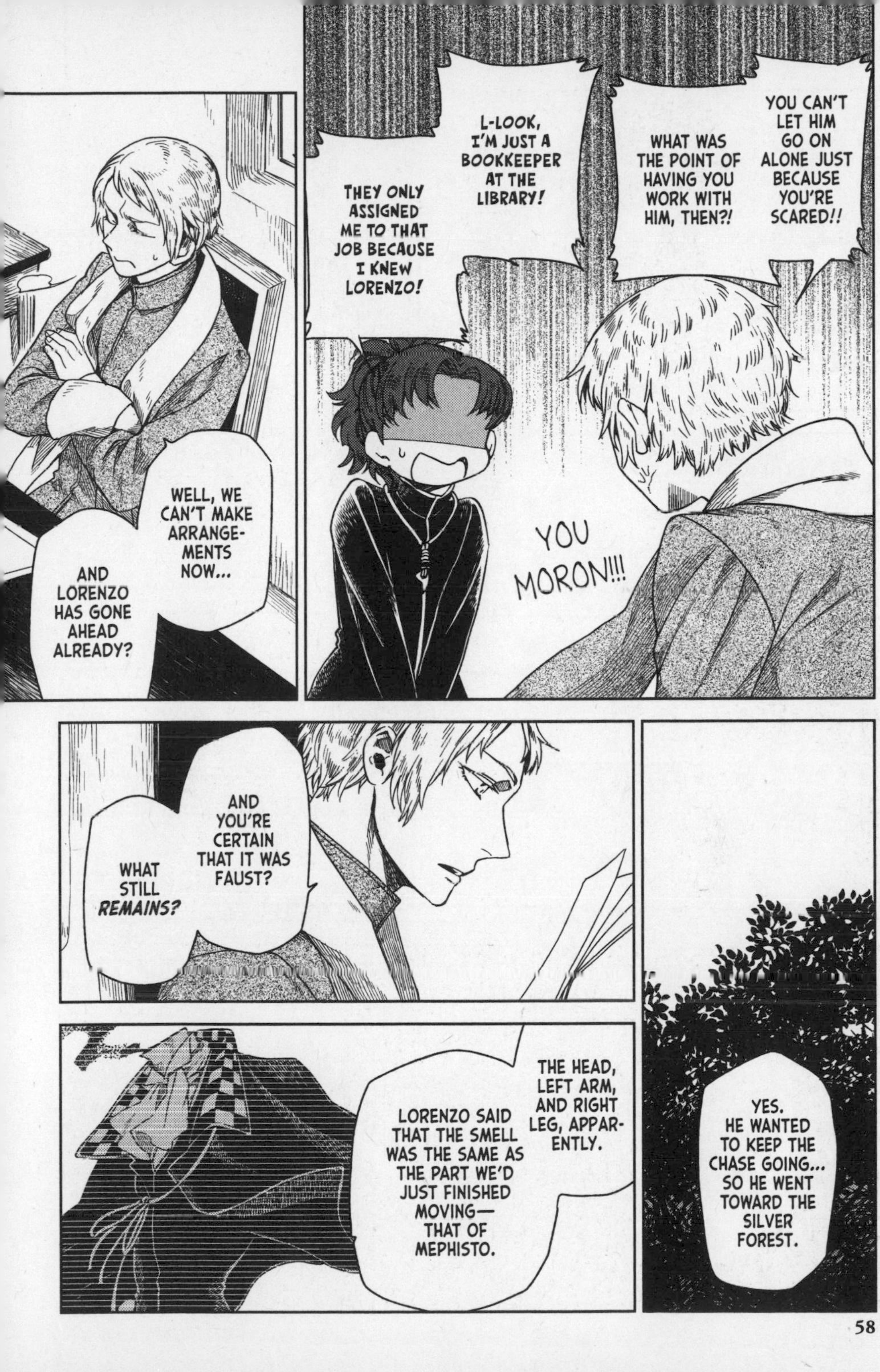
YOU CAN'T LET HIM GO ON ALONE JUST BECAUSE YOU'RE SCARED!!
WHAT WAS THE POINT OF HAVING YOU WORK WITH HIM, THEN?!
YOU MORON!!!
L-LOOK, I'M JUST A BOOKKEEPER AT THE LIBRARY!
THEY ONLY ASSIGNED ME TO THAT JOB BECAUSE I KNEW LORENZO!
WELL, WE CAN'T MAKE ARRANGE-MENTS NOW...
AND LORENZO HAS GONE AHEAD ALREADY?
YES. HE WANTED TO KEEP THE CHASE GOING... SO HE WENT TOWARD THE SILVER FOREST.
AND YOU'RE CERTAIN THAT IT WAS FAUST?
WHAT STILL *REMAINS?*
THE HEAD, LEFT ARM, AND RIGHT LEG, APPAR-ENTLY.
LORENZO SAID THAT THE SMELL WAS THE SAME AS THE PART WE'D JUST FINISHED MOVING—THAT OF MEPHISTO.

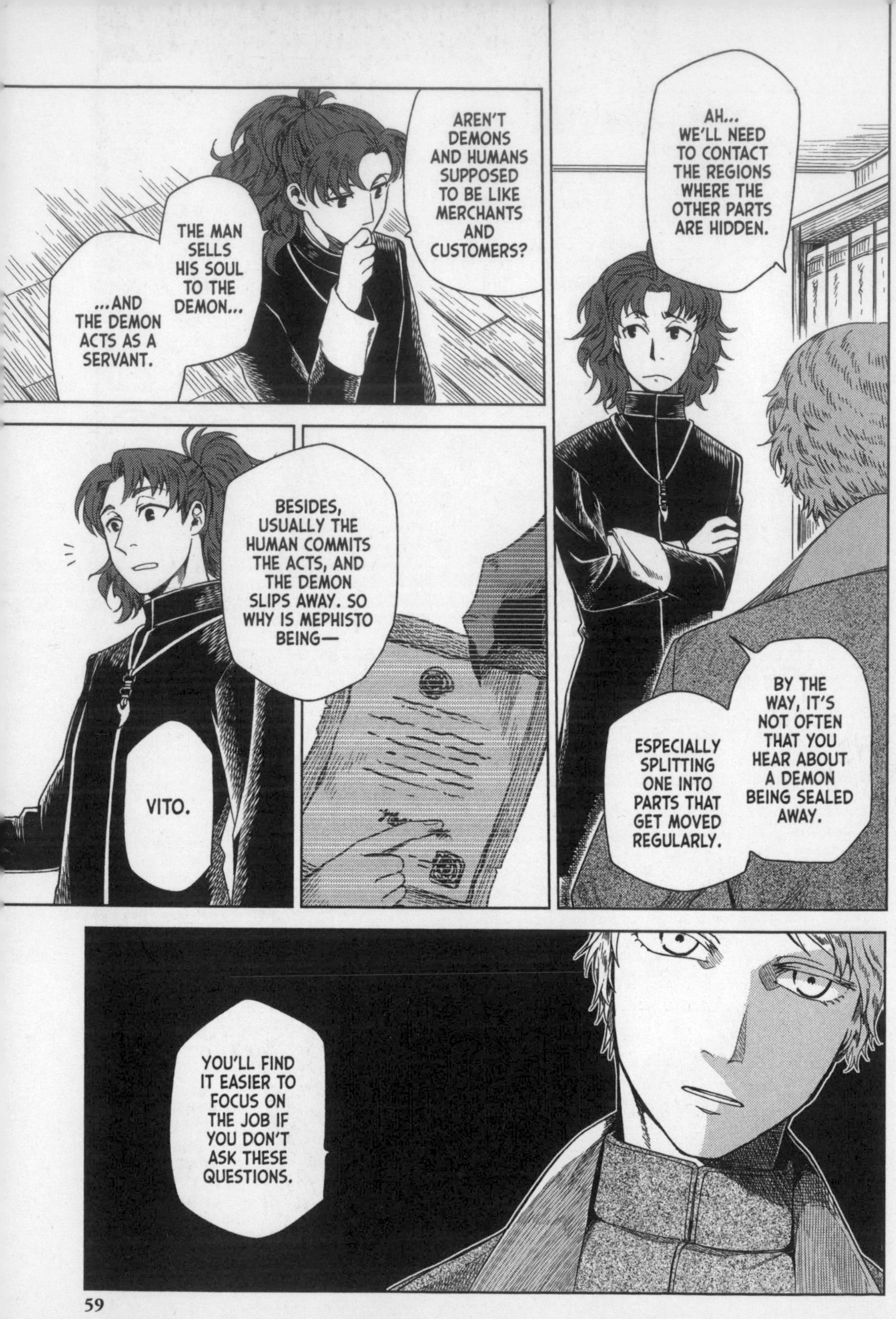
AH... WE'LL NEED TO CONTACT THE REGIONS WHERE THE OTHER PARTS ARE HIDDEN.
BY THE WAY, IT'S NOT OFTEN THAT YOU HEAR ABOUT A DEMON BEING SEALED AWAY.
ESPECIALLY SPLITTING ONE INTO PARTS THAT GET MOVED REGULARLY.
AREN'T DEMONS AND HUMANS SUPPOSED TO BE LIKE MERCHANTS AND CUSTOMERS?
THE MAN SELLS HIS SOUL TO THE DEMON...
...AND THE DEMON ACTS AS A SERVANT.
BESIDES, USUALLY THE HUMAN COMMITS THE ACTS, AND THE DEMON SLIPS AWAY. SO WHY IS MEPHISTO BEING—
VITO.
YOU'LL FIND IT EASIER TO FOCUS ON THE JOB IF YOU DON'T ASK THESE QUESTIONS.

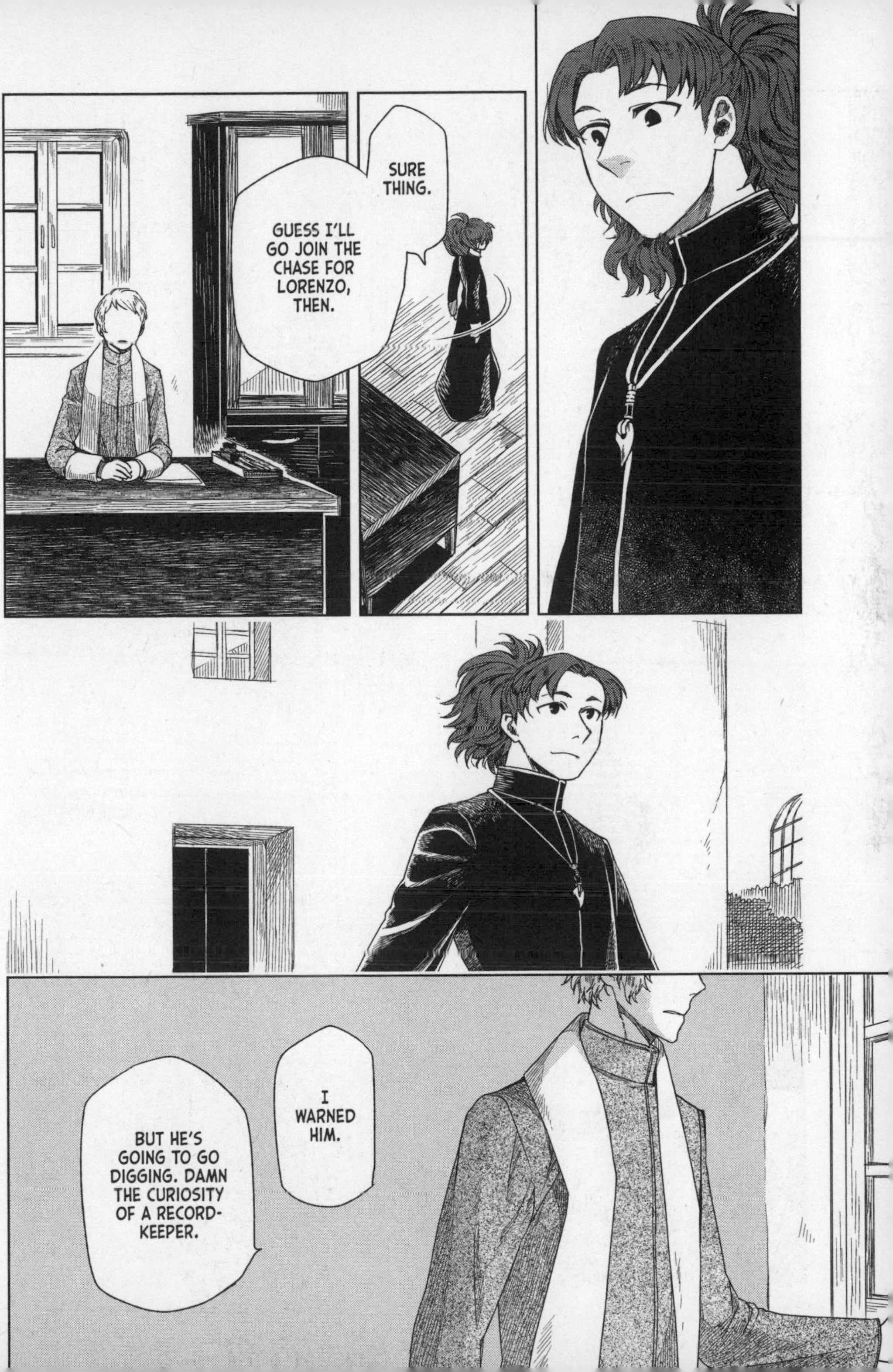
SURE THING.
GUESS I'LL GO JOIN THE CHASE FOR LORENZO, THEN.
I WARNED HIM.
BUT HE'S GOING TO GO DIGGING. DAMN THE CURIOSITY OF A RECORD-KEEPER.

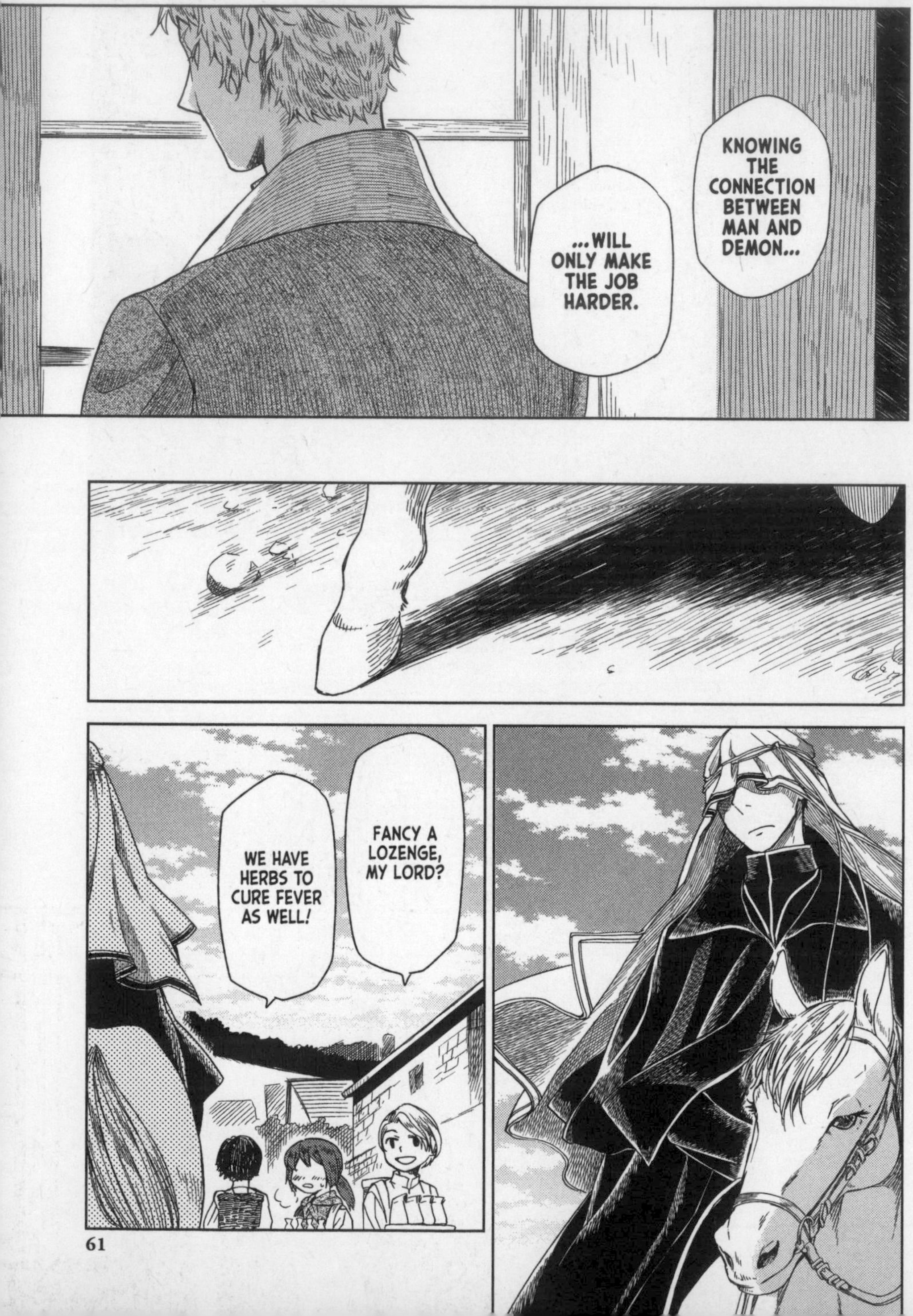
KNOWING THE CONNECTION BETWEEN MAN AND DEMON...
...WILL ONLY MAKE THE JOB HARDER.
FANCY A LOZENGE, MY LORD?
WE HAVE HERBS TO CURE FEVER AS WELL!

ARE YOU ALL RIGHT, MARTINA?

YOU HAVEN'T LOOKED WELL ALL DAY.

I'M FINE! LET'S HURRY UP AND SELL ALL OF THESE!

CHIRP CHIRP

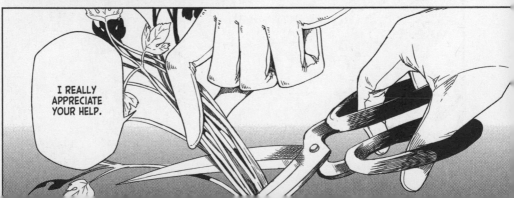

I REALLY APPRECIATE YOUR HELP.

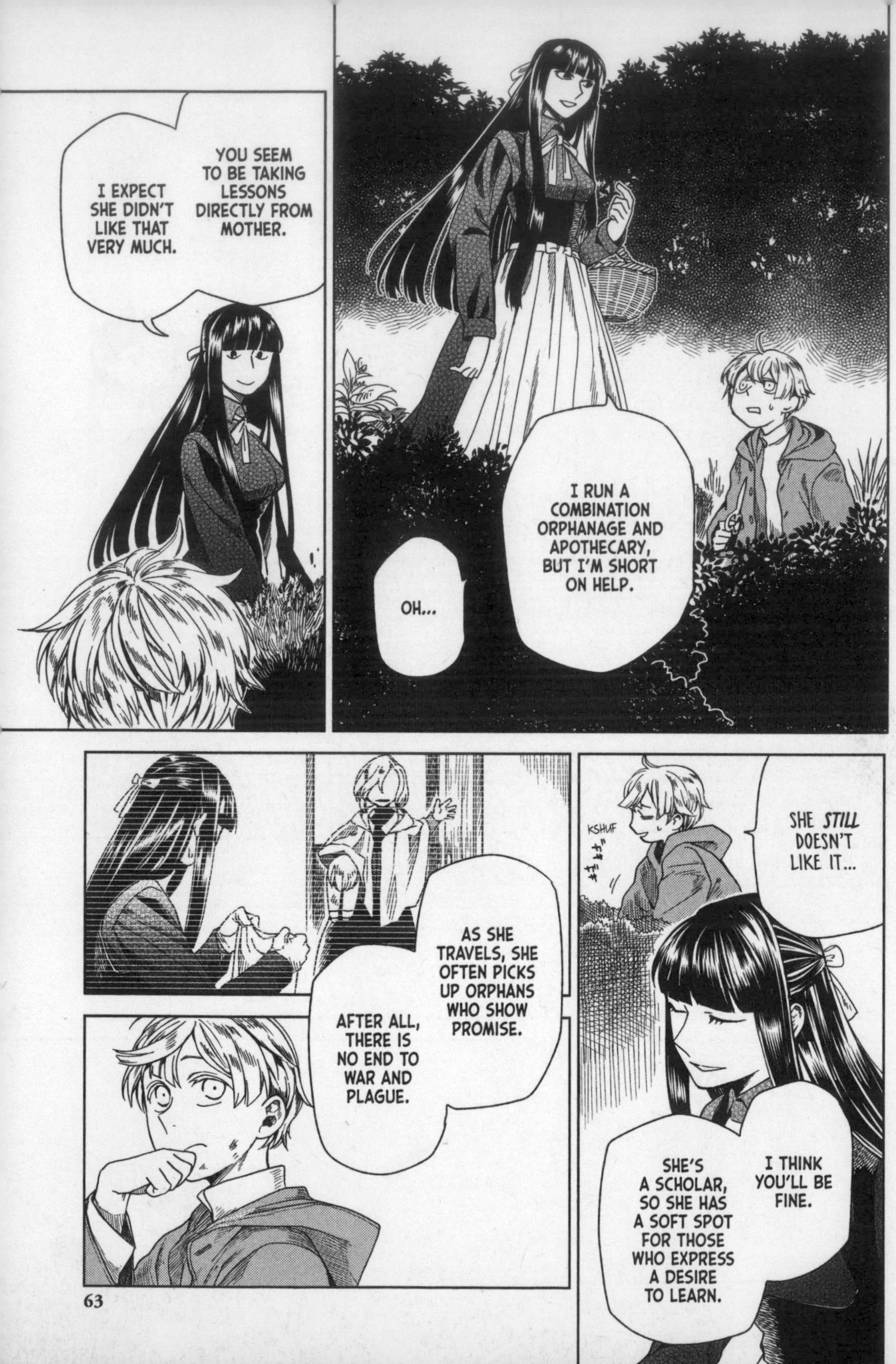
I RUN A COMBINATION ORPHANAGE AND APOTHECARY, BUT I'M SHORT ON HELP.
OH...
YOU SEEM TO BE TAKING LESSONS DIRECTLY FROM MOTHER.
I EXPECT SHE DIDN'T LIKE THAT VERY MUCH.
SHE *STILL* DOESN'T LIKE IT...
KSHUF
I THINK YOU'LL BE FINE.
SHE'S A SCHOLAR, SO SHE HAS A SOFT SPOT FOR THOSE WHO EXPRESS A DESIRE TO LEARN.
AS SHE TRAVELS, SHE OFTEN PICKS UP ORPHANS WHO SHOW PROMISE.
AFTER ALL, THERE IS NO END TO WAR AND PLAGUE.

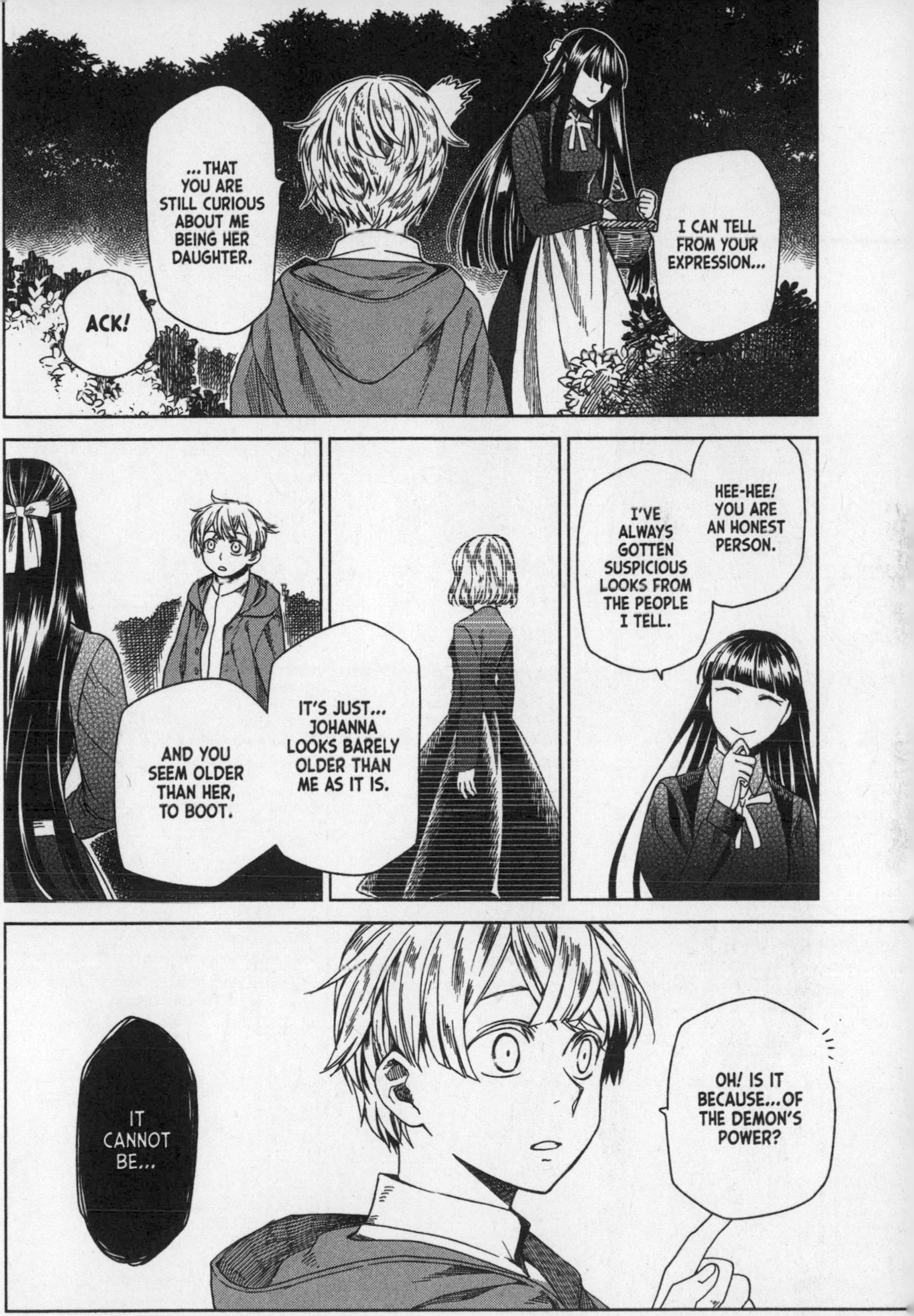
I CAN TELL FROM YOUR EXPRESSION...
...THAT YOU ARE STILL CURIOUS ABOUT ME BEING HER DAUGHTER.
ACK!
HEE-HEE! YOU ARE AN HONEST PERSON.
I'VE ALWAYS GOTTEN SUSPICIOUS LOOKS FROM THE PEOPLE I TELL.
IT'S JUST... JOHANNA LOOKS BARELY OLDER THAN ME AS IT IS.
AND YOU SEEM OLDER THAN HER, TO BOOT.
OH! IS IT BECAUSE...OF THE DEMON'S POWER?
IT CANNOT BE...

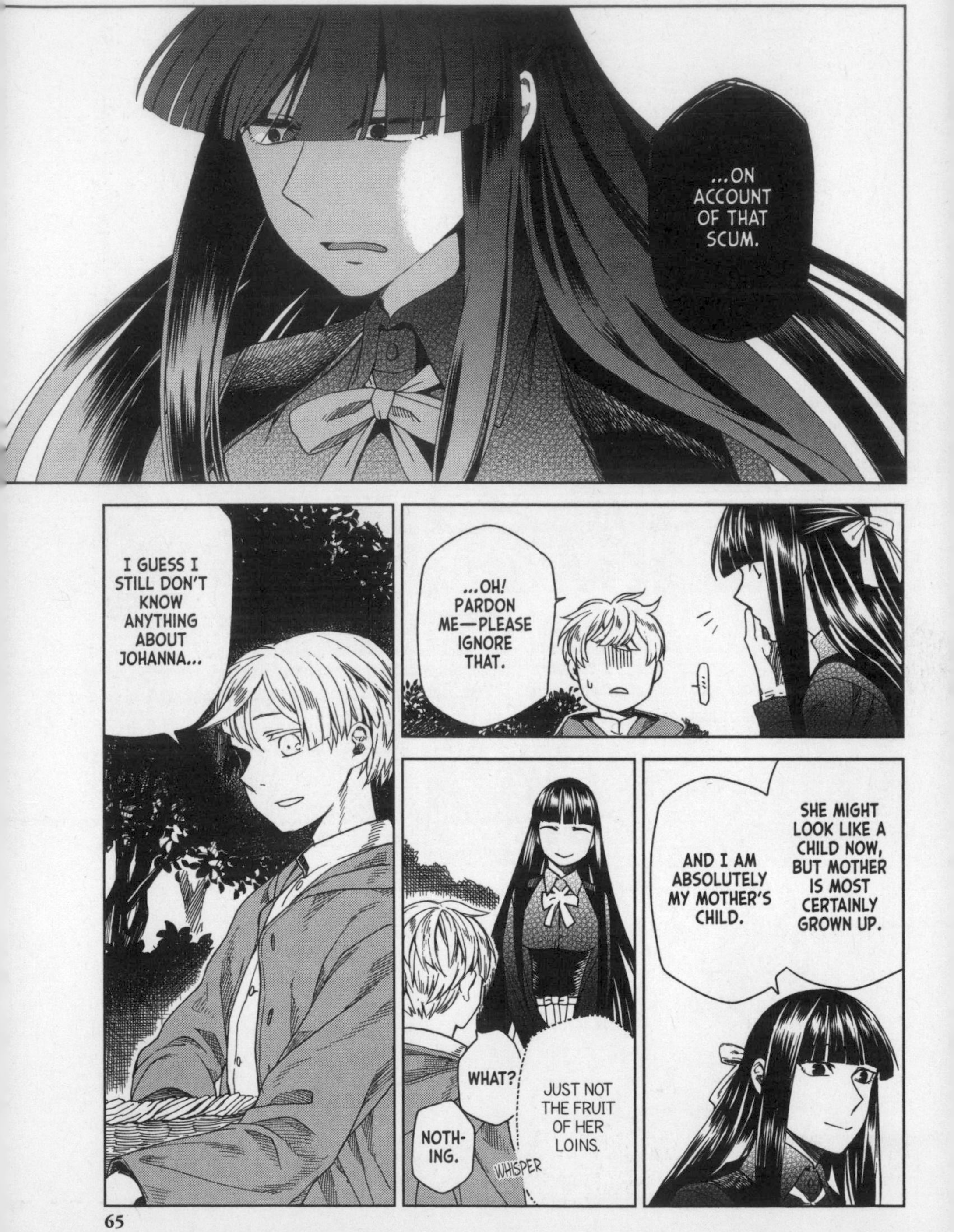
...ON ACCOUNT OF THAT SCUM.
...OH! PARDON ME—PLEASE IGNORE THAT.
SHE MIGHT LOOK LIKE A CHILD NOW, BUT MOTHER IS MOST CERTAINLY GROWN UP.
AND I AM ABSOLUTELY MY MOTHER'S CHILD.
JUST NOT THE FRUIT OF HER LOINS.
WHISPER
WHAT?
NOTH-ING.
I GUESS I STILL DON'T KNOW ANYTHING ABOUT JOHANNA...

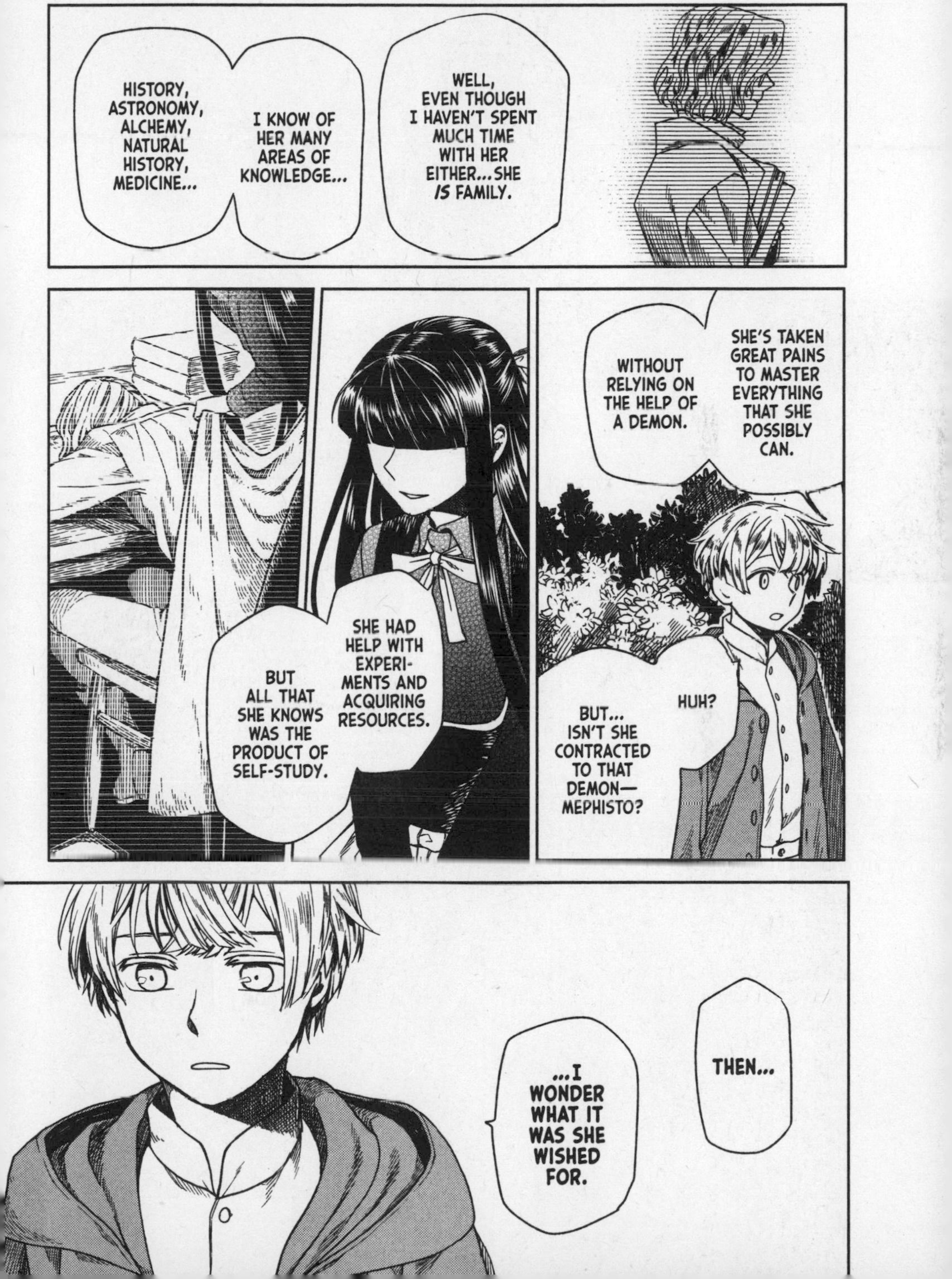
WELL, EVEN THOUGH I HAVEN'T SPENT MUCH TIME WITH HER EITHER...SHE *IS* FAMILY.
I KNOW OF HER MANY AREAS OF KNOWLEDGE...
HISTORY, ASTRONOMY, ALCHEMY, NATURAL HISTORY, MEDICINE...
SHE'S TAKEN GREAT PAINS TO MASTER EVERYTHING THAT SHE POSSIBLY CAN.
WITHOUT RELYING ON THE HELP OF A DEMON.
HUH?
BUT... ISN'T SHE CONTRACTED TO THAT DEMON—MEPHISTO?
SHE HAD HELP WITH EXPERI-MENTS AND ACQUIRING RESOURCES.
BUT ALL THAT SHE KNOWS WAS THE PRODUCT OF SELF-STUDY.
THEN...
...I WONDER WHAT IT WAS SHE WISHED FOR.

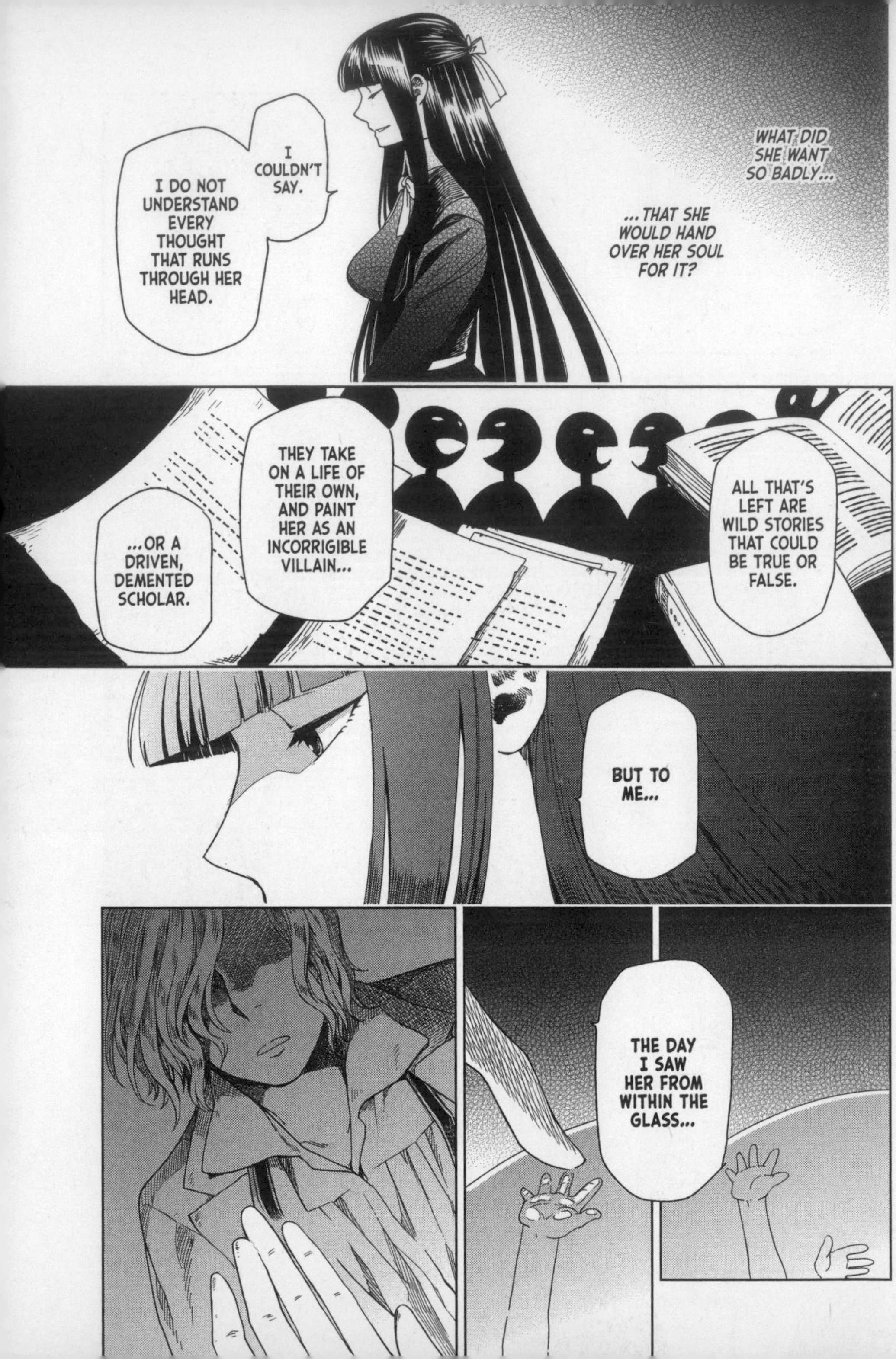
WHAT DID SHE WANT SO BADLY...
...THAT SHE WOULD HAND OVER HER SOUL FOR IT?
I COULDN'T SAY.
I DO NOT UNDERSTAND EVERY THOUGHT THAT RUNS THROUGH HER HEAD.
ALL THAT'S LEFT ARE WILD STORIES THAT COULD BE TRUE OR FALSE.
THEY TAKE ON A LIFE OF THEIR OWN, AND PAINT HER AS AN INCORRIGIBLE VILLAIN...
...OR A DRIVEN, DEMENTED SCHOLAR.
BUT TO ME...
THE DAY I SAW HER FROM WITHIN THE GLASS...

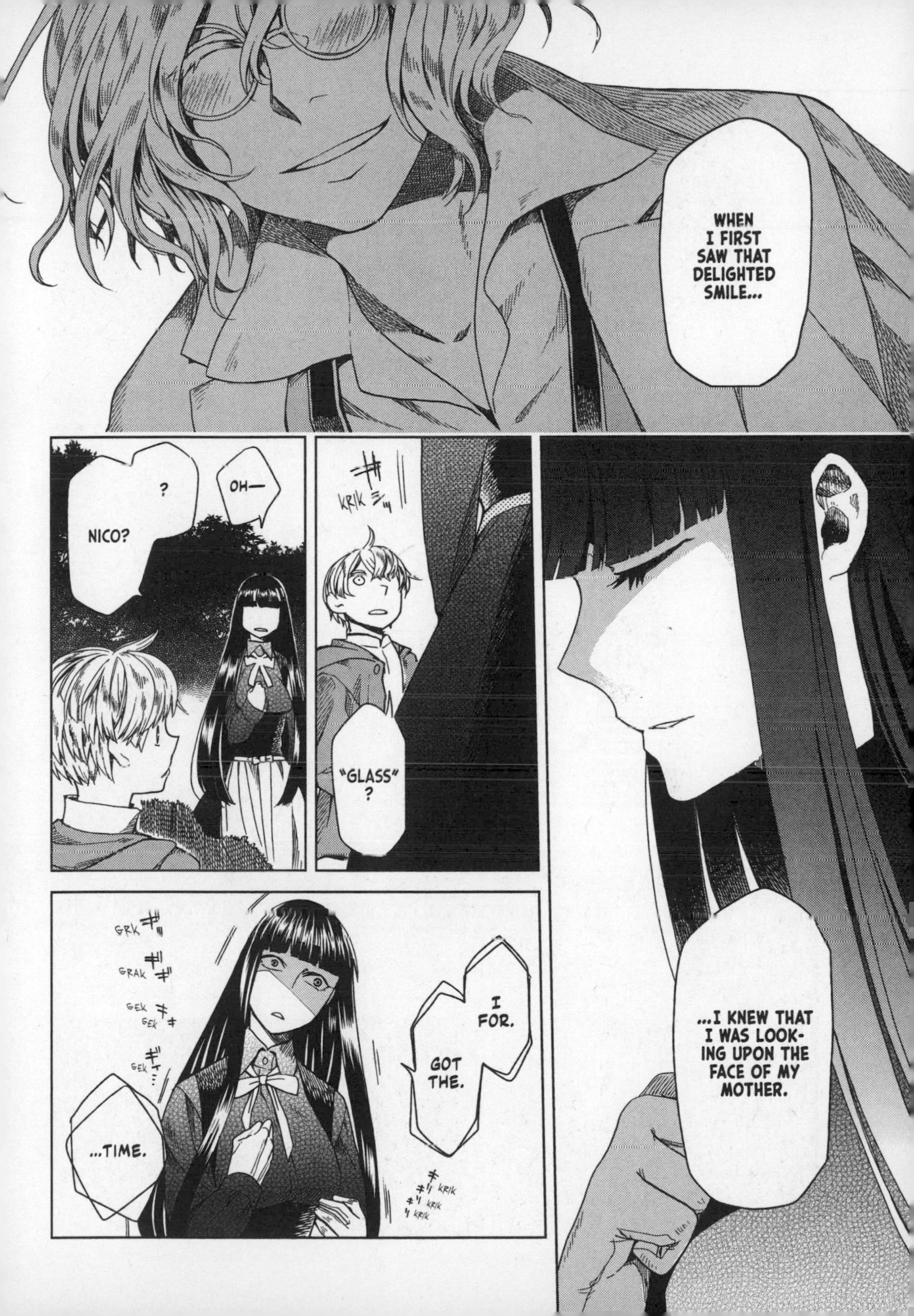
WHEN I FIRST SAW THAT DELIGHTED SMILE...
...I KNEW THAT I WAS LOOKING UPON THE FACE OF MY MOTHER.
KRIK
"GLASS"?
OH—
?
NICO?
I FOR.
GOT THE.
GRK
GRAK
GEK GEK
GEK
...TIME.
KRIK KRIK KRIK

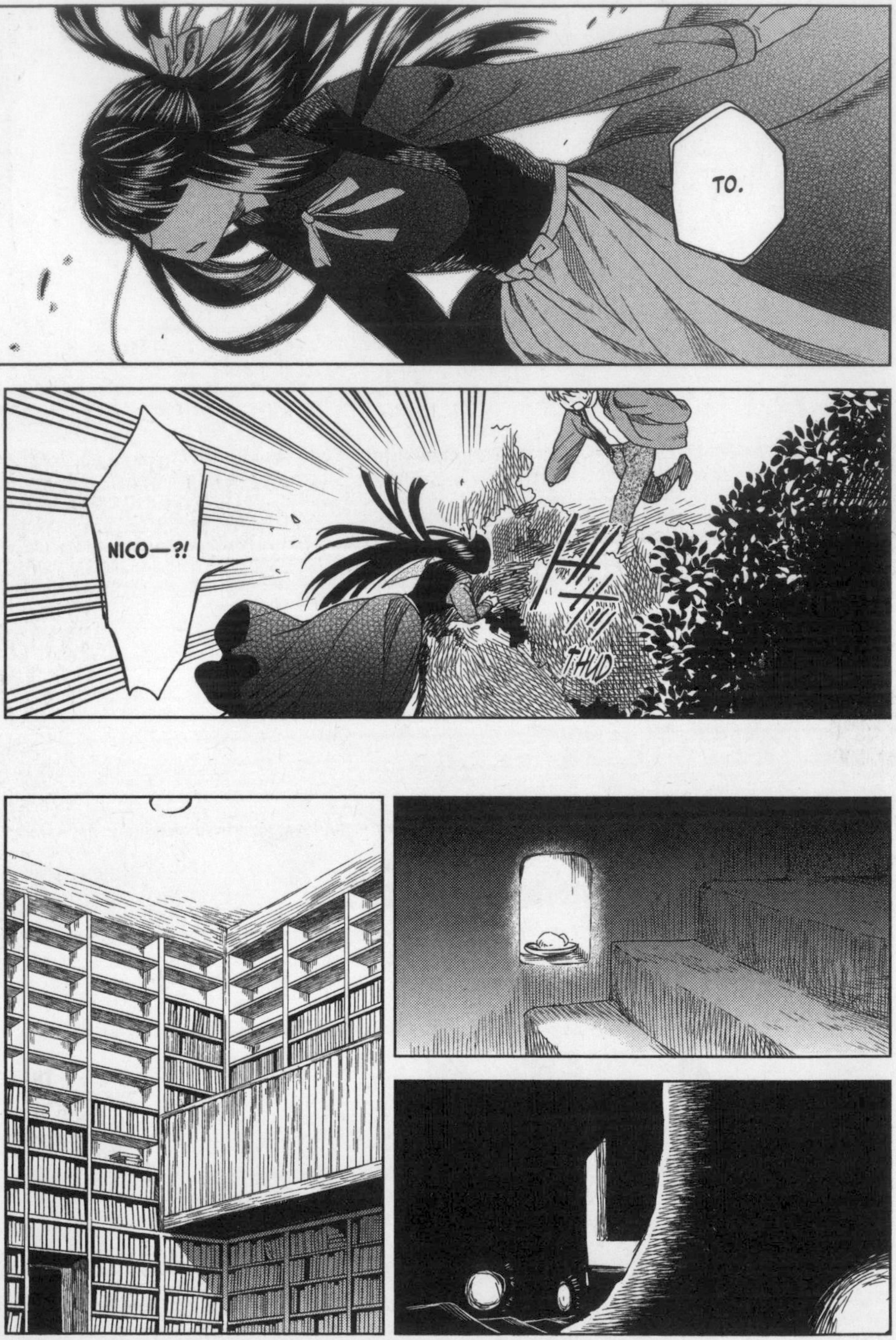
TO.
NICO—?!
THUD

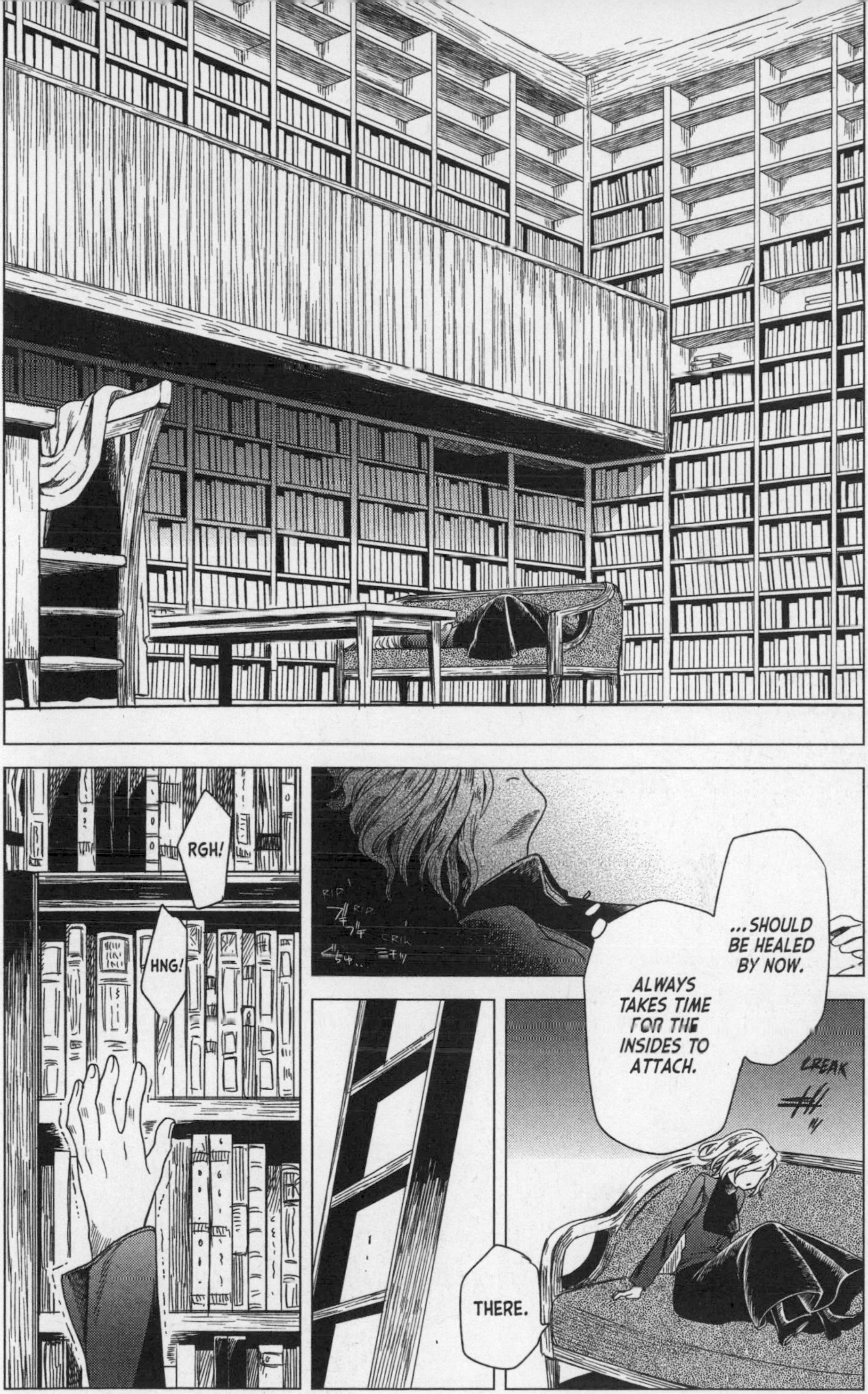
RIP RIP
CRIK
...SHOULD BE HEALED BY NOW.
ALWAYS TAKES TIME FOR THE INSIDES TO ATTACH.
CREAK
THERE.
RGH!
HNG!

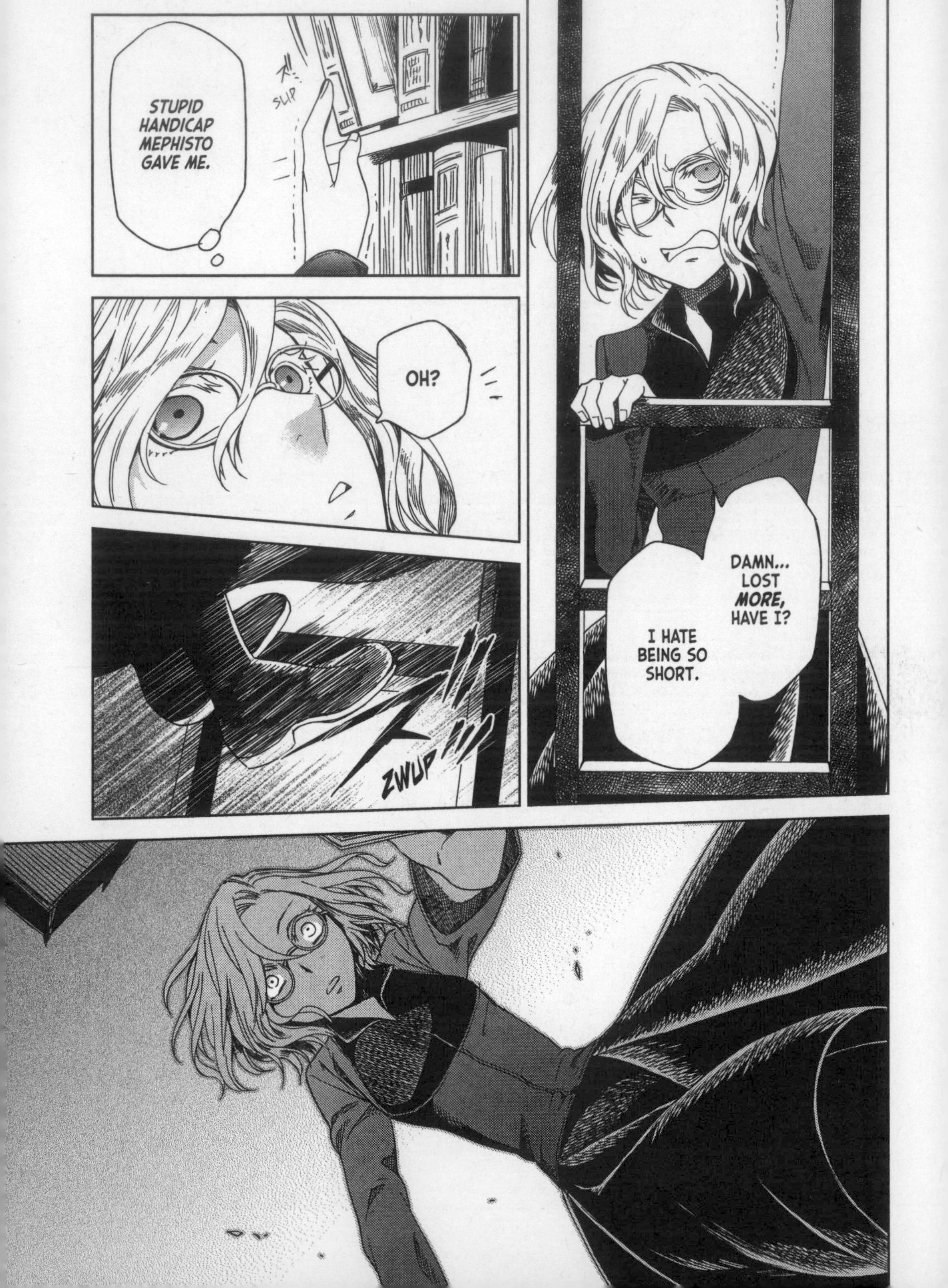
DAMN... LOST MORE, HAVE I?
I HATE BEING SO SHORT.
STUPID HANDICAP MEPHISTO GAVE ME.
SLIP
OH?
ZWUP

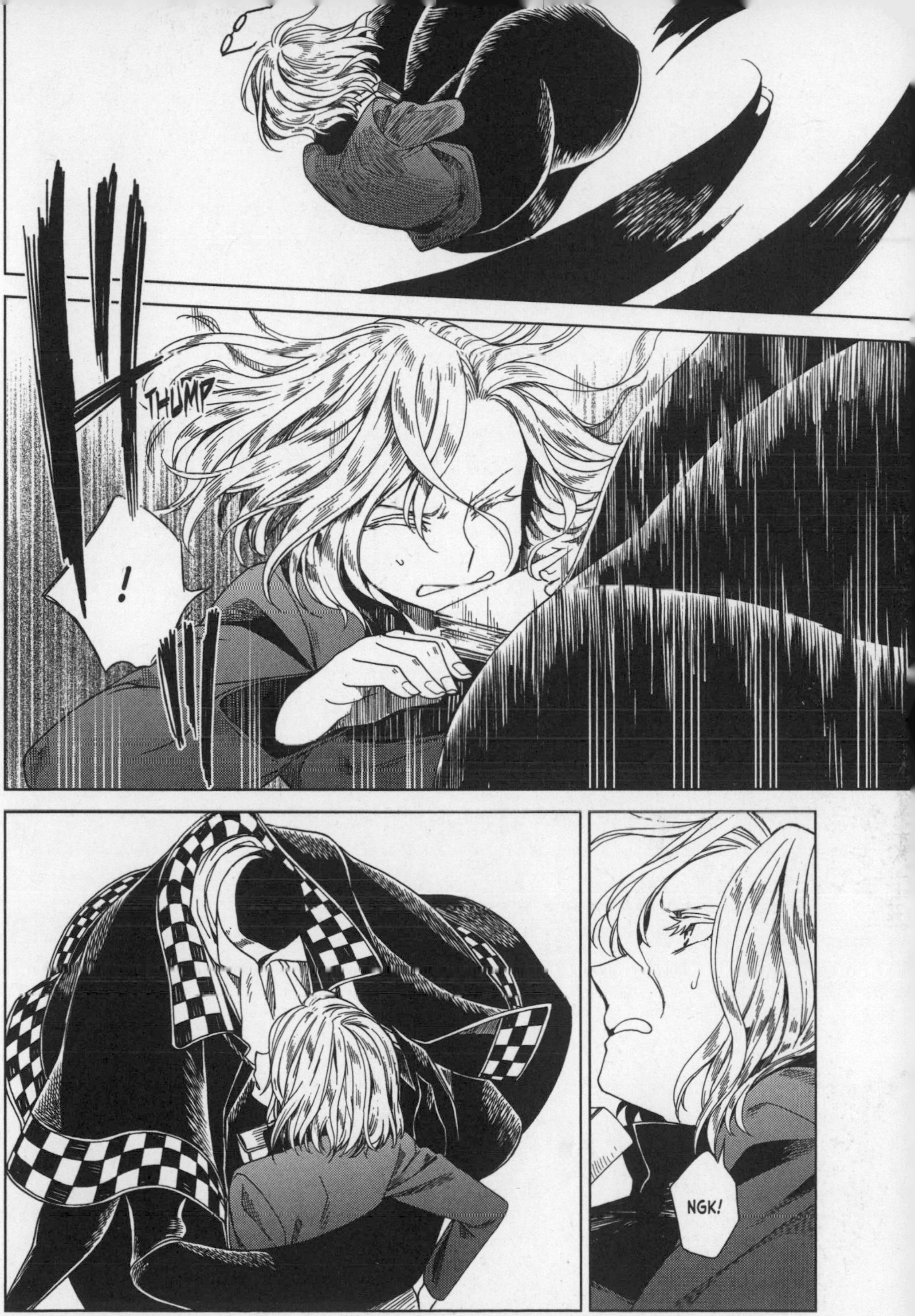
THUMP
!
NGK!

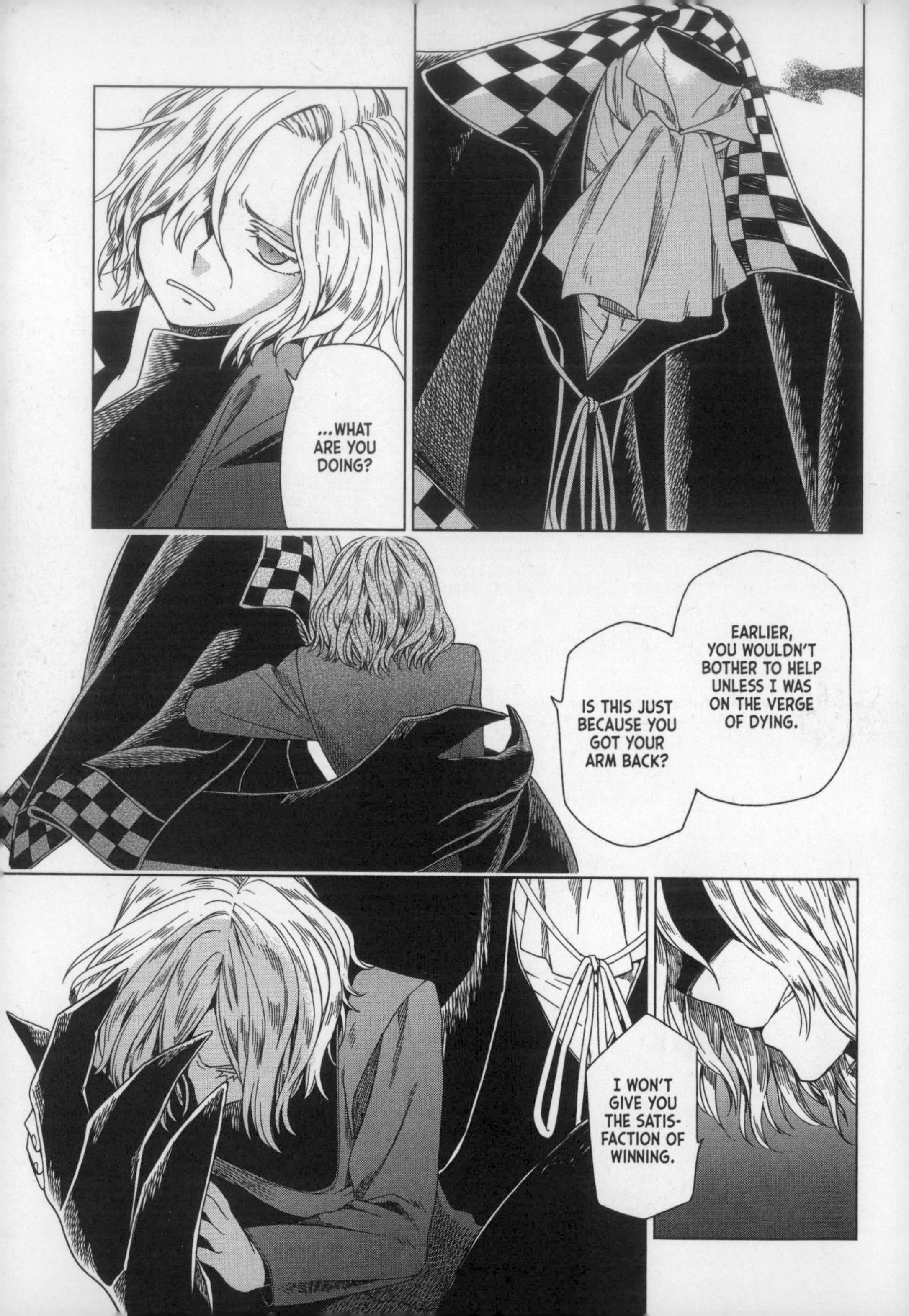
...WHAT ARE YOU DOING?
EARLIER, YOU WOULDN'T BOTHER TO HELP UNLESS I WAS ON THE VERGE OF DYING.
IS THIS JUST BECAUSE YOU GOT YOUR ARM BACK?
I WON'T GIVE YOU THE SATIS-FACTION OF WINNING.

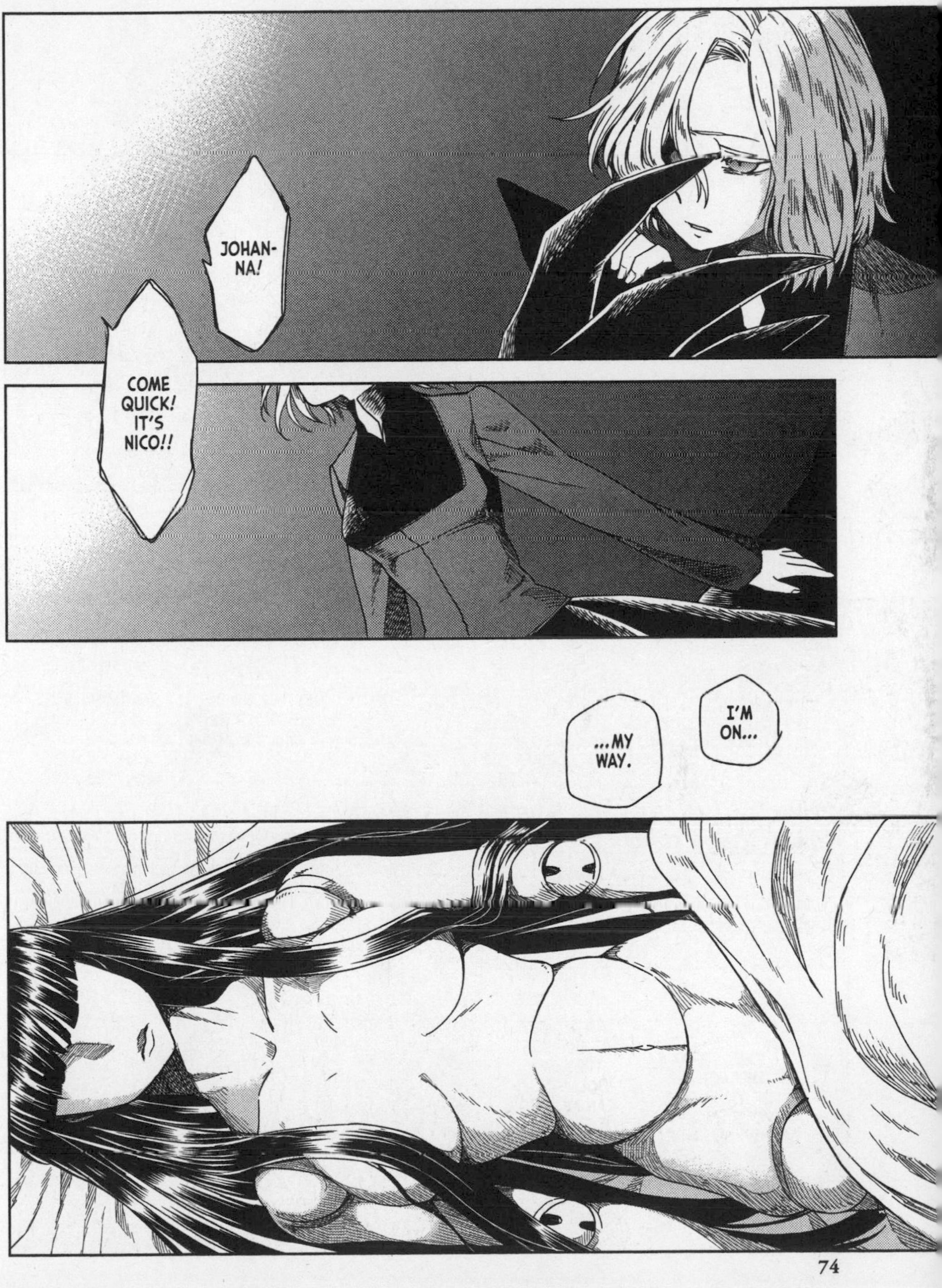
JOHAN-NA!
COME QUICK! IT'S NICO!!
I'M ON...
...MY WAY.

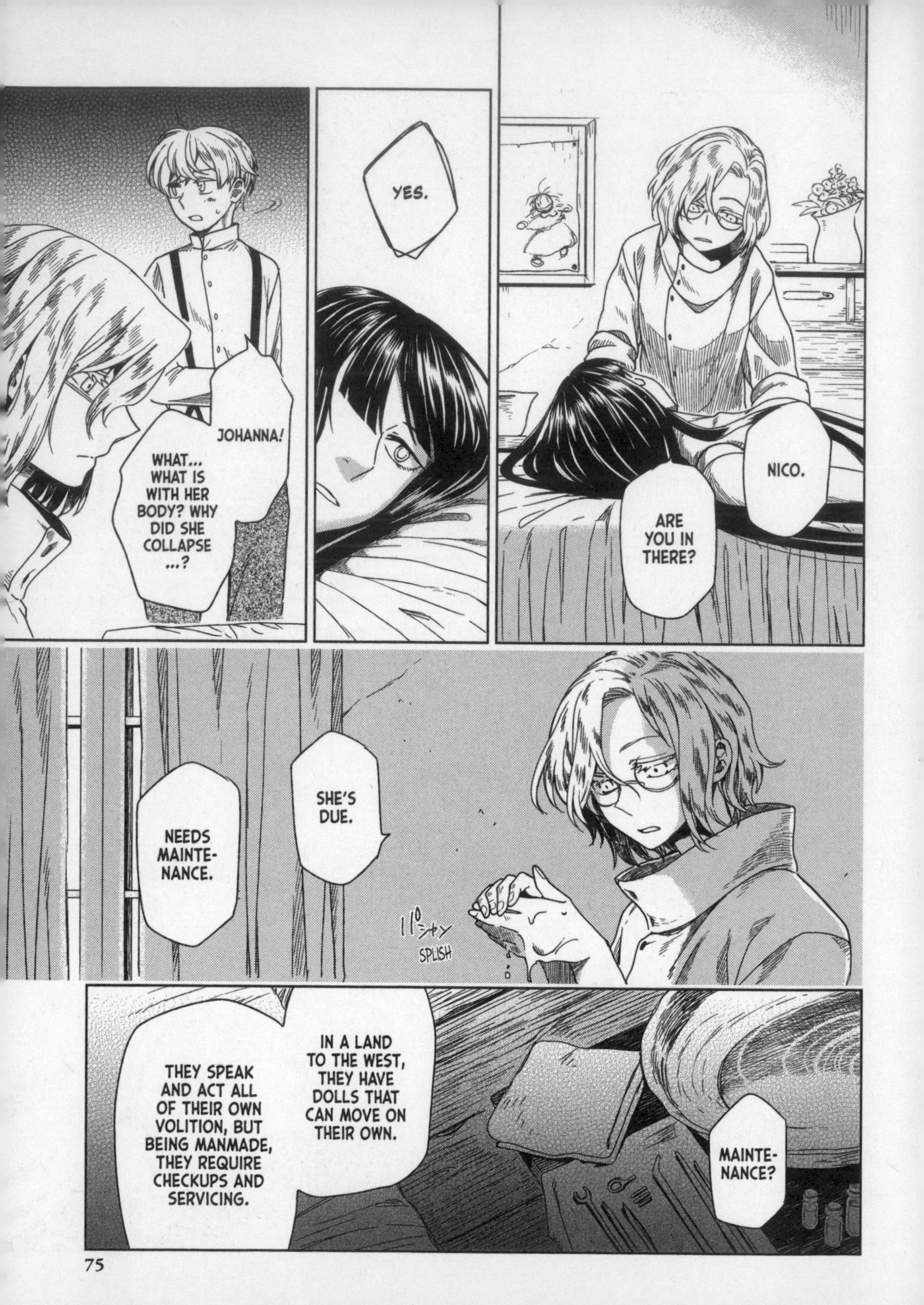
NICO.
ARE YOU IN THERE?
YES.
JOHANNA!
WHAT... WHAT IS WITH HER BODY? WHY DID SHE COLLAPSE ...?
SHE'S DUE.
NEEDS MAINTE-NANCE.
パシャ
SPLISH
MAINTE-NANCE?
IN A LAND TO THE WEST, THEY HAVE DOLLS THAT CAN MOVE ON THEIR OWN.
THEY SPEAK AND ACT ALL OF THEIR OWN VOLITION, BUT BEING MANMADE, THEY REQUIRE CHECKUPS AND SERVICING.

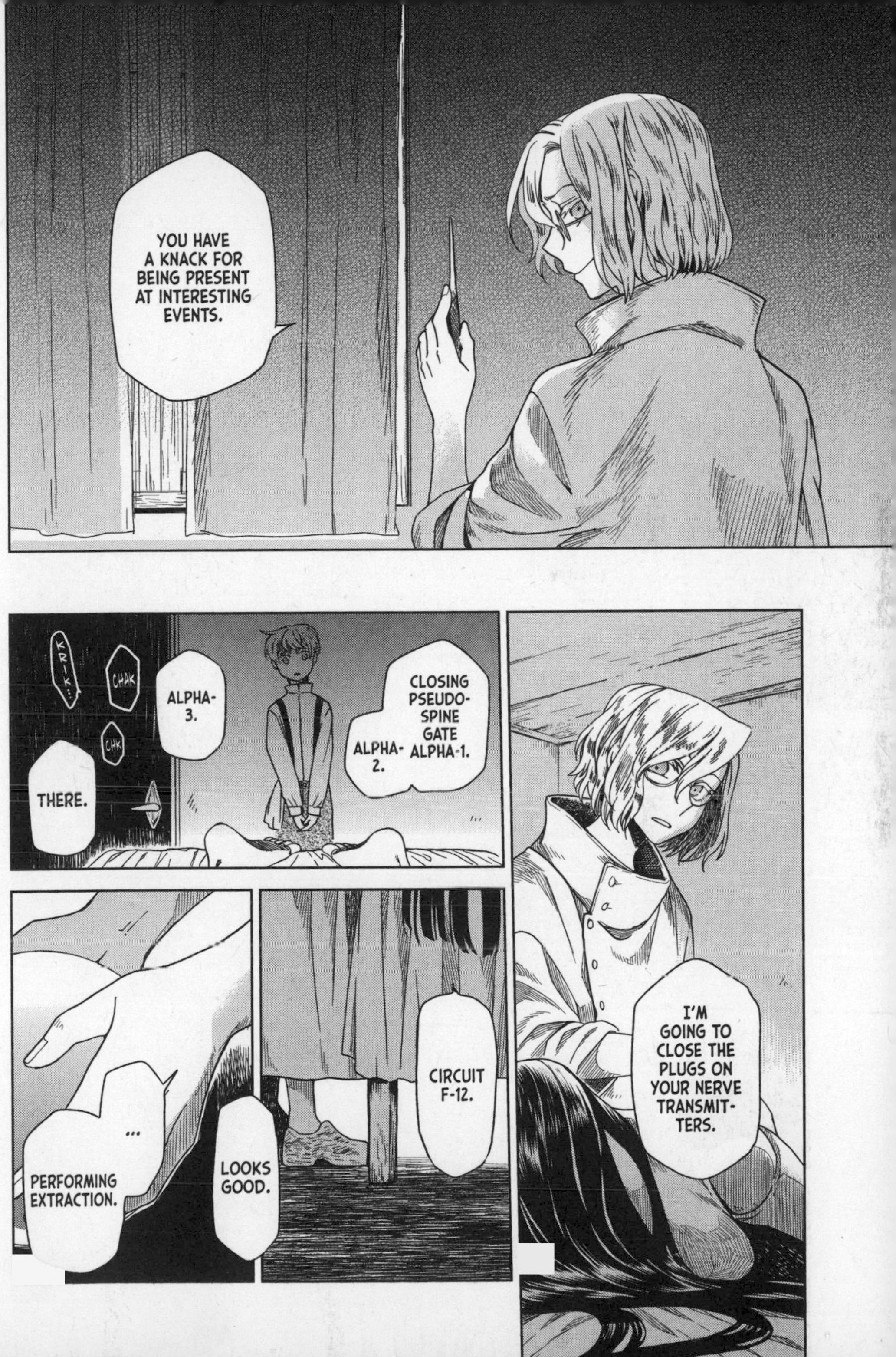
YOU HAVE A KNACK FOR BEING PRESENT AT INTERESTING EVENTS.
I'M GOING TO CLOSE THE PLUGS ON YOUR NERVE TRANSMIT-TERS.
CLOSING PSEUDO-SPINE GATE ALPHA-1.
ALPHA-2.
ALPHA-3.
CHAK
CHK
KRIK...
THERE.
CIRCUIT F-12.
LOOKS GOOD.
...
PERFORMING EXTRACTION.

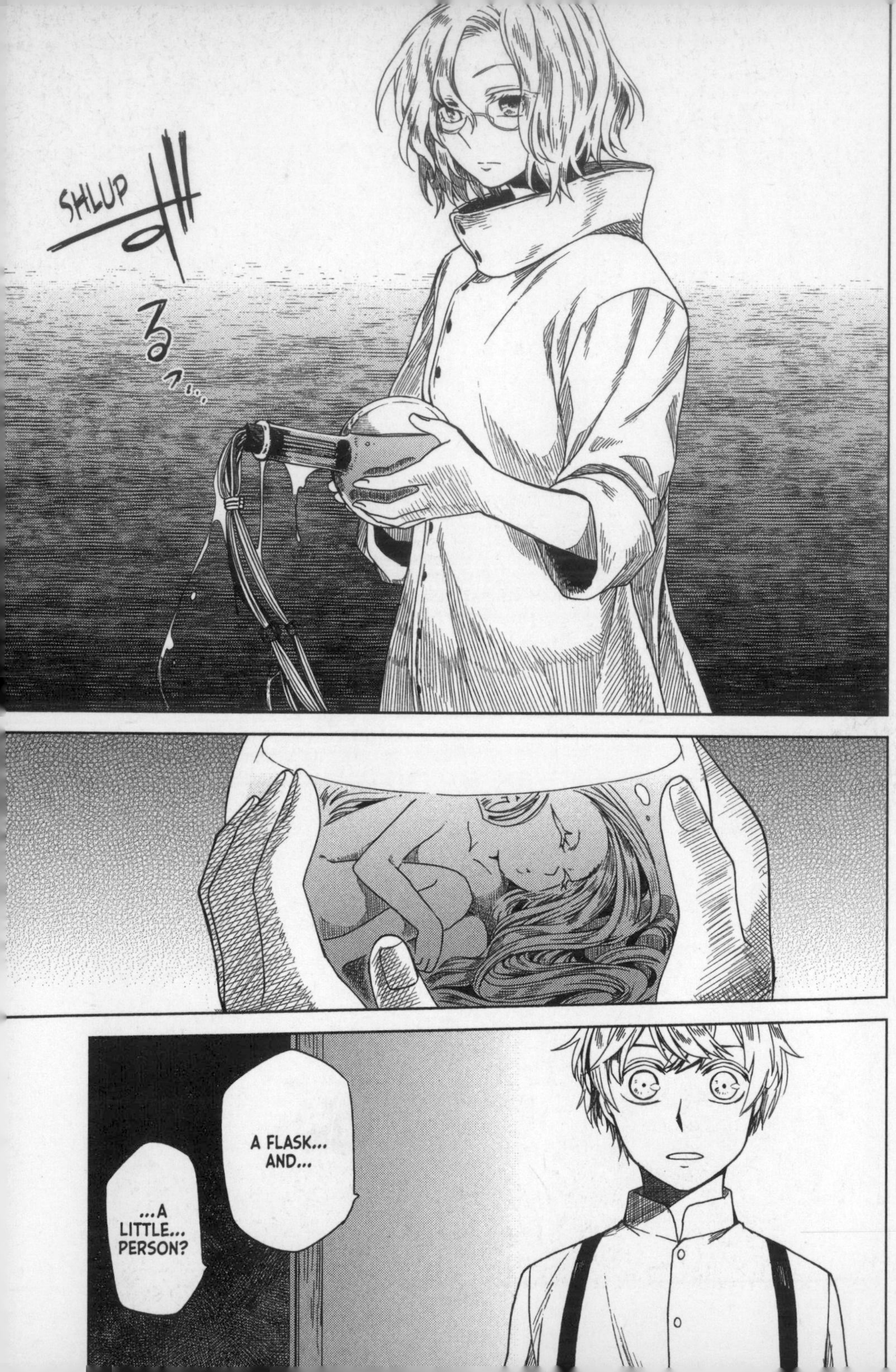
SHLUP
A FLASK... AND...
...A LITTLE... PERSON?

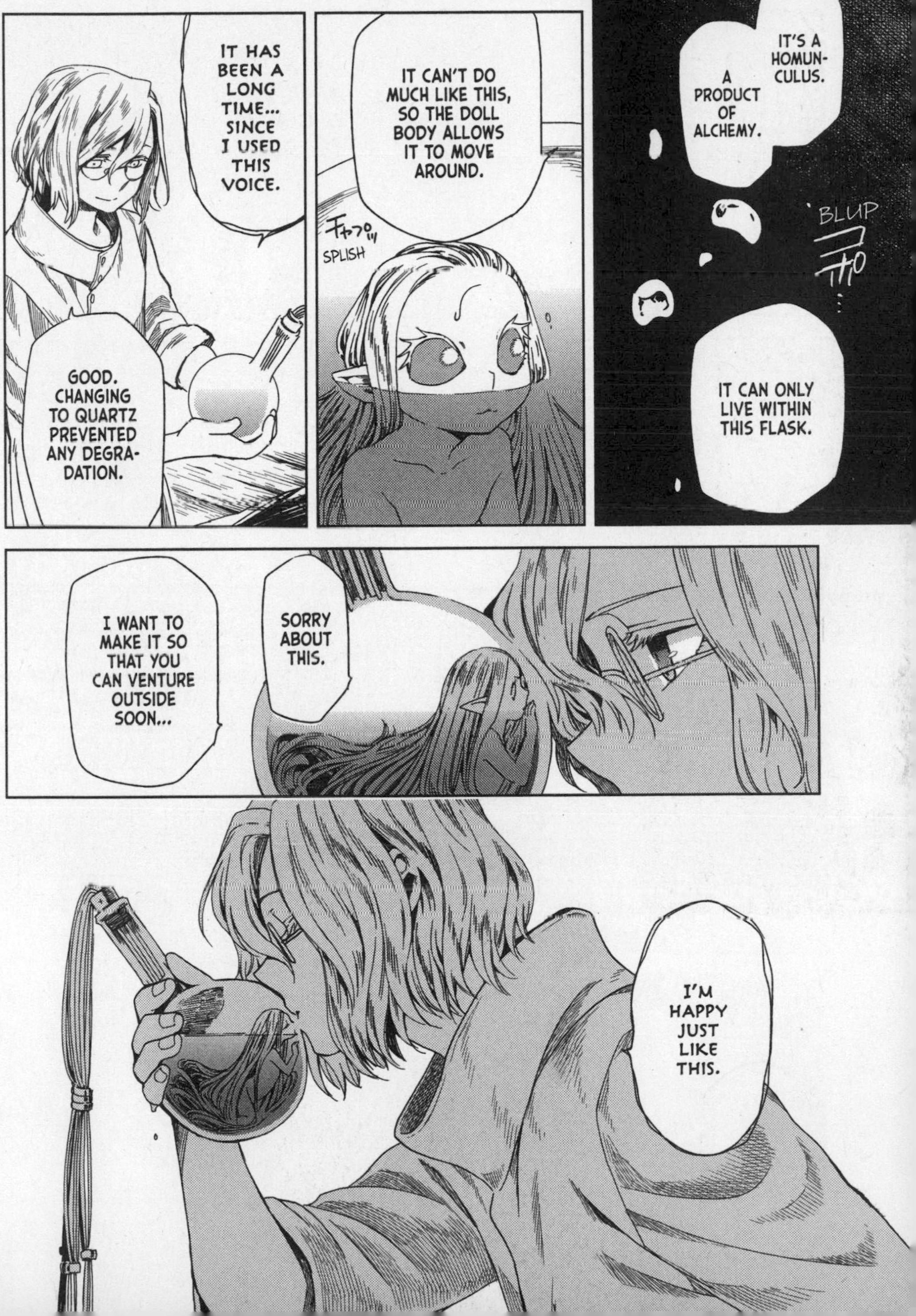
IT'S A HOMUN-CULUS.
A PRODUCT OF ALCHEMY.
BLUP
IT CAN ONLY LIVE WITHIN THIS FLASK.
IT CAN'T DO MUCH LIKE THIS, SO THE DOLL BODY ALLOWS IT TO MOVE AROUND.
SPLISH
IT HAS BEEN A LONG TIME... SINCE I USED THIS VOICE.
GOOD. CHANGING TO QUARTZ PREVENTED ANY DEGRA-DATION.
SORRY ABOUT THIS.
I WANT TO MAKE IT SO THAT YOU CAN VENTURE OUTSIDE SOON...
I'M HAPPY JUST LIKE THIS.

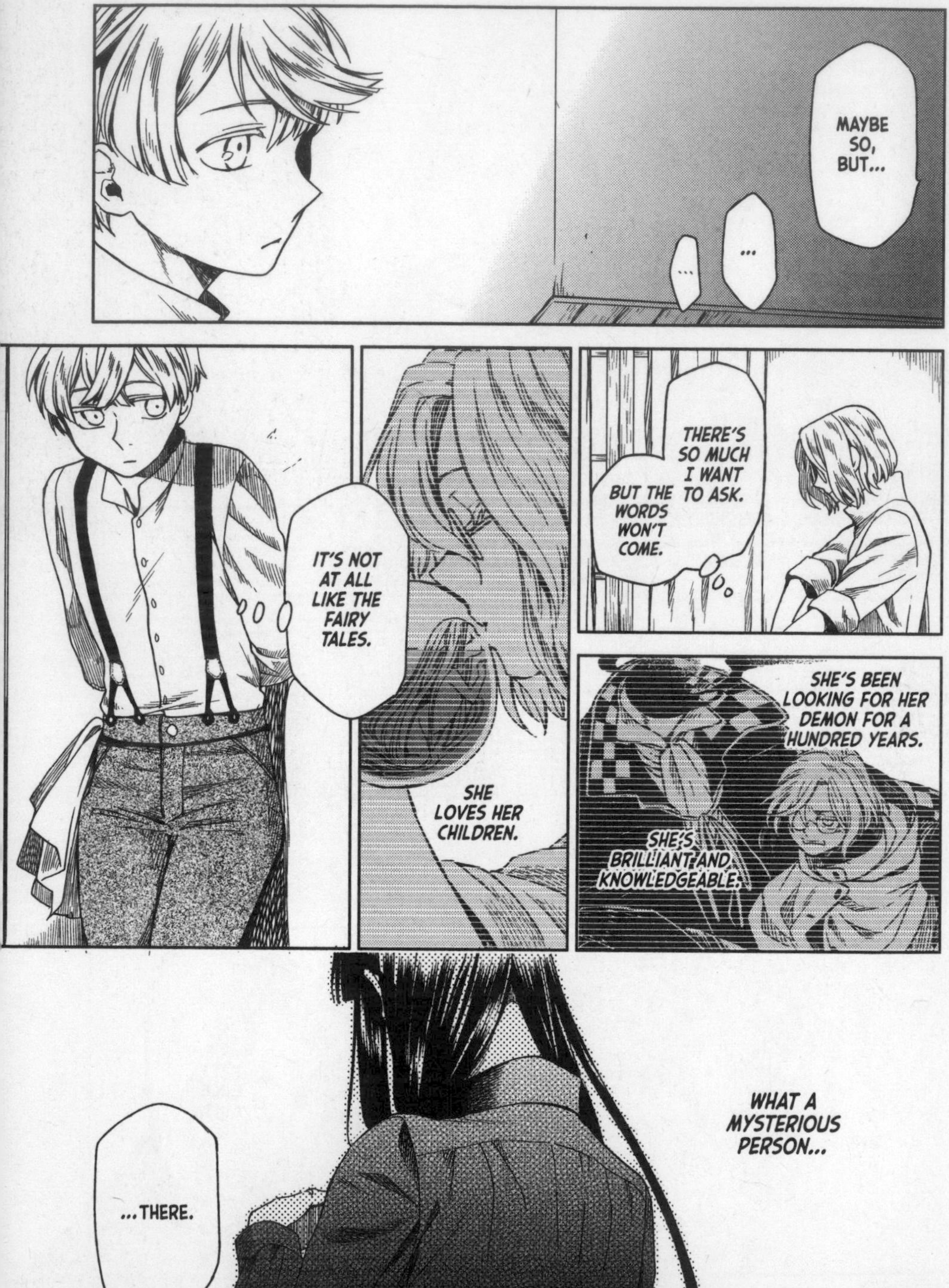
MAYBE SO, BUT...
...
...
THERE'S SO MUCH I WANT TO ASK.
BUT THE WORDS WON'T COME.
SHE'S BEEN LOOKING FOR HER DEMON FOR A HUNDRED YEARS.
SHE'S BRILLIANT AND KNOWLEDGEABLE.
SHE LOVES HER CHILDREN.
IT'S NOT AT ALL LIKE THE FAIRY TALES.
WHAT A MYSTERIOUS PERSON...
...THERE.

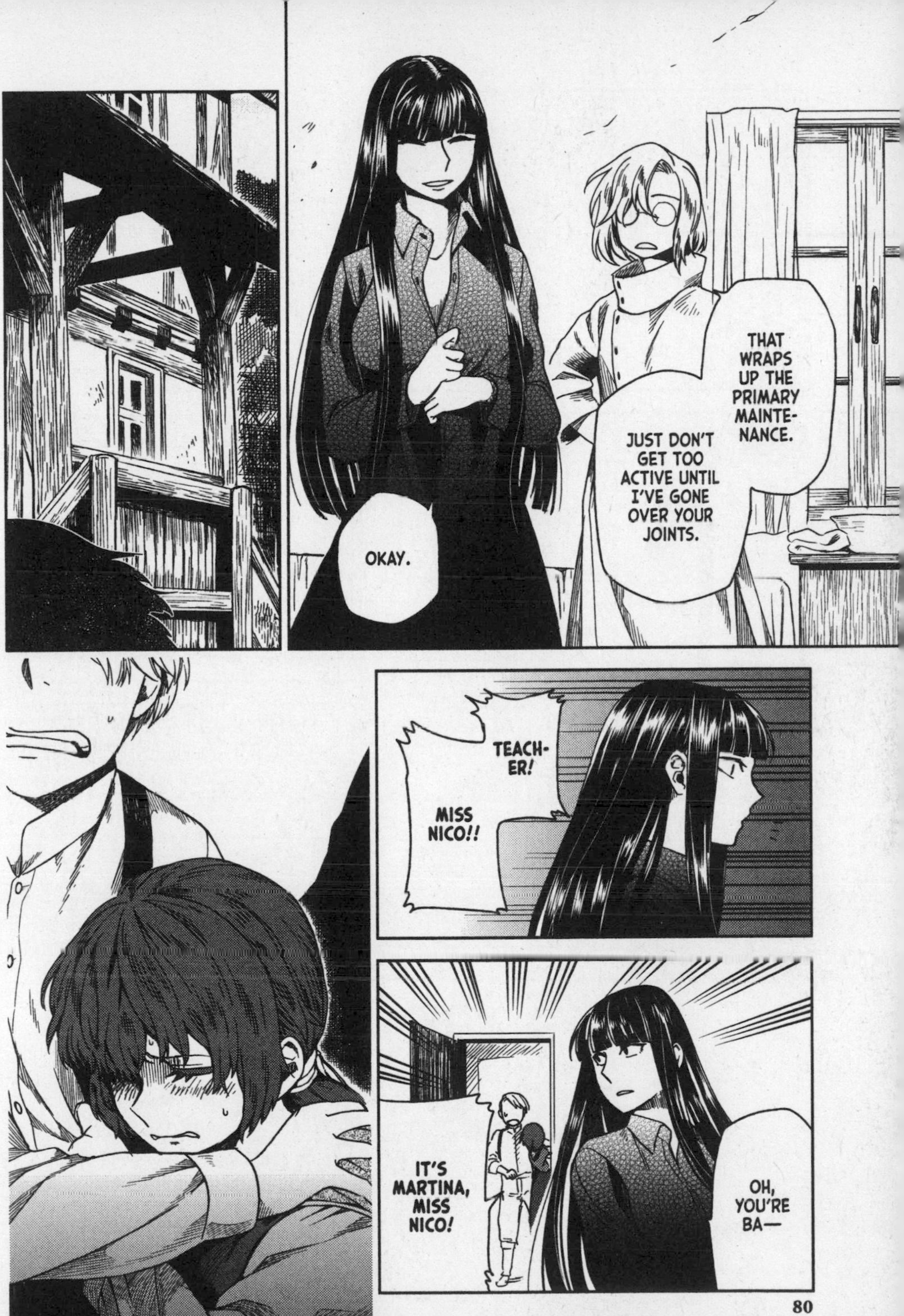
THAT WRAPS UP THE PRIMARY MAINTE-NANCE.
JUST DON'T GET TOO ACTIVE UNTIL I'VE GONE OVER YOUR JOINTS.
OKAY.
TEACH-ER!
MISS NICO!!
OH, YOU'RE BA—
IT'S MARTINA, MISS NICO!

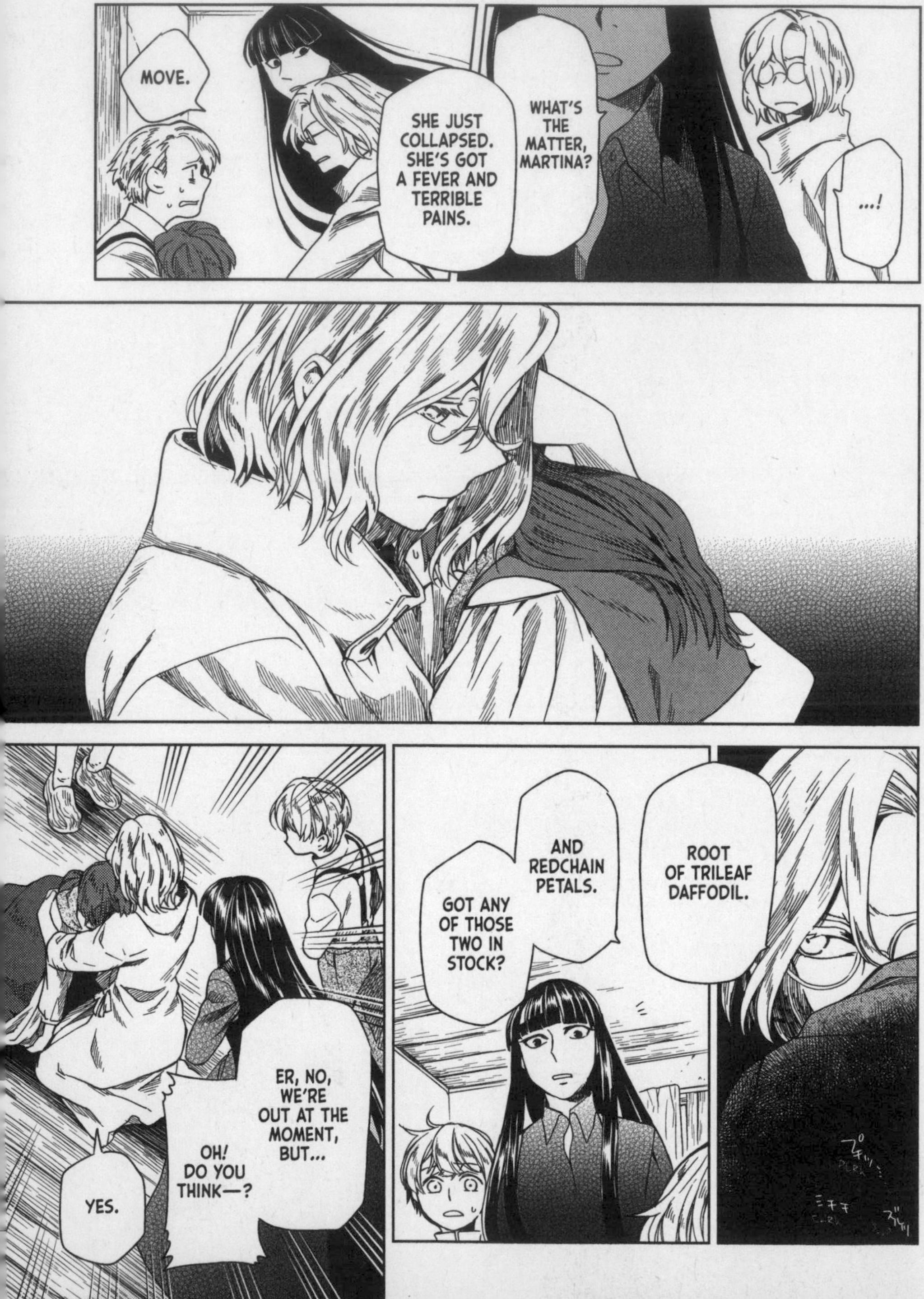
...!
WHAT'S THE MATTER, MARTINA?
SHE JUST COLLAPSED. SHE'S GOT A FEVER AND TERRIBLE PAINS.
MOVE.
ROOT OF TRILEAF DAFFODIL.
AND REDCHAIN PETALS.
GOT ANY OF THOSE TWO IN STOCK?
ER, NO, WE'RE OUT AT THE MOMENT, BUT...
OH! DO YOU THINK—?
YES.

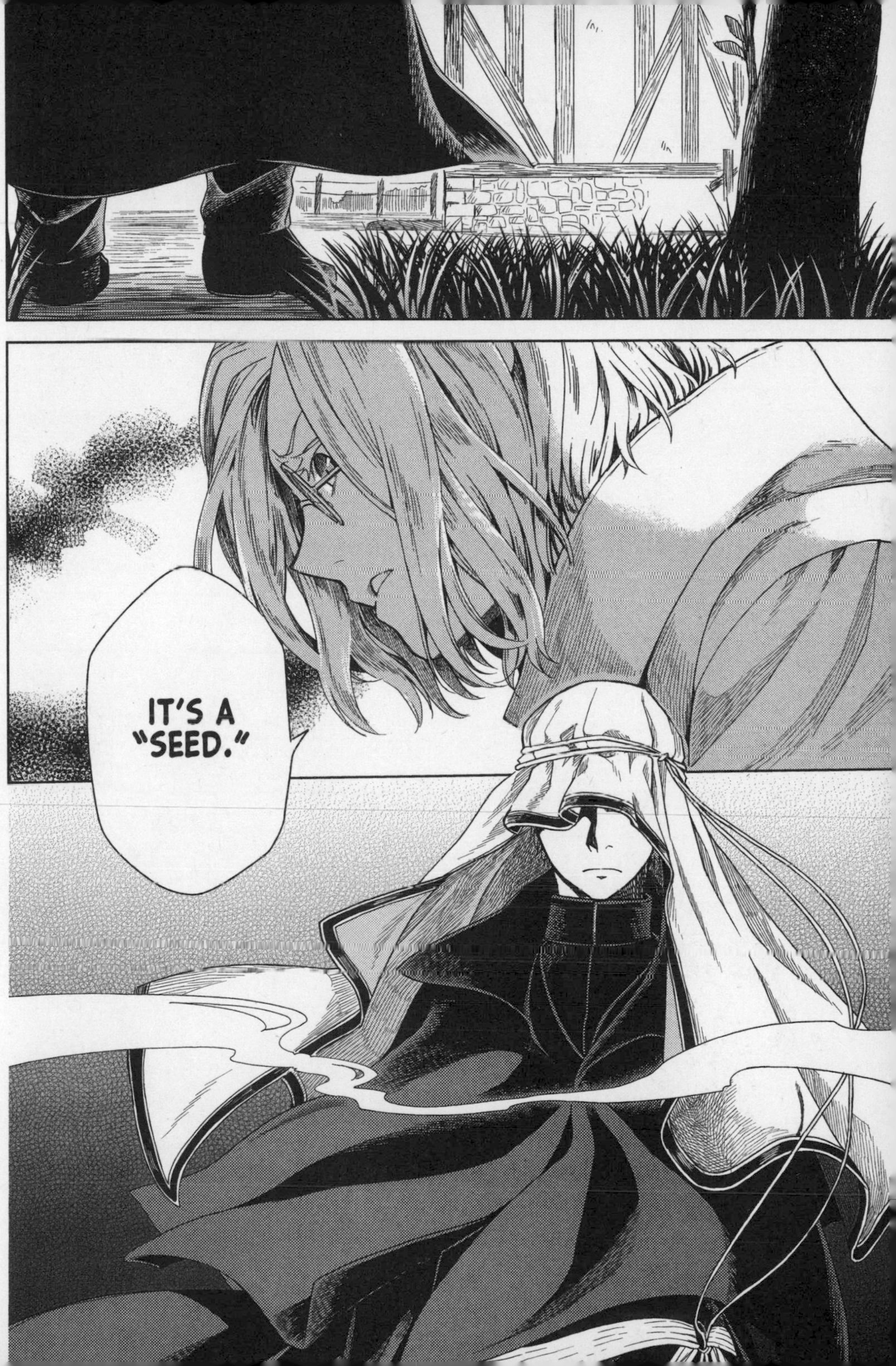
IT'S A "SEED."

STUNT PRACTICE

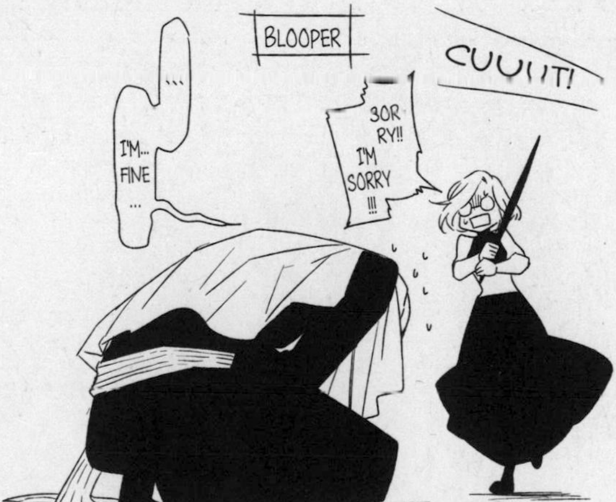
CUUUT!
BLOOPER
SORRY!! I'M SORRY!!!
...
I'M... FINE ...

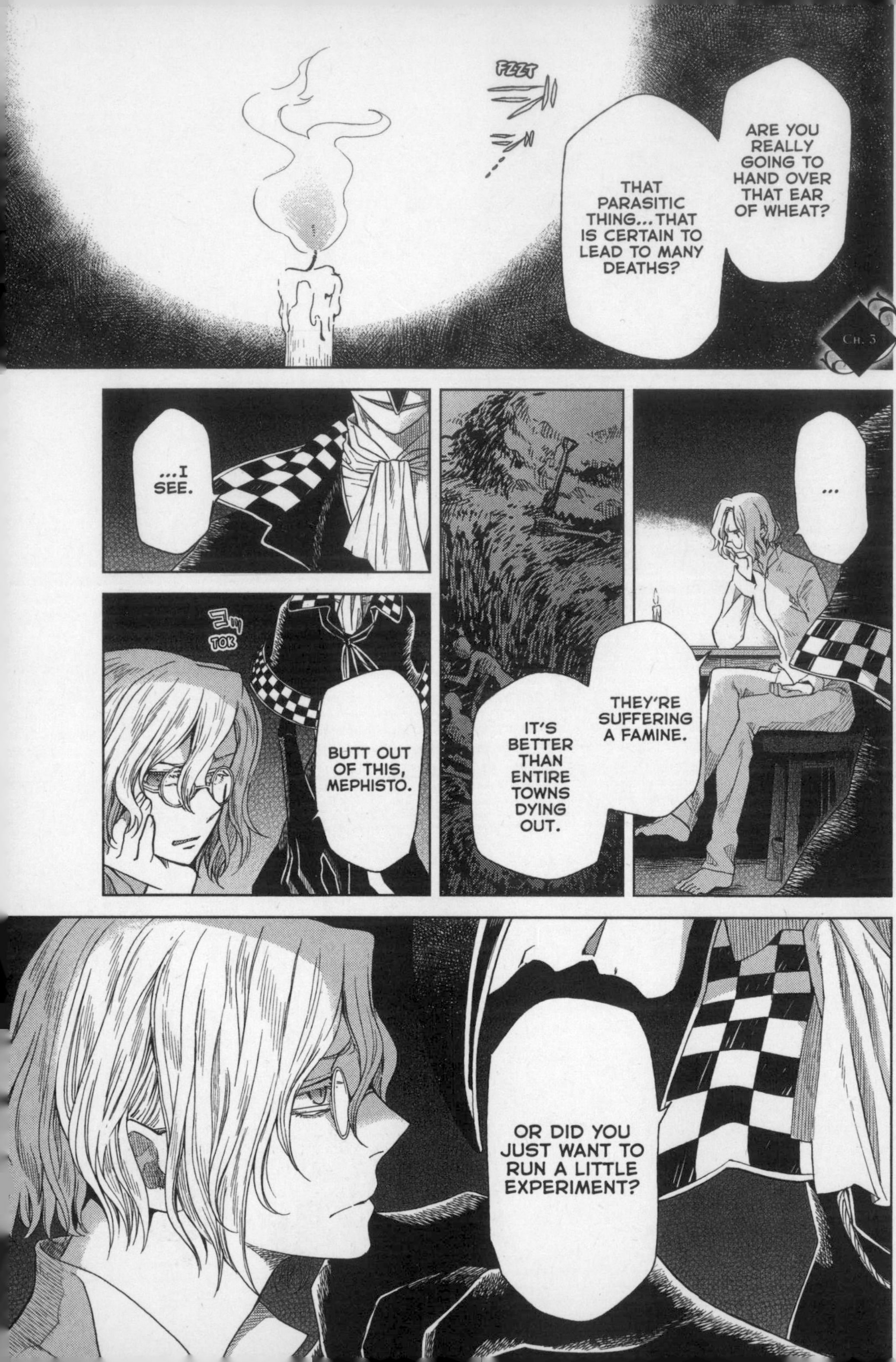
FZZT
ARE YOU REALLY GOING TO HAND OVER THAT EAR OF WHEAT?
THAT PARASITIC THING... THAT IS CERTAIN TO LEAD TO MANY DEATHS?
...
THEY'RE SUFFERING A FAMINE.
IT'S BETTER THAN ENTIRE TOWNS DYING OUT.
...I SEE.
TOK
BUTT OUT OF THIS, MEPHISTO.
OR DID YOU JUST WANT TO RUN A LITTLE EXPERIMENT?

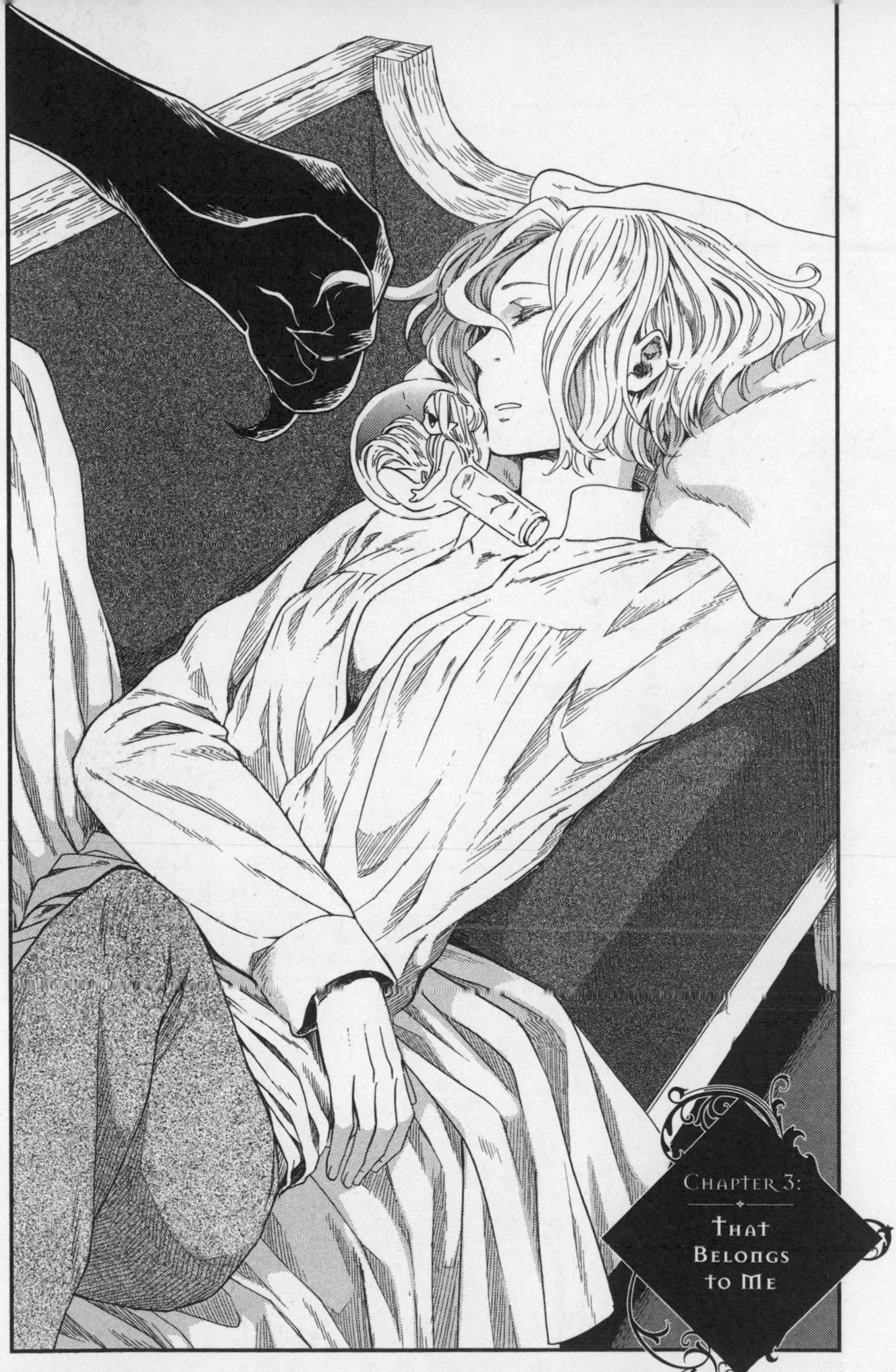
Chapter 3:
That Belongs to Me

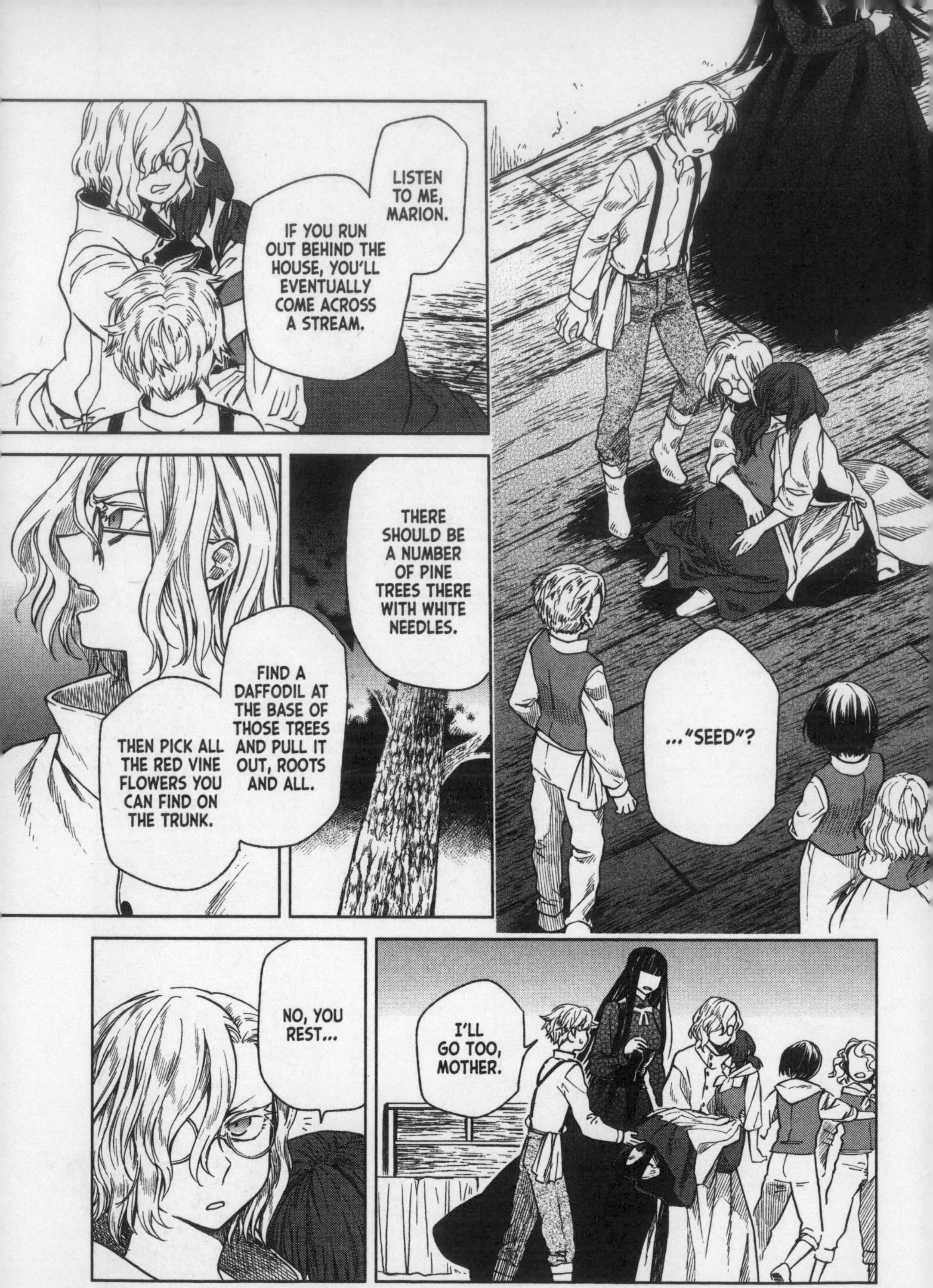
..."SEED"?
LISTEN TO ME, MARION.
IF YOU RUN OUT BEHIND THE HOUSE, YOU'LL EVENTUALLY COME ACROSS A STREAM.
THERE SHOULD BE A NUMBER OF PINE TREES THERE WITH WHITE NEEDLES.
FIND A DAFFODIL AT THE BASE OF THOSE TREES AND PULL IT OUT, ROOTS AND ALL.
THEN PICK ALL THE RED VINE FLOWERS YOU CAN FIND ON THE TRUNK.
I'LL GO TOO, MOTHER.
NO, YOU REST...

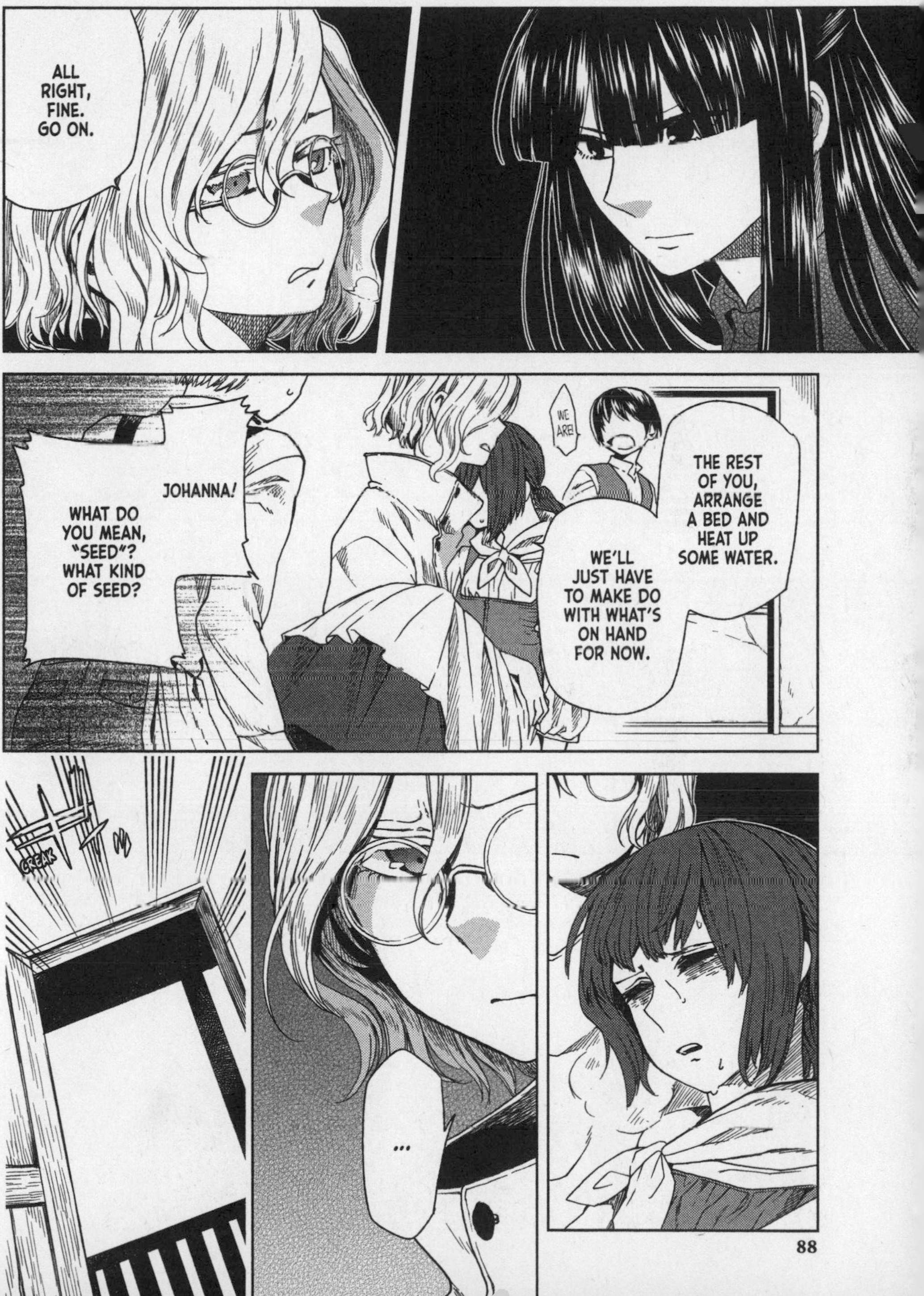
ALL RIGHT, FINE. GO ON.
THE REST OF YOU, ARRANGE A BED AND HEAT UP SOME WATER.
WE'LL JUST HAVE TO MAKE DO WITH WHAT'S ON HAND FOR NOW.
WE ARE!
JOHANNA!
WHAT DO YOU MEAN, "SEED"? WHAT KIND OF SEED?
...
CREAK

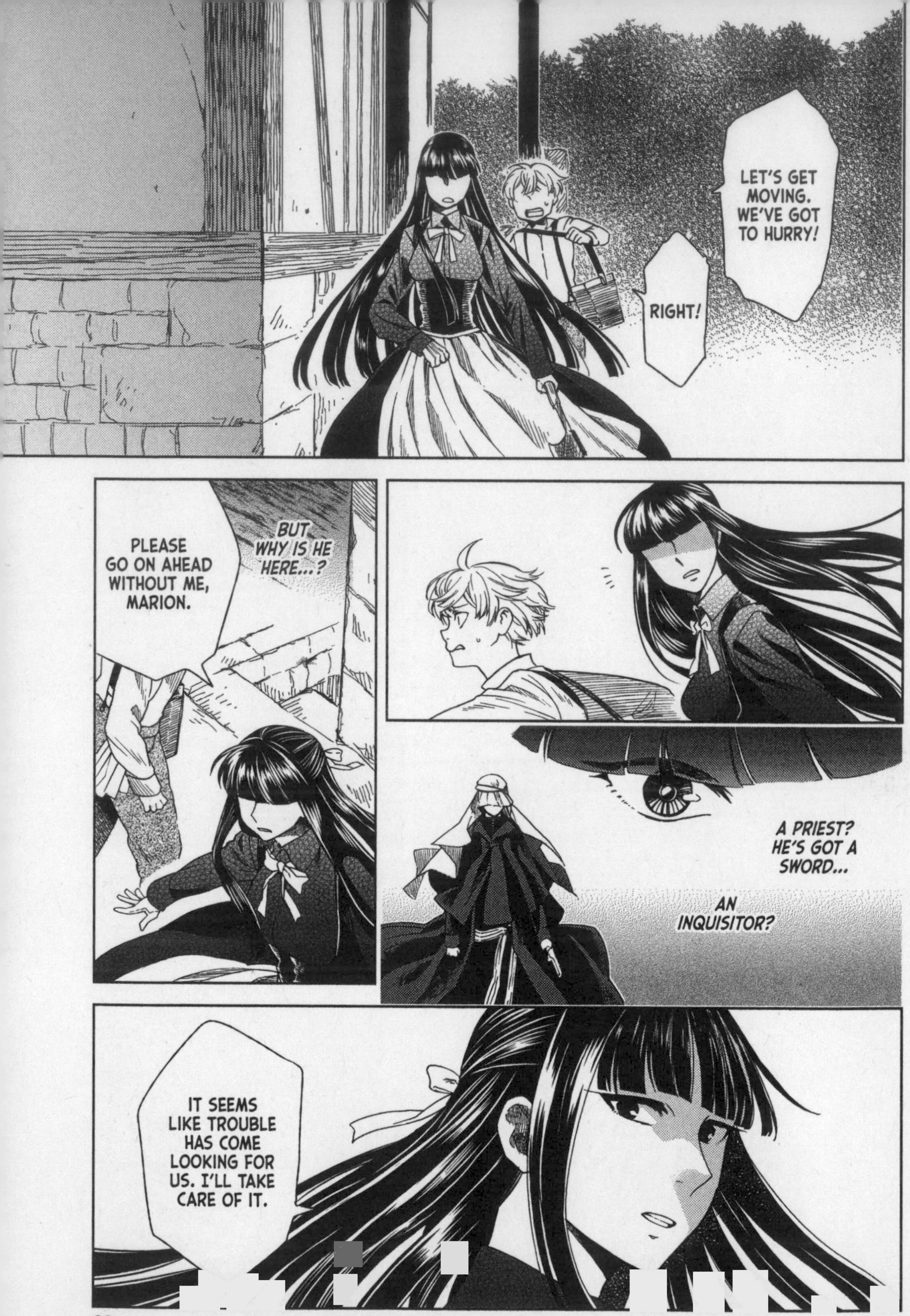
LET'S GET MOVING. WE'VE GOT TO HURRY!
RIGHT!
A PRIEST? HE'S GOT A SWORD...
AN INQUISITOR?
BUT WHY IS HE HERE...?
PLEASE GO ON AHEAD WITHOUT ME, MARION.
IT SEEMS LIKE TROUBLE HAS COME LOOKING FOR US. I'LL TAKE CARE OF IT.

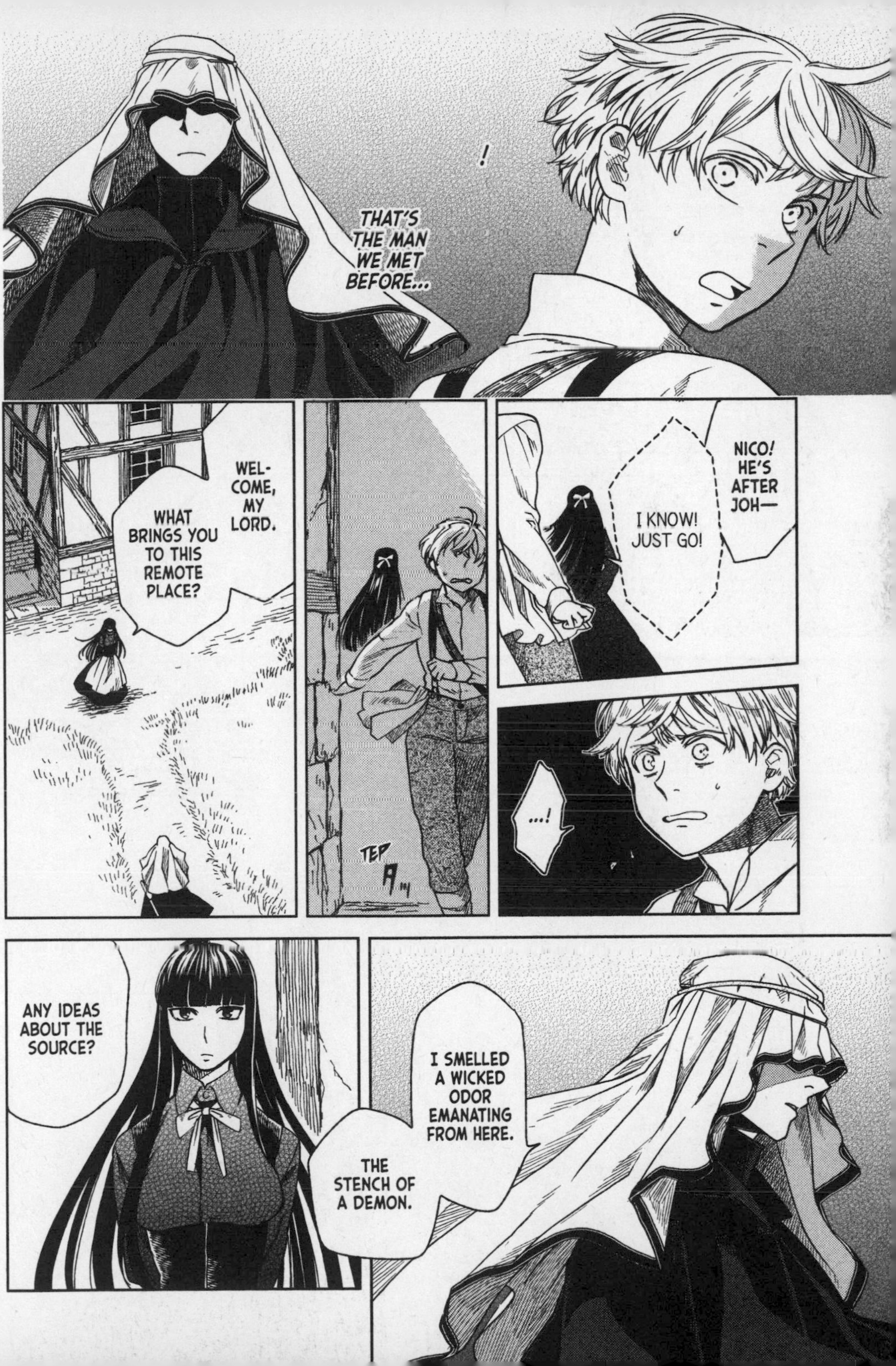
!
THAT'S THE MAN WE MET BEFORE...
NICO! HE'S AFTER JOH—
I KNOW! JUST GO!
...!
TEP
WEL-COME, MY LORD.
WHAT BRINGS YOU TO THIS REMOTE PLACE?
I SMELLED A WICKED ODOR EMANATING FROM HERE.
THE STENCH OF A DEMON.
ANY IDEAS ABOUT THE SOURCE?

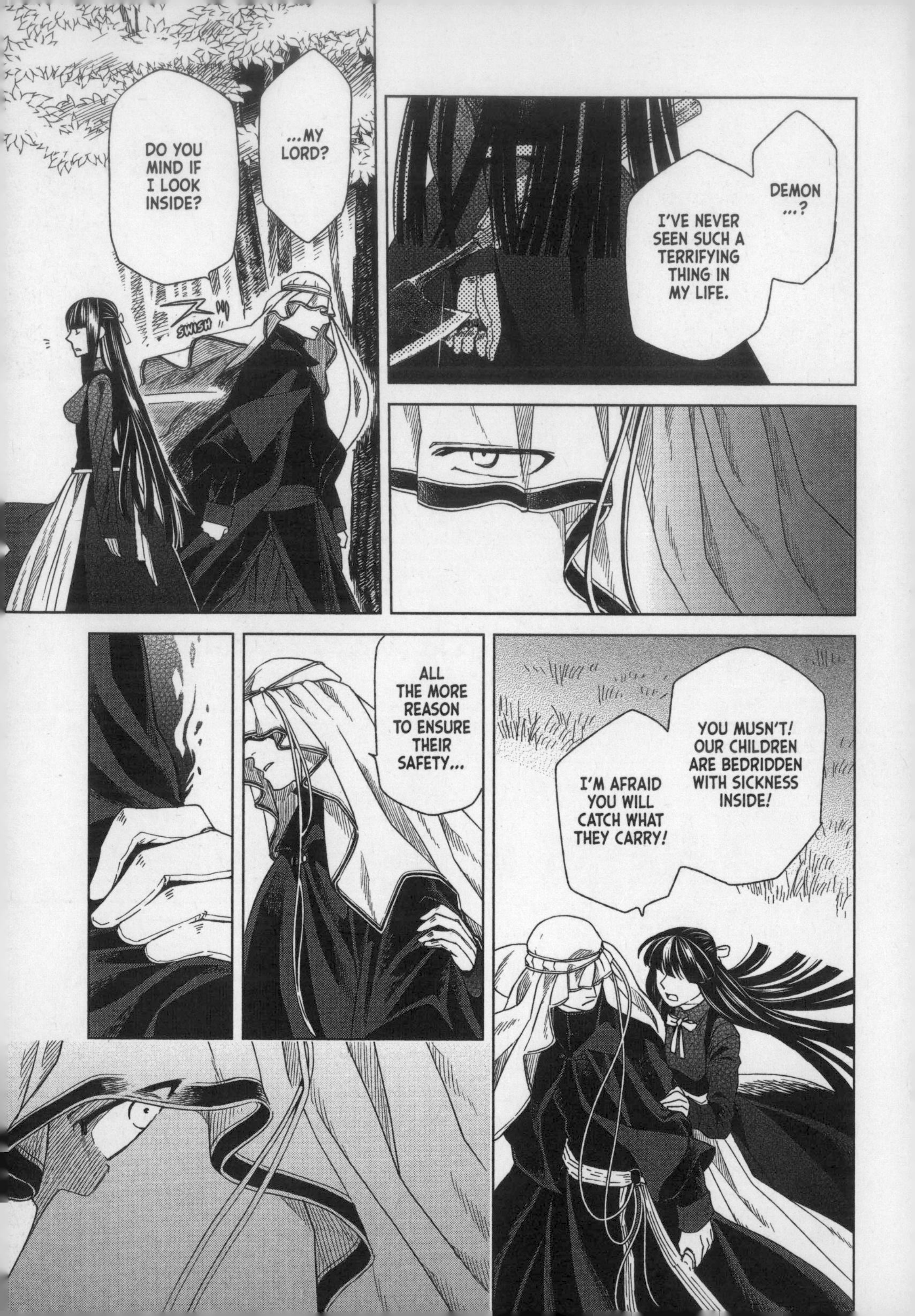
DEMON ...?
I'VE NEVER SEEN SUCH A TERRIFYING THING IN MY LIFE.
...MY LORD?
DO YOU MIND IF I LOOK INSIDE?
SWISH
YOU MUSN'T! OUR CHILDREN ARE BEDRIDDEN WITH SICKNESS INSIDE!
I'M AFRAID YOU WILL CATCH WHAT THEY CARRY!
ALL THE MORE REASON TO ENSURE THEIR SAFETY...

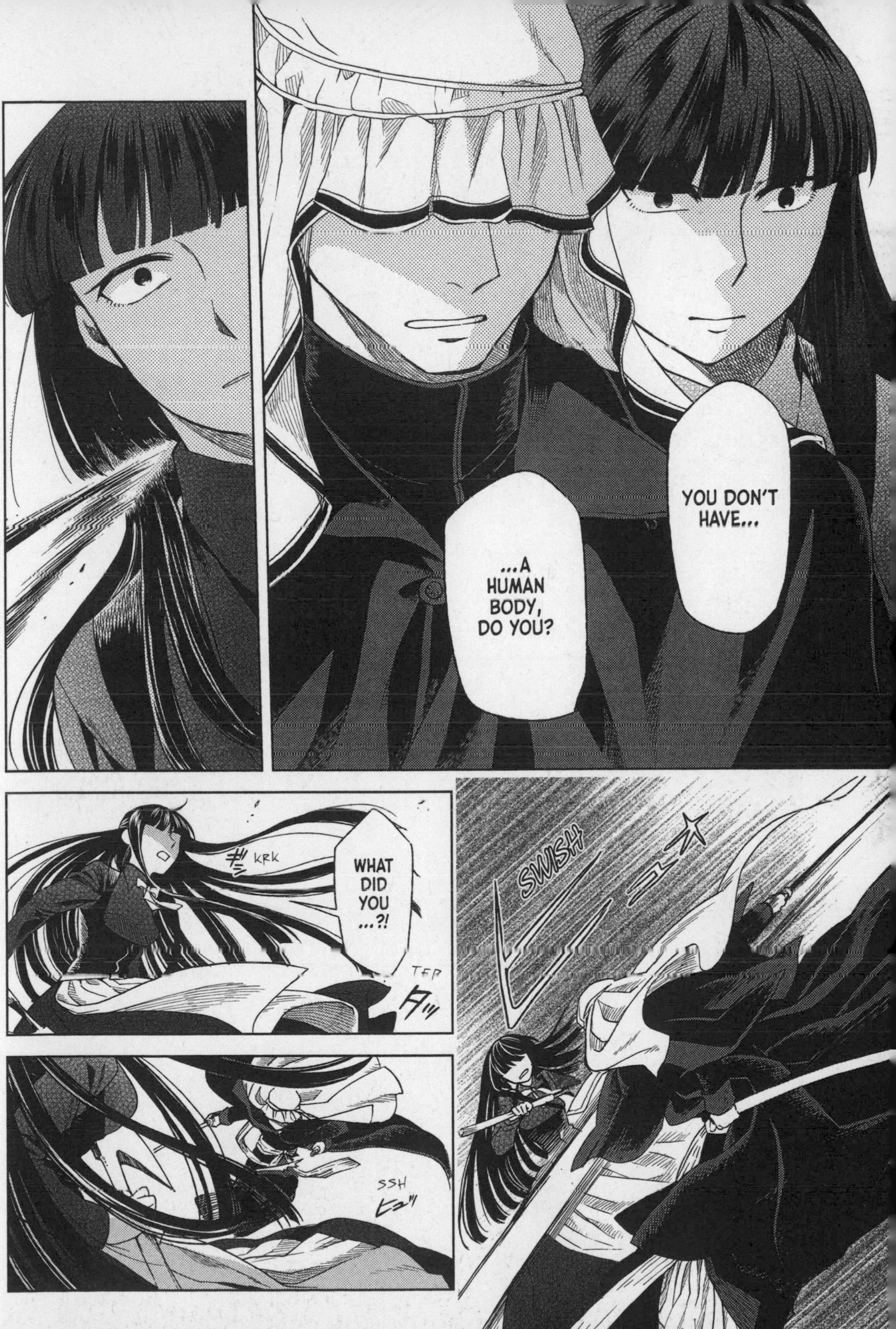
YOU DON'T HAVE...
...A HUMAN BODY, DO YOU?
SWISH
KRK
WHAT DID YOU ...?!
TEP
SSH

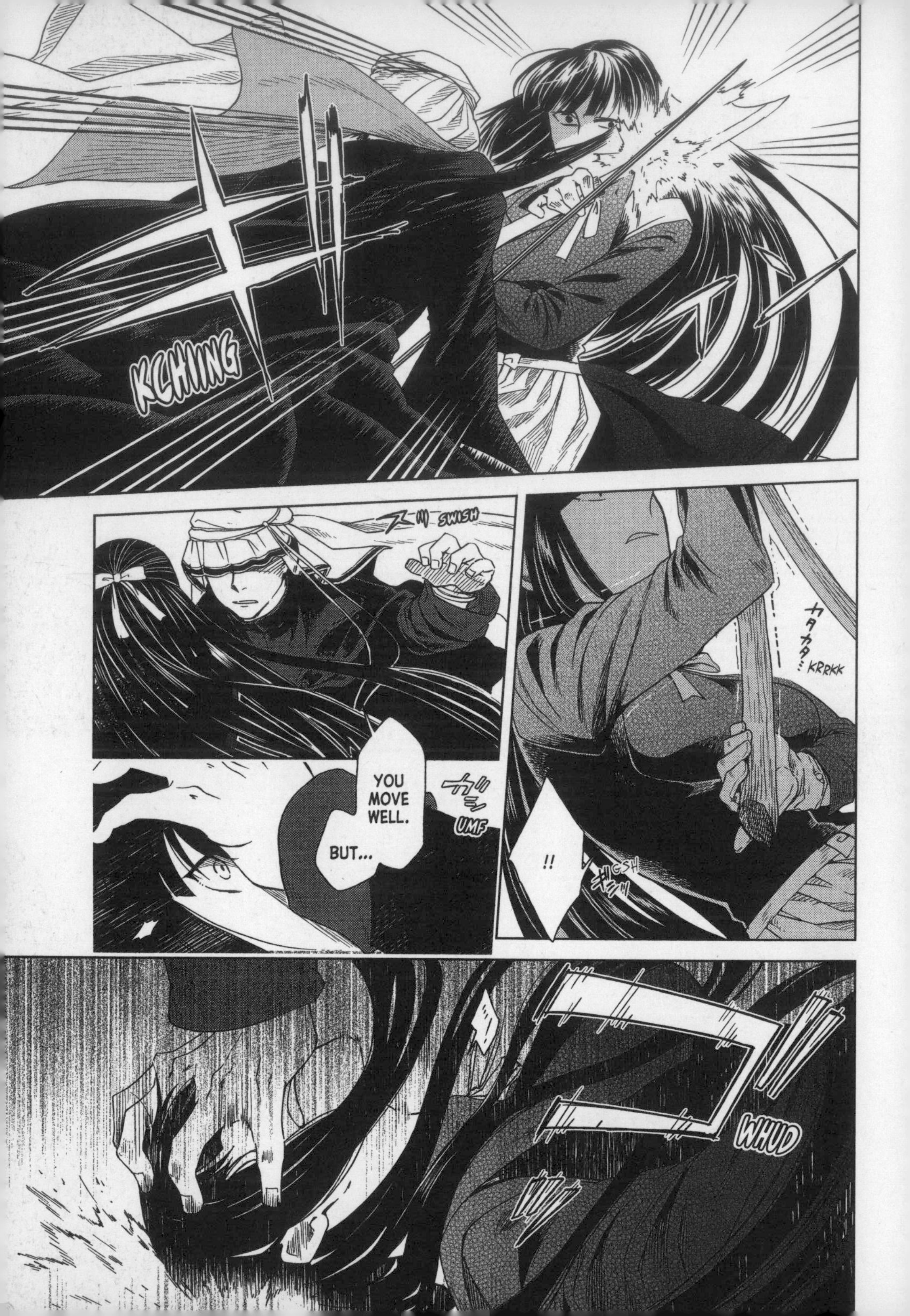
KCHIING
カタカタ KRRKK
!!
GSH
SWISH
YOU MOVE WELL.
BUT...
UMF
WHUD

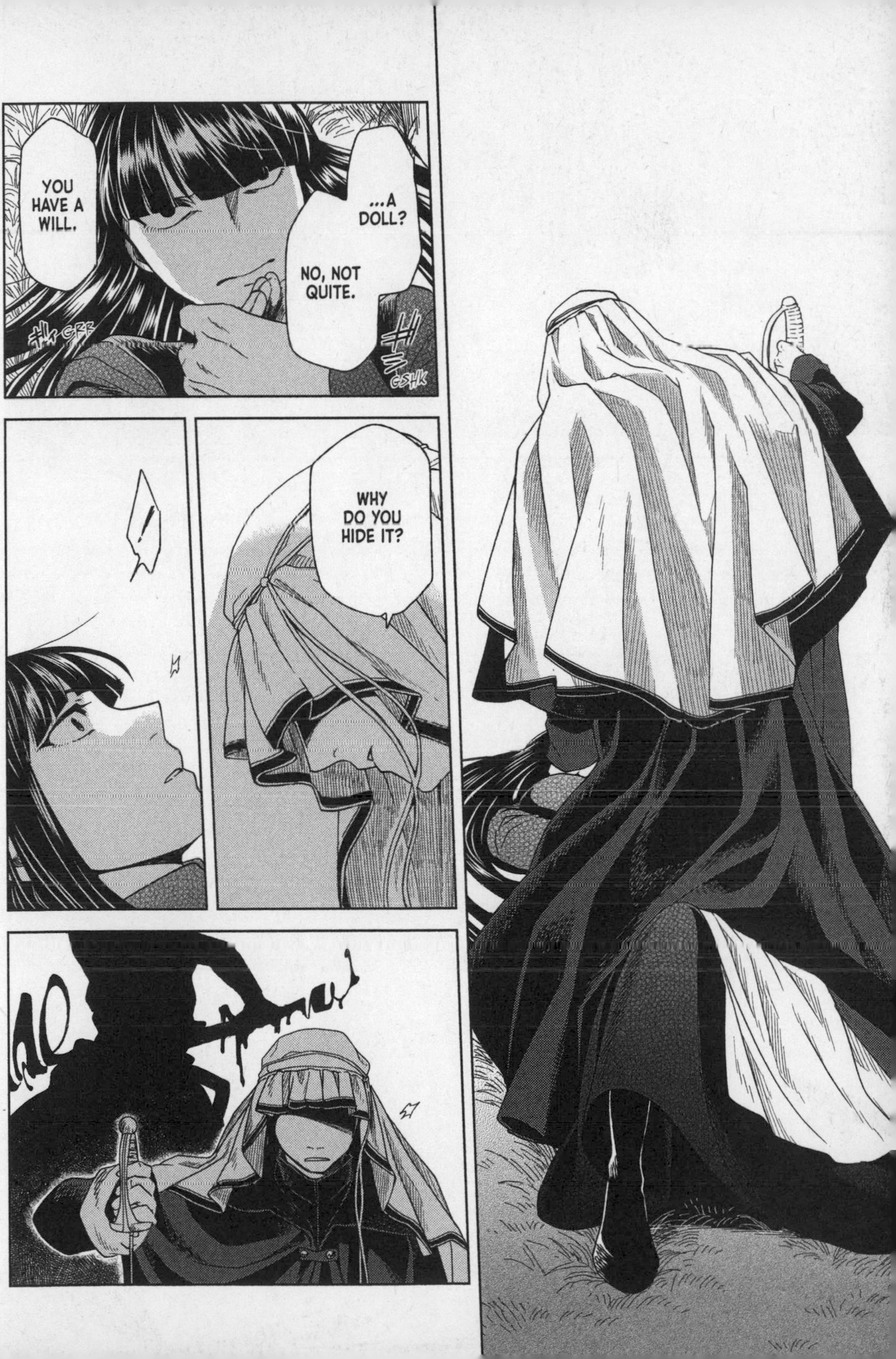
...A DOLL?
NO, NOT QUITE.
GSHK
YOU HAVE A WILL.
GRB
WHY DO YOU HIDE IT?
!

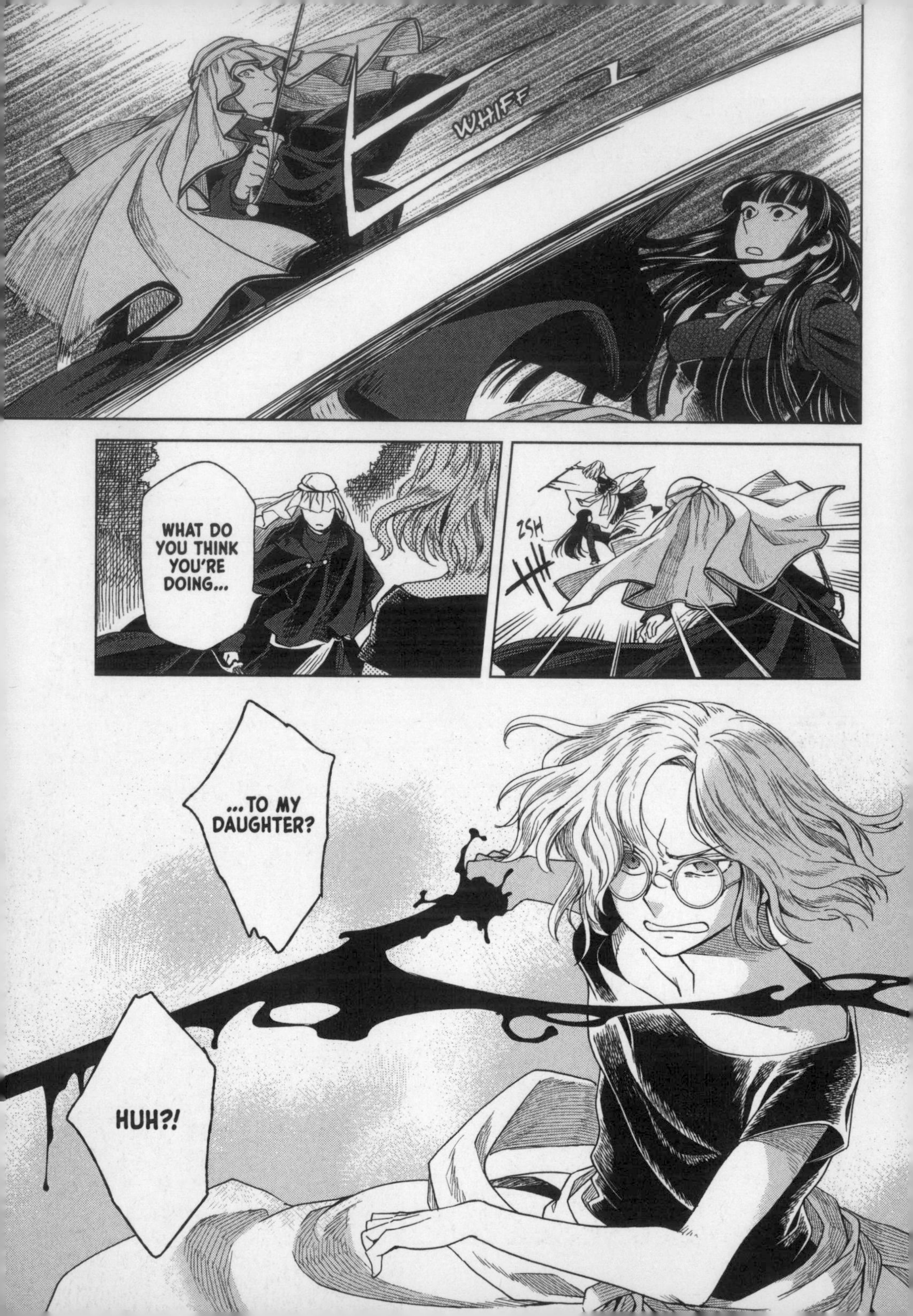
WHIFF
ZSH
WHAT DO YOU THINK YOU'RE DOING...
...TO MY DAUGHTER?
HUH?!

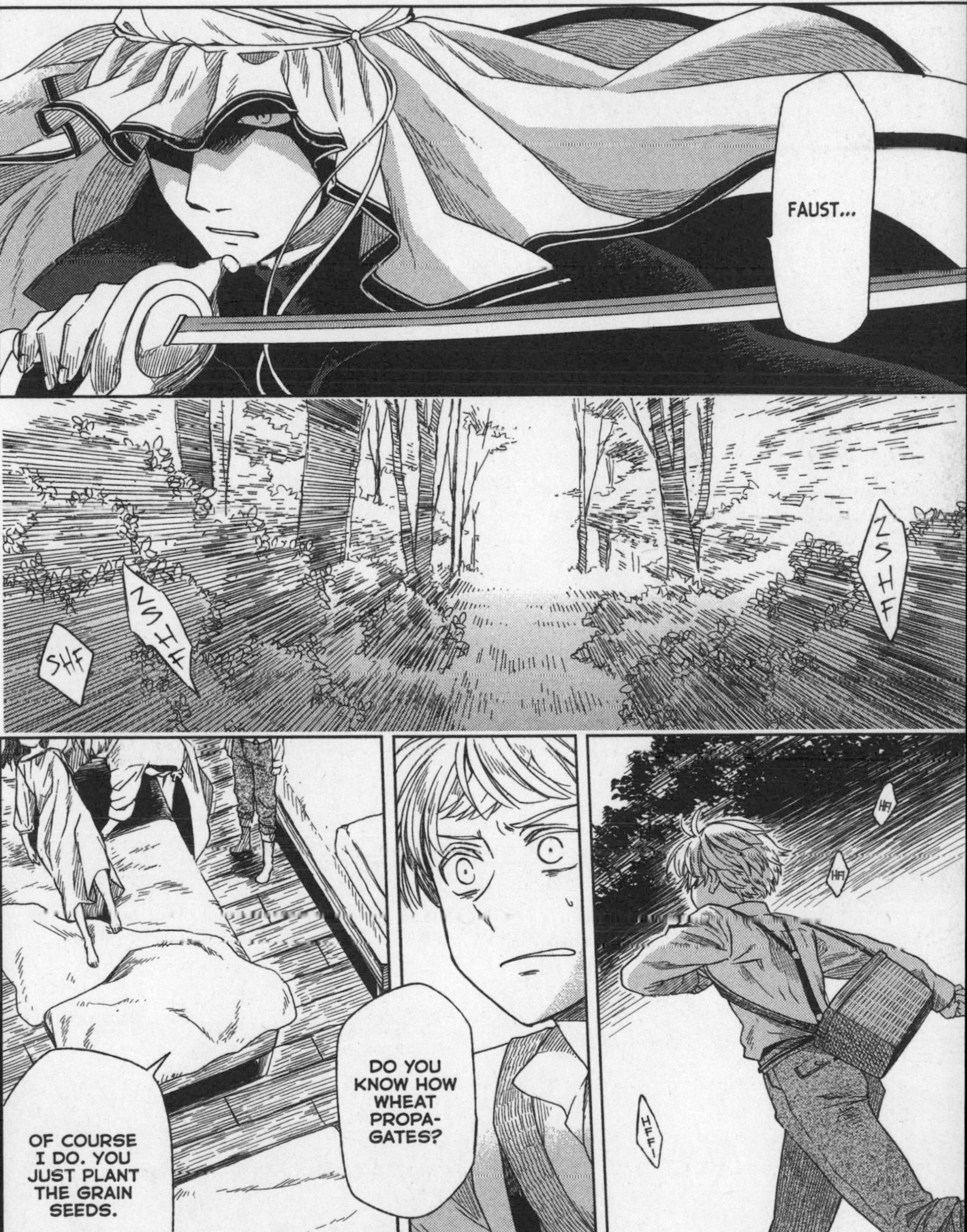
FAUST...
ZSHF
ZSHF
SHF
HF!
HF!
HFF!
DO YOU KNOW HOW WHEAT PROPAGATES?
OF COURSE I DO. YOU JUST PLANT THE GRAIN SEEDS.

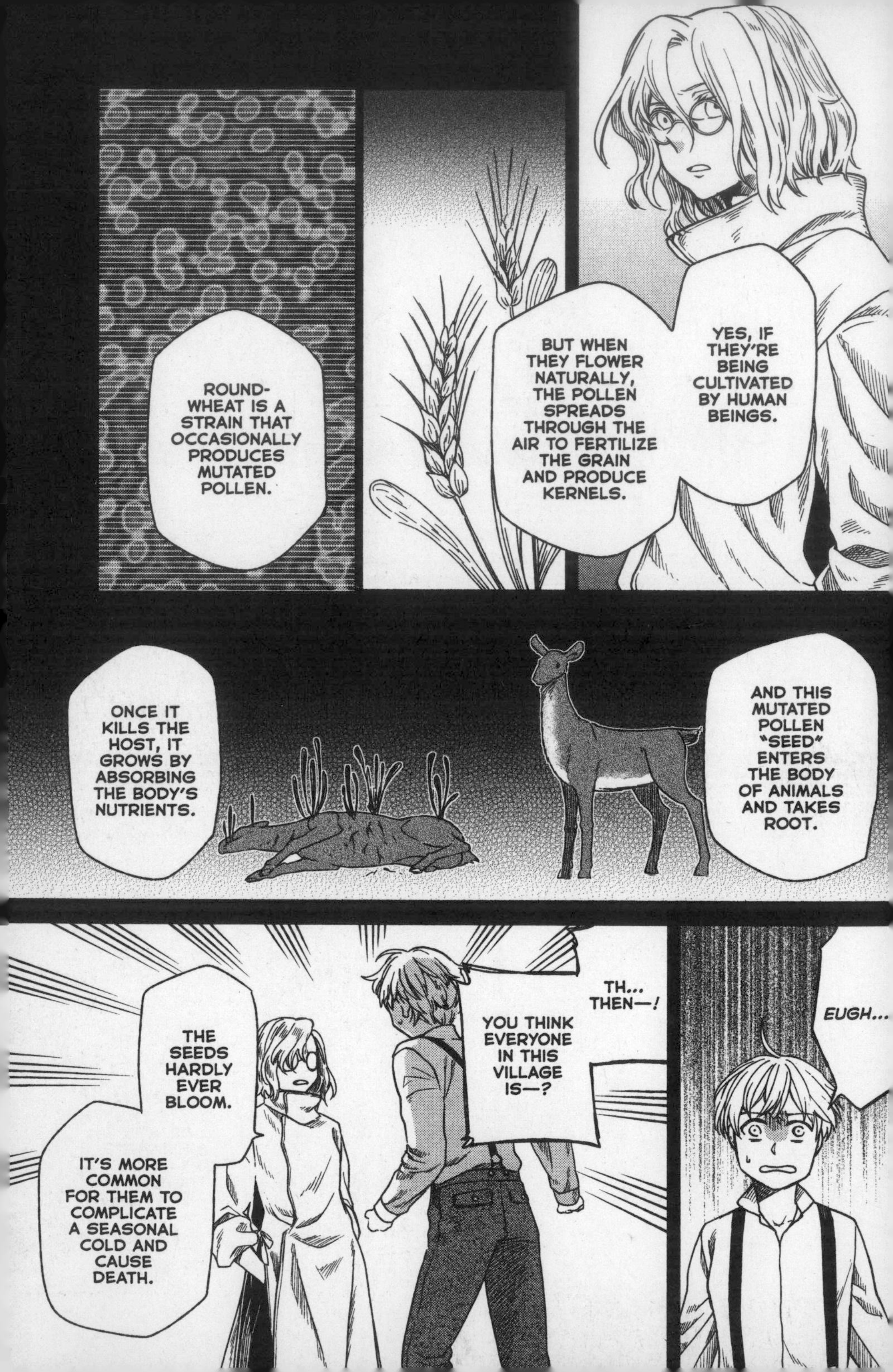
YES, IF THEY'RE BEING CULTIVATED BY HUMAN BEINGS.
BUT WHEN THEY FLOWER NATURALLY, THE POLLEN SPREADS THROUGH THE AIR TO FERTILIZE THE GRAIN AND PRODUCE KERNELS.
ROUND-WHEAT IS A STRAIN THAT OCCASIONALLY PRODUCES MUTATED POLLEN.
AND THIS MUTATED POLLEN "SEED" ENTERS THE BODY OF ANIMALS AND TAKES ROOT.
ONCE IT KILLS THE HOST, IT GROWS BY ABSORBING THE BODY'S NUTRIENTS.
EUGH...
TH... THEN—!
YOU THINK EVERYONE IN THIS VILLAGE IS—?
THE SEEDS HARDLY EVER BLOOM.
IT'S MORE COMMON FOR THEM TO COMPLICATE A SEASONAL COLD AND CAUSE DEATH.

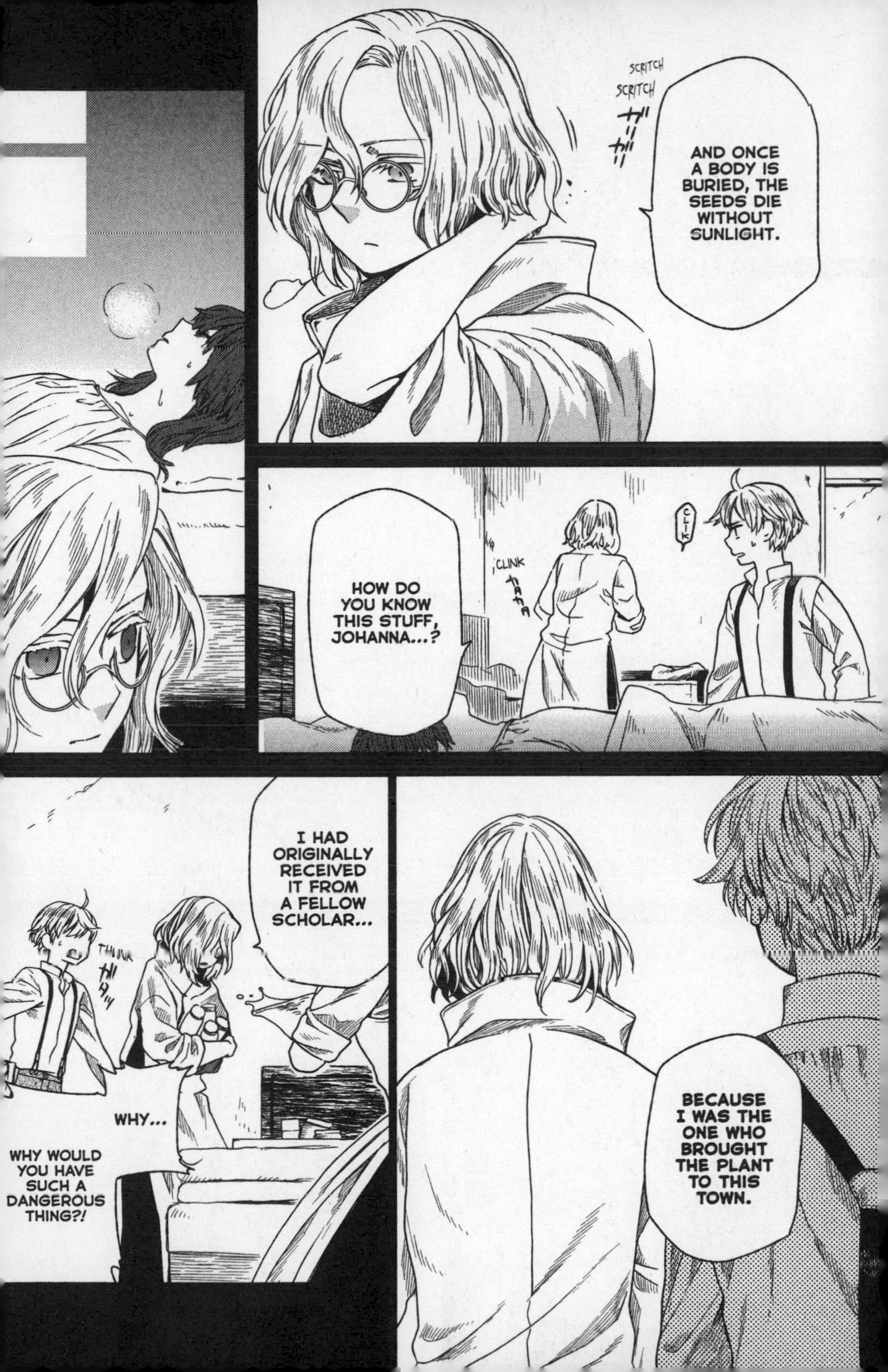
SCRITCH
SCRITCH
AND ONCE A BODY IS BURIED, THE SEEDS DIE WITHOUT SUNLIGHT.
CLIK
CLINK
HOW DO YOU KNOW THIS STUFF, JOHANNA...?
BECAUSE I WAS THE ONE WHO BROUGHT THE PLANT TO THIS TOWN.
I HAD ORIGINALLY RECEIVED IT FROM A FELLOW SCHOLAR...
THUNK
WHY...
WHY WOULD YOU HAVE SUCH A DANGEROUS THING?!

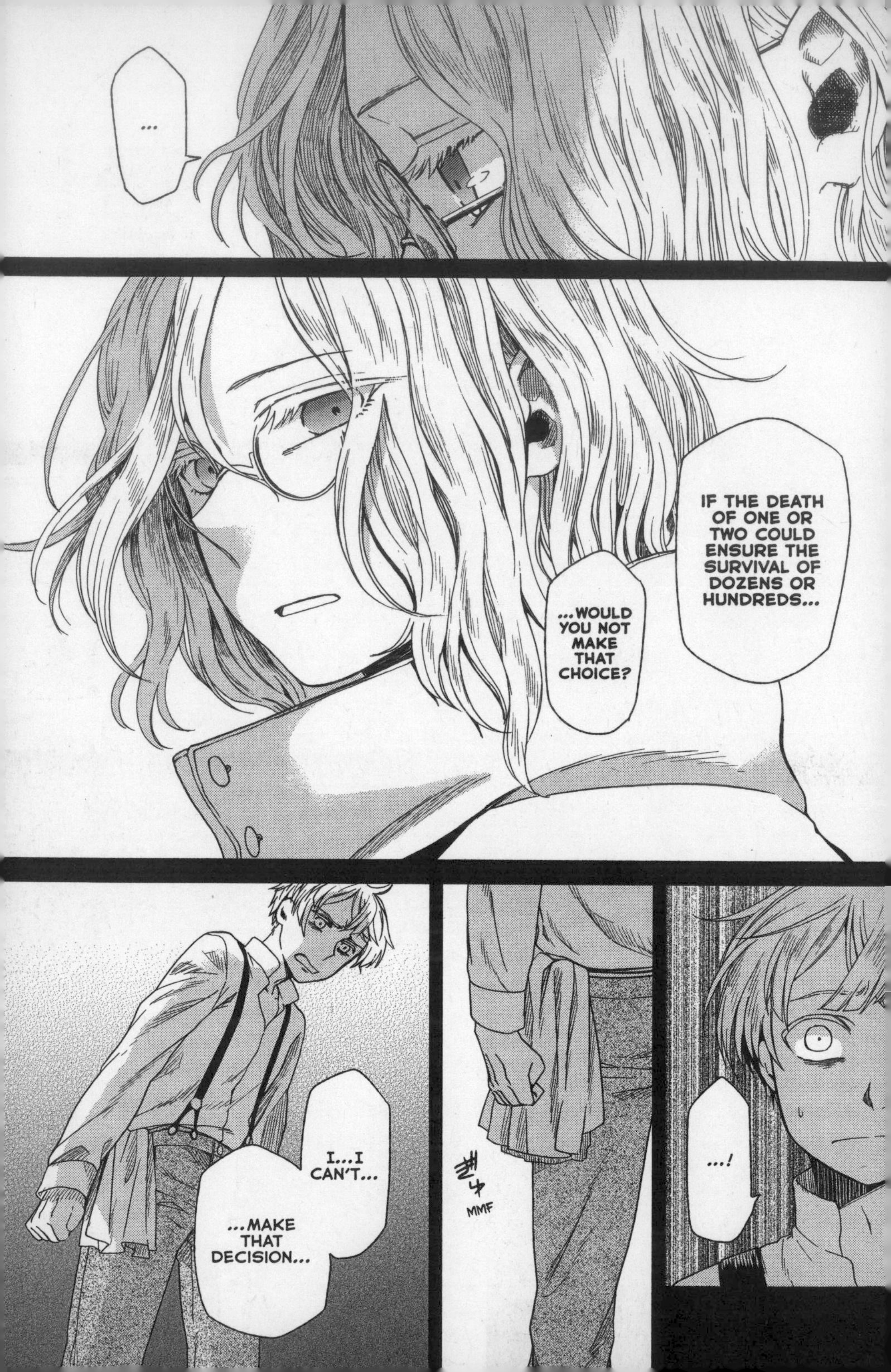
...
IF THE DEATH OF ONE OR TWO COULD ENSURE THE SURVIVAL OF DOZENS OR HUNDREDS...
...WOULD YOU NOT MAKE THAT CHOICE?
...!
MMF
I...I CAN'T...
...MAKE THAT DECISION...

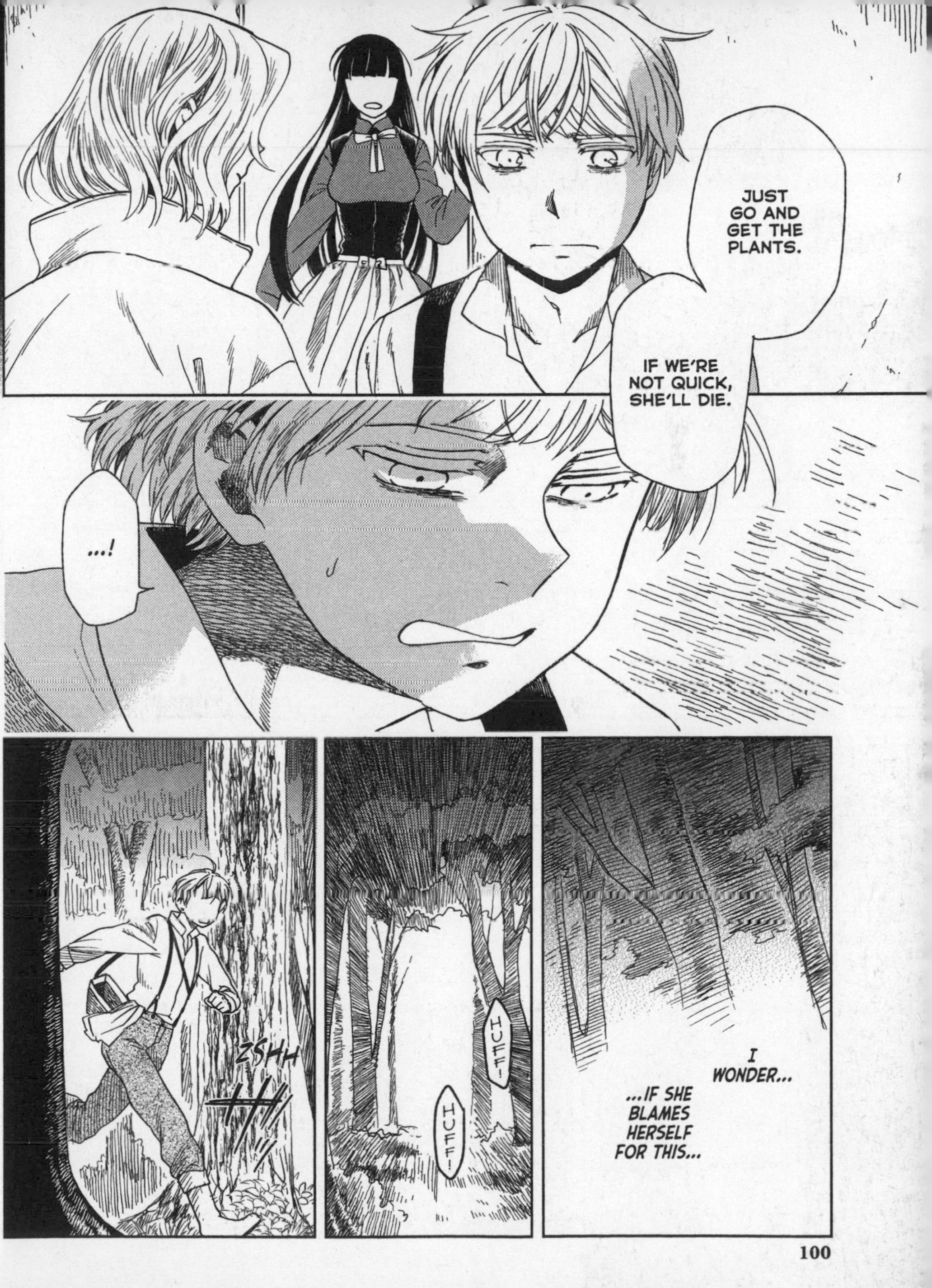
JUST GO AND GET THE PLANTS.
IF WE'RE NOT QUICK, SHE'LL DIE.
...!
I WONDER...
...IF SHE BLAMES HERSELF FOR THIS...
HUFF!
HUFF!
ZSHH

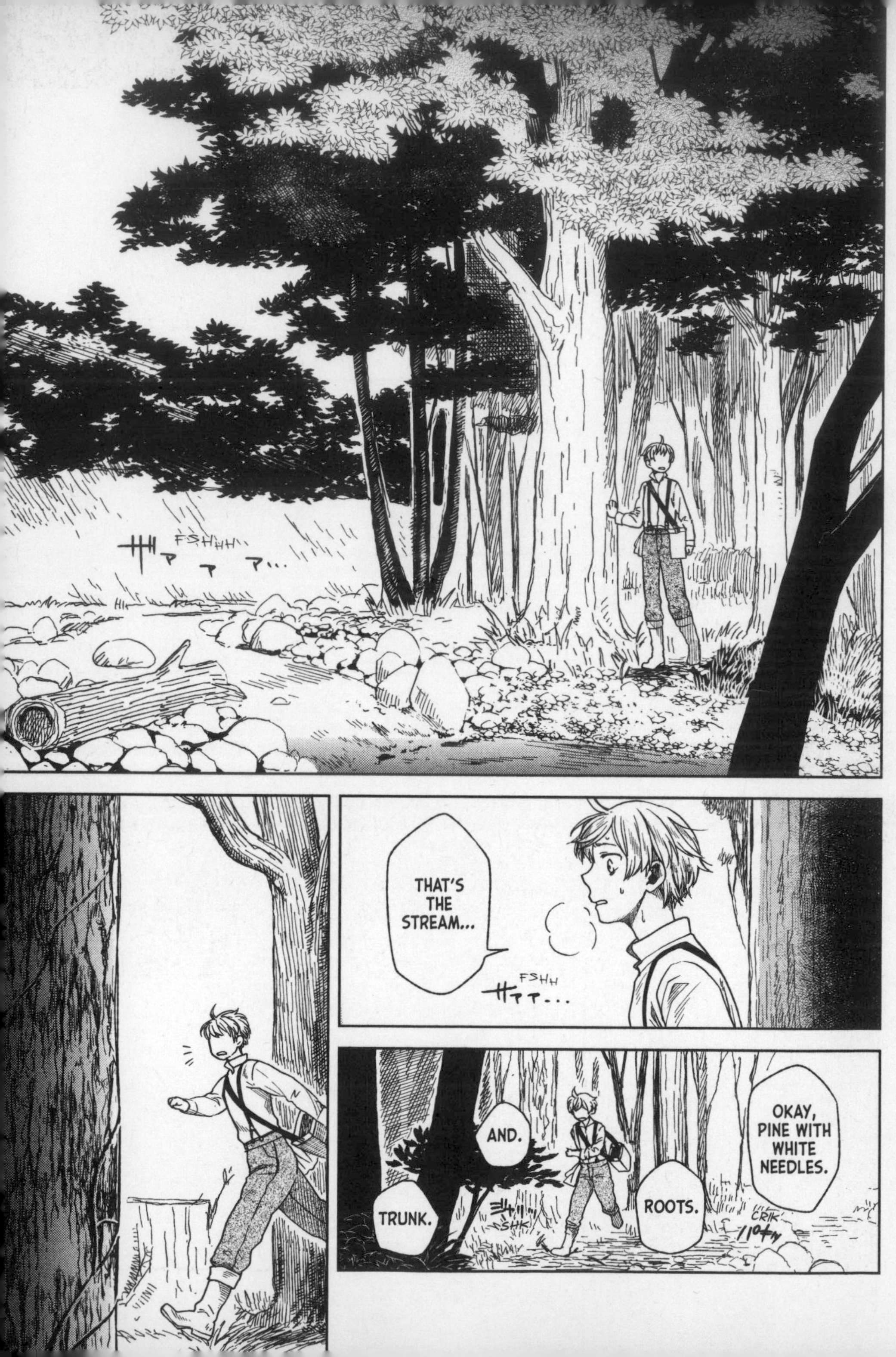

FSHHH...
THAT'S THE STREAM...
FSHH...
OKAY, PINE WITH WHITE NEEDLES.
ROOTS.
CRIK
AND.
TRUNK.
SHK

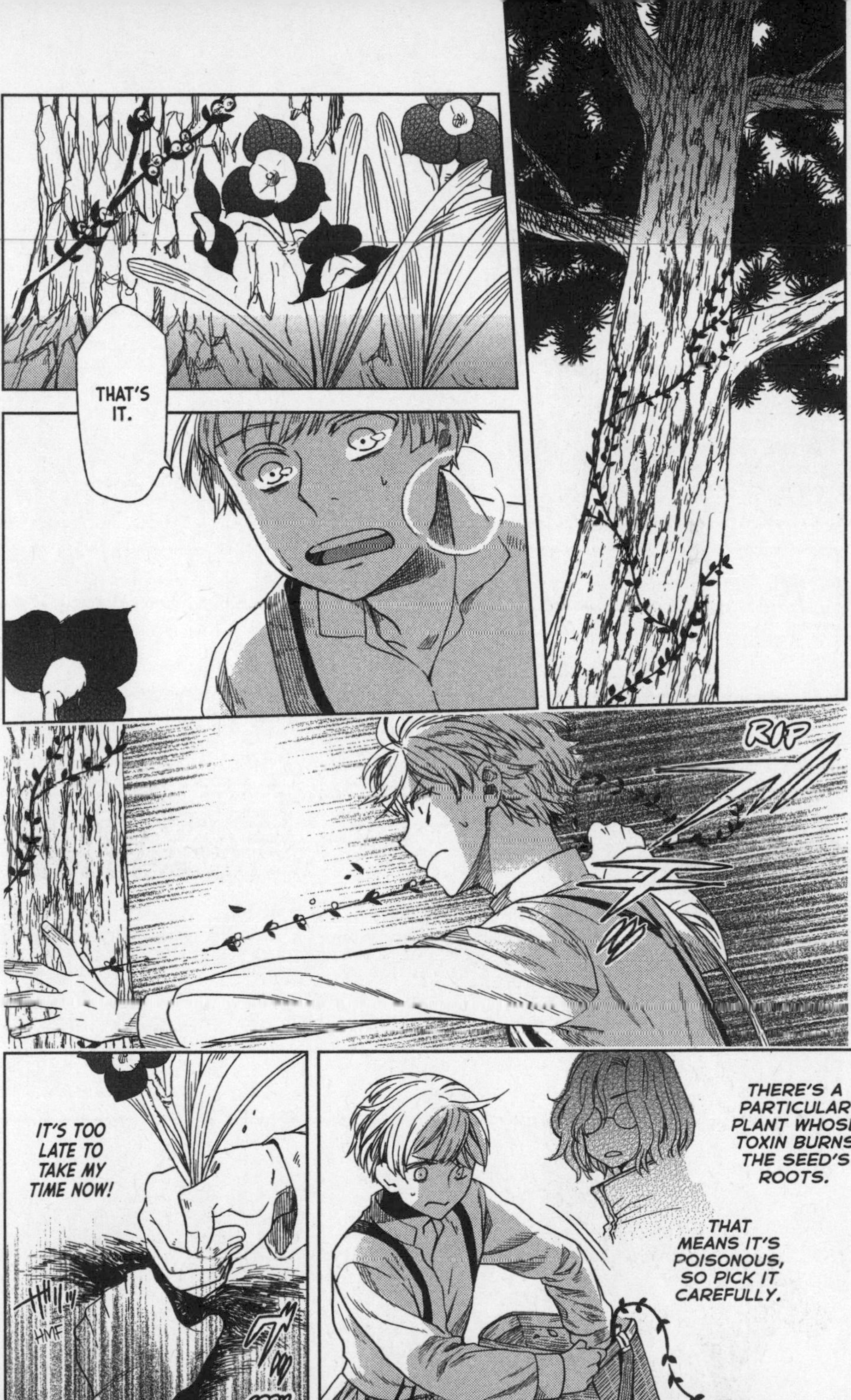
THAT'S IT.
RIP
THERE'S A PARTICULAR PLANT WHOSE TOXIN BURNS THE SEED'S ROOTS.
THAT MEANS IT'S POISONOUS, SO PICK IT CAREFULLY.
IT'S TOO LATE TO TAKE MY TIME NOW!
HMF
GRRK

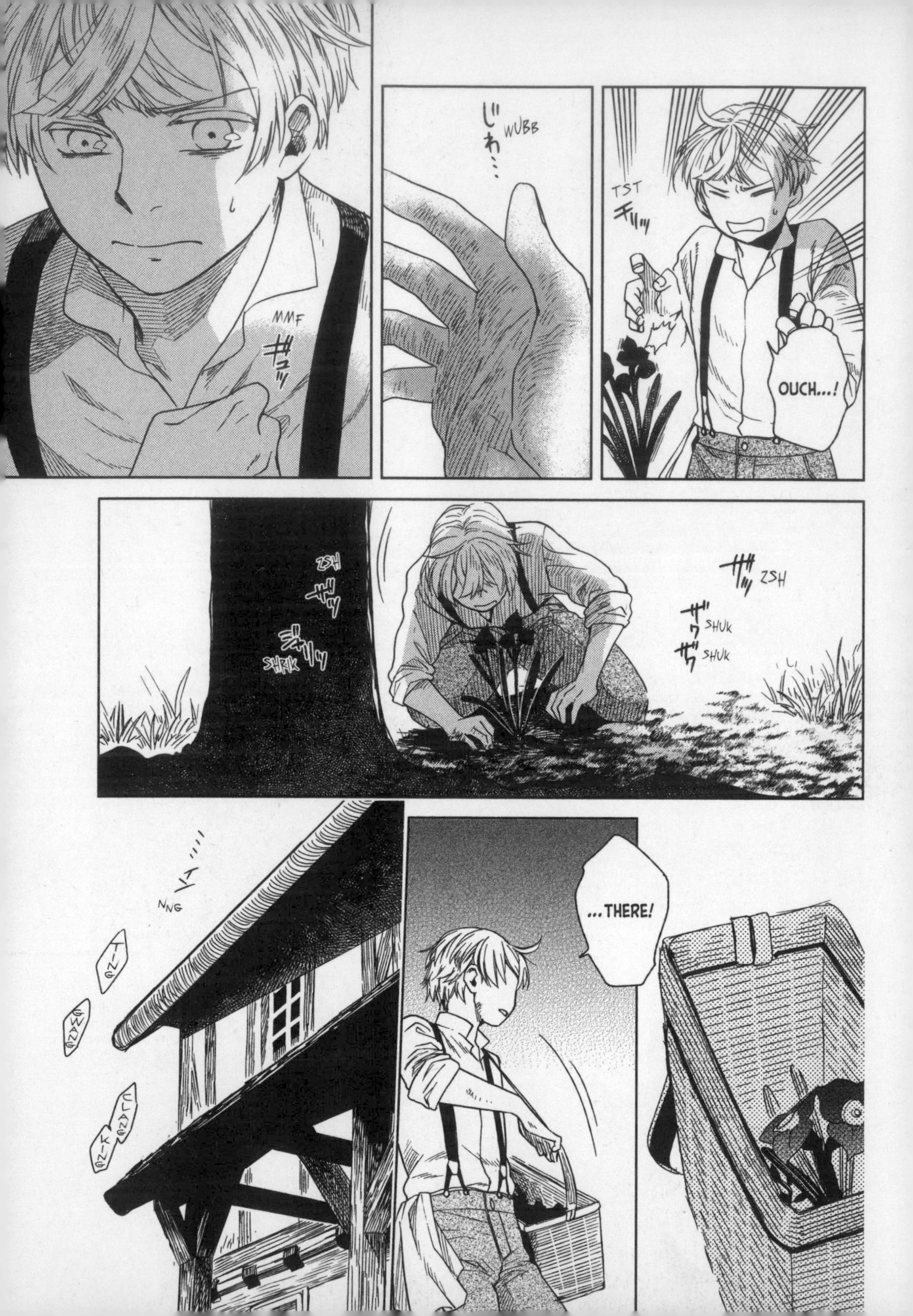
TST
チッ
OUCH...!
じわ…
WUBB
MMF
ギュッ
ザッ
ZSH
ザク
SHUK
ザク
SHUK
ZSH
ザッ
ジャリッ
SHRIK
...THERE!
NNG
TING
GWANG
CLANG
KING

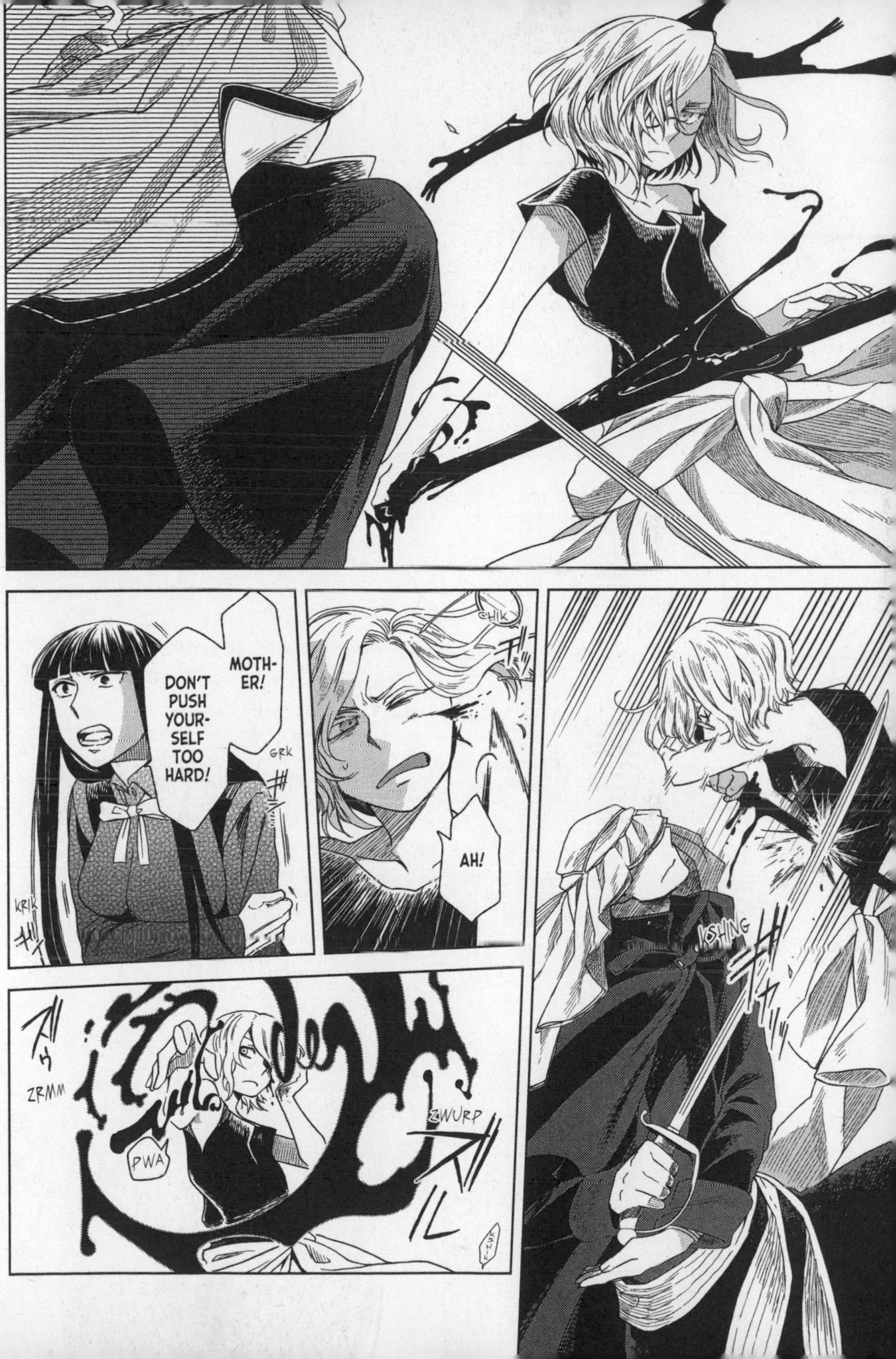
SHING
KRIK
CHIK
AH!
MOTHER!
DON'T PUSH YOURSELF TOO HARD!
GRK
KRIK
ZWURP
ZRMM
PWA

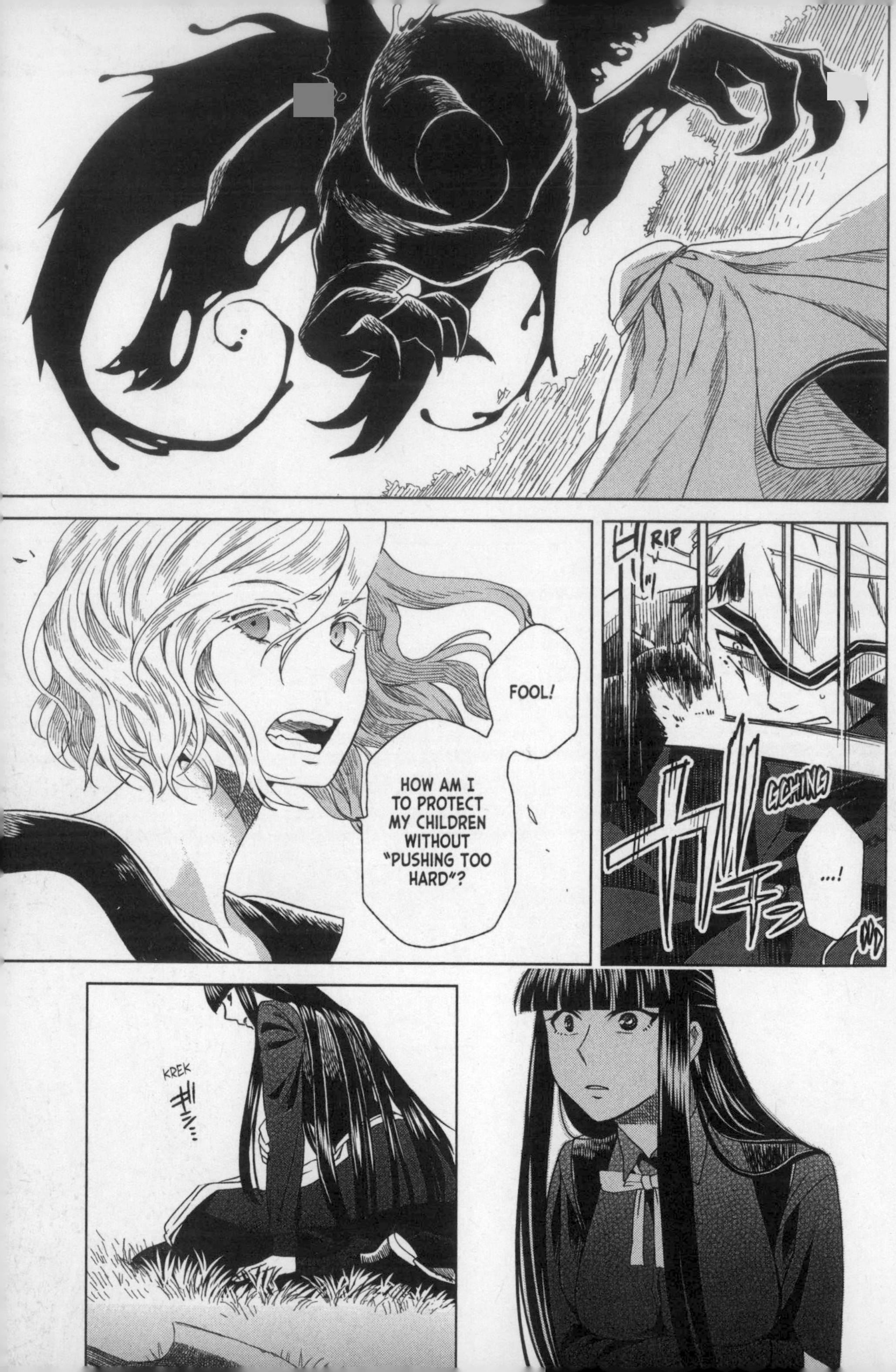
RIP
GCHING
...!
FOOL!
HOW AM I TO PROTECT MY CHILDREN WITHOUT "PUSHING TOO HARD"?
KREK

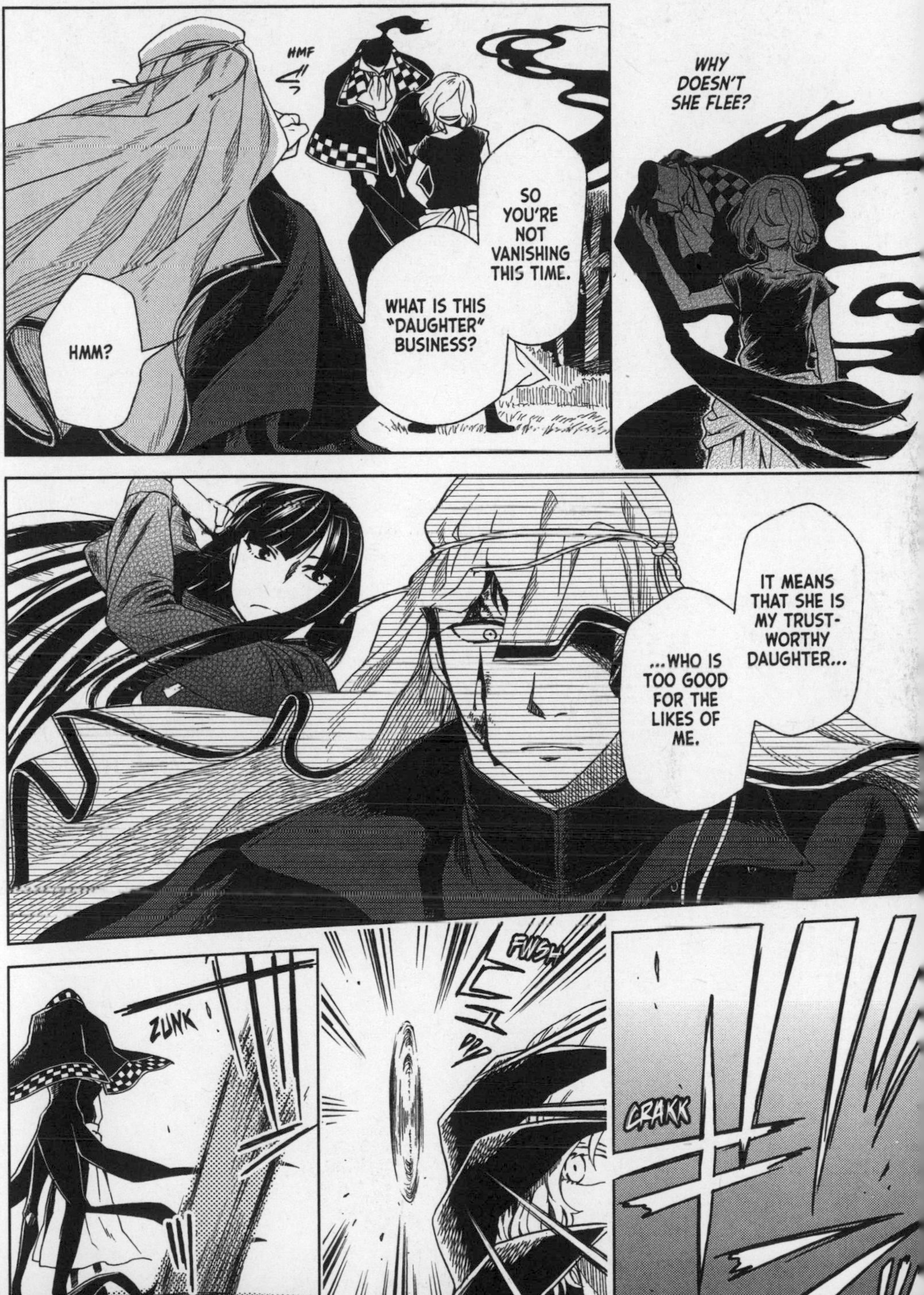
WHY DOESN'T SHE FLEE?
HMF
SO YOU'RE NOT VANISHING THIS TIME.
WHAT IS THIS "DAUGHTER" BUSINESS?
HMM?
IT MEANS THAT SHE IS MY TRUST-WORTHY DAUGHTER...
...WHO IS TOO GOOD FOR THE LIKES OF ME.
CRAKK
FWSH
ZUNK

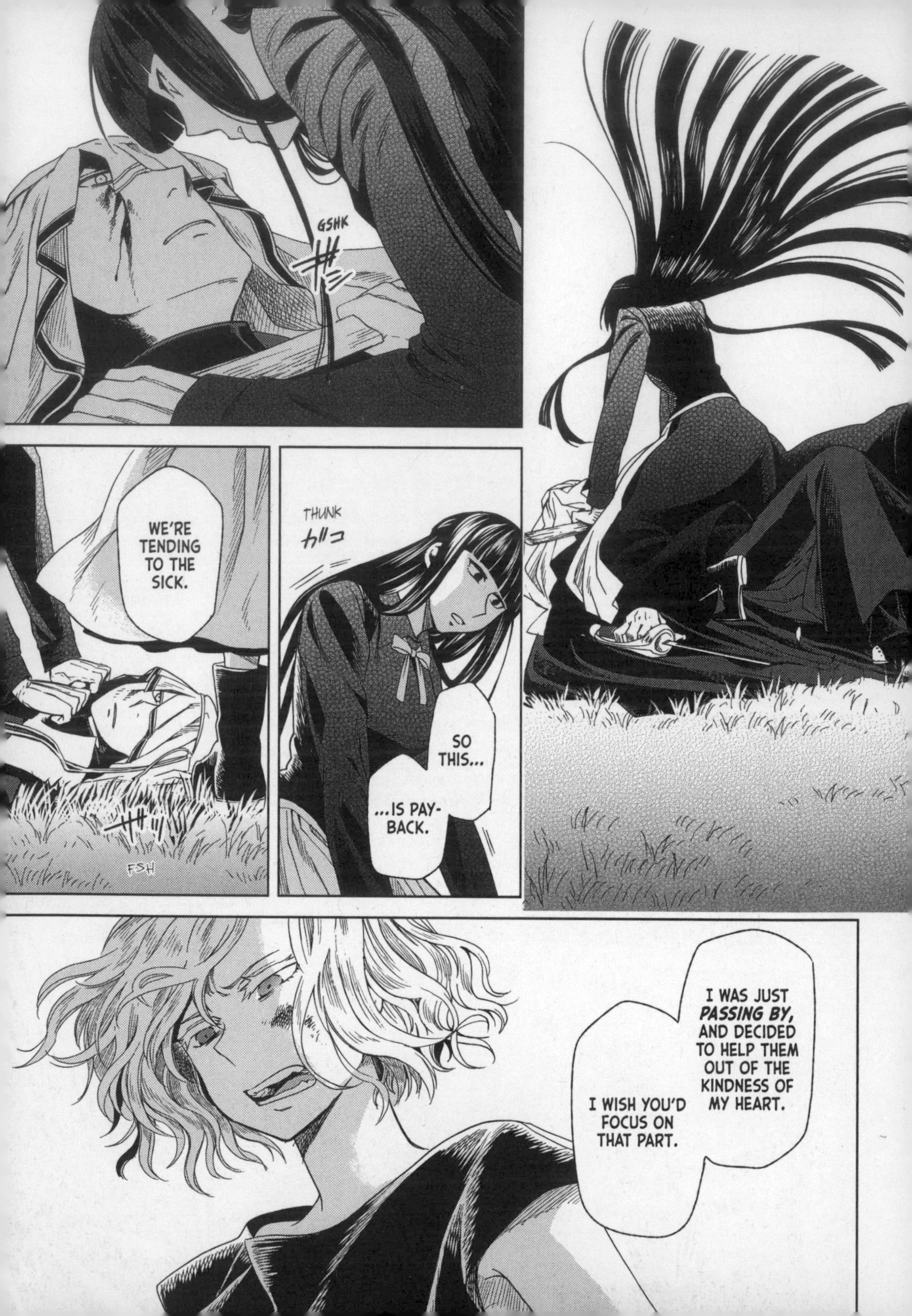
GSHK
THUNK
SO THIS...
...IS PAY-BACK.
WE'RE TENDING TO THE SICK.
FSH
I WAS JUST *PASSING BY,* AND DECIDED TO HELP THEM OUT OF THE KINDNESS OF MY HEART.
I WISH YOU'D FOCUS ON THAT PART.

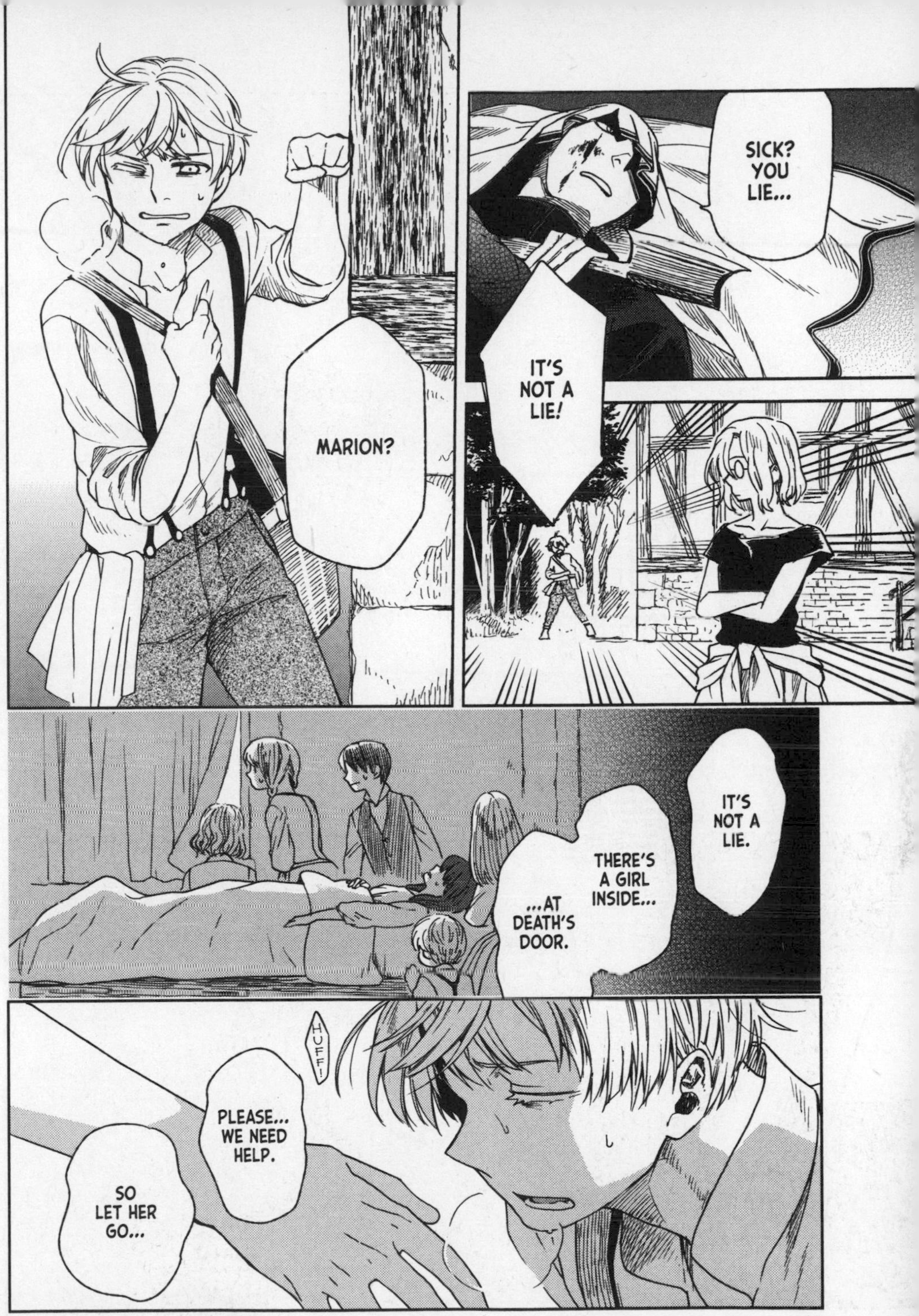
SICK? YOU LIE...
IT'S NOT A LIE!
MARION?
IT'S NOT A LIE.
THERE'S A GIRL INSIDE...
...AT DEATH'S DOOR.
HUFF!
PLEASE... WE NEED HELP.
SO LET HER GO...

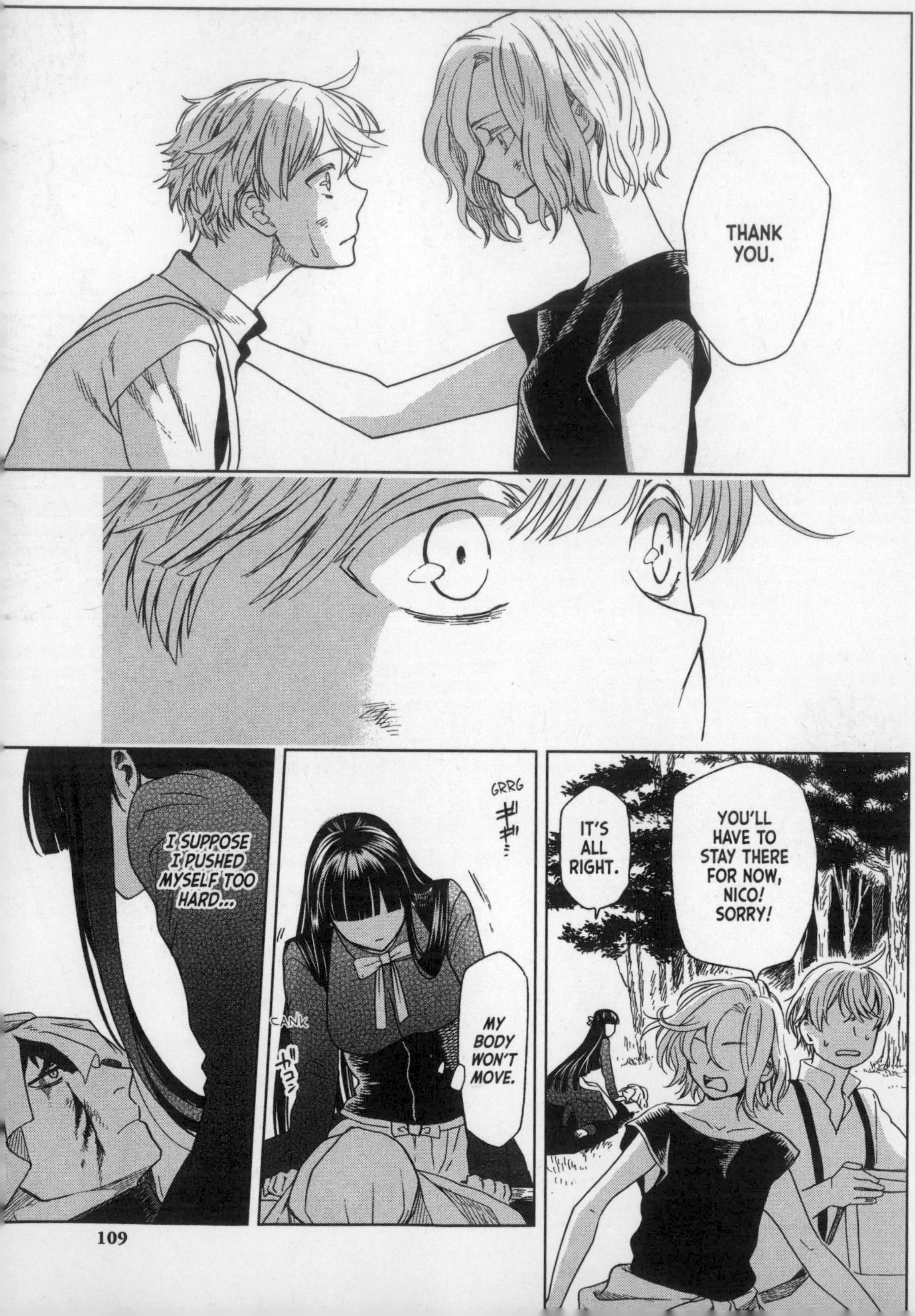
THANK YOU.
YOU'LL HAVE TO STAY THERE FOR NOW, NICO! SORRY!
IT'S ALL RIGHT.
GRRG
MY BODY WON'T MOVE.
CANK
I SUPPOSE I PUSHED MYSELF TOO HARD...

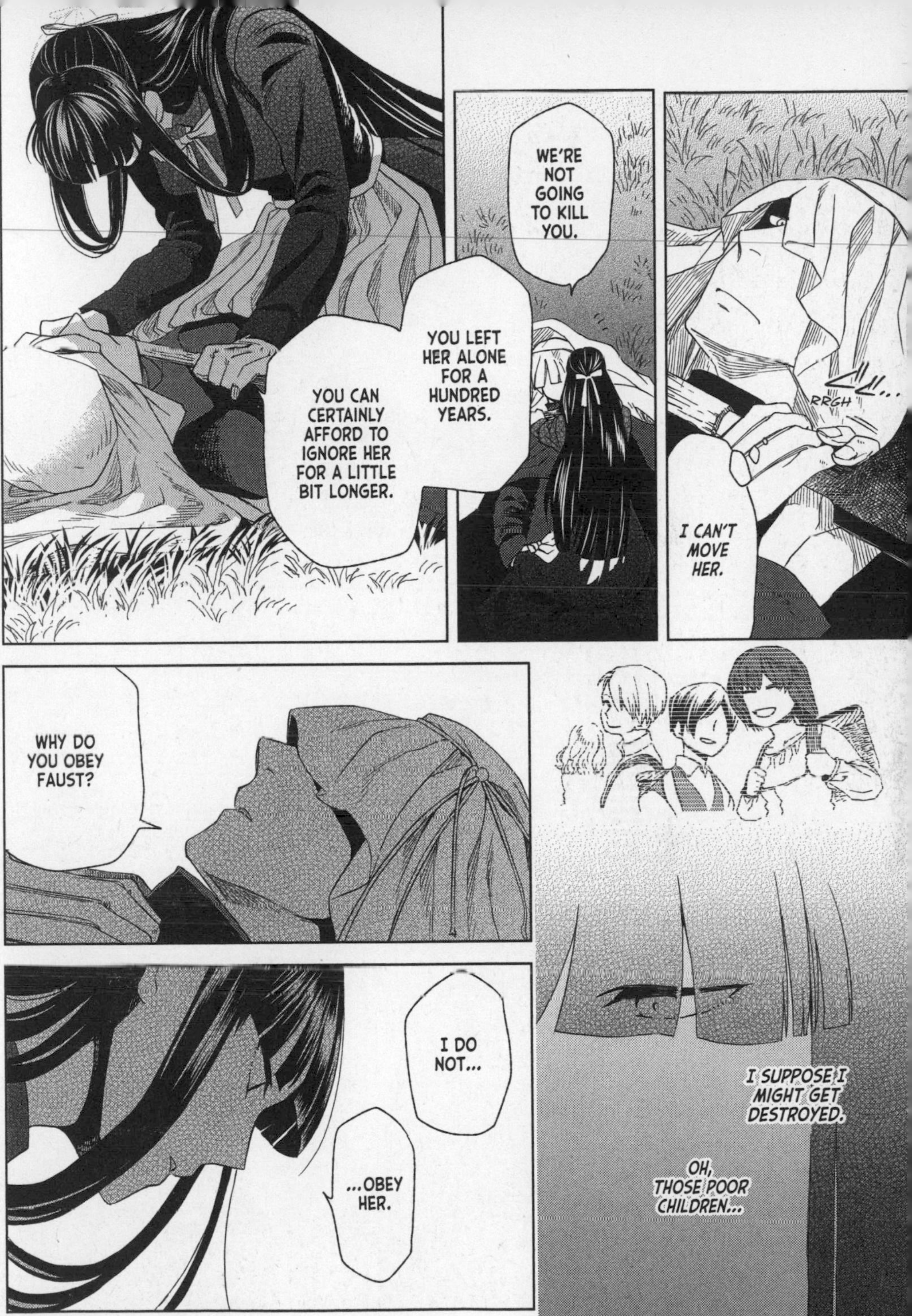
RRGH
I CAN'T MOVE HER.
WE'RE NOT GOING TO KILL YOU.
YOU LEFT HER ALONE FOR A HUNDRED YEARS.
YOU CAN CERTAINLY AFFORD TO IGNORE HER FOR A LITTLE BIT LONGER.
I SUPPOSE I MIGHT GET DESTROYED.
OH, THOSE POOR CHILDREN...
WHY DO YOU OBEY FAUST?
I DO NOT...
...OBEY HER.

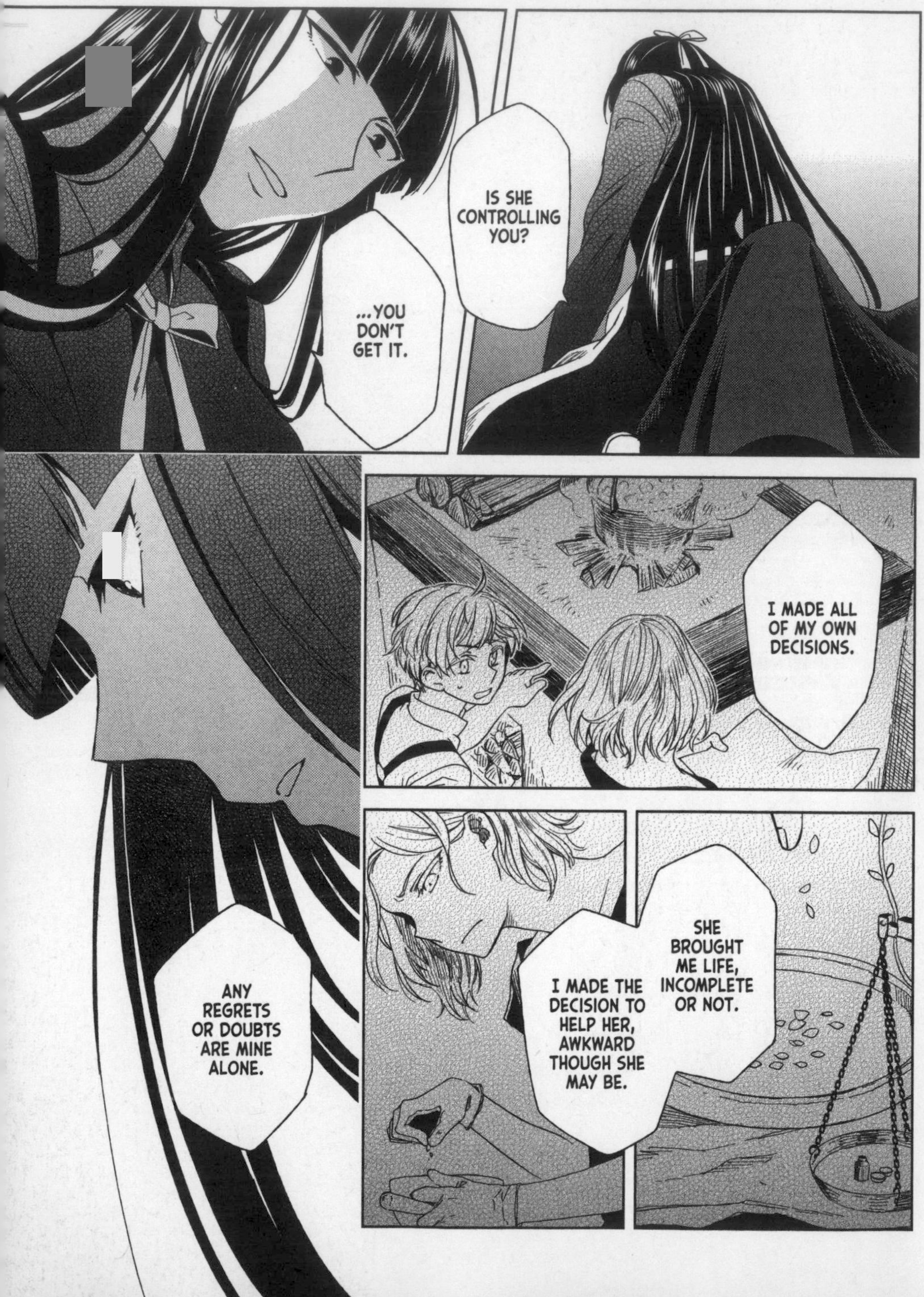
IS SHE CONTROLLING YOU?
...YOU DON'T GET IT.
I MADE ALL OF MY OWN DECISIONS.
SHE BROUGHT ME LIFE, INCOMPLETE OR NOT.
I MADE THE DECISION TO HELP HER, AWKWARD THOUGH SHE MAY BE.
ANY REGRETS OR DOUBTS ARE MINE ALONE.

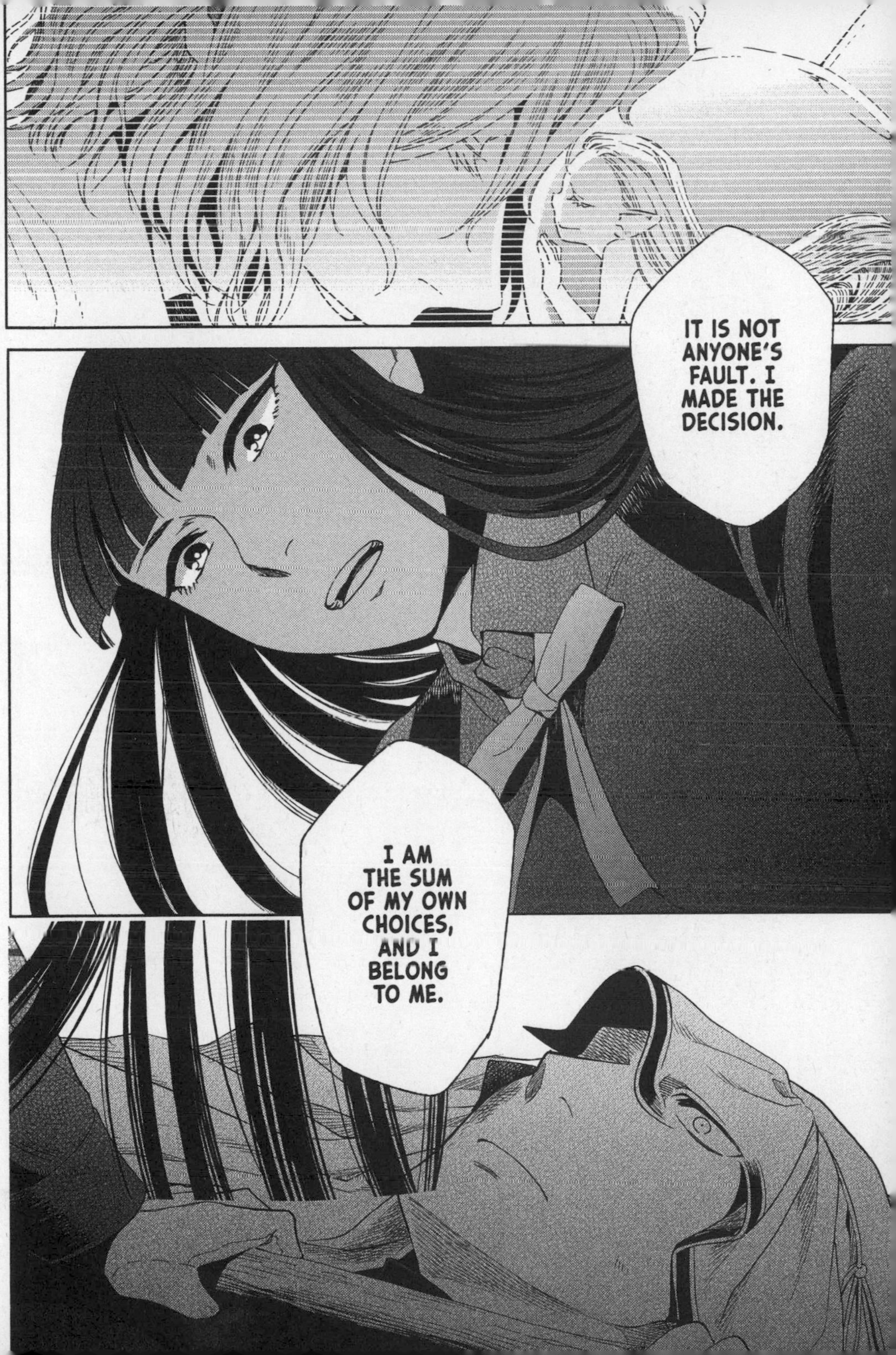
IT IS NOT ANYONE'S FAULT. I MADE THE DECISION.
I AM THE SUM OF MY OWN CHOICES, AND I BELONG TO ME.

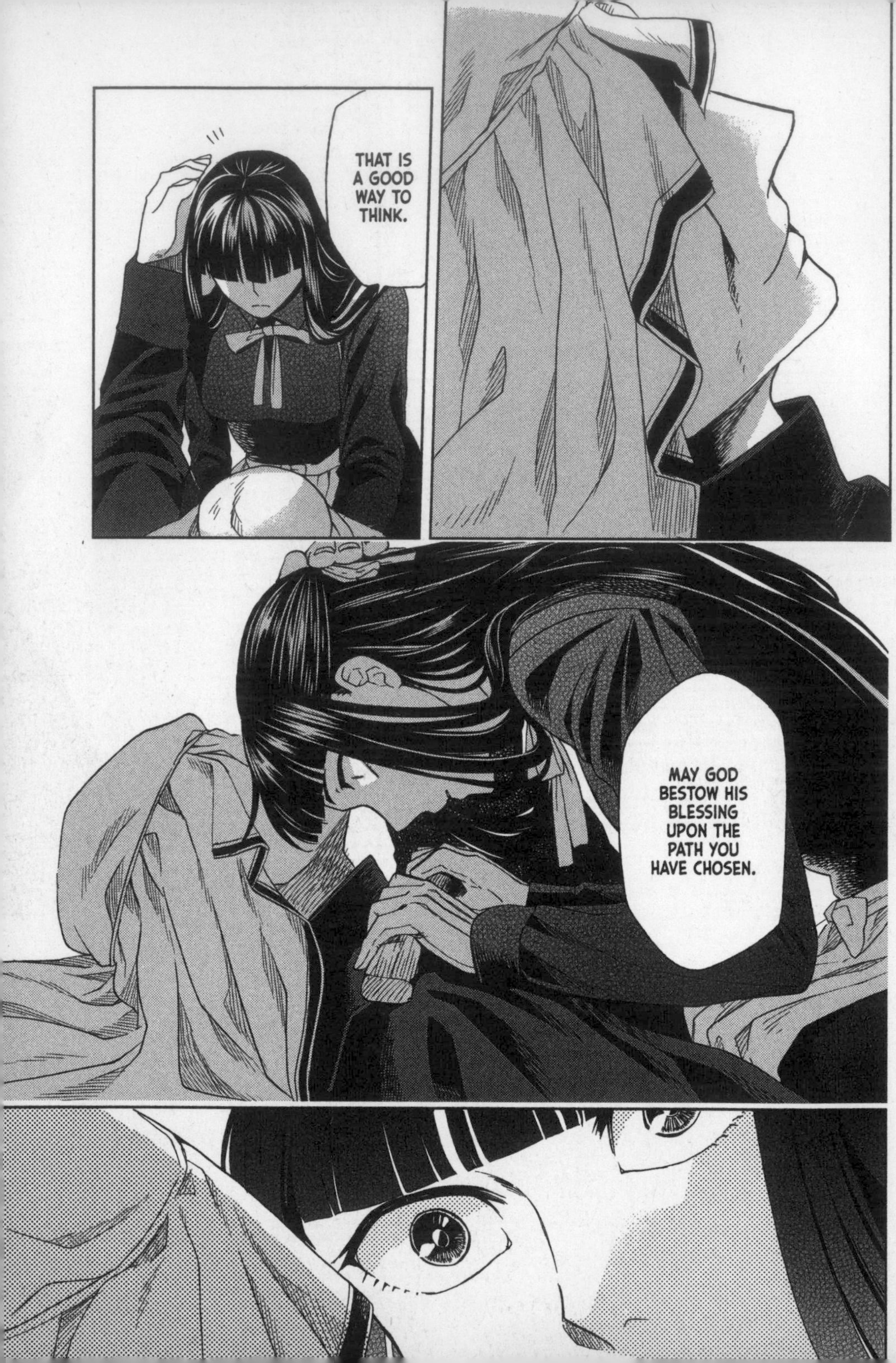
THAT IS A GOOD WAY TO THINK.
MAY GOD BESTOW HIS BLESSING UPON THE PATH YOU HAVE CHOSEN.

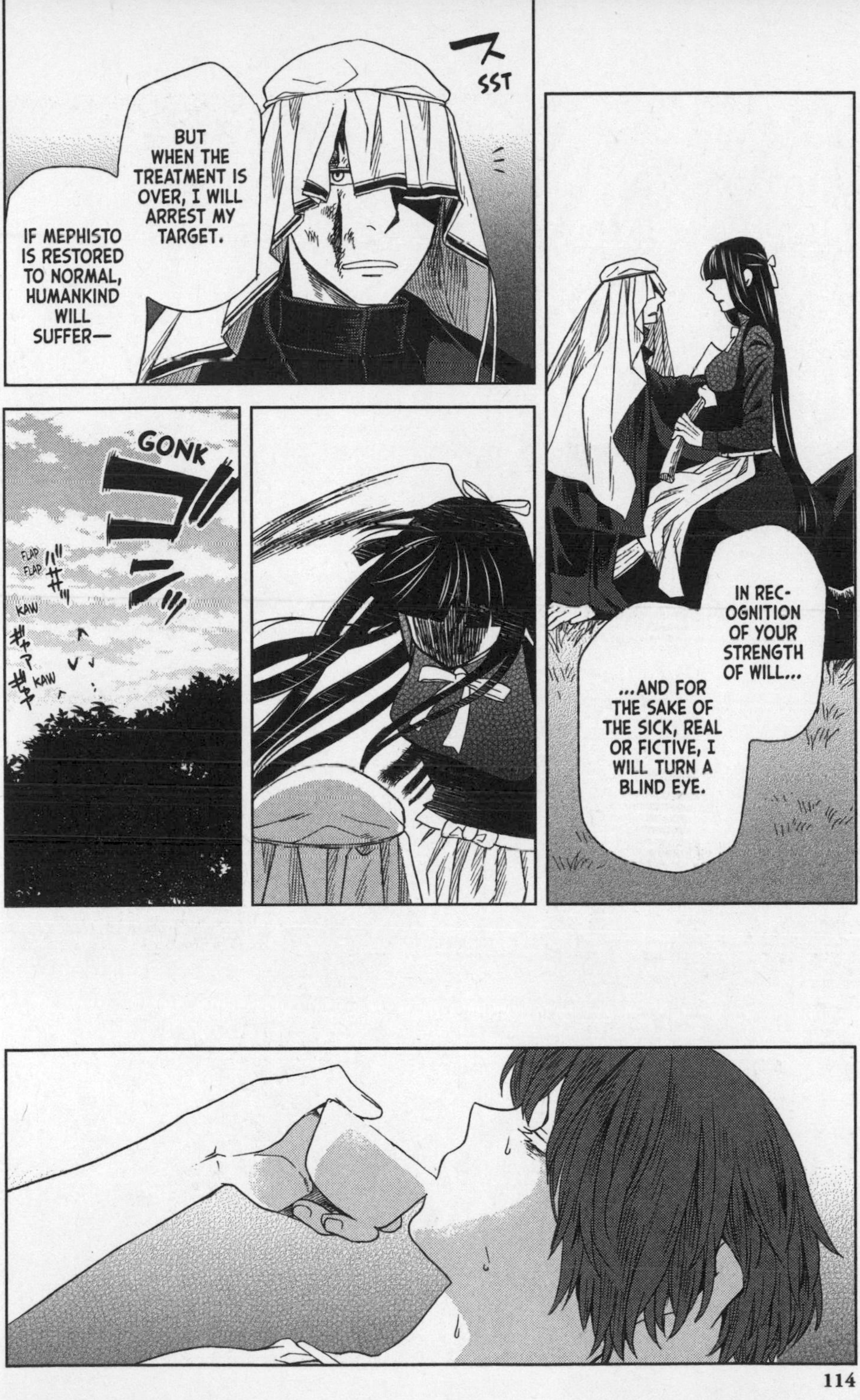
IN RECOGNITION OF YOUR STRENGTH OF WILL...
...AND FOR THE SAKE OF THE SICK, REAL OR FICTIVE, I WILL TURN A BLIND EYE.
SST
BUT WHEN THE TREATMENT IS OVER, I WILL ARREST MY TARGET.
IF MEPHISTO IS RESTORED TO NORMAL, HUMANKIND WILL SUFFER—
GONK
FLAP FLAP
KAW
KAW

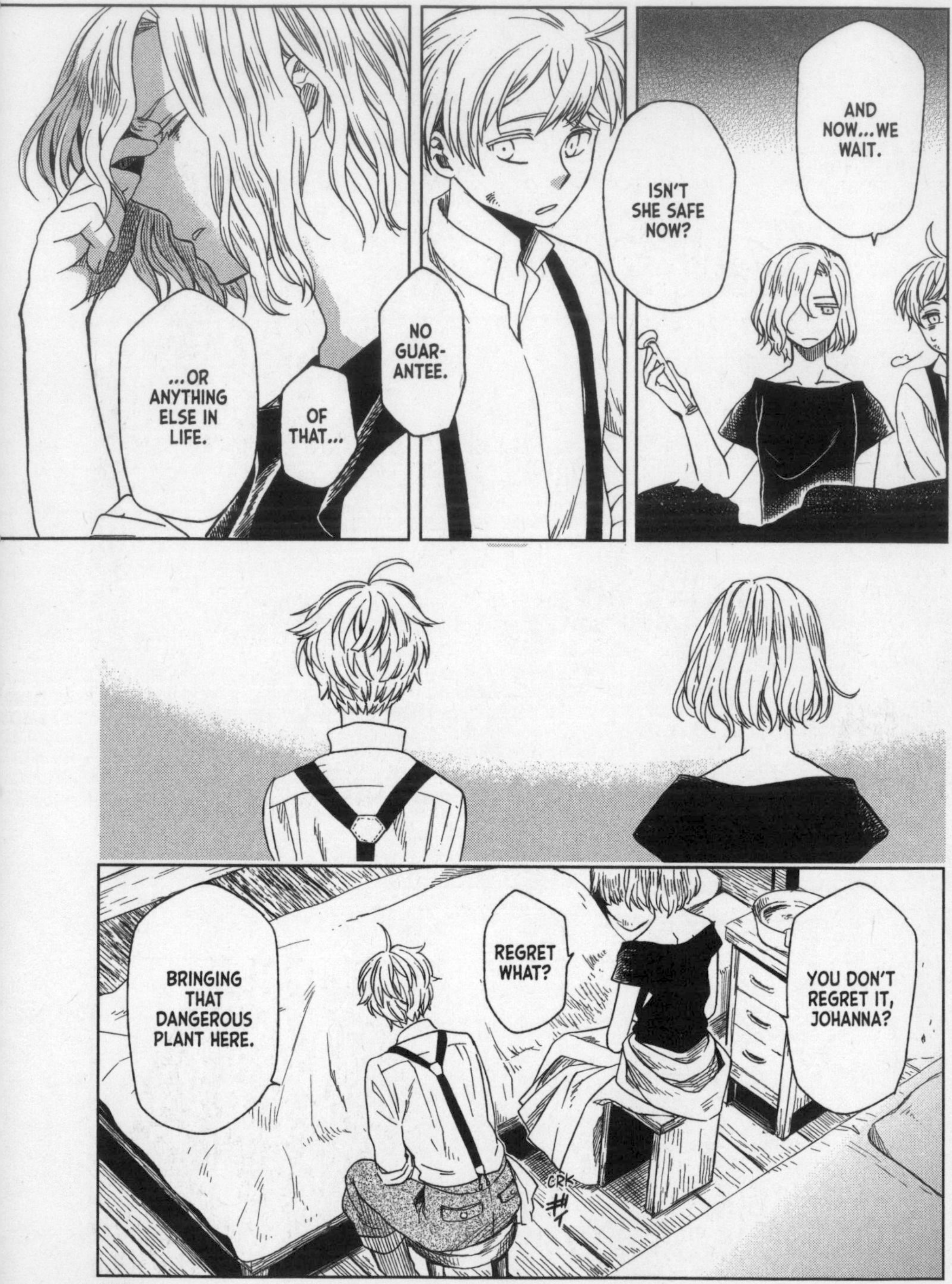
AND NOW...WE WAIT.
ISN'T SHE SAFE NOW?
NO GUAR-ANTEE.
OF THAT...
...OR ANYTHING ELSE IN LIFE.
YOU DON'T REGRET IT, JOHANNA?
REGRET WHAT?
BRINGING THAT DANGEROUS PLANT HERE.
CRK

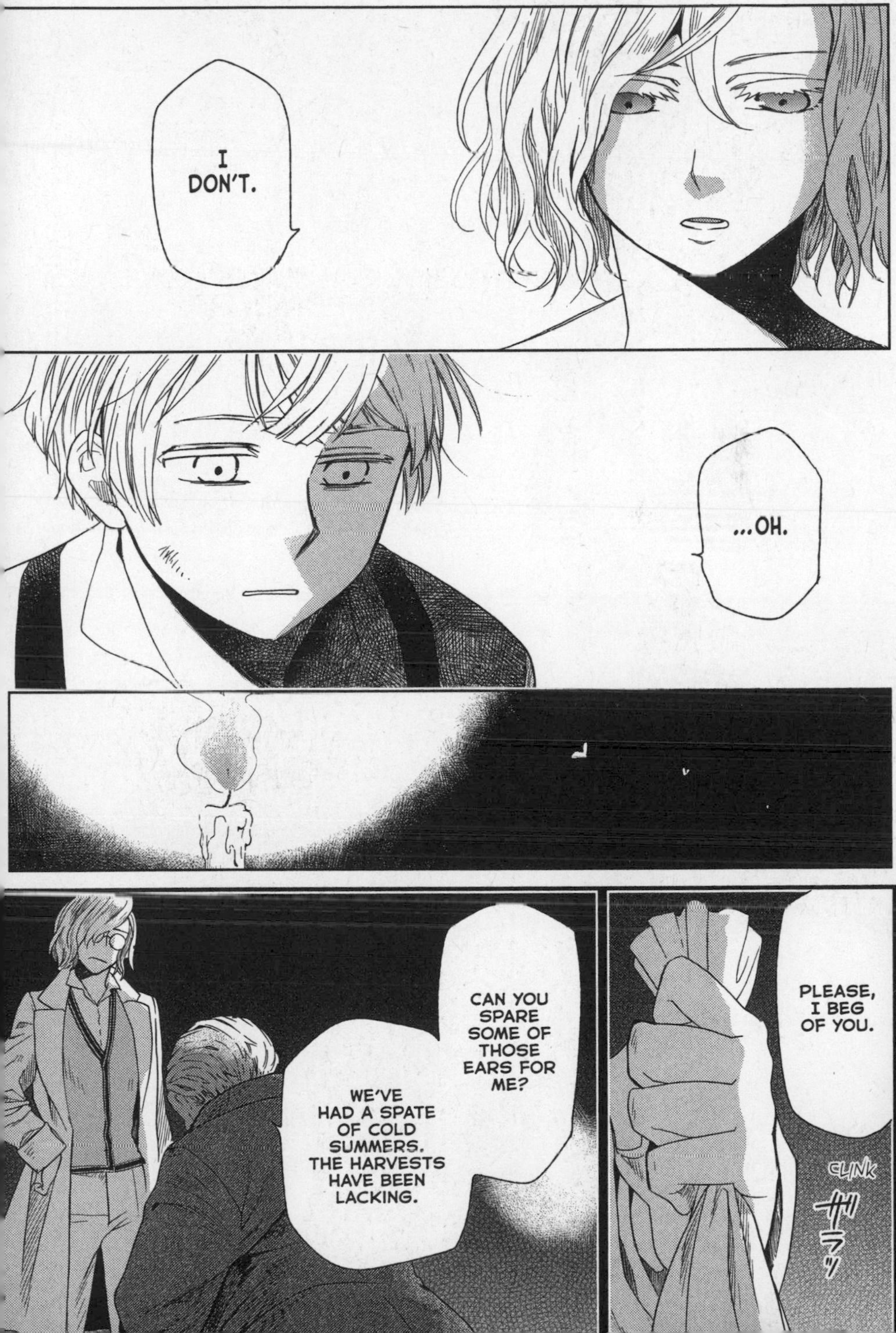
I DON'T.
...OH.
PLEASE, I BEG OF YOU.
CLINK
ガラッ
CAN YOU SPARE SOME OF THOSE EARS FOR ME?
WE'VE HAD A SPATE OF COLD SUMMERS. THE HARVESTS HAVE BEEN LACKING.

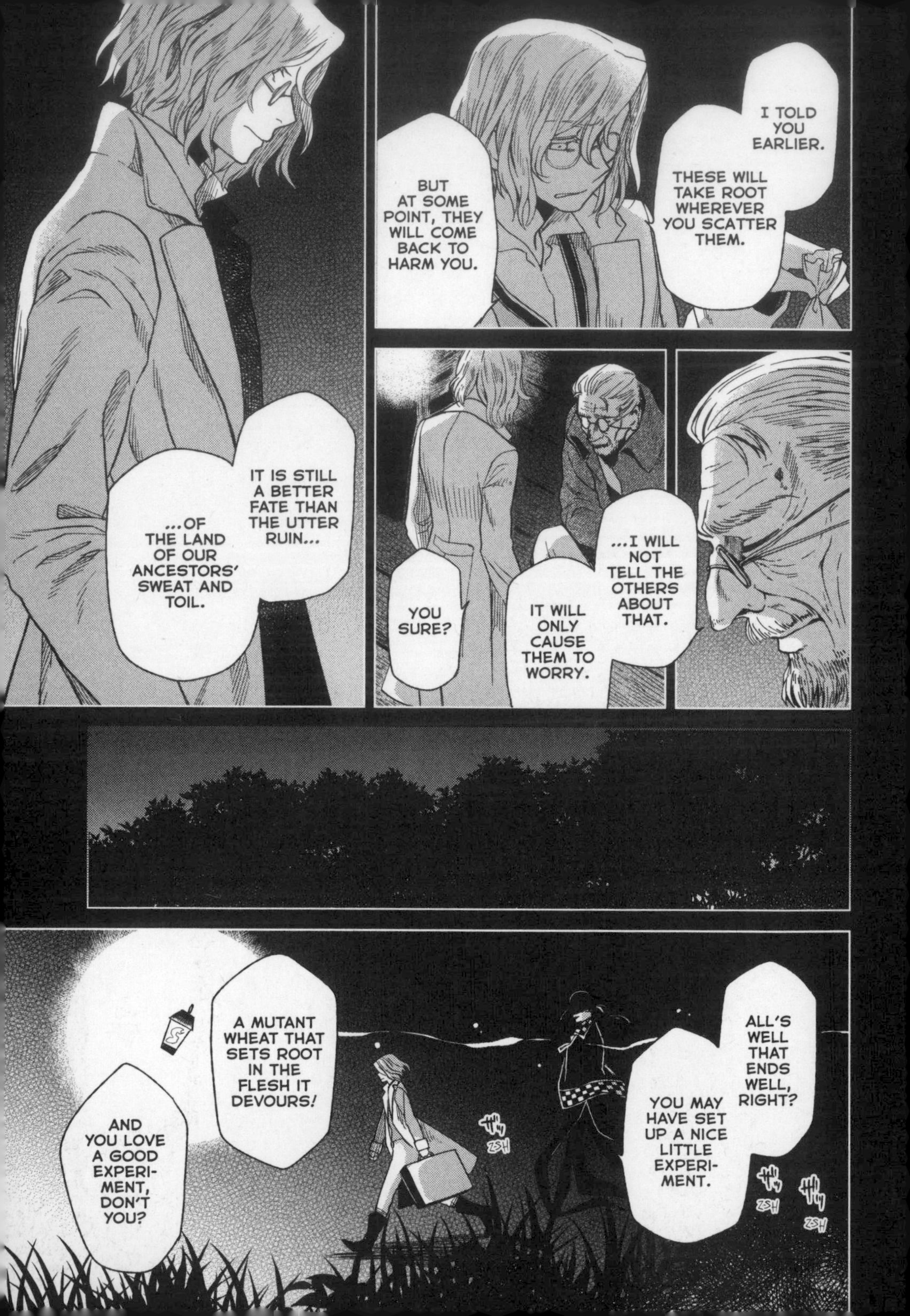
I TOLD YOU EARLIER.
THESE WILL TAKE ROOT WHEREVER YOU SCATTER THEM.
BUT AT SOME POINT, THEY WILL COME BACK TO HARM YOU.
...I WILL NOT TELL THE OTHERS ABOUT THAT.
IT WILL ONLY CAUSE THEM TO WORRY.
YOU SURE?
IT IS STILL A BETTER FATE THAN THE UTTER RUIN...
...OF THE LAND OF OUR ANCESTORS' SWEAT AND TOIL.
ALL'S WELL THAT ENDS WELL, RIGHT?
YOU MAY HAVE SET UP A NICE LITTLE EXPERI-MENT.
ZSH
ZSH
ZSH
A MUTANT WHEAT THAT SETS ROOT IN THE FLESH IT DEVOURS!
AND YOU LOVE A GOOD EXPERI-MENT, DON'T YOU?

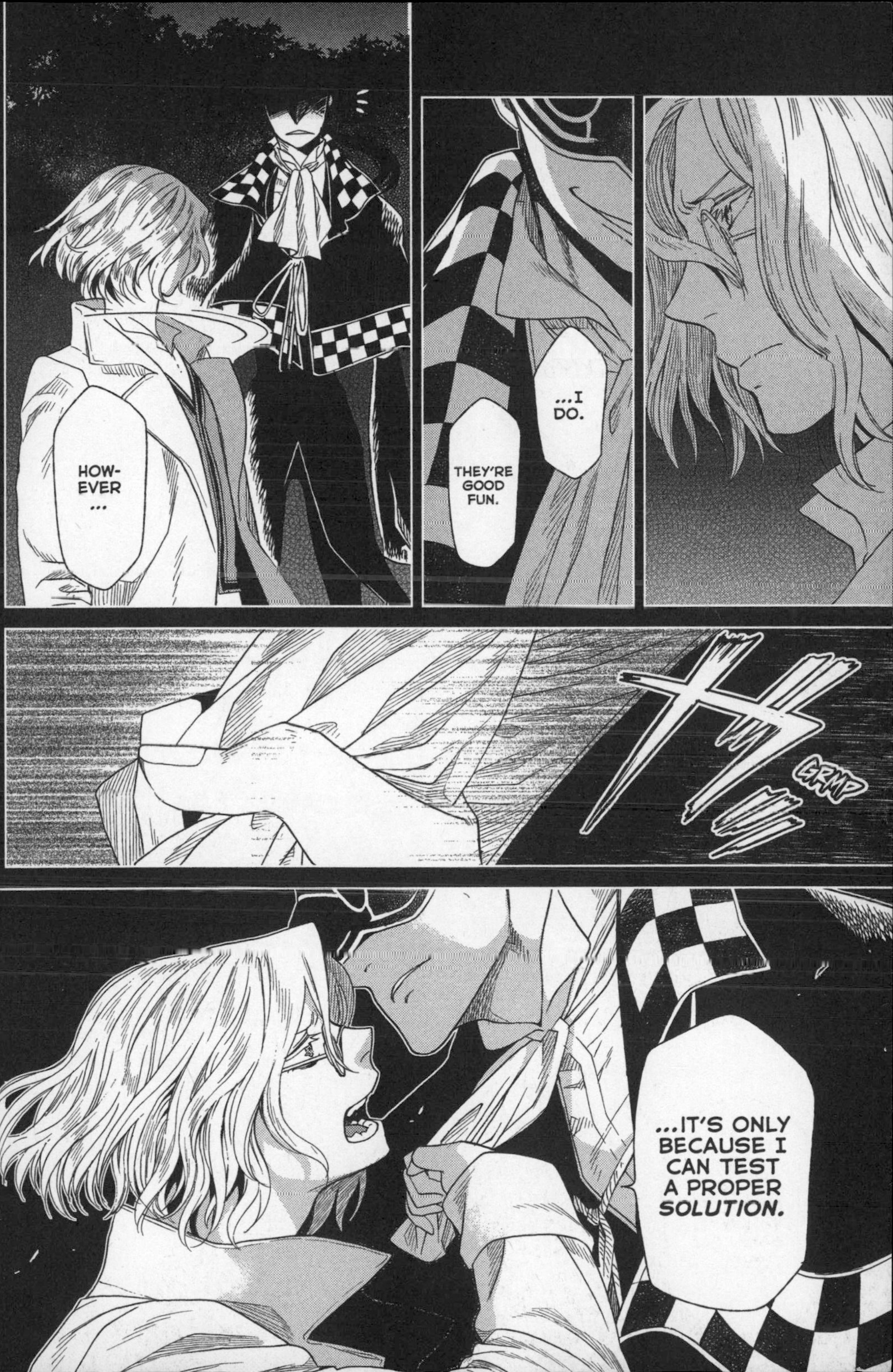
...I DO.
THEY'RE GOOD FUN.
HOW-EVER ...
GRMP
...IT'S ONLY BECAUSE I CAN TEST A PROPER SOLUTION.

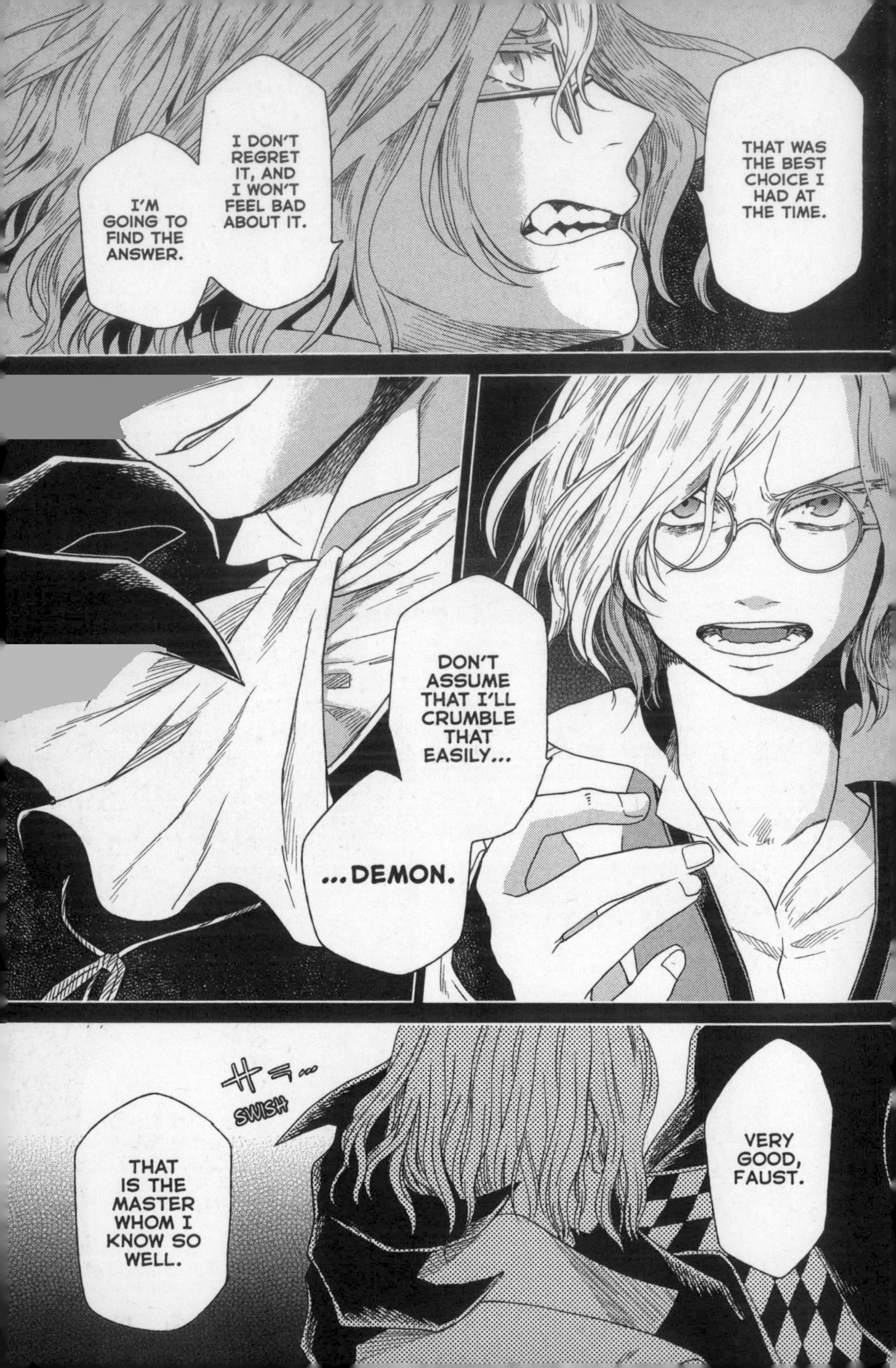
THAT WAS THE BEST CHOICE I HAD AT THE TIME.
I DON'T REGRET IT, AND I WON'T FEEL BAD ABOUT IT.
I'M GOING TO FIND THE ANSWER.
DON'T ASSUME THAT I'LL CRUMBLE THAT EASILY...
...DEMON.
VERY GOOD, FAUST.
ササ…
SWISH
THAT IS THE MASTER WHOM I KNOW SO WELL.

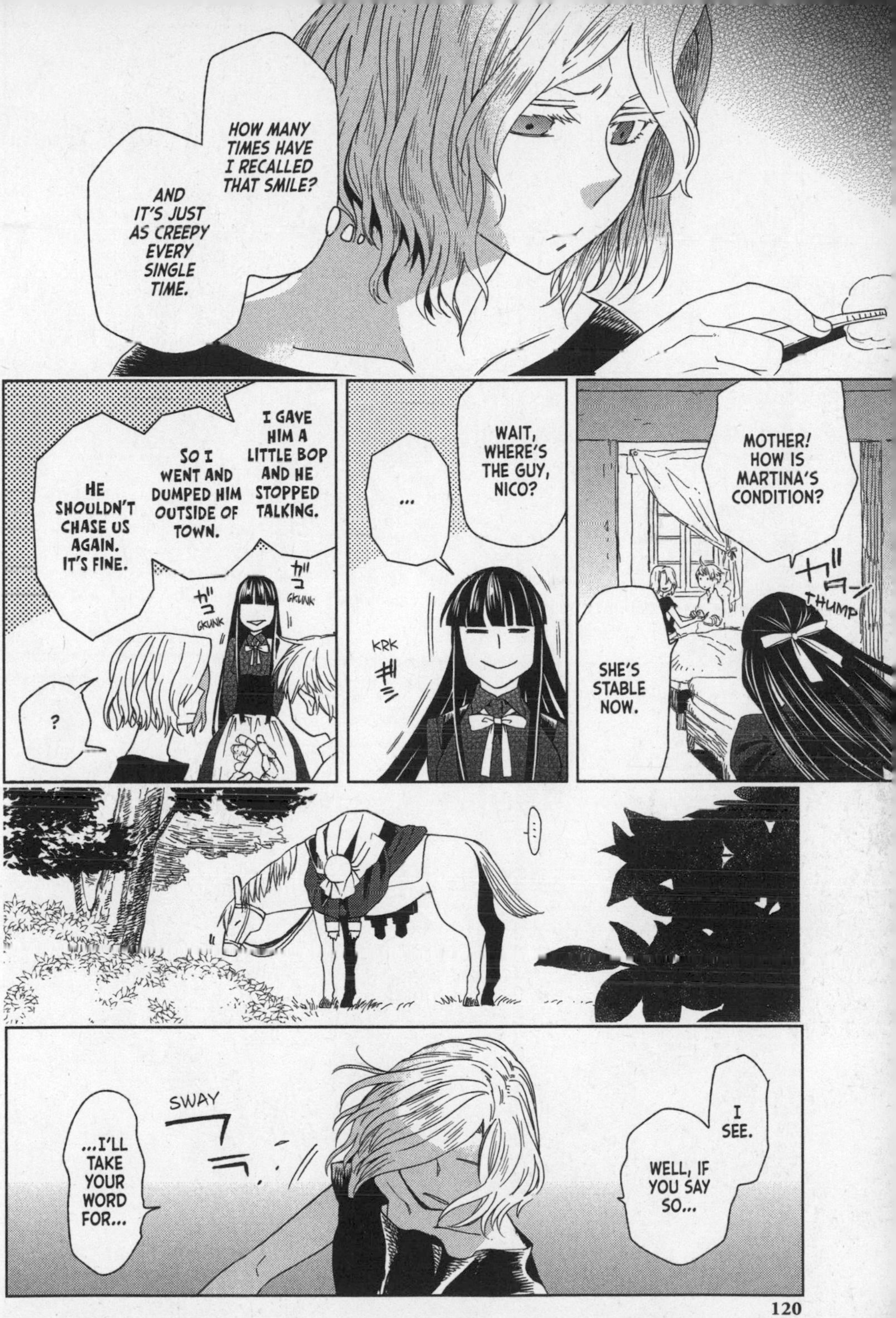
HOW MANY TIMES HAVE I RECALLED THAT SMILE?
AND IT'S JUST AS CREEPY EVERY SINGLE TIME.
MOTHER! HOW IS MARTINA'S CONDITION?
THUMP
SHE'S STABLE NOW.
WAIT, WHERE'S THE GUY, NICO?
KRK
...
I GAVE HIM A LITTLE BOP AND HE STOPPED TALKING.
SO I WENT AND DUMPED HIM OUTSIDE OF TOWN.
HE SHOULDN'T CHASE US AGAIN. IT'S FINE.
GKUNK
GKUNK
?
...
I SEE.
WELL, IF YOU SAY SO...
SWAY
...I'LL TAKE YOUR WORD FOR...

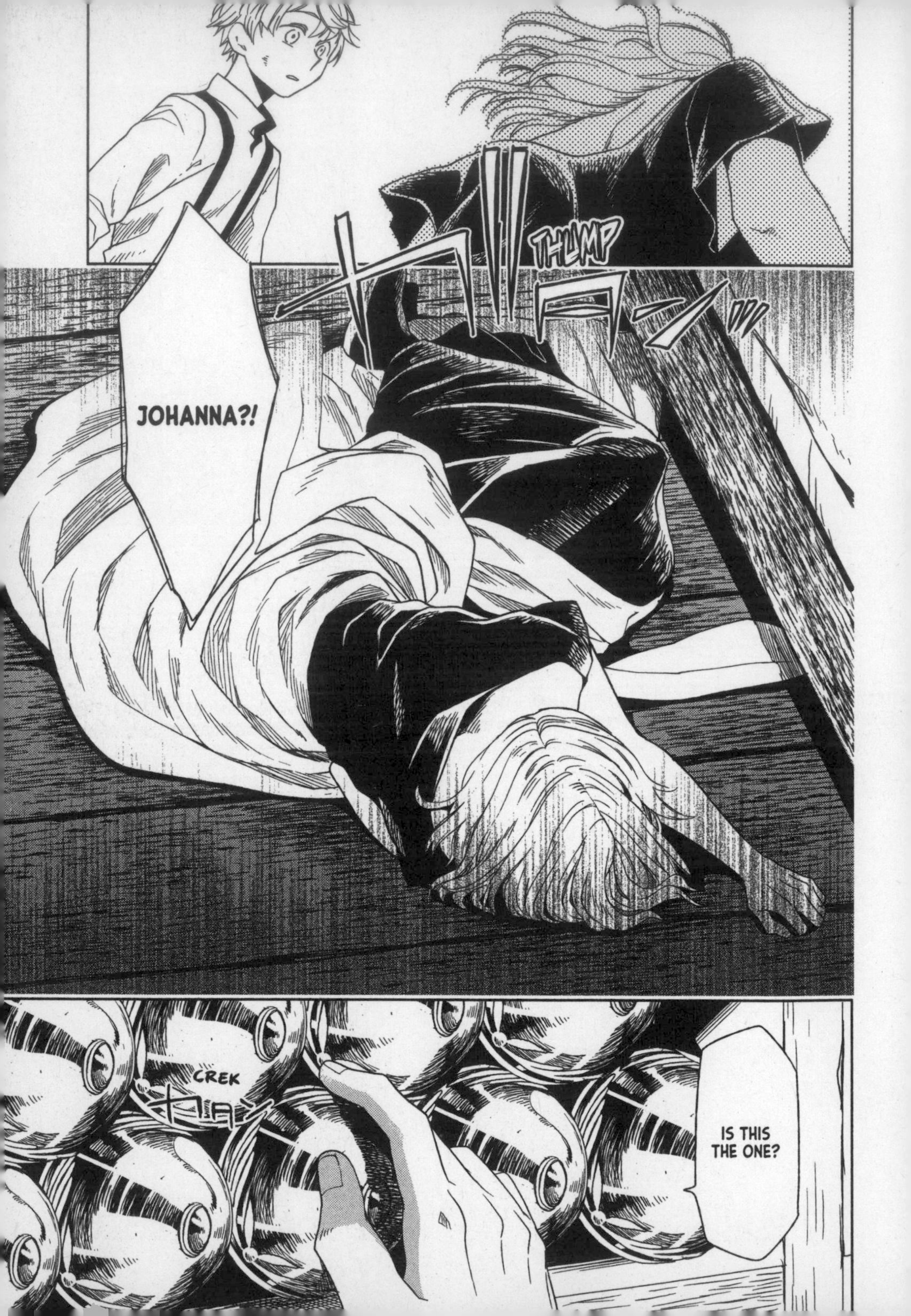
THUMP
JOHANNA?!
CREK
IS THIS THE ONE?

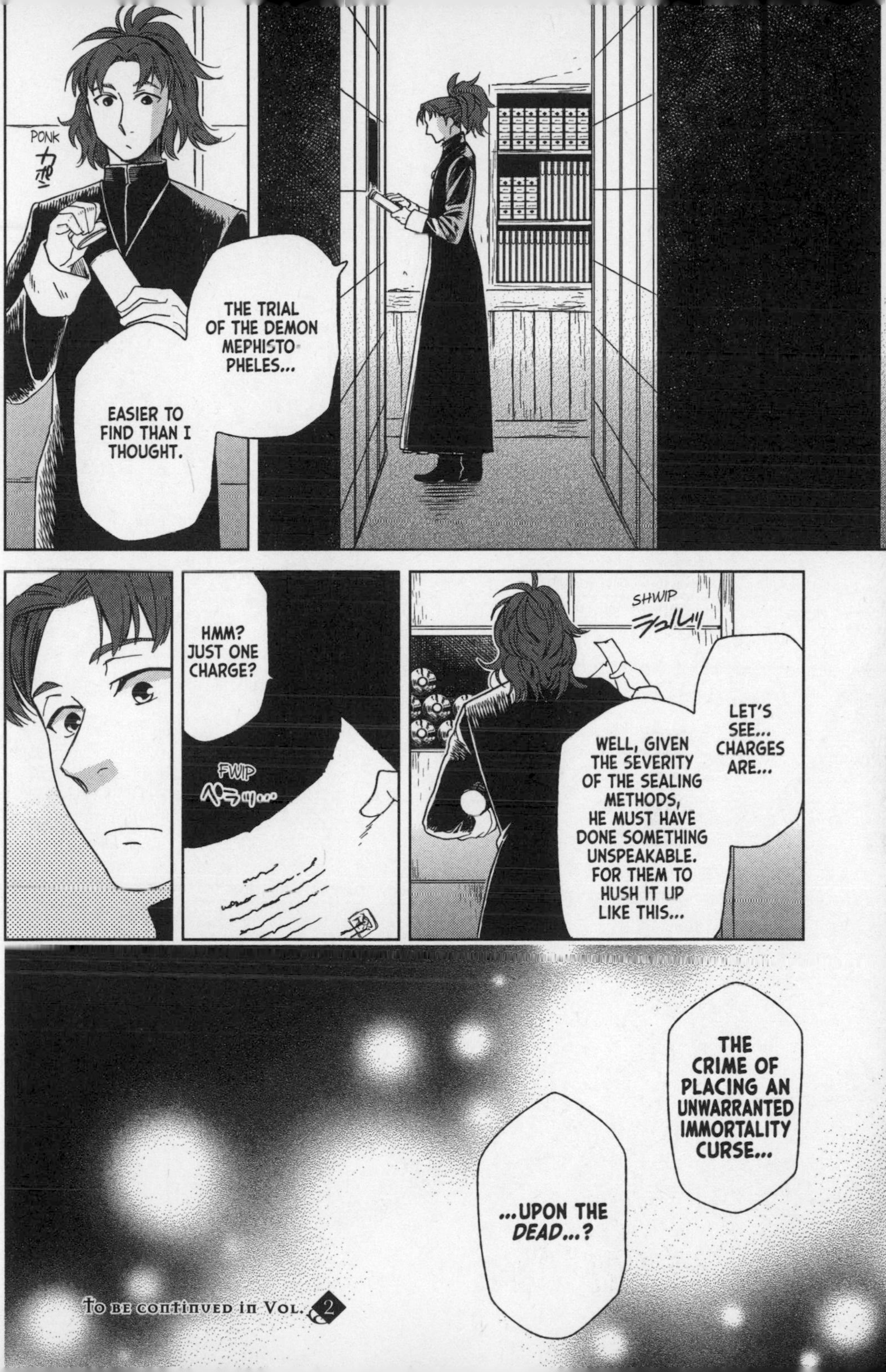
PONK
THE TRIAL OF THE DEMON MEPHISTO PHELES...
EASIER TO FIND THAN I THOUGHT.
SHWIP
LET'S SEE... CHARGES ARE...
WELL, GIVEN THE SEVERITY OF THE SEALING METHODS, HE MUST HAVE DONE SOMETHING UNSPEAKABLE. FOR THEM TO HUSH IT UP LIKE THIS...
HMM? JUST ONE CHARGE?
FWIP
THE CRIME OF PLACING AN UNWARRANTED IMMORTALITY CURSE...
...UPON THE *DEAD*...?
To be continued in Vol. 2

FAMILY CASTING

BETWEEN
SCENES

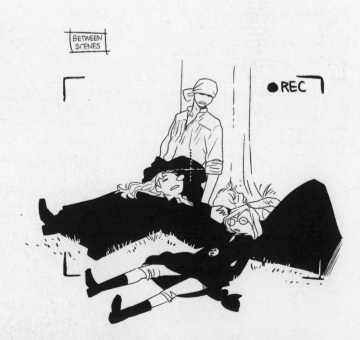

● REC

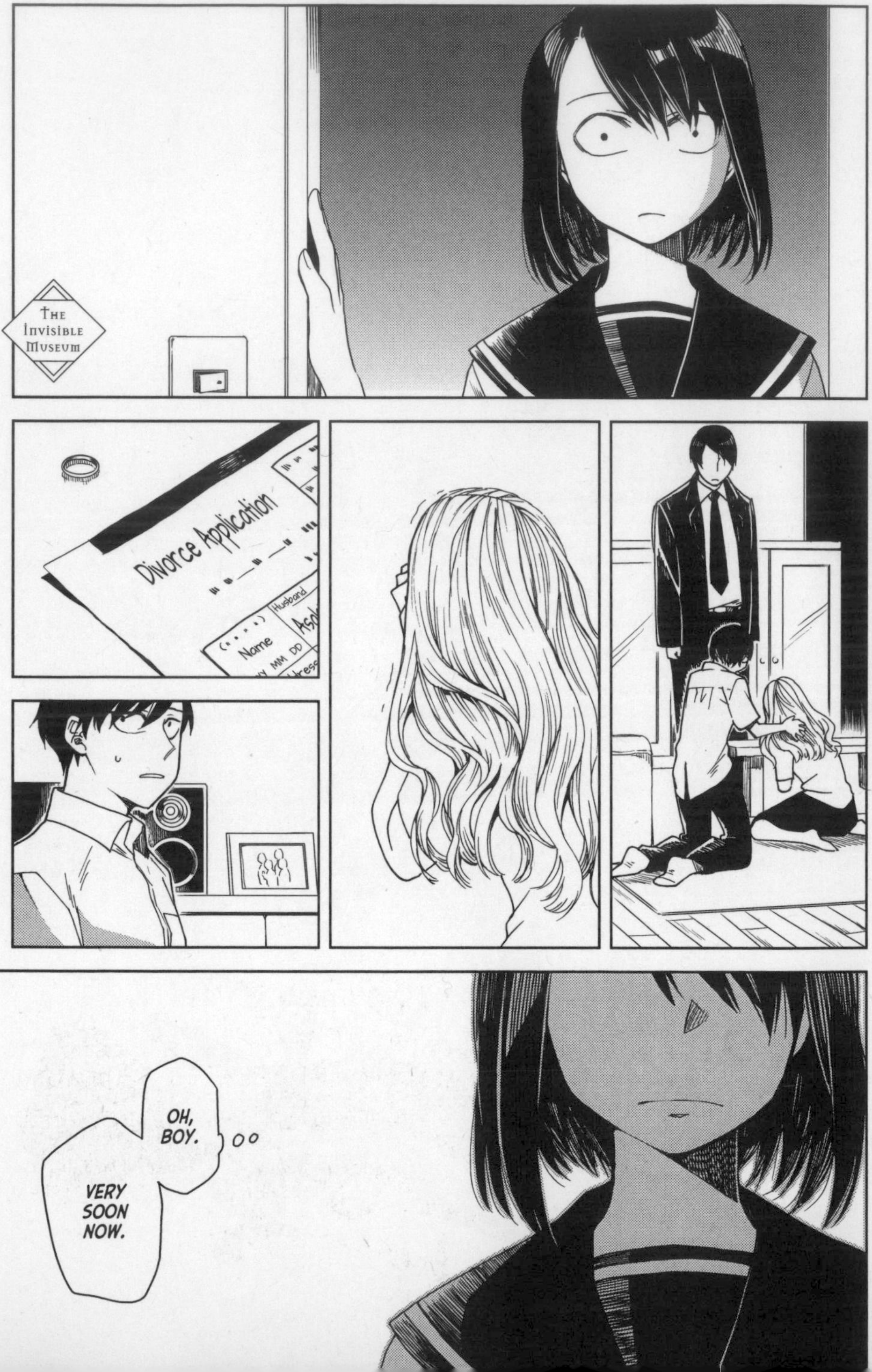
The Invisible Museum
Divorce Application
Husband
Name
MM DD
OH, BOY.
VERY SOON NOW.

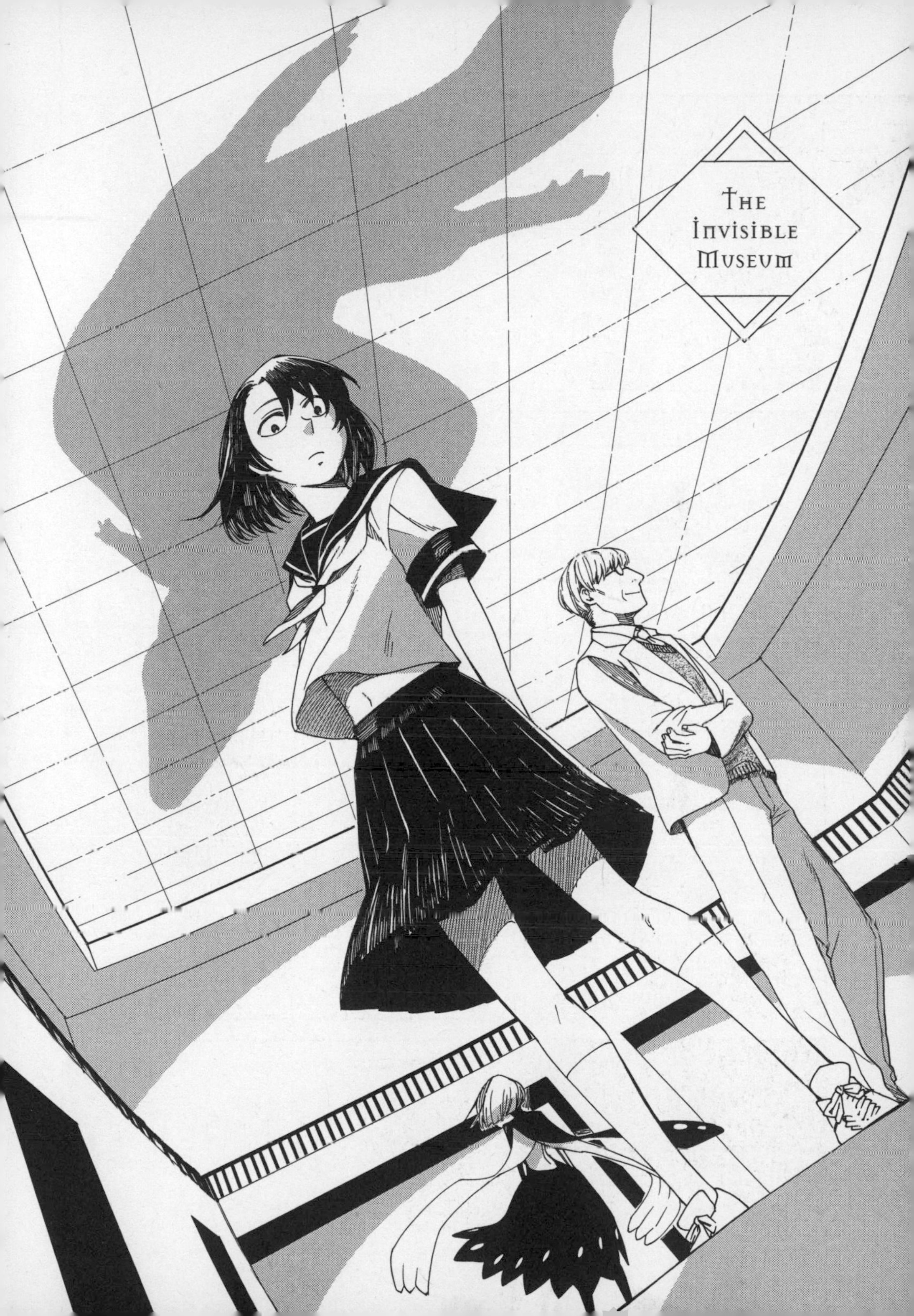
THE
INVISIBLE
MUSEUM

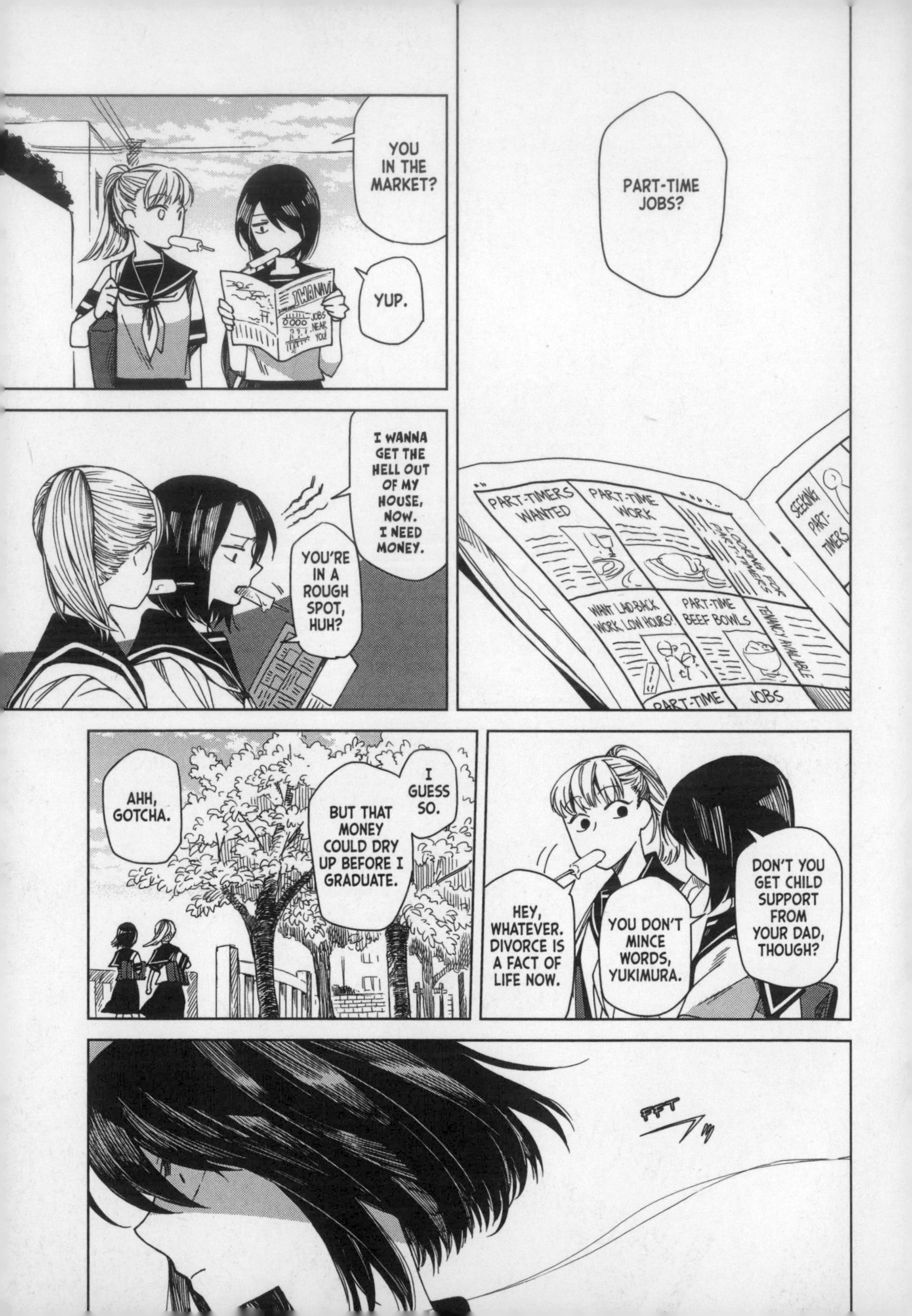
PART-TIME JOBS?
PART-TIMERS WANTED
PART-TIME WORK
LOOKING FOR PART-TIMERS
SEEKING PART-TIMERS
WANT LAID-BACK WORK, LOW HOURS?
PART-TIME BEEF BOWLS
TENANCY AVAILABLE
PART-TIME JOBS
YOU IN THE MARKET?
YUP.
JOBS NEAR YOU!
I WANNA GET THE HELL OUT OF MY HOUSE, NOW. I NEED MONEY.
YOU'RE IN A ROUGH SPOT, HUH?
DON'T YOU GET CHILD SUPPORT FROM YOUR DAD, THOUGH?
YOU DON'T MINCE WORDS, YUKIMURA.
HEY, WHATEVER. DIVORCE IS A FACT OF LIFE NOW.
I GUESS SO.
BUT THAT MONEY COULD DRY UP BEFORE I GRADUATE.
AHH, GOTCHA.
FFT

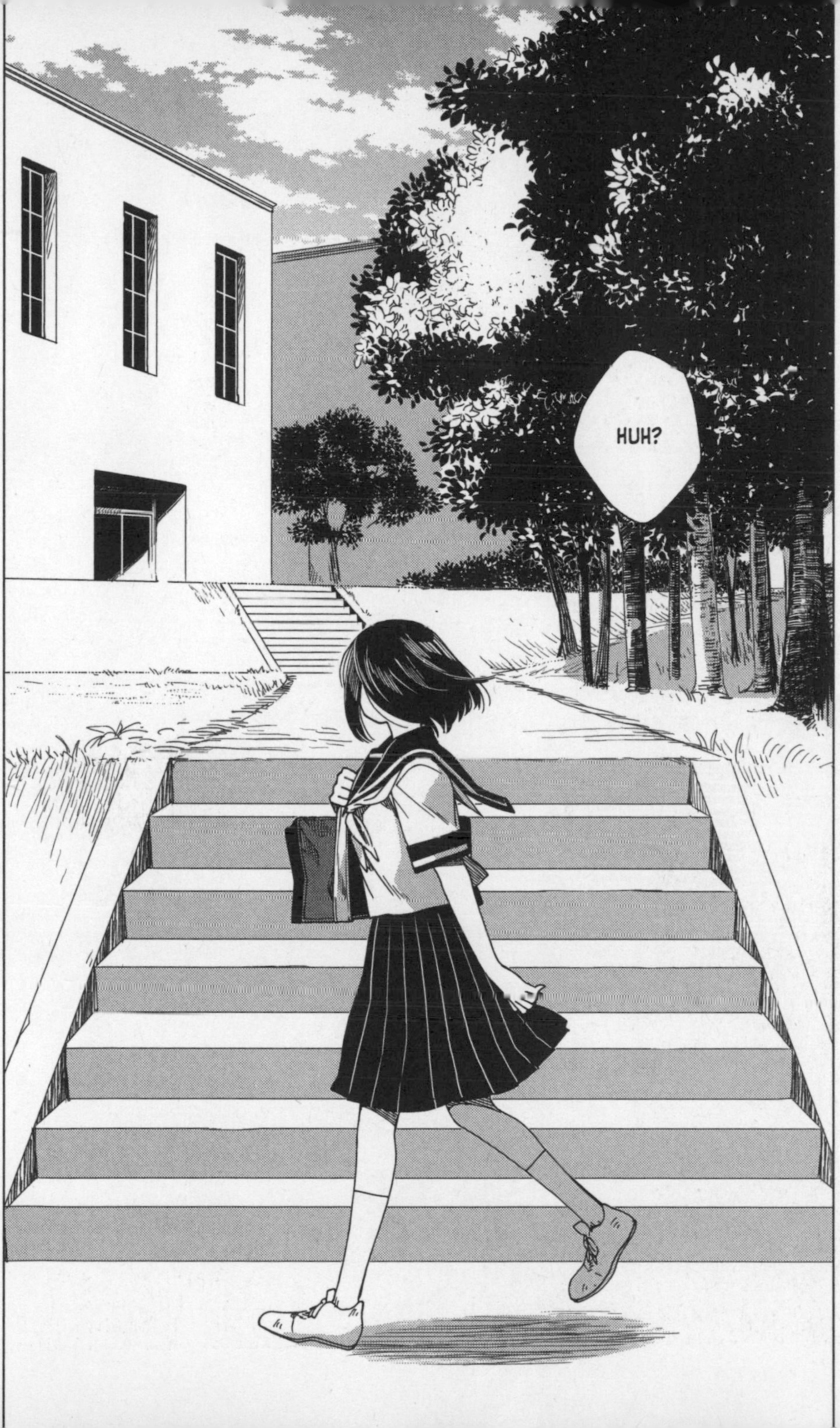
HUH?

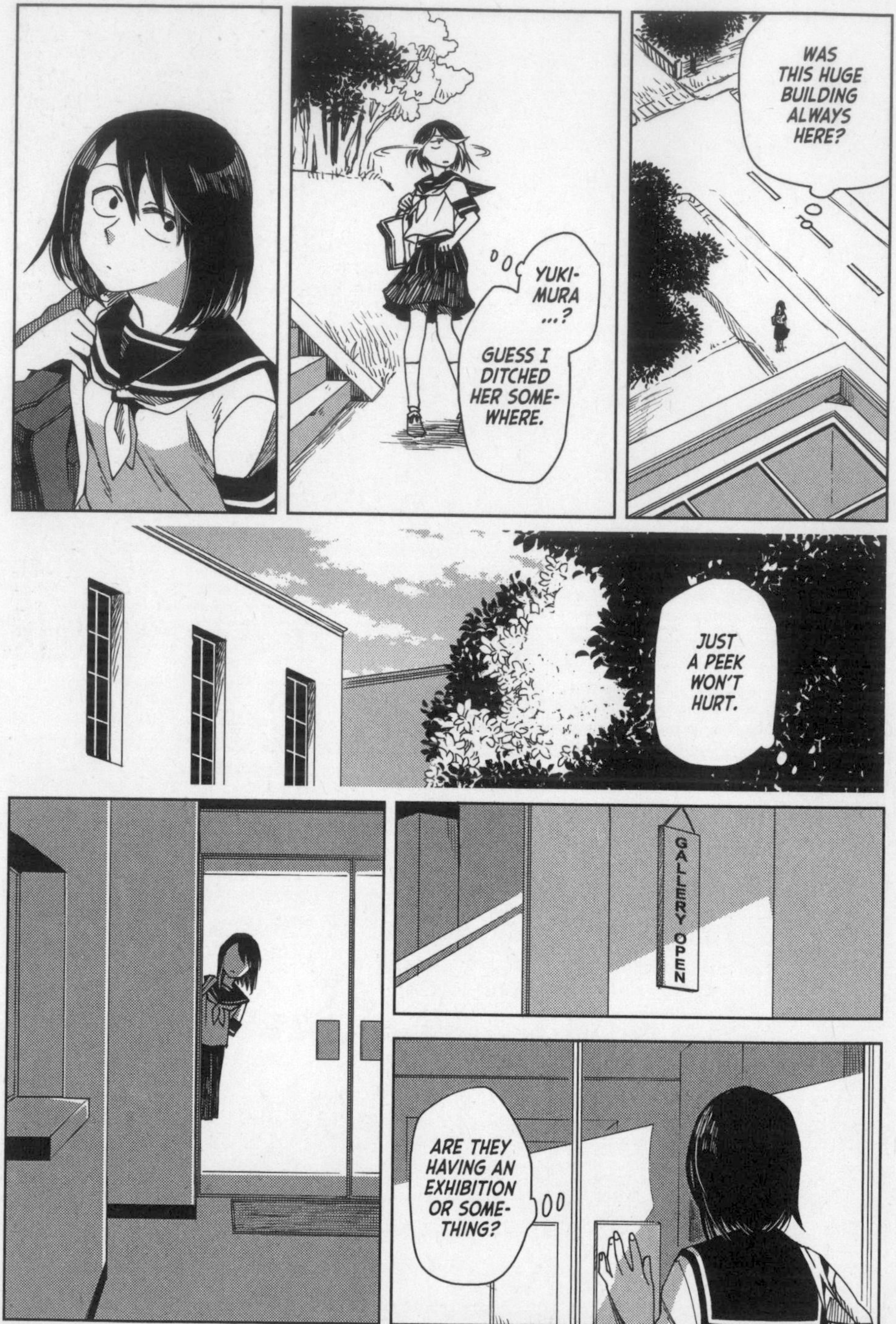
WAS THIS HUGE BUILDING ALWAYS HERE?
YUKI-MURA ...?
GUESS I DITCHED HER SOME-WHERE.
JUST A PEEK WON'T HURT.
GALLERY OPEN
ARE THEY HAVING AN EXHIBITION OR SOME-THING?

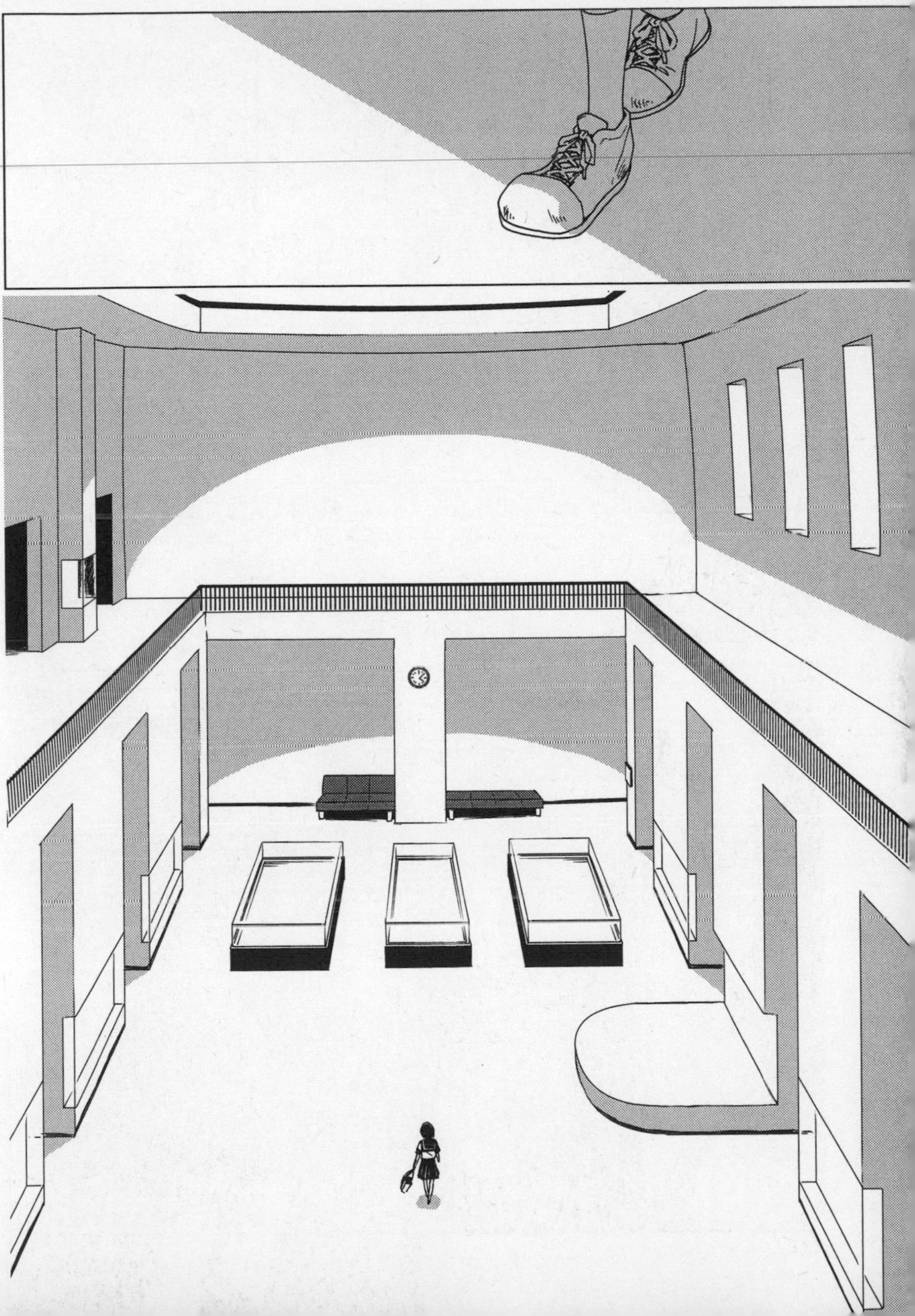

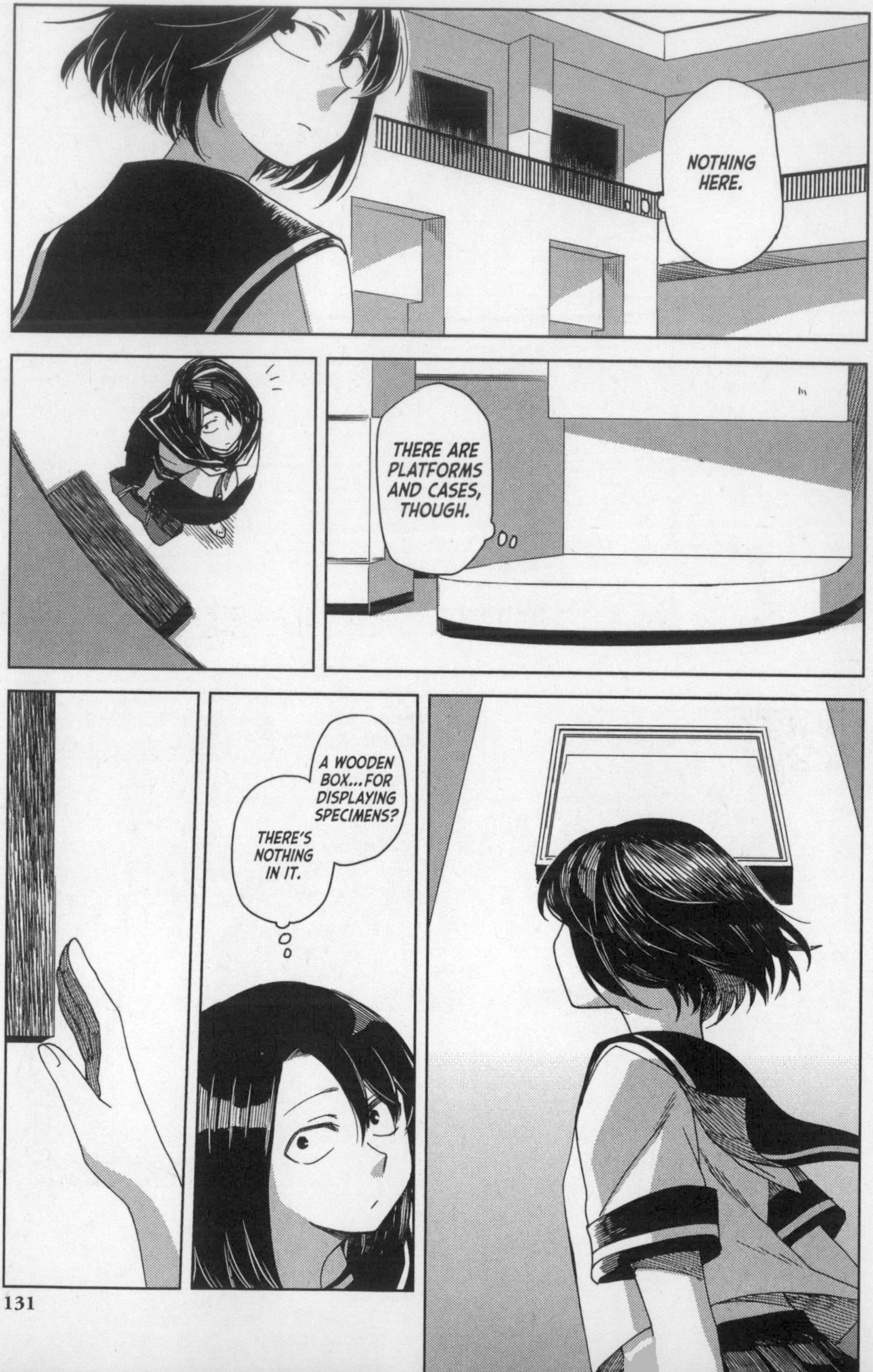
NOTHING HERE.
THERE ARE PLATFORMS AND CASES, THOUGH.
A WOODEN BOX...FOR DISPLAYING SPECIMENS?
THERE'S NOTHING IN IT.

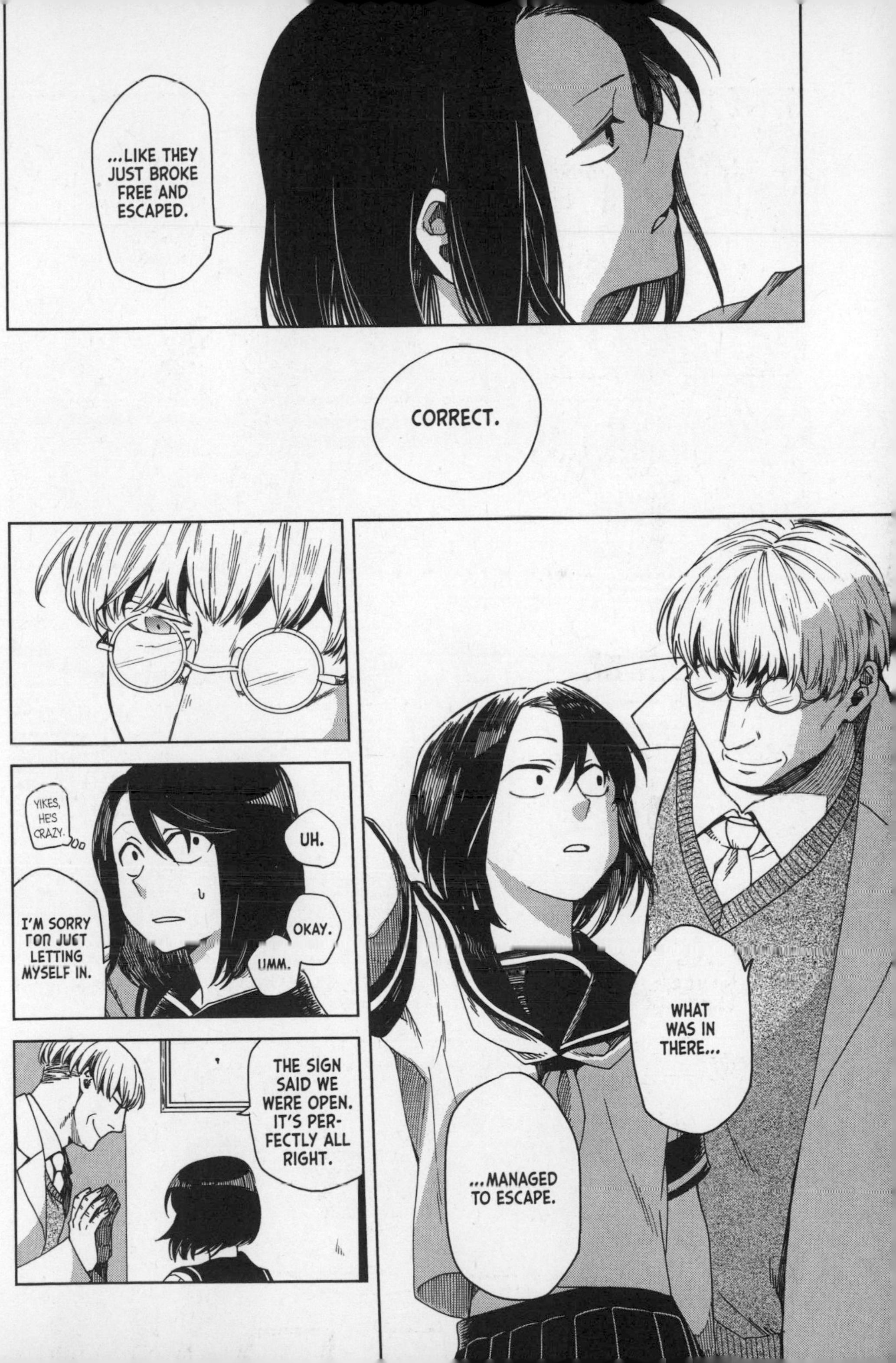
...LIKE THEY JUST BROKE FREE AND ESCAPED.
CORRECT.
WHAT WAS IN THERE...
...MANAGED TO ESCAPE.
UH.
OKAY.
UMM.
YIKES, HE'S CRAZY.
I'M SORRY FOR JUST LETTING MYSELF IN.
THE SIGN SAID WE WERE OPEN. IT'S PER-FECTLY ALL RIGHT.

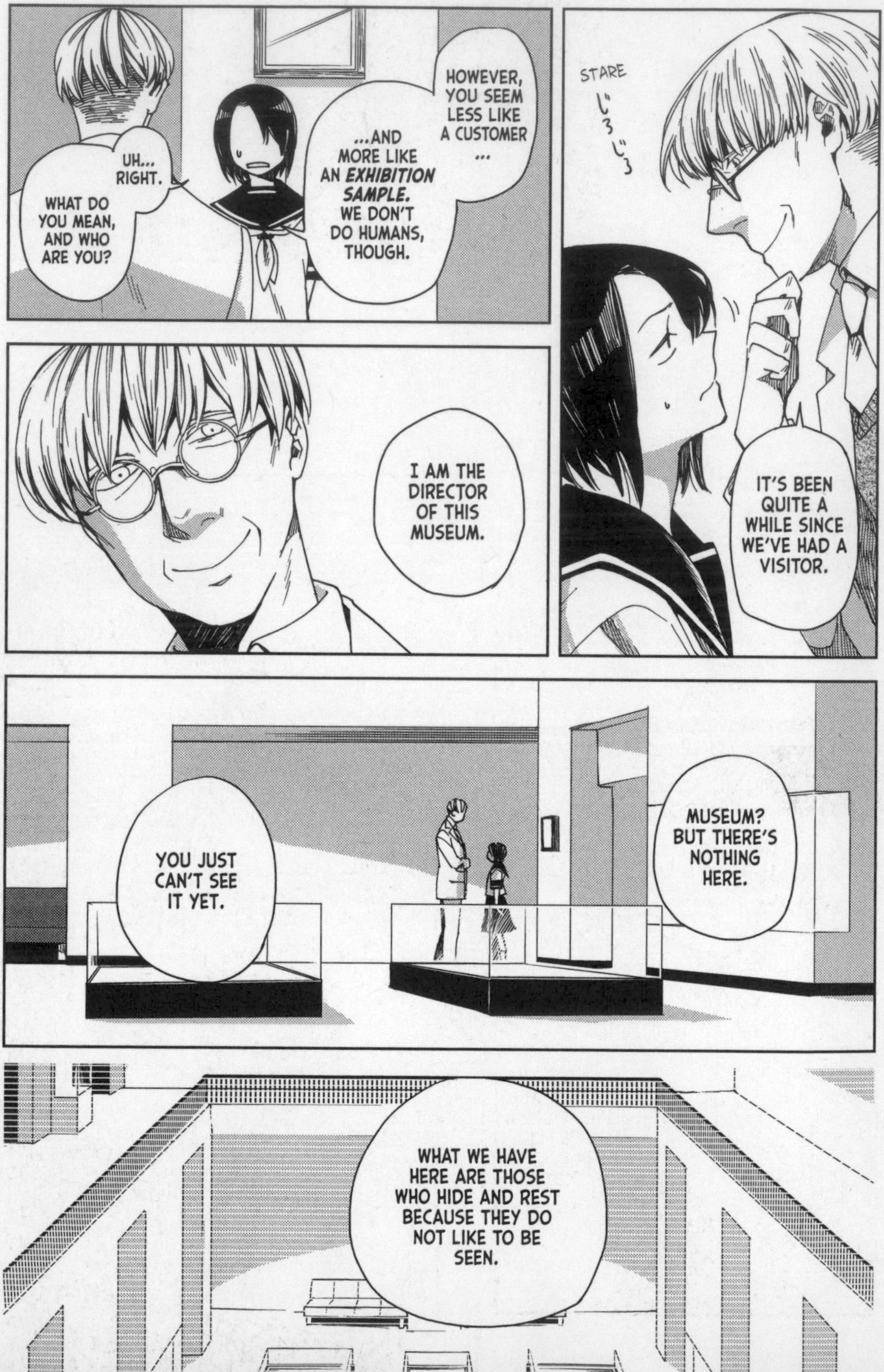
STARE
じろじろ
IT'S BEEN QUITE A WHILE SINCE WE'VE HAD A VISITOR.
HOWEVER, YOU SEEM LESS LIKE A CUSTOMER ...
...AND MORE LIKE AN *EXHIBITION SAMPLE.* WE DON'T DO HUMANS, THOUGH.
UH... RIGHT.
WHAT DO YOU MEAN, AND WHO ARE YOU?
I AM THE DIRECTOR OF THIS MUSEUM.
MUSEUM? BUT THERE'S NOTHING HERE.
YOU JUST CAN'T SEE IT YET.
WHAT WE HAVE HERE ARE THOSE WHO HIDE AND REST BECAUSE THEY DO NOT LIKE TO BE SEEN.

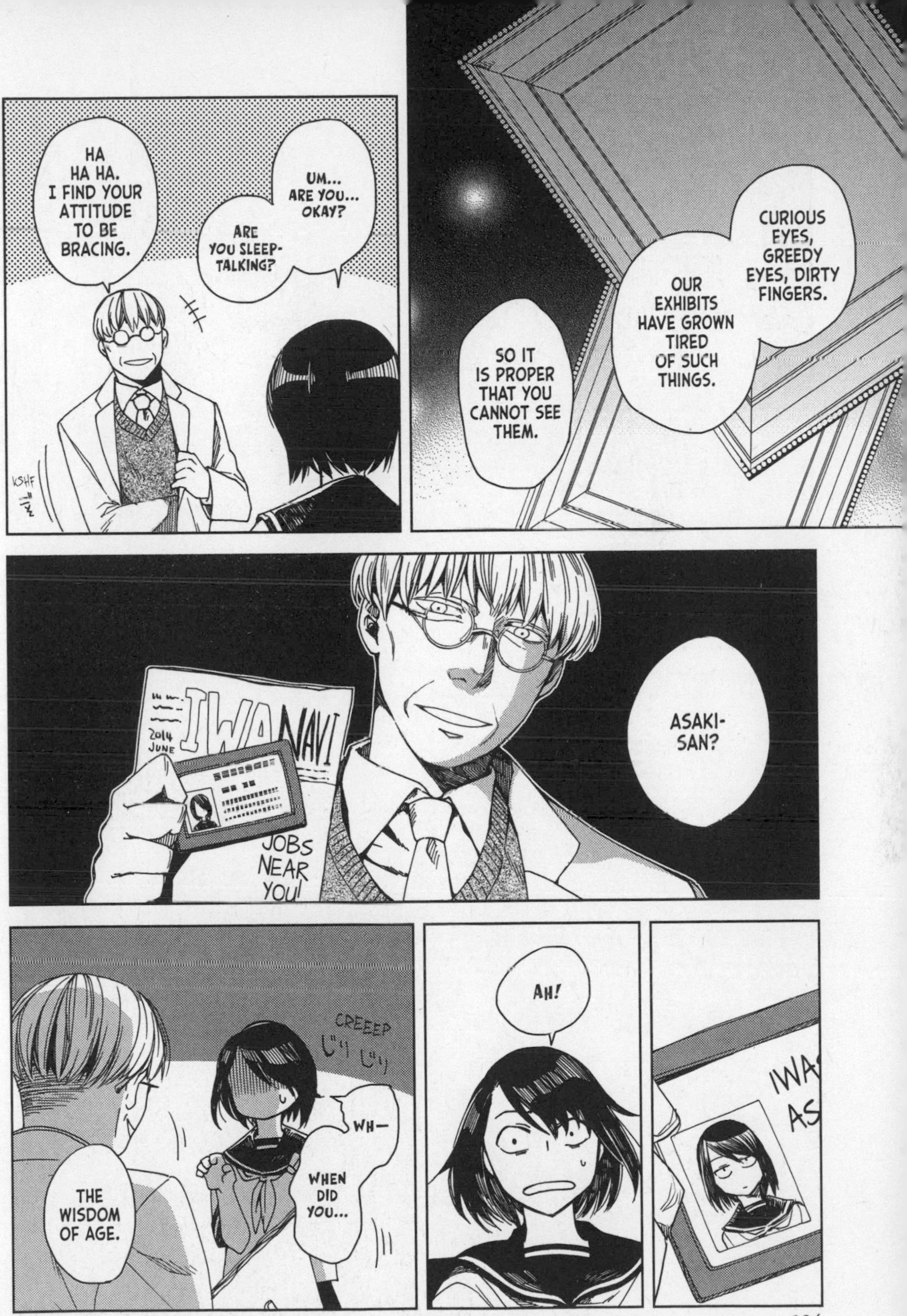
CURIOUS EYES, GREEDY EYES, DIRTY FINGERS.
OUR EXHIBITS HAVE GROWN TIRED OF SUCH THINGS.
SO IT IS PROPER THAT YOU CANNOT SEE THEM.
UM... ARE YOU... OKAY?
ARE YOU SLEEP-TALKING?
HA HA HA. I FIND YOUR ATTITUDE TO BE BRACING.
KSHF
ASAKI-SAN?
IWANAVI
2014 JUNE
JOBS NEAR YOU!
AH!
CREEEP
じり じり
WH—
WHEN DID YOU...
THE WISDOM OF AGE.

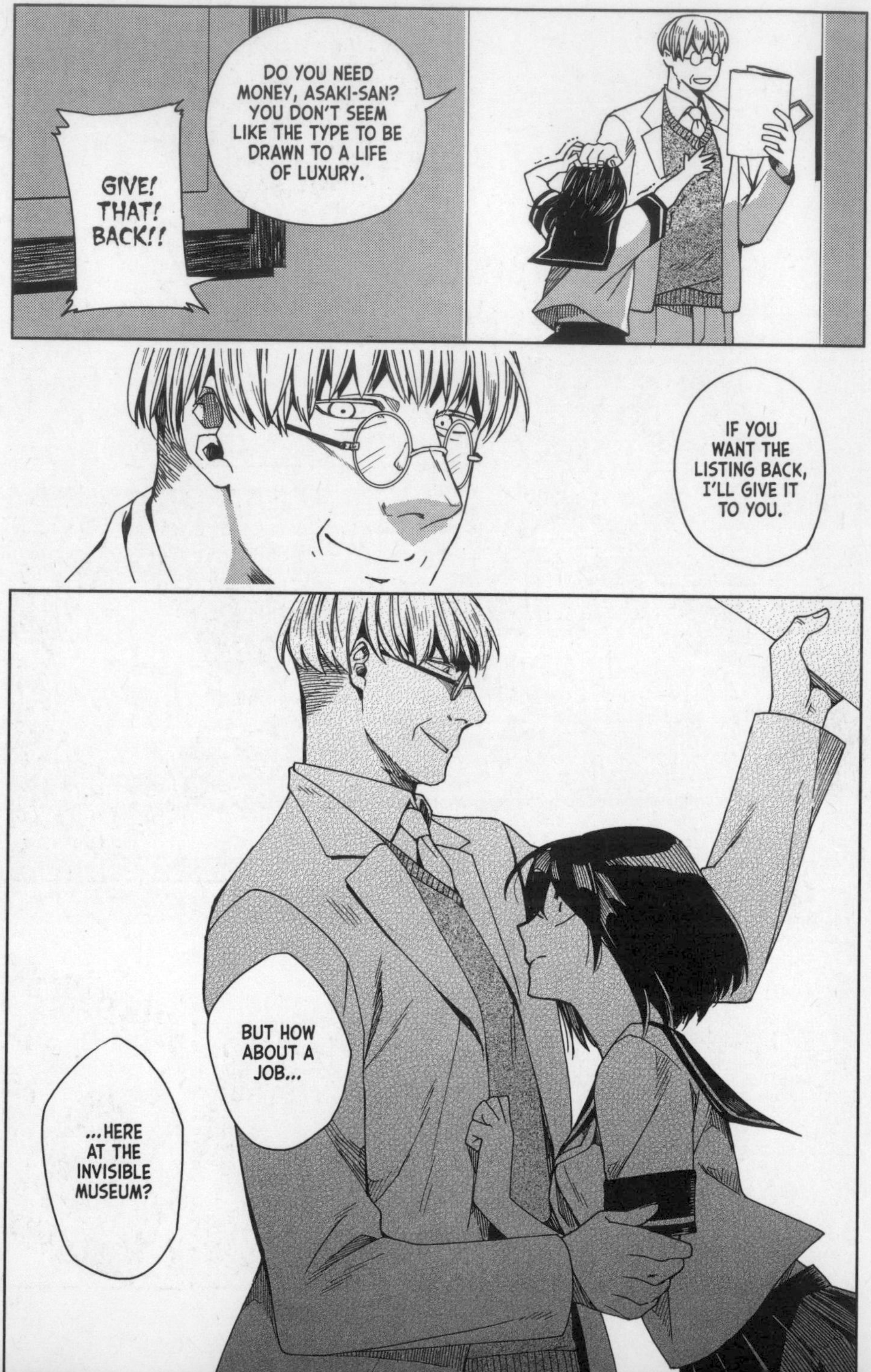
DO YOU NEED MONEY, ASAKI-SAN? YOU DON'T SEEM LIKE THE TYPE TO BE DRAWN TO A LIFE OF LUXURY.
GIVE! THAT! BACK!!
IF YOU WANT THE LISTING BACK, I'LL GIVE IT TO YOU.
BUT HOW ABOUT A JOB...
...HERE AT THE INVISIBLE MUSEUM?

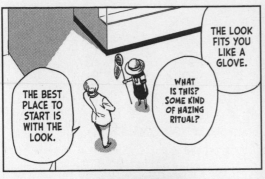

THE LOOK FITS YOU LIKE A GLOVE.
WHAT IS THIS? SOME KIND OF HAZING RITUAL?
THE BEST PLACE TO START IS WITH THE LOOK.
THERE WAS A BUTTERFLY IN THAT DISPLAY CASE.
BUTTER-FLY?
IT WAS SUCH A PERFECT SPECIMEN THAT IT'D BEEN SOLD TIME AND TIME AGAIN. SO DESIRABLE THAT IT PROMPTED QUARRELS.
EVENTUALLY IT GREW SO TIRED OF THE ATTENTION THAT IT WENT INVISIBLE TO AVOID IT.
THAT WAS HOW IT LANDED HERE AT THE MUSEUM.
IF IT'S INVISIBLE, HOW DID IT GET TRANSPORTED HERE?
I CAN SEE BETTER THAN MOST.
WHY?
I'M THE DIREC-TOR.
THAT'S NOT AN ANSWER.
ALL I CAN TELL YOU IS THAT I WAS BORN THIS WAY.
...

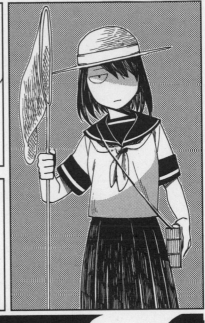

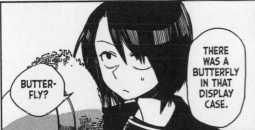

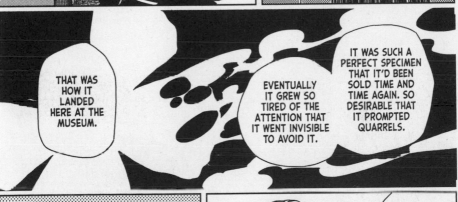

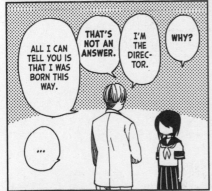

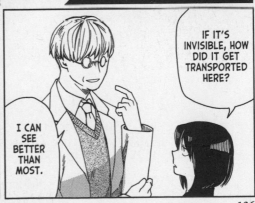

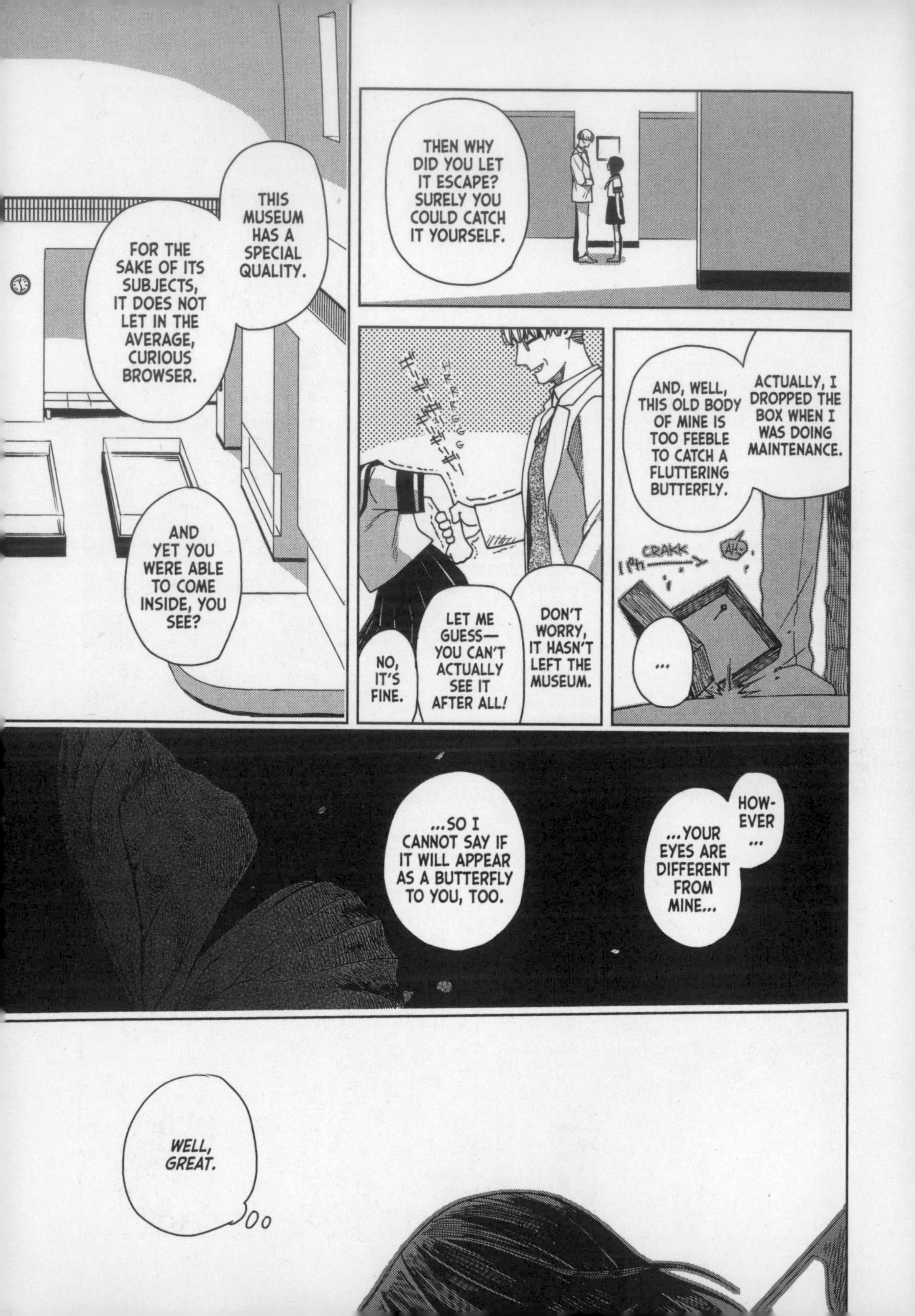
THEN WHY DID YOU LET IT ESCAPE? SURELY YOU COULD CATCH IT YOURSELF.
ACTUALLY, I DROPPED THE BOX WHEN I WAS DOING MAINTENANCE.
AND, WELL, THIS OLD BODY OF MINE IS TOO FEEBLE TO CATCH A FLUTTERING BUTTERFLY.
CRAKK
AH-
...
DON'T WORRY, IT HASN'T LEFT THE MUSEUM.
HRRRGG
LET ME GUESS— YOU CAN'T ACTUALLY SEE IT AFTER ALL!
NO, IT'S FINE.
THIS MUSEUM HAS A SPECIAL QUALITY.
FOR THE SAKE OF ITS SUBJECTS, IT DOES NOT LET IN THE AVERAGE, CURIOUS BROWSER.
AND YET YOU WERE ABLE TO COME INSIDE, YOU SEE?
HOW-EVER...
...YOUR EYES ARE DIFFERENT FROM MINE...
...SO I CANNOT SAY IF IT WILL APPEAR AS A BUTTERFLY TO YOU, TOO.
WELL, GREAT.

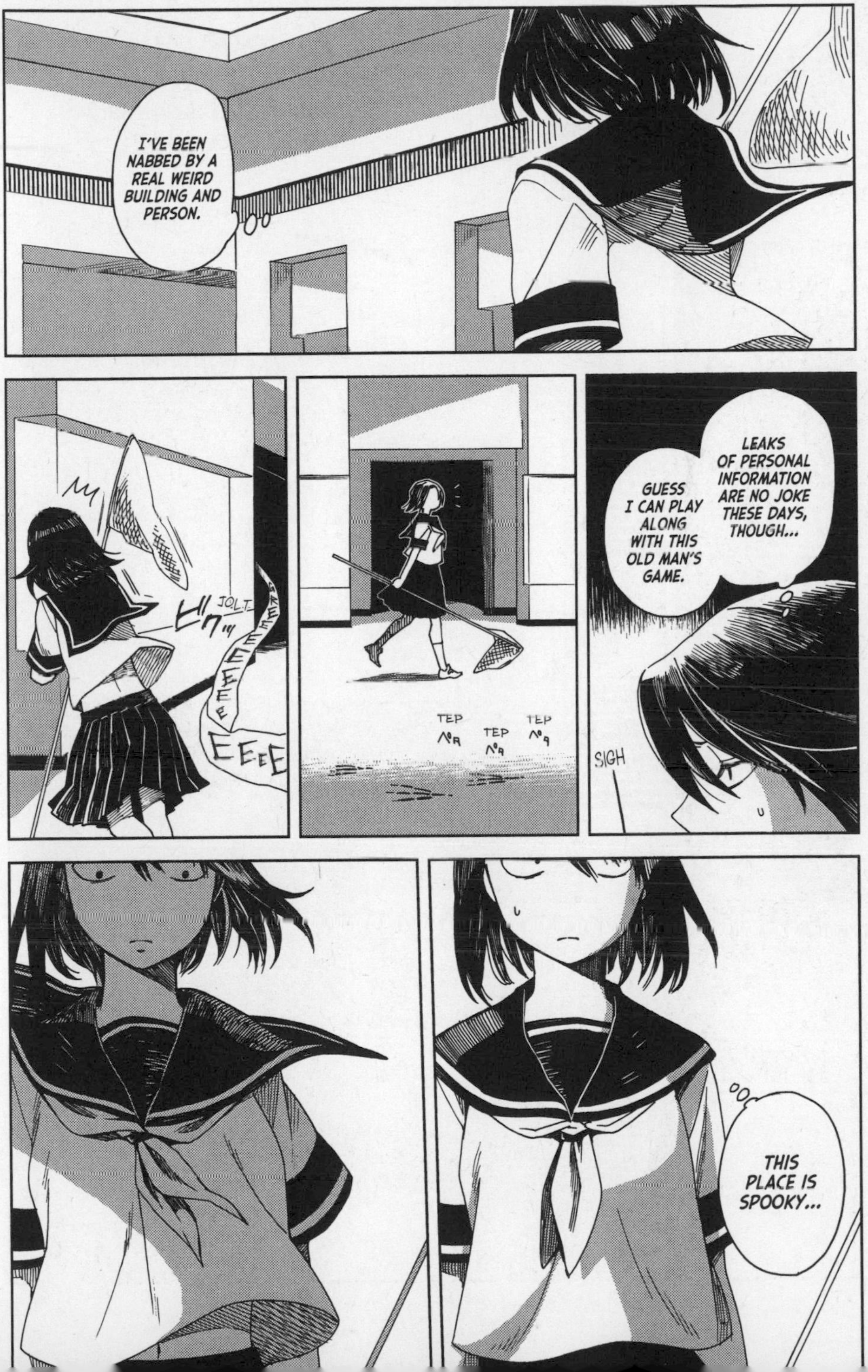

I'VE BEEN NABBED BY A REAL WEIRD BUILDING AND PERSON.
LEAKS OF PERSONAL INFORMATION ARE NO JOKE THESE DAYS, THOUGH...
GUESS I CAN PLAY ALONG WITH THIS OLD MAN'S GAME.
SIGH
TEP
TEP
TEP
JOLT
THIS PLACE IS SPOOKY...

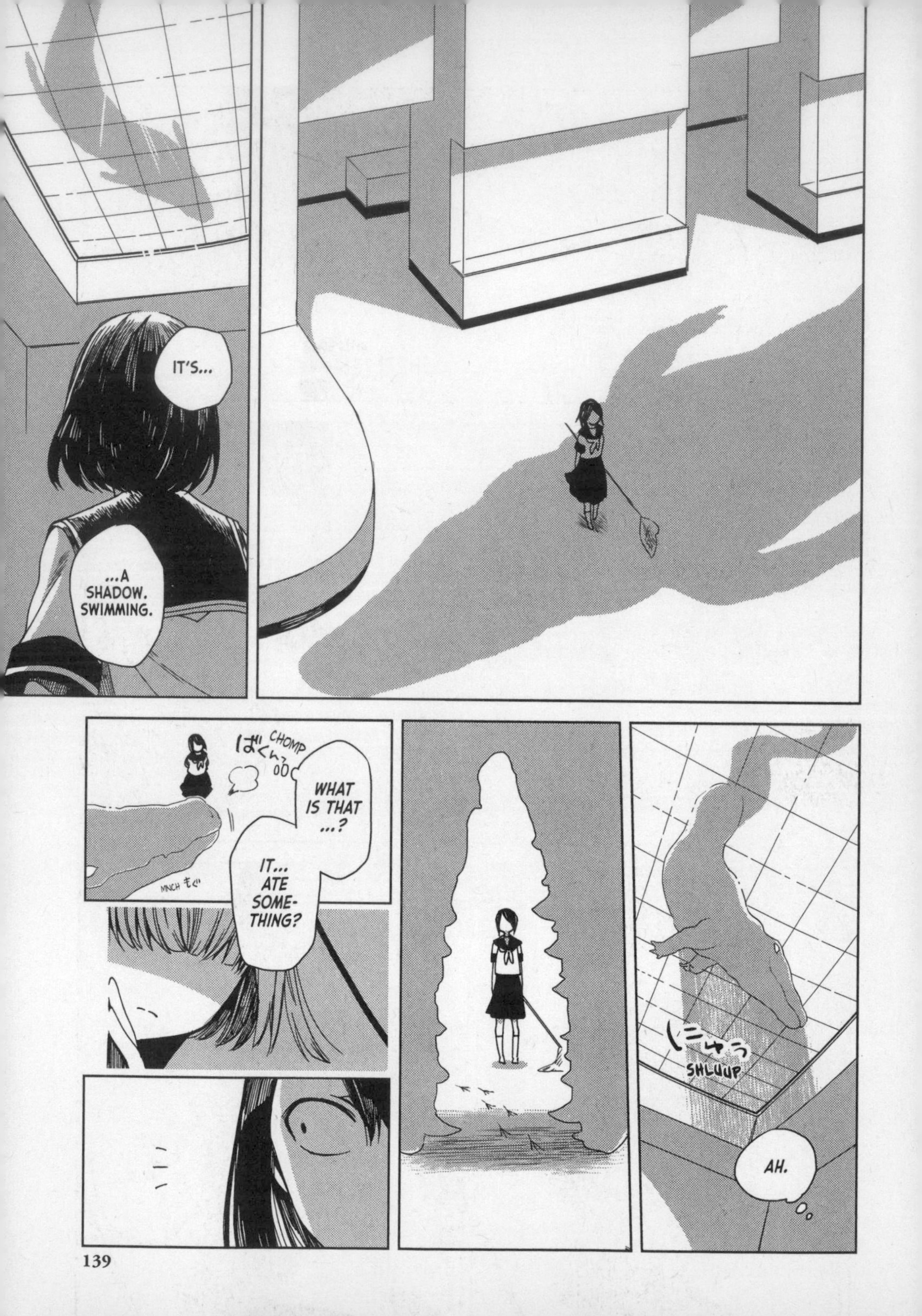
IT'S...
...A SHADOW. SWIMMING.
SHLUUP
AH.
ぱくんっ
CHOMP
MNCH もぐ
WHAT IS THAT ...?
IT... ATE SOMETHING?

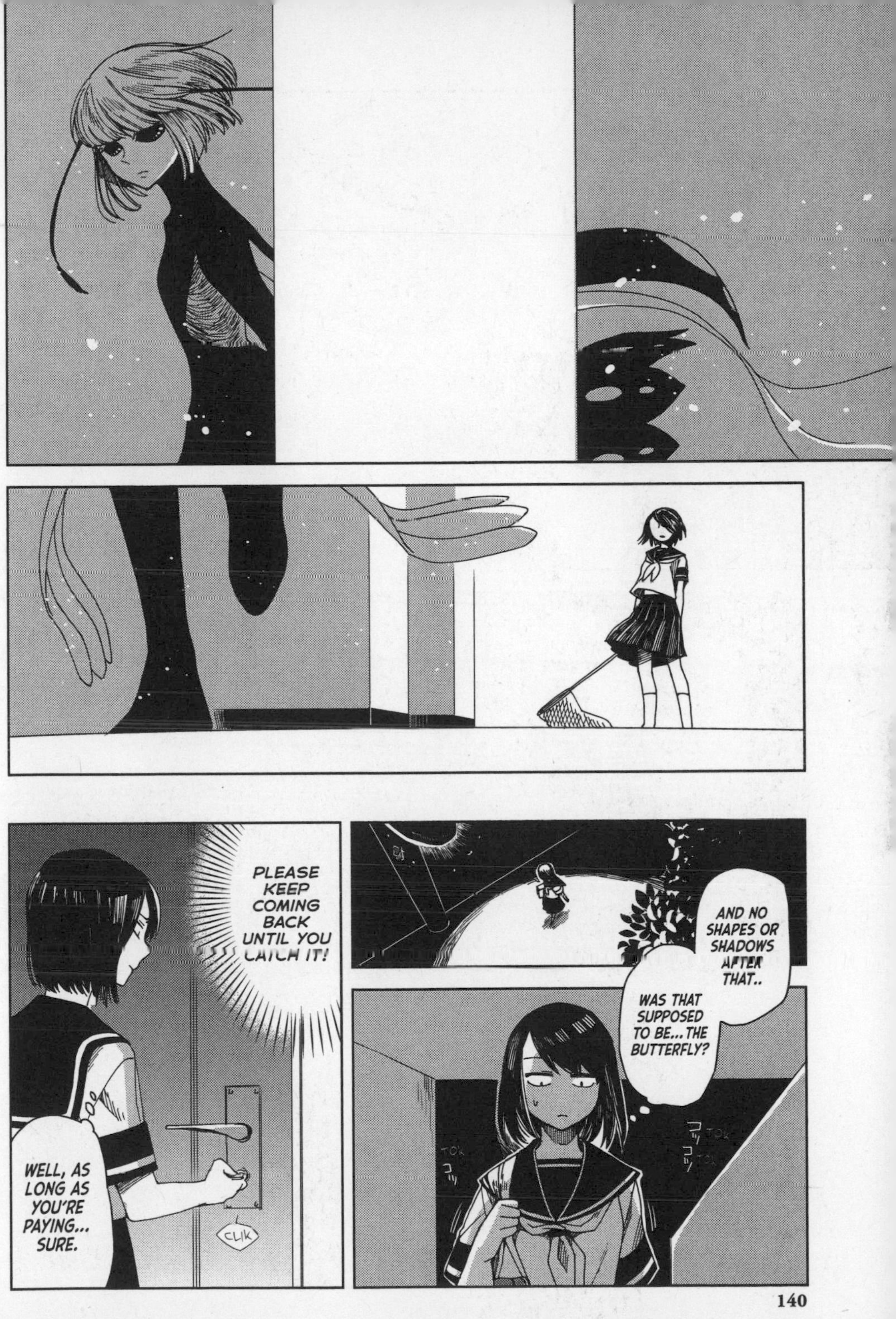
AND NO SHAPES OR SHADOWS AFTER THAT..
WAS THAT SUPPOSED TO BE... THE BUTTERFLY?
TOK
TOK
PLEASE KEEP COMING BACK UNTIL YOU CATCH IT!
WELL, AS LONG AS YOU'RE PAYING... SURE.
CLIK

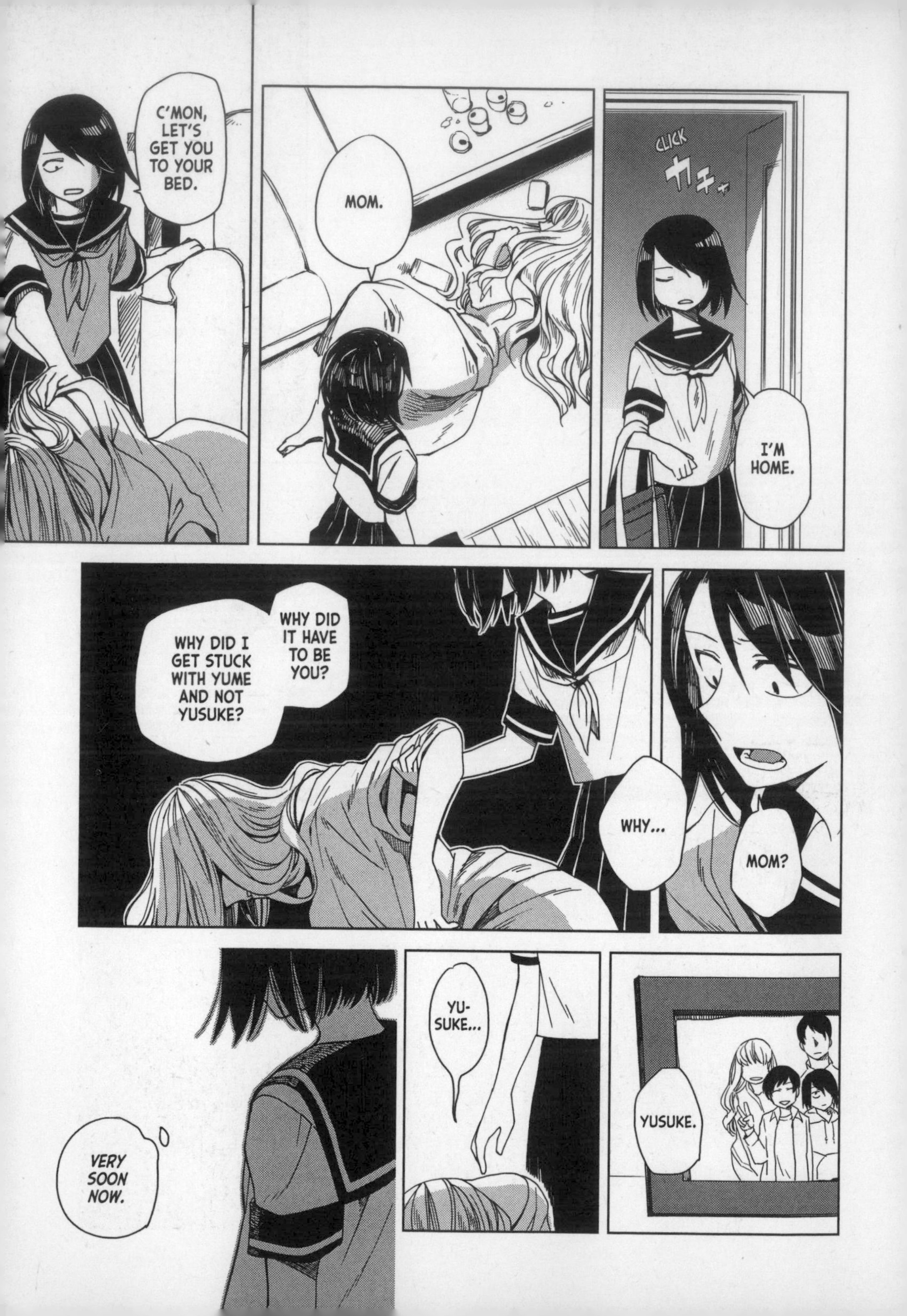
CLICK
カチャ
I'M HOME.
MOM.
C'MON, LET'S GET YOU TO YOUR BED.
WHY...
MOM?
WHY DID IT HAVE TO BE YOU?
WHY DID I GET STUCK WITH YUME AND NOT YUSUKE?
YUSUKE.
YU-SUKE...
VERY SOON NOW.

SWISH
ひらり

WHOOSH

WHOOSH

SWISH
ひらり

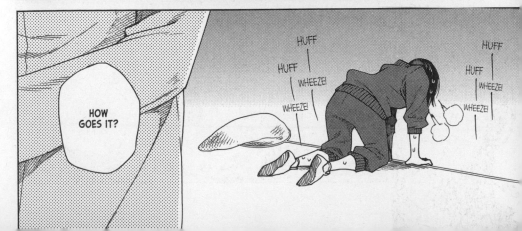

HOW
GOES IT?

HUFF

HUFF

WHEEZE!

WHEEZE!

HUFF

HUFF

WHEEZE!

WHEEZE!

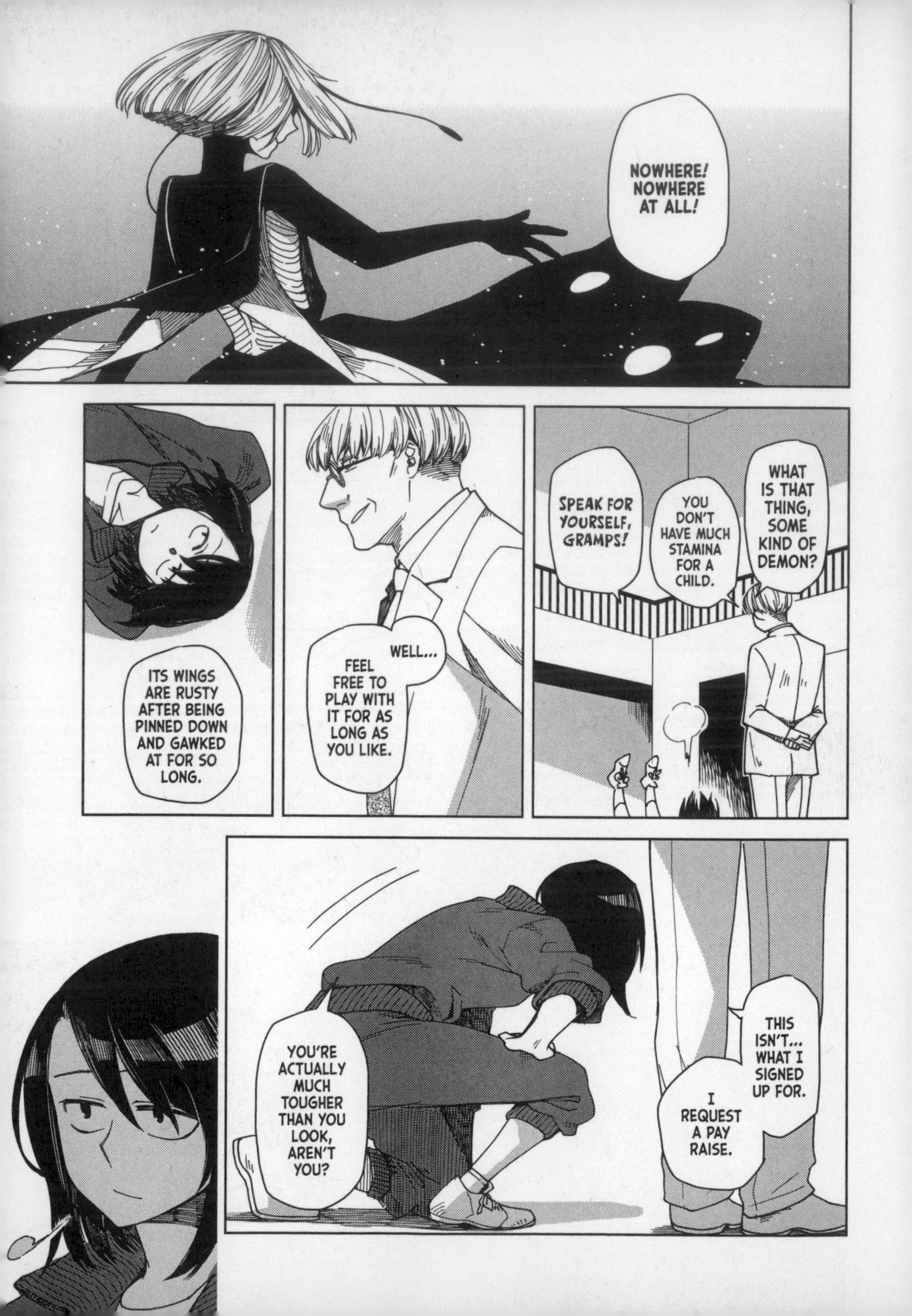
NOWHERE! NOWHERE AT ALL!
WHAT IS THAT THING, SOME KIND OF DEMON?
YOU DON'T HAVE MUCH STAMINA FOR A CHILD.
SPEAK FOR YOURSELF, GRAMPS!
WELL...
FEEL FREE TO PLAY WITH IT FOR AS LONG AS YOU LIKE.
ITS WINGS ARE RUSTY AFTER BEING PINNED DOWN AND GAWKED AT FOR SO LONG.
THIS ISN'T... WHAT I SIGNED UP FOR.
I REQUEST A PAY RAISE.
YOU'RE ACTUALLY MUCH TOUGHER THAN YOU LOOK, AREN'T YOU?

DAY
SEVEN

DAY
FIVE

DAY
THREE

DAY
TEN

FWSH

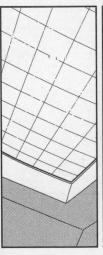

I'M GETTING OWNED BY A GODDAMN BUTTERFLY.

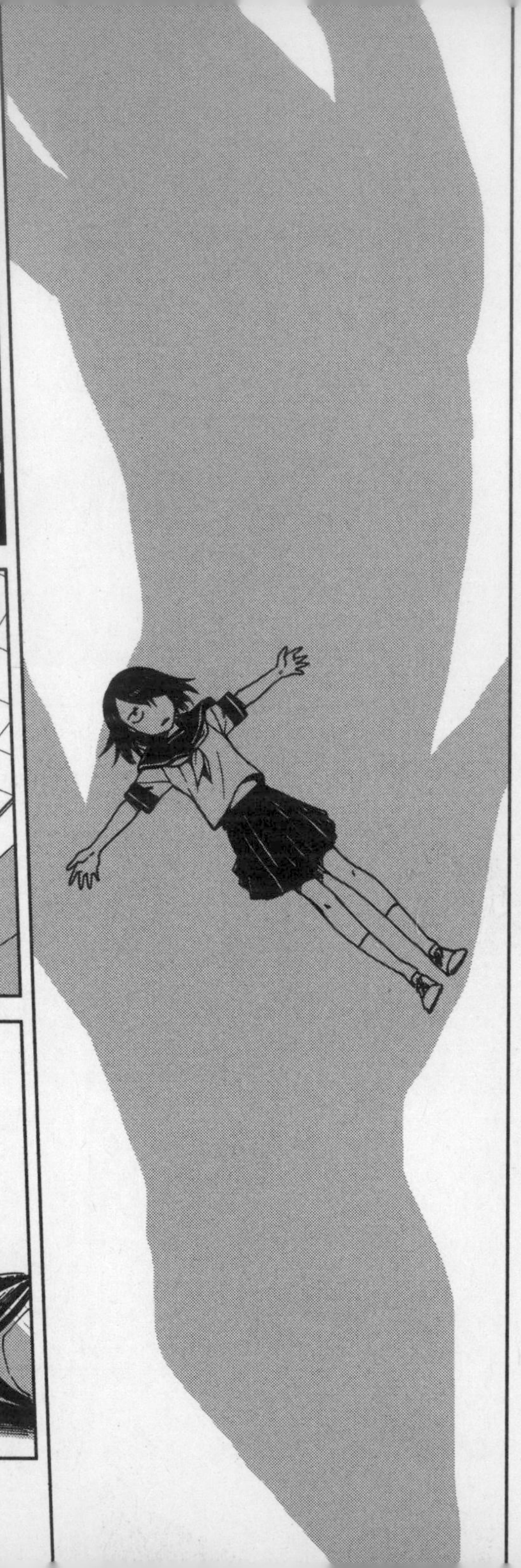

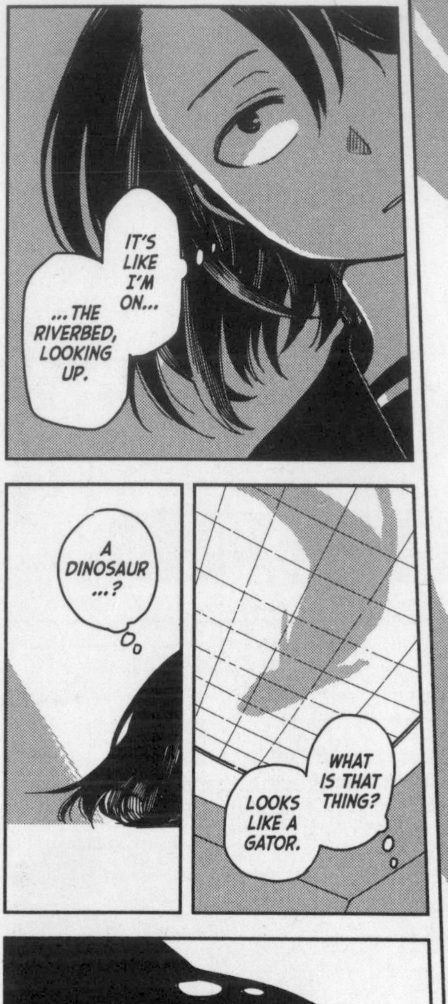
IT'S LIKE I'M ON...
...THE RIVERBED, LOOKING UP.
WHAT IS THAT THING?
LOOKS LIKE A GATOR.
A DINOSAUR ...?

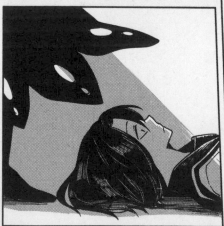

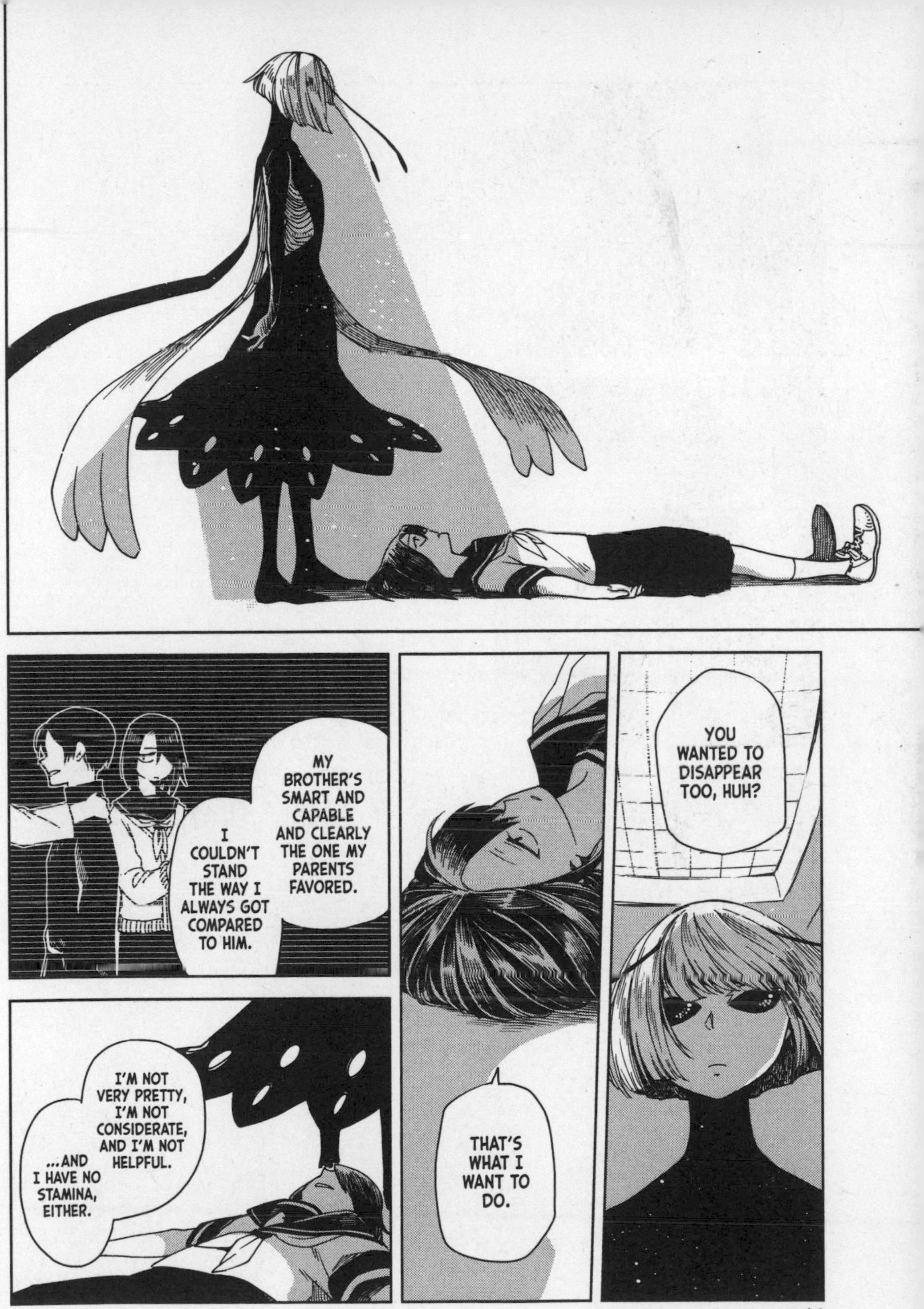
YOU WANTED TO DISAPPEAR TOO, HUH?
THAT'S WHAT I WANT TO DO.
MY BROTHER'S SMART AND CAPABLE AND CLEARLY THE ONE MY PARENTS FAVORED.
I COULDN'T STAND THE WAY I ALWAYS GOT COMPARED TO HIM.
I'M NOT VERY PRETTY, I'M NOT CONSIDERATE, AND I'M NOT HELPFUL.
...AND I HAVE NO STAMINA, EITHER.

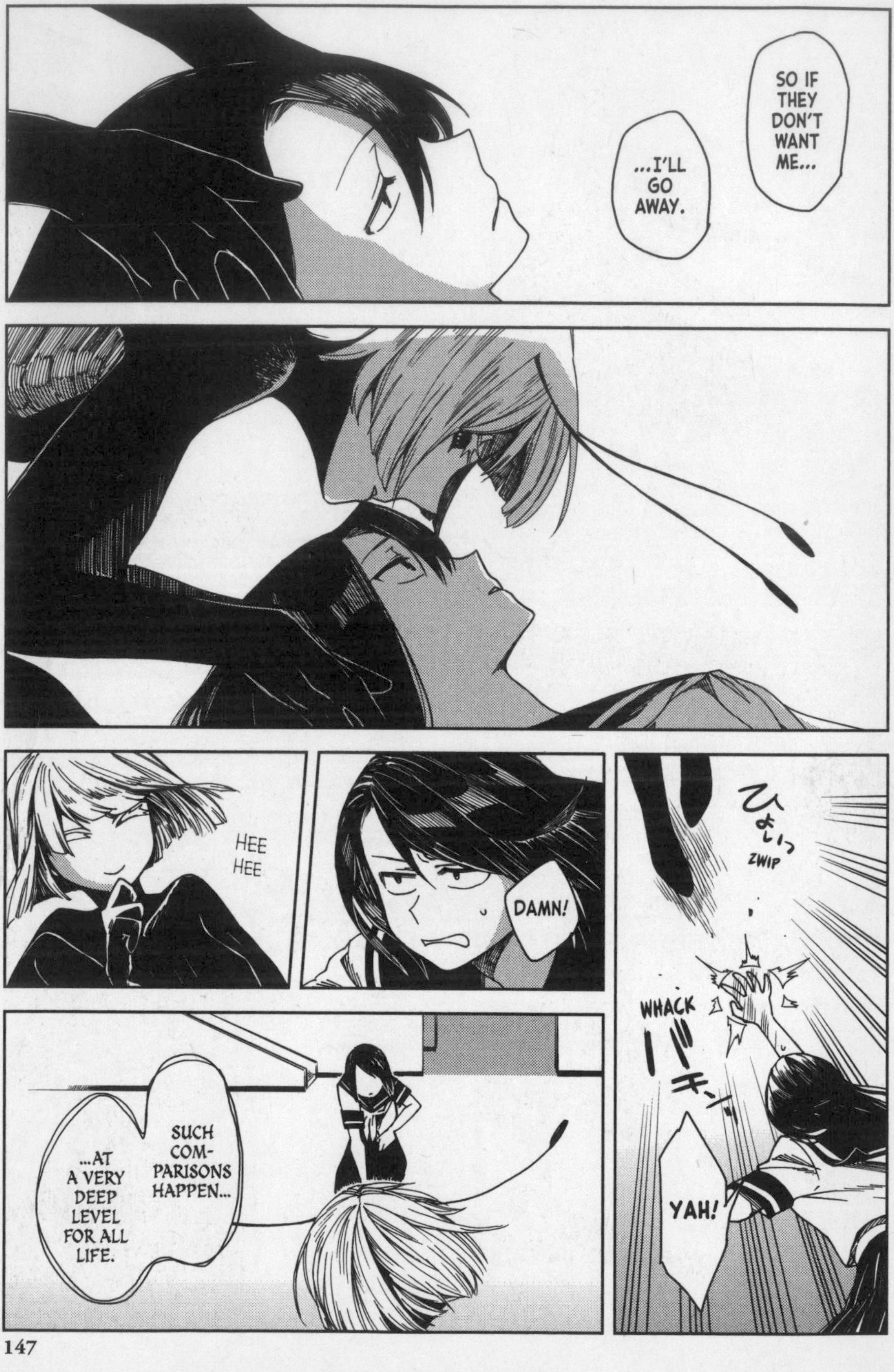
SO IF THEY DON'T WANT ME...
...I'LL GO AWAY.
ひょいっ
ZWIP
WHACK
バチーッ
YAH!
DAMN!
HEE HEE
SUCH COM-PARISONS HAPPEN...
...AT A VERY DEEP LEVEL FOR ALL LIFE.

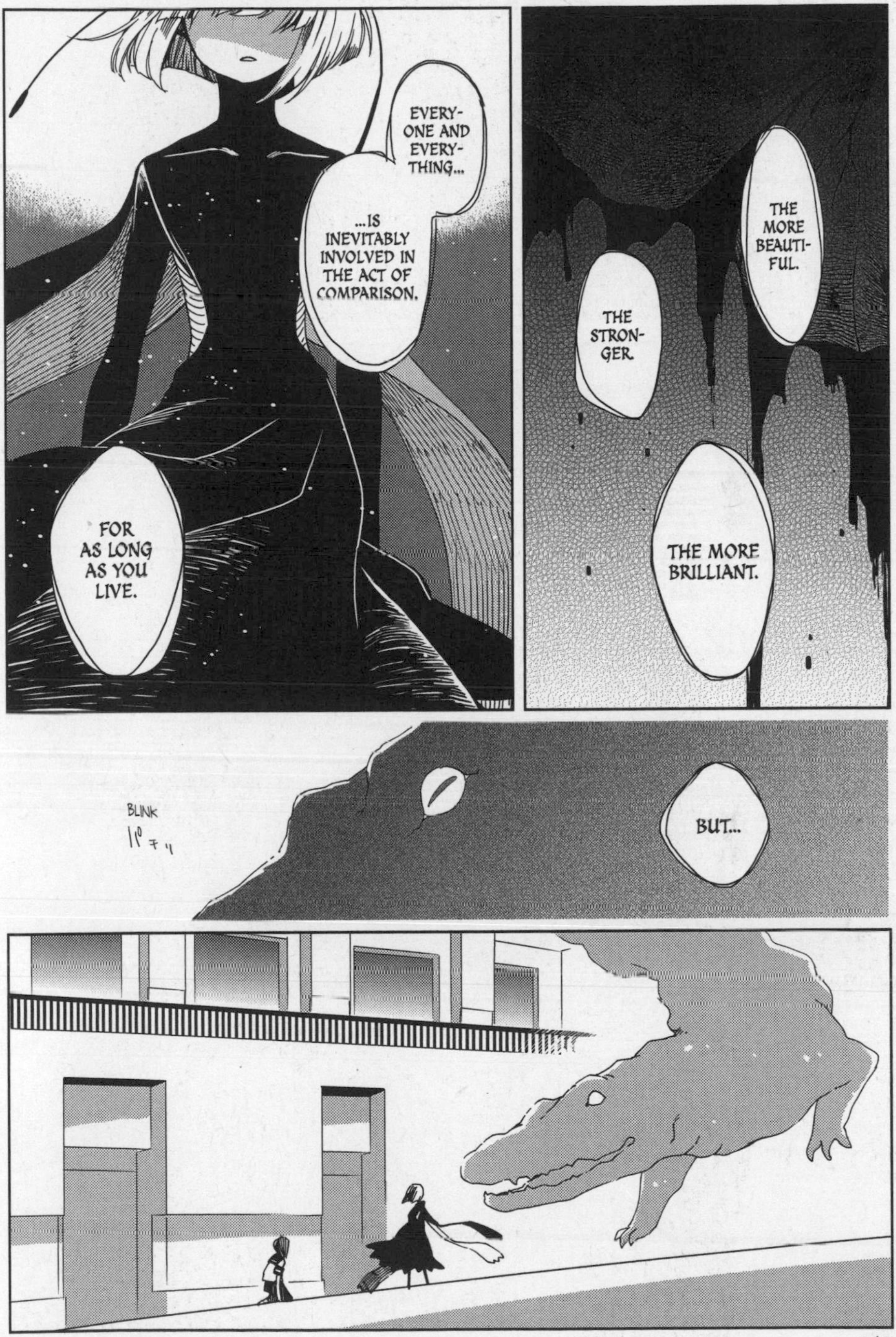
THE MORE BEAUTIFUL.
THE STRONGER.
THE MORE BRILLIANT.
EVERYONE AND EVERYTHING...
...IS INEVITABLY INVOLVED IN THE ACT OF COMPARISON.
FOR AS LONG AS YOU LIVE.
BUT...
BLINK
パチッ

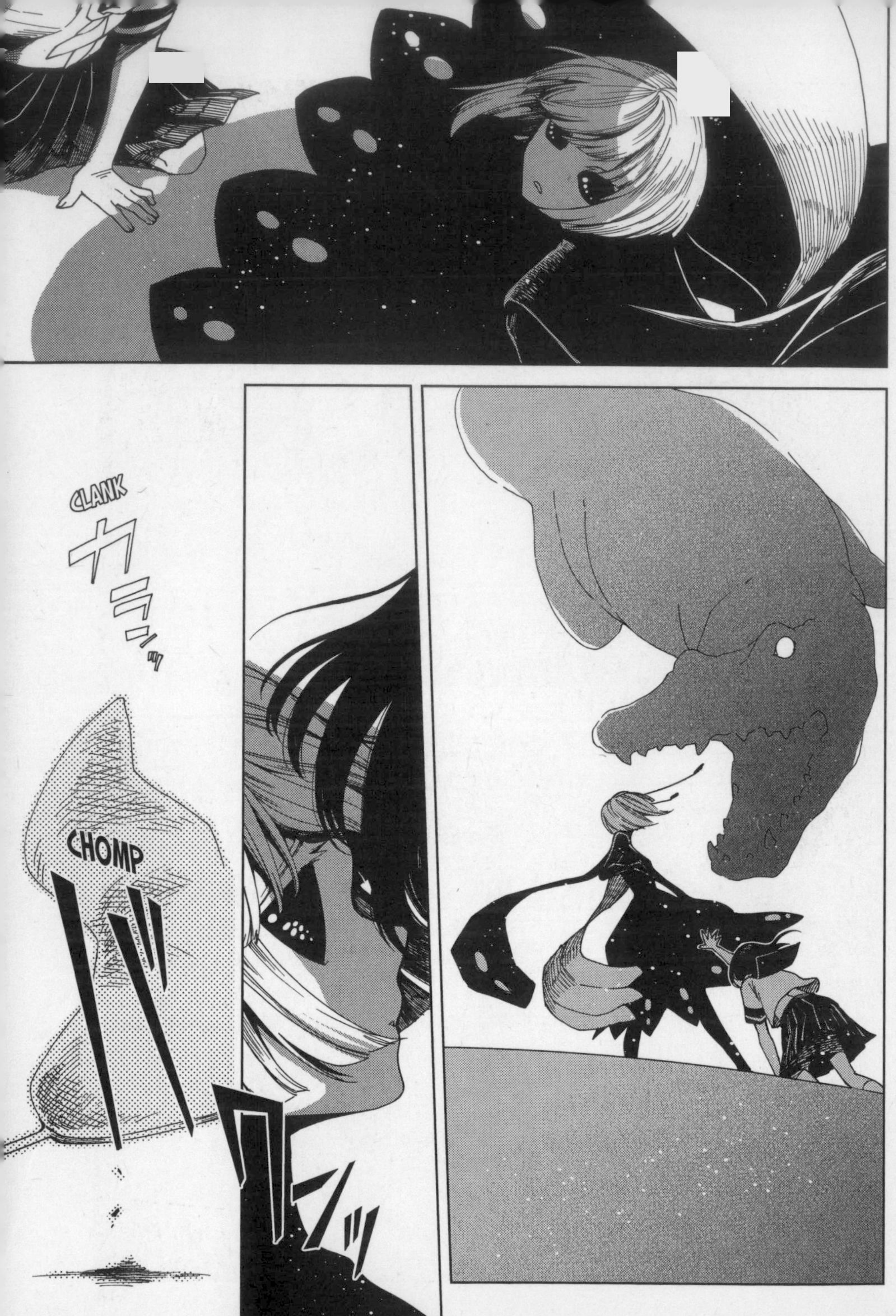
CLANK
カラン
CHOMP

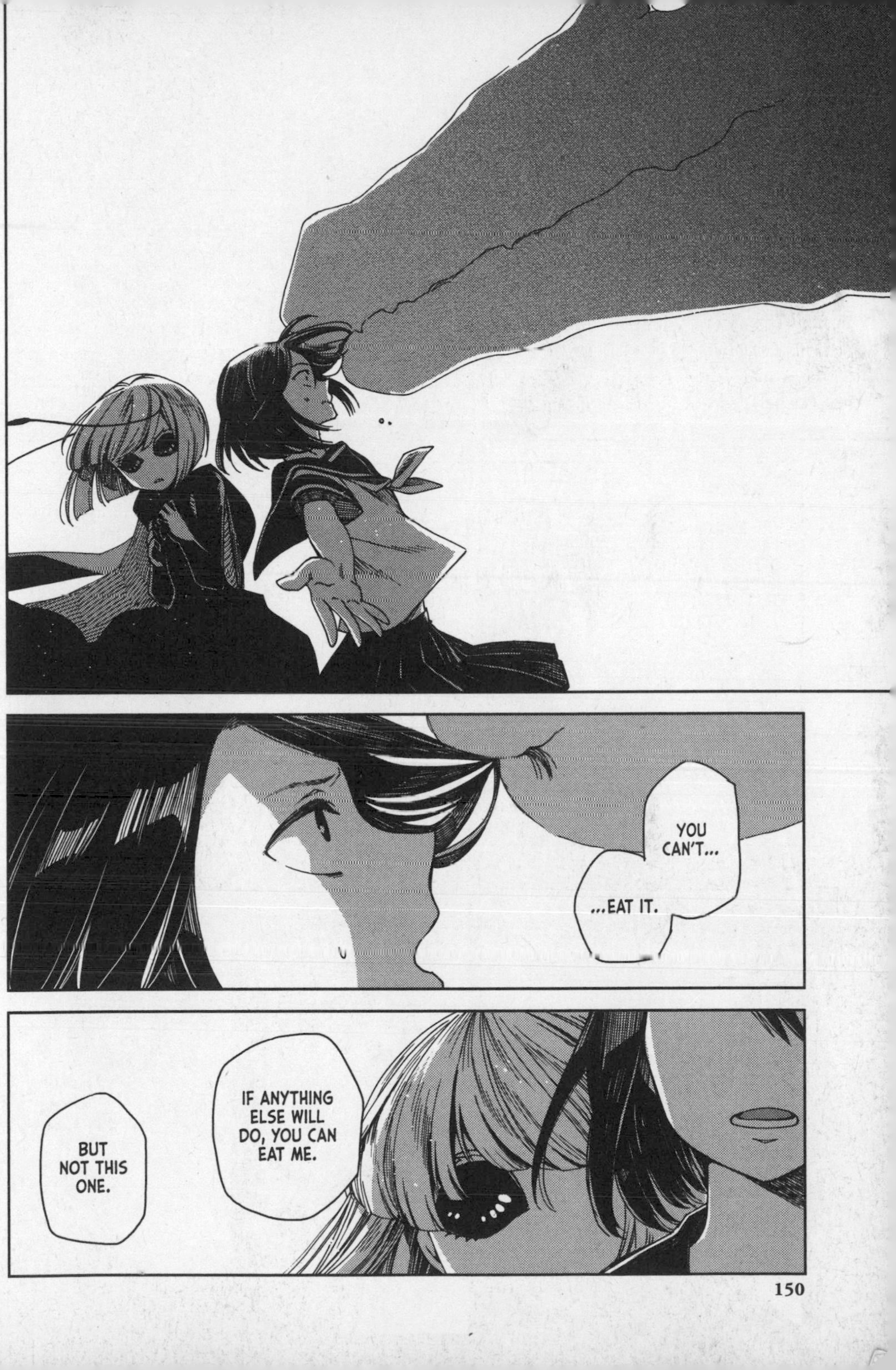
YOU CAN'T...
...EAT IT.
IF ANYTHING ELSE WILL DO, YOU CAN EAT ME.
BUT NOT THIS ONE.

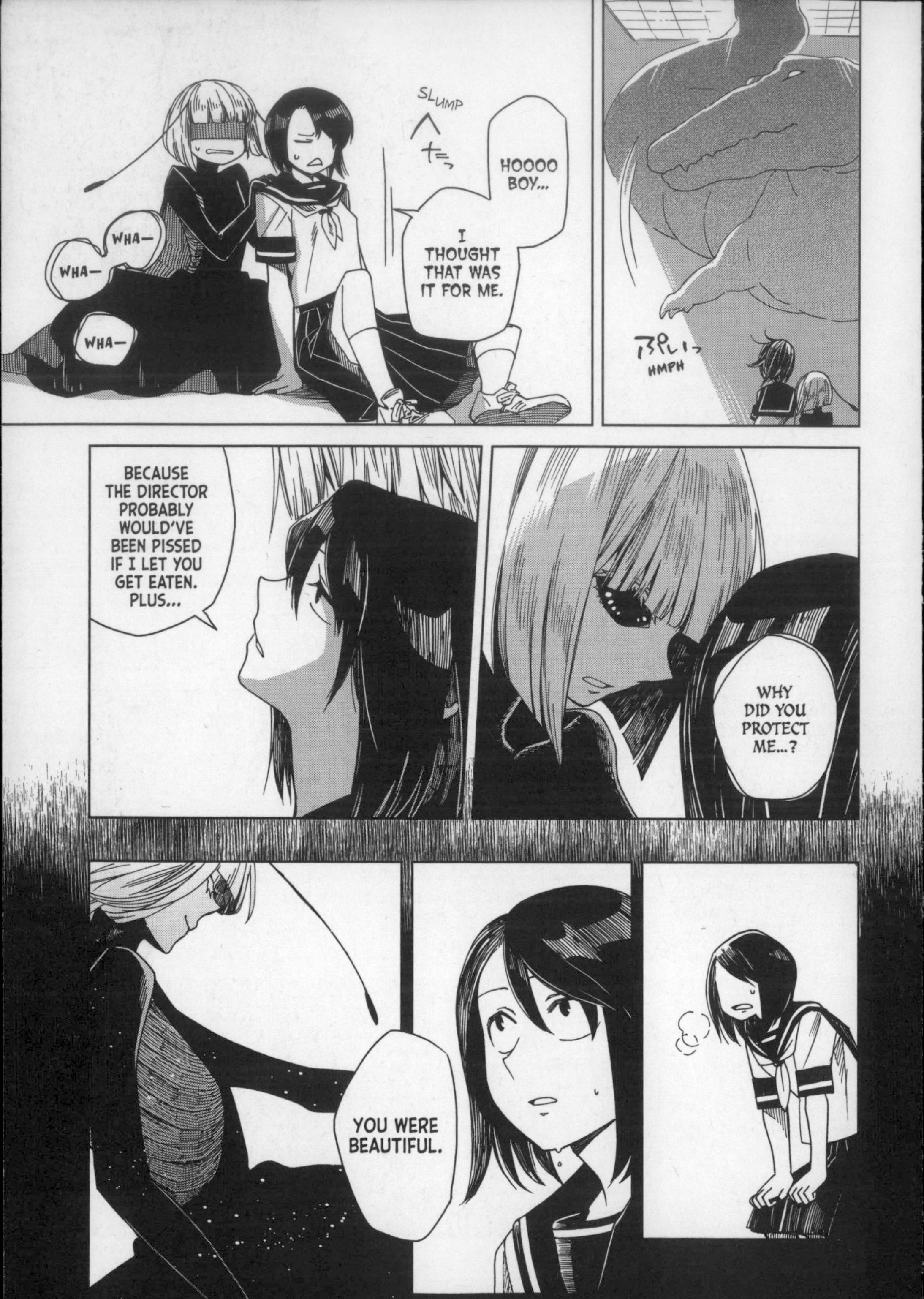
HMPH
HOOOO BOY...
I THOUGHT THAT WAS IT FOR ME.
SLUMP
WHA—
WHA—
WHA—
WHY DID YOU PROTECT ME...?
BECAUSE THE DIRECTOR PROBABLY WOULD'VE BEEN PISSED IF I LET YOU GET EATEN. PLUS...
YOU WERE BEAUTIFUL.

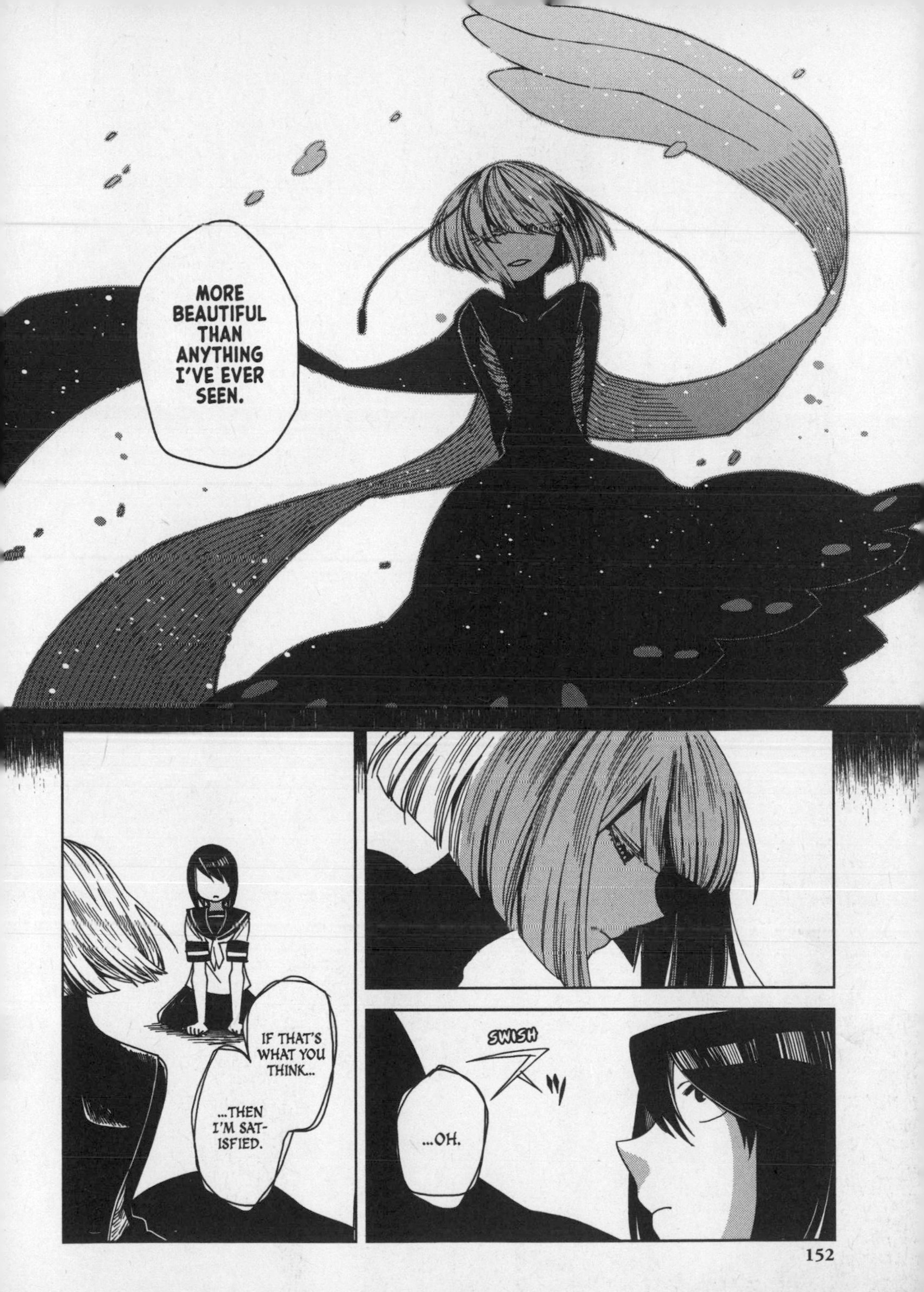
MORE BEAUTIFUL THAN ANYTHING I'VE EVER SEEN.
SWISH
...OH.
IF THAT'S WHAT YOU THINK...
...THEN I'M SAT-ISFIED.

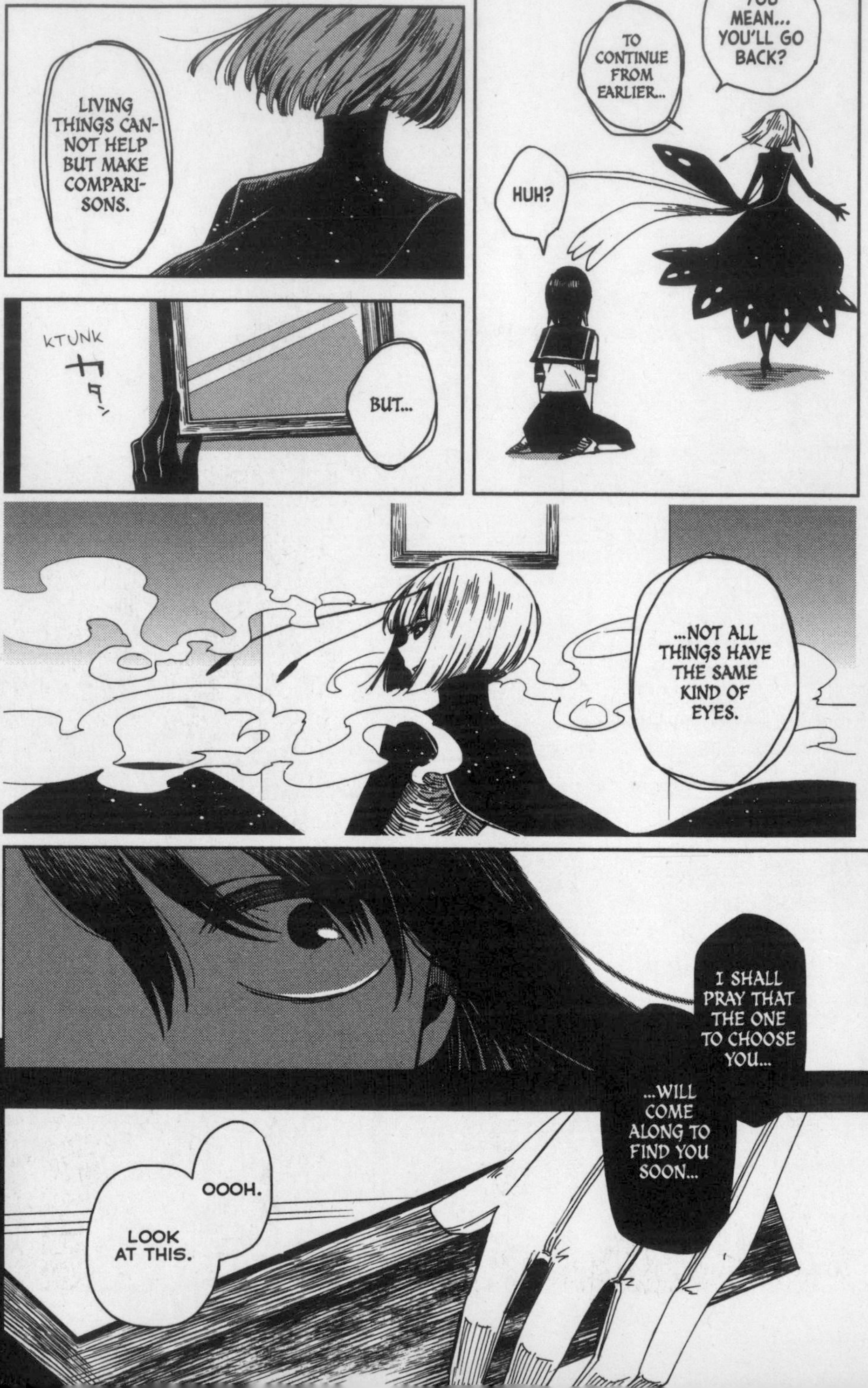
YOU MEAN... YOU'LL GO BACK?
TO CONTINUE FROM EARLIER...
HUH?
LIVING THINGS CANNOT HELP BUT MAKE COMPARISONS.
KTUNK
BUT...
...NOT ALL THINGS HAVE THE SAME KIND OF EYES.
I SHALL PRAY THAT THE ONE TO CHOOSE YOU...
...WILL COME ALONG TO FIND YOU SOON...
OOOH.
LOOK AT THIS.

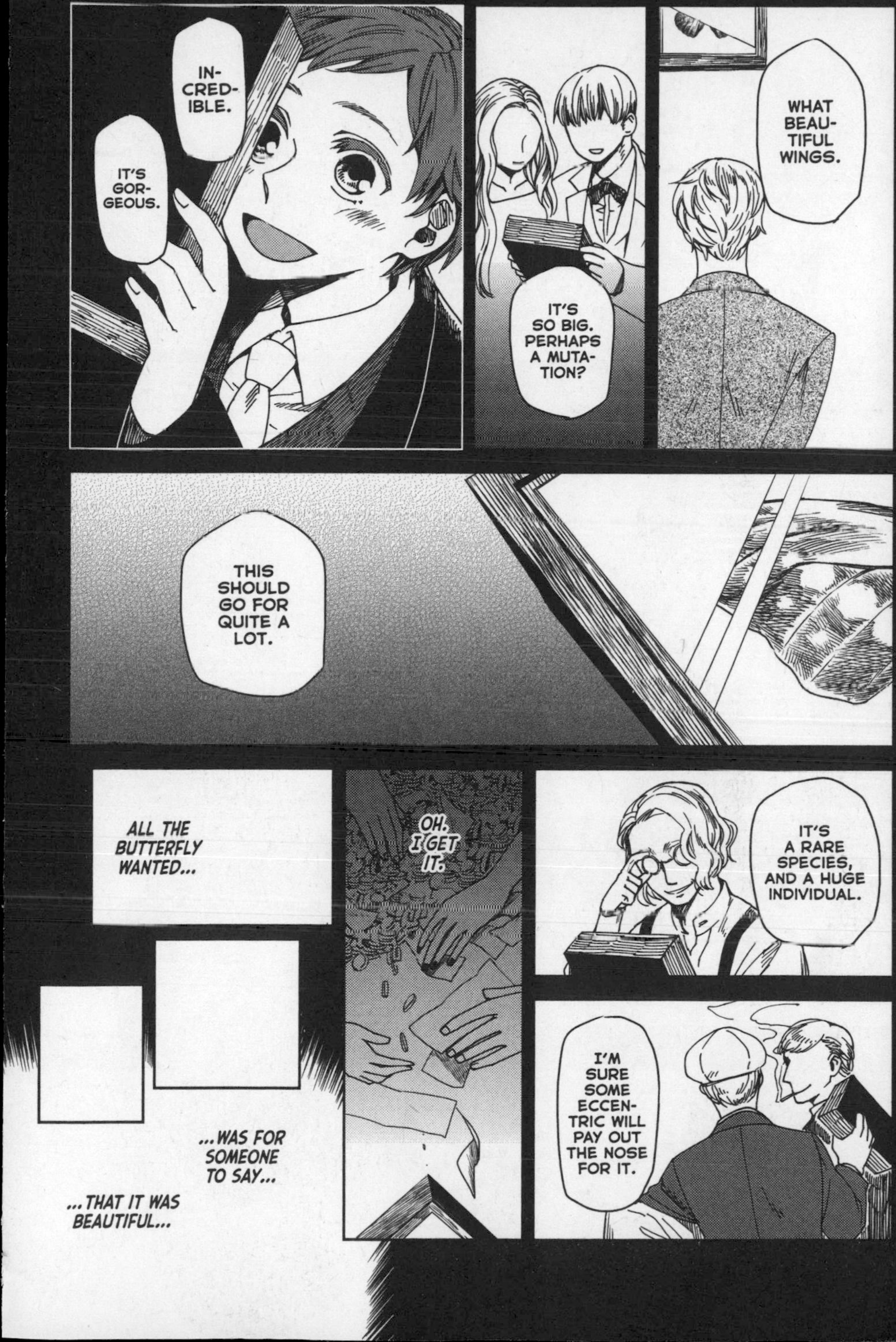
WHAT BEAUTIFUL WINGS.
IT'S SO BIG. PERHAPS A MUTATION?
INCREDIBLE.
IT'S GORGEOUS.
THIS SHOULD GO FOR QUITE A LOT.
IT'S A RARE SPECIES, AND A HUGE INDIVIDUAL.
I'M SURE SOME ECCENTRIC WILL PAY OUT THE NOSE FOR IT.
OH. I GET IT.
ALL THE BUTTERFLY WANTED...
...WAS FOR SOMEONE TO SAY...
...THAT IT WAS BEAUTIFUL...

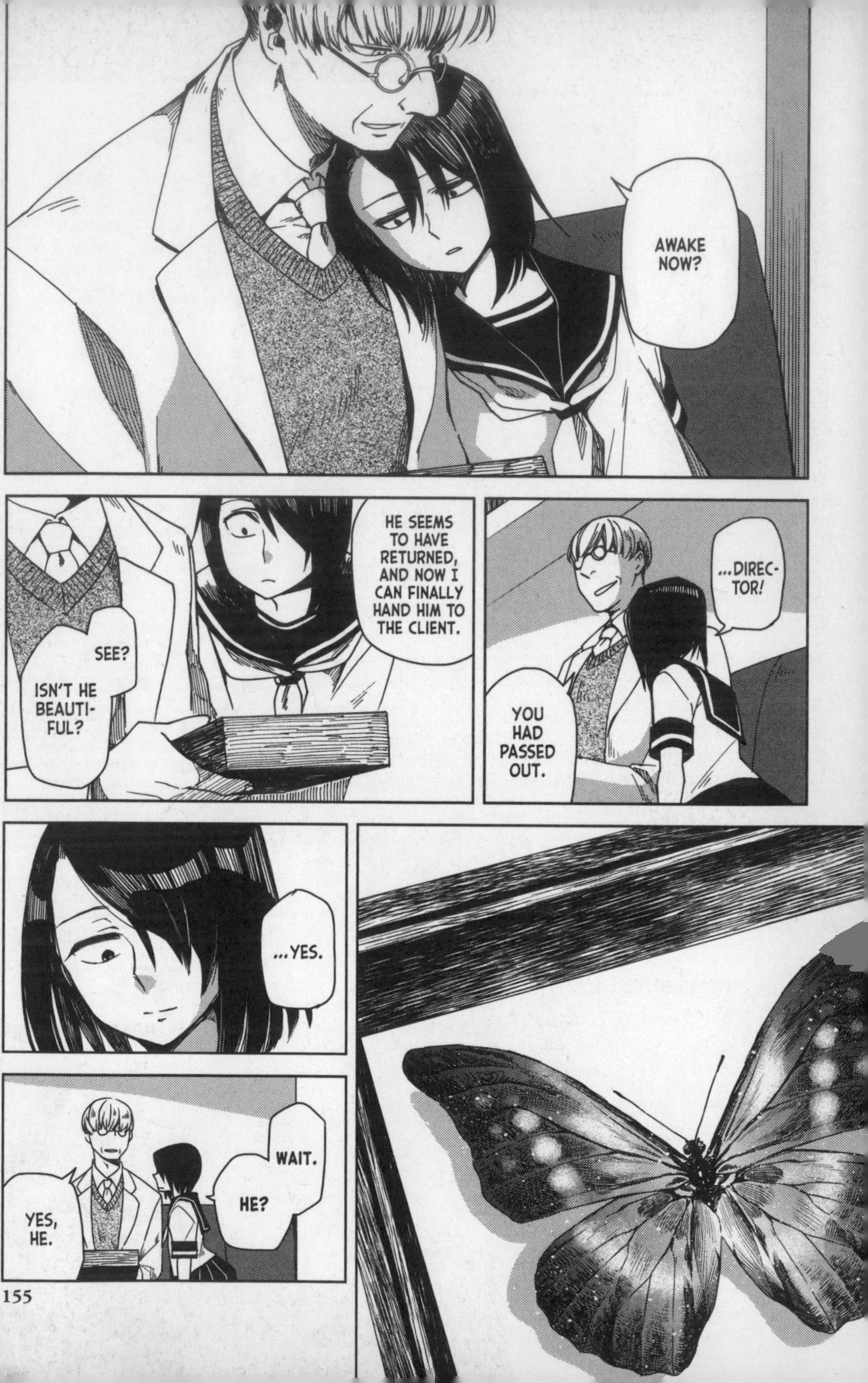
AWAKE NOW?
...DIREC-TOR!
YOU HAD PASSED OUT.
HE SEEMS TO HAVE RETURNED, AND NOW I CAN FINALLY HAND HIM TO THE CLIENT.
SEE?
ISN'T HE BEAUTI-FUL?
...YES.
WAIT.
HE?
YES, HE.

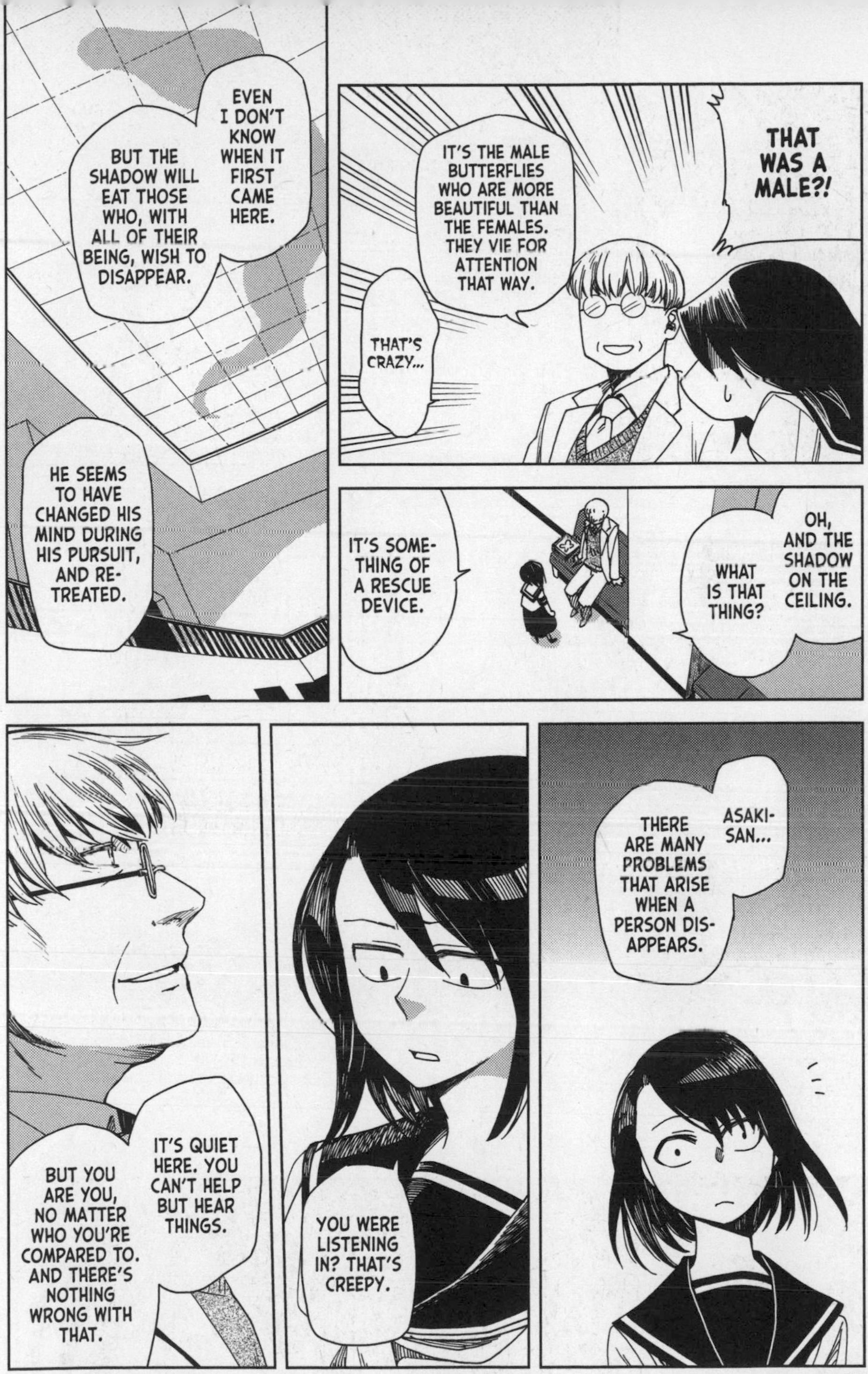
THAT WAS A MALE?!
IT'S THE MALE BUTTERFLIES WHO ARE MORE BEAUTIFUL THAN THE FEMALES. THEY VIE FOR ATTENTION THAT WAY.
THAT'S CRAZY...
OH, AND THE SHADOW ON THE CEILING.
WHAT IS THAT THING?
IT'S SOME-THING OF A RESCUE DEVICE.
EVEN I DON'T KNOW WHEN IT FIRST CAME HERE.
BUT THE SHADOW WILL EAT THOSE WHO, WITH ALL OF THEIR BEING, WISH TO DISAPPEAR.
HE SEEMS TO HAVE CHANGED HIS MIND DURING HIS PURSUIT, AND RE-TREATED.
ASAKI-SAN...
THERE ARE MANY PROBLEMS THAT ARISE WHEN A PERSON DIS-APPEARS.
YOU WERE LISTENING IN? THAT'S CREEPY.
IT'S QUIET HERE. YOU CAN'T HELP BUT HEAR THINGS.
BUT YOU ARE YOU, NO MATTER WHO YOU'RE COMPARED TO. AND THERE'S NOTHING WRONG WITH THAT.

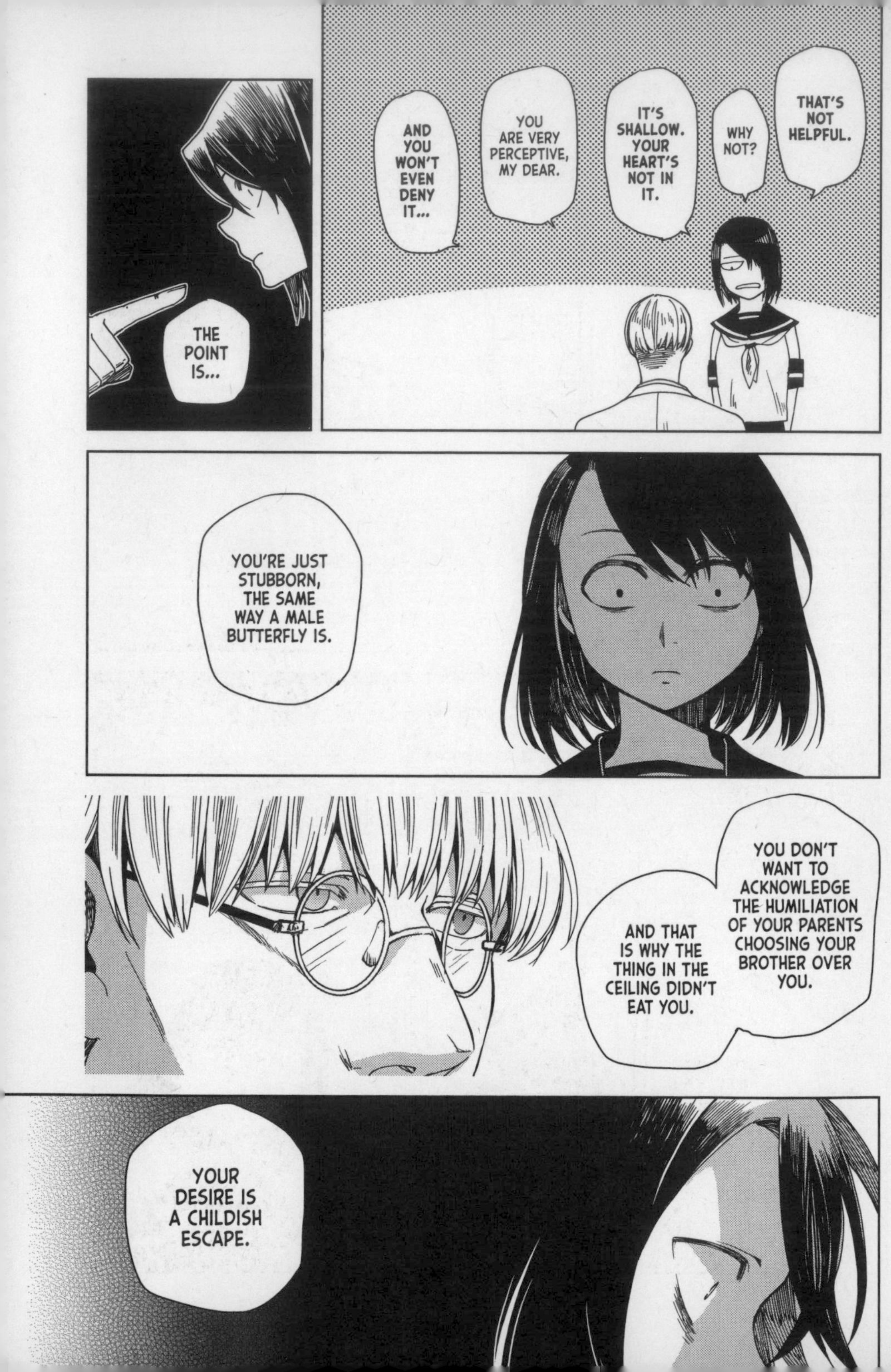
THAT'S NOT HELPFUL.
WHY NOT?
IT'S SHALLOW. YOUR HEART'S NOT IN IT.
YOU ARE VERY PERCEPTIVE, MY DEAR.
AND YOU WON'T EVEN DENY IT...
THE POINT IS...
YOU'RE JUST STUBBORN, THE SAME WAY A MALE BUTTERFLY IS.
YOU DON'T WANT TO ACKNOWLEDGE THE HUMILIATION OF YOUR PARENTS CHOOSING YOUR BROTHER OVER YOU.
AND THAT IS WHY THE THING IN THE CEILING DIDN'T EAT YOU.
YOUR DESIRE IS A CHILDISH ESCAPE.

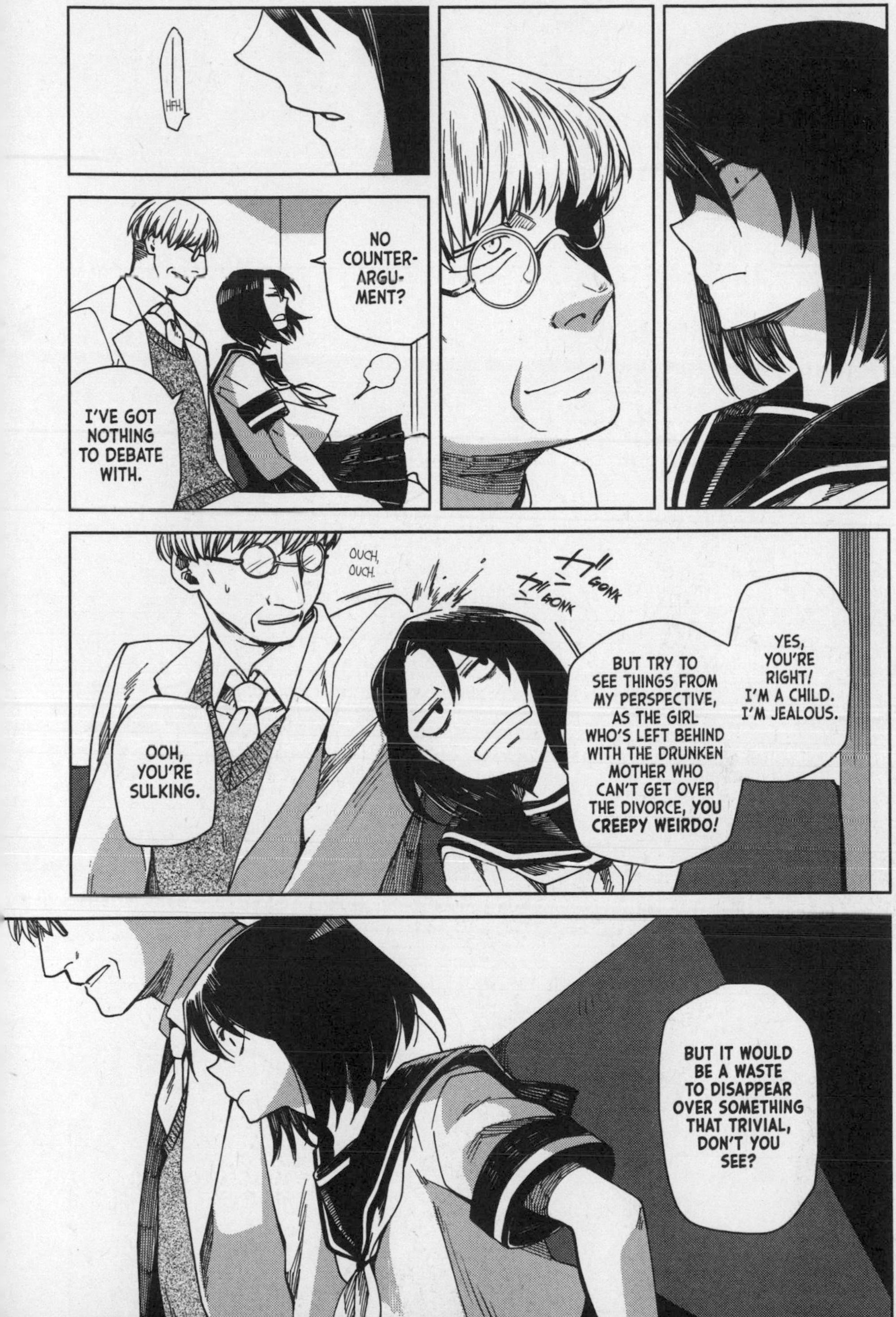
HFH.
NO COUNTER-ARGUMENT?
I'VE GOT NOTHING TO DEBATE WITH.
YES, YOU'RE RIGHT! I'M A CHILD. I'M JEALOUS.
GONK
GONK
BUT TRY TO SEE THINGS FROM MY PERSPECTIVE, AS THE GIRL WHO'S LEFT BEHIND WITH THE DRUNKEN MOTHER WHO CAN'T GET OVER THE DIVORCE, YOU CREEPY WEIRDO!
OUCH, OUCH.
OOH, YOU'RE SULKING.
BUT IT WOULD BE A WASTE TO DISAPPEAR OVER SOMETHING THAT TRIVIAL, DON'T YOU SEE?

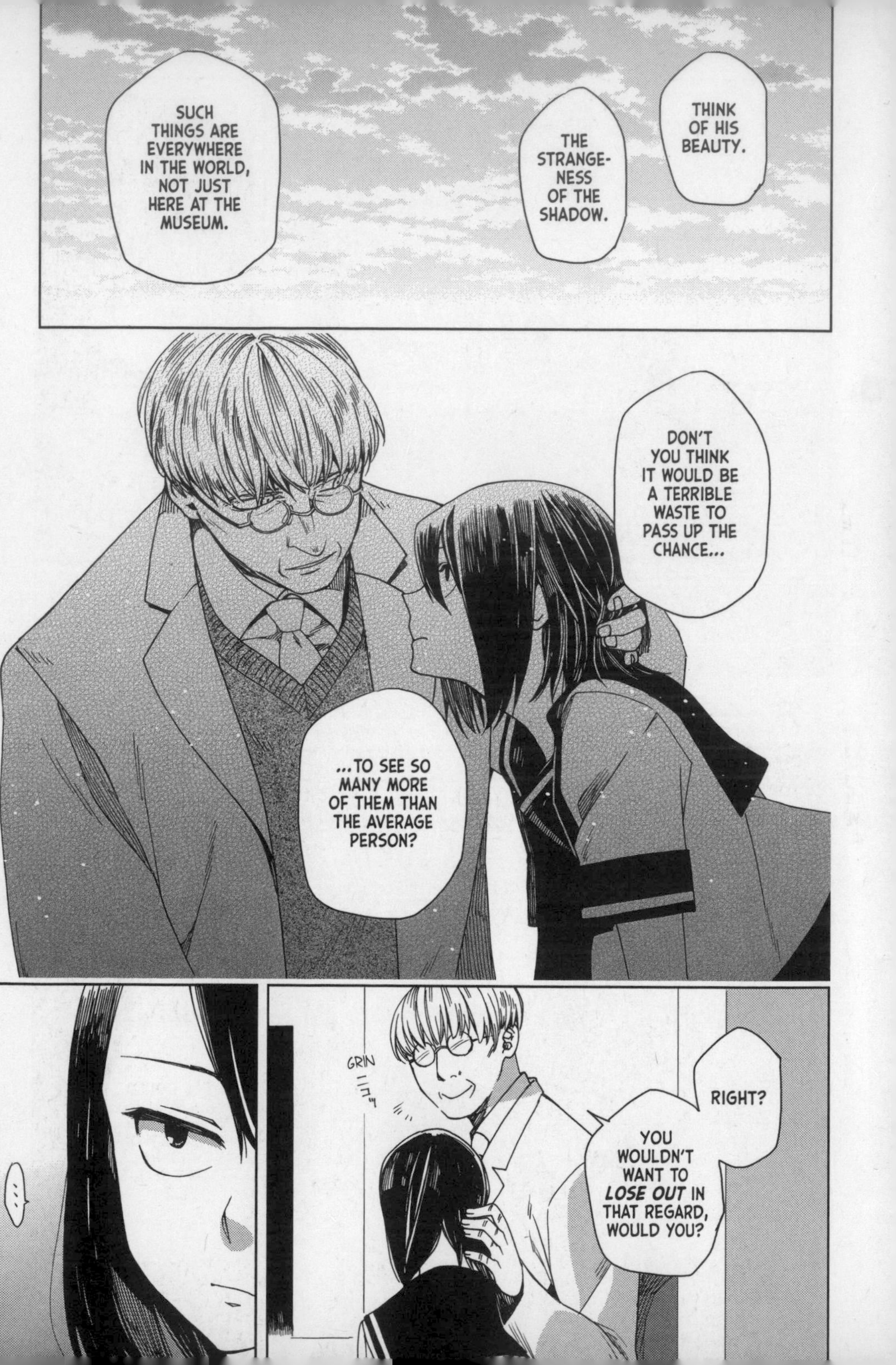
THINK OF HIS BEAUTY.
THE STRANGENESS OF THE SHADOW.
SUCH THINGS ARE EVERYWHERE IN THE WORLD, NOT JUST HERE AT THE MUSEUM.
DON'T YOU THINK IT WOULD BE A TERRIBLE WASTE TO PASS UP THE CHANCE...
...TO SEE SO MANY MORE OF THEM THAN THE AVERAGE PERSON?
RIGHT?
YOU WOULDN'T WANT TO ***LOSE OUT*** IN THAT REGARD, WOULD YOU?
GRIN
...

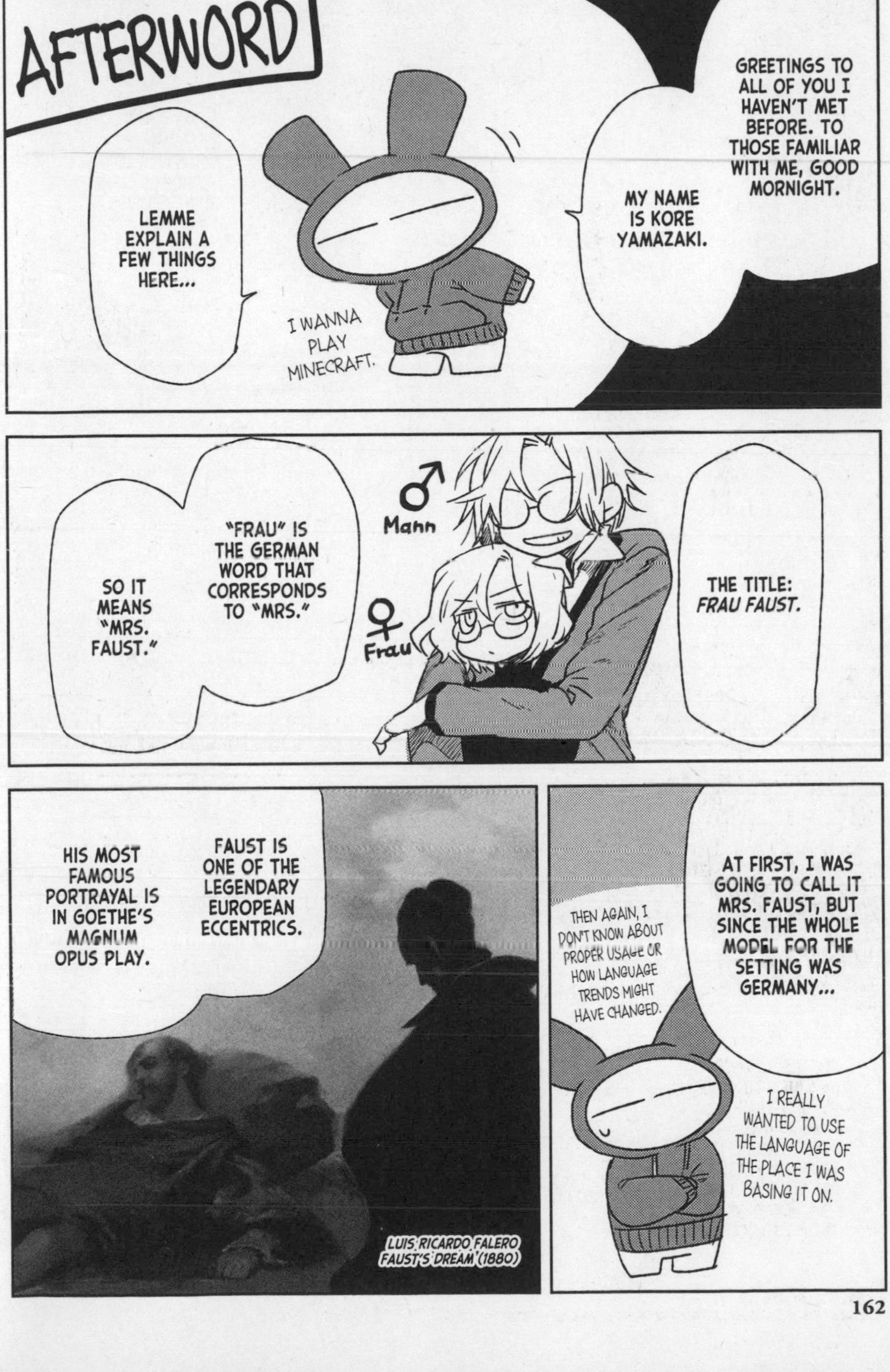
AFTERWORD
GREETINGS TO ALL OF YOU I HAVEN'T MET BEFORE. TO THOSE FAMILIAR WITH ME, GOOD MORNIGHT.
MY NAME IS KORE YAMAZAKI.
LEMME EXPLAIN A FEW THINGS HERE...
I WANNA PLAY MINECRAFT.
THE TITLE: *FRAU FAUST.*
♂ Mann
♀ Frau
"FRAU" IS THE GERMAN WORD THAT CORRESPONDS TO "MRS."
SO IT MEANS "MRS. FAUST."
AT FIRST, I WAS GOING TO CALL IT MRS. FAUST, BUT SINCE THE WHOLE MODEL FOR THE SETTING WAS GERMANY...
THEN AGAIN, I DON'T KNOW ABOUT PROPER USAGE OR HOW LANGUAGE TRENDS MIGHT HAVE CHANGED.
I REALLY WANTED TO USE THE LANGUAGE OF THE PLACE I WAS BASING IT ON.
FAUST IS ONE OF THE LEGENDARY EUROPEAN ECCENTRICS.
HIS MOST FAMOUS PORTRAYAL IS IN GOETHE'S MAGNUM OPUS PLAY.
LUIS RICARDO FALERO
FAUST'S DREAM (1880)

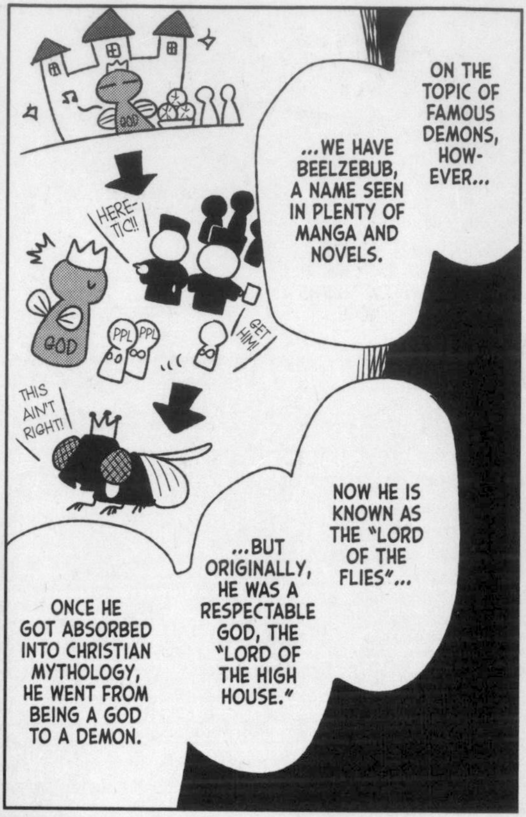
ON THE TOPIC OF FAMOUS DEMONS, HOWEVER...
...WE HAVE BEELZEBUB, A NAME SEEN IN PLENTY OF MANGA AND NOVELS.
GOD
HERETIC!!
GOD
PPL
PPL
GET HIM!
THIS AIN'T RIGHT!
NOW HE IS KNOWN AS THE "LORD OF THE FLIES"...
...BUT ORIGINALLY, HE WAS A RESPECTABLE GOD, THE "LORD OF THE HIGH HOUSE."
ONCE HE GOT ABSORBED INTO CHRISTIAN MYTHOLOGY, HE WENT FROM BEING A GOD TO A DEMON.

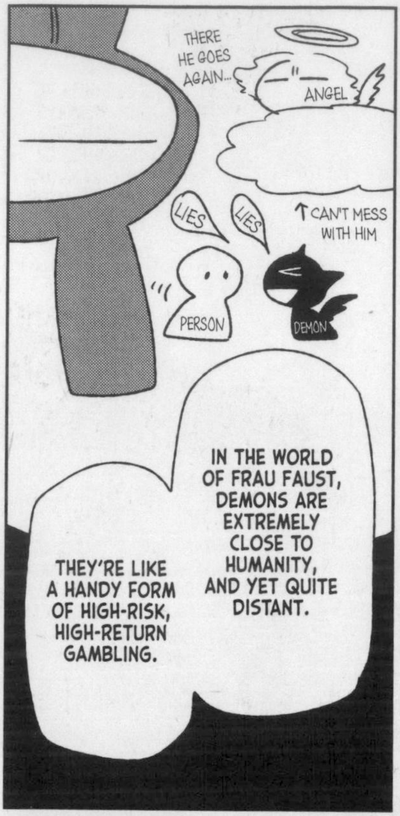
THERE HE GOES AGAIN...
ANGEL
↑CAN'T MESS WITH HIM
LIES
LIES
PERSON
DEMON
IN THE WORLD OF FRAU FAUST, DEMONS ARE EXTREMELY CLOSE TO HUMANITY, AND YET QUITE DISTANT.
THEY'RE LIKE A HANDY FORM OF HIGH-RISK, HIGH-RETURN GAMBLING.

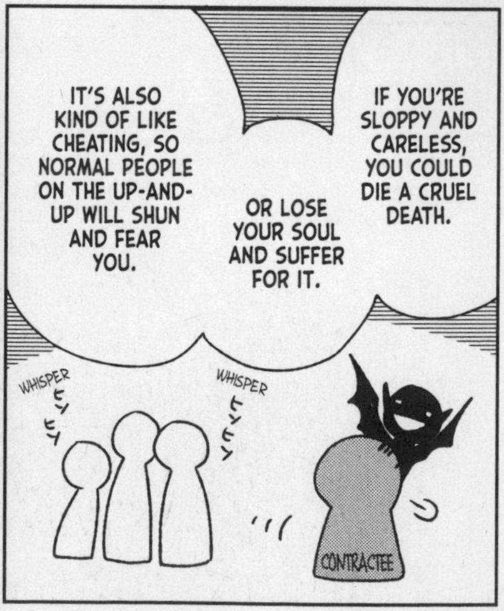
IF YOU'RE SLOPPY AND CARELESS, YOU COULD DIE A CRUEL DEATH.
OR LOSE YOUR SOUL AND SUFFER FOR IT.
IT'S ALSO KIND OF LIKE CHEATING, SO NORMAL PEOPLE ON THE UP-AND-UP WILL SHUN AND FEAR YOU.
WHISPER
WHISPER
CONTRACTEE

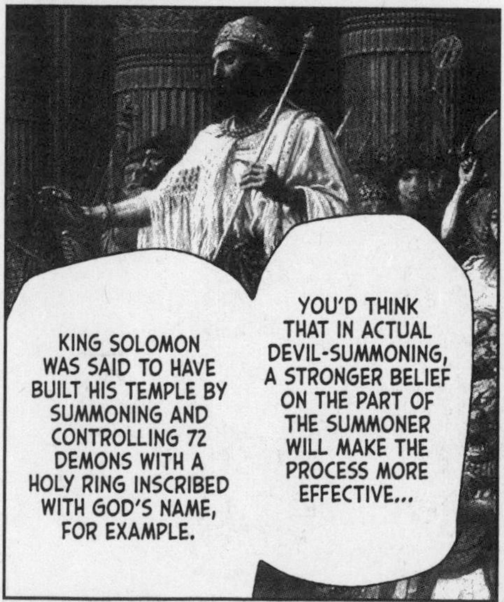
YOU'D THINK THAT IN ACTUAL DEVIL-SUMMONING, A STRONGER BELIEF ON THE PART OF THE SUMMONER WILL MAKE THE PROCESS MORE EFFECTIVE...
KING SOLOMON WAS SAID TO HAVE BUILT HIS TEMPLE BY SUMMONING AND CONTROLLING 72 DEMONS WITH A HOLY RING INSCRIBED WITH GOD'S NAME, FOR EXAMPLE.

EDWARD JOHN POYNTER
THE VISIT OF THE QUEEN OF SHEBA TO KING SOLOMON (1890)

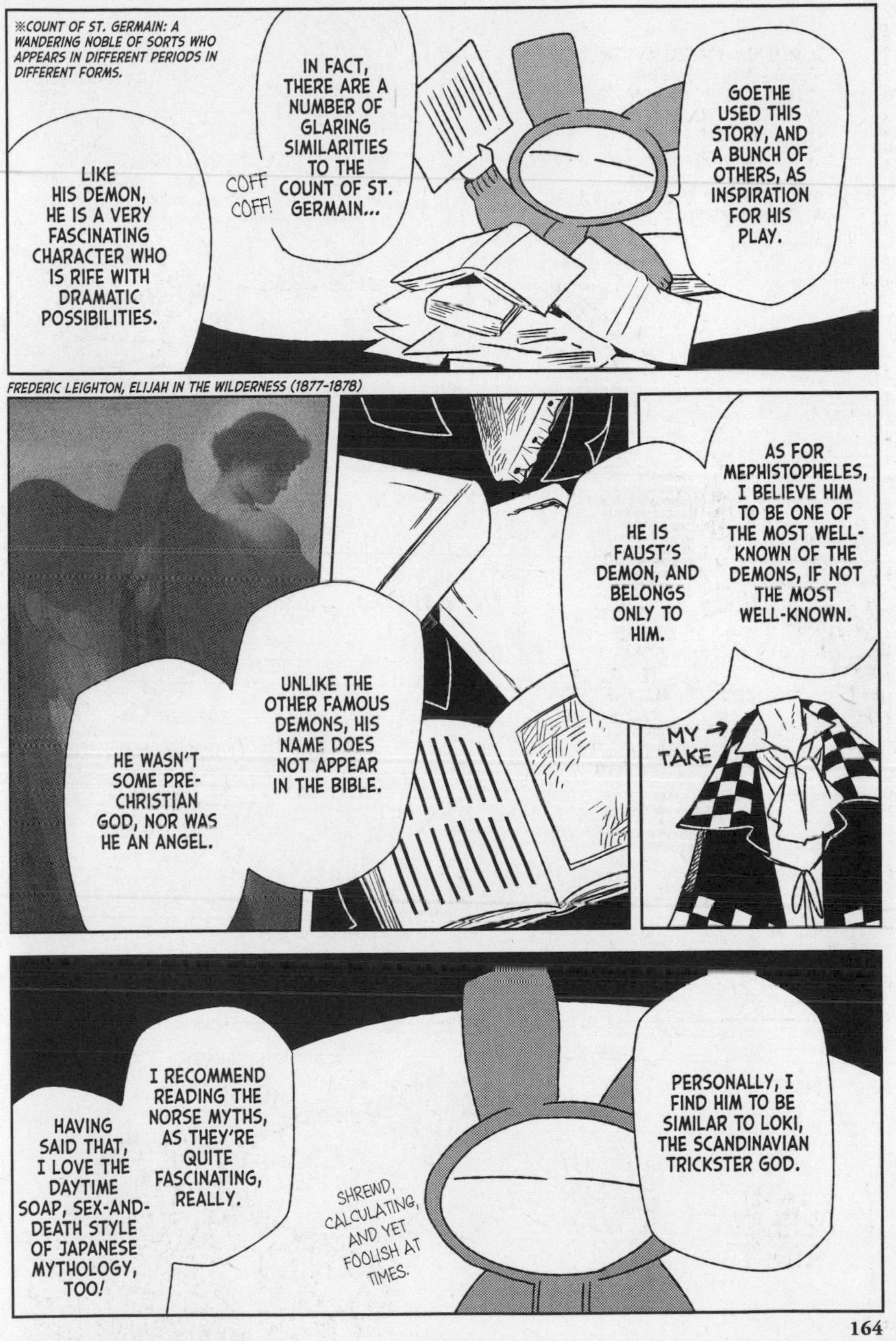
GOETHE USED THIS STORY, AND A BUNCH OF OTHERS, AS INSPIRATION FOR HIS PLAY.
IN FACT, THERE ARE A NUMBER OF GLARING SIMILARITIES TO THE COUNT OF ST. GERMAIN...
COFF COFF!
LIKE HIS DEMON, HE IS A VERY FASCINATING CHARACTER WHO IS RIFE WITH DRAMATIC POSSIBILITIES.
※COUNT OF ST. GERMAIN: A WANDERING NOBLE OF SORTS WHO APPEARS IN DIFFERENT PERIODS IN DIFFERENT FORMS.
AS FOR MEPHISTOPHELES, I BELIEVE HIM TO BE ONE OF THE MOST WELL-KNOWN OF THE DEMONS, IF NOT THE MOST WELL-KNOWN.
HE IS FAUST'S DEMON, AND BELONGS ONLY TO HIM.
MY TAKE
UNLIKE THE OTHER FAMOUS DEMONS, HIS NAME DOES NOT APPEAR IN THE BIBLE.
FREDERIC LEIGHTON, ELIJAH IN THE WILDERNESS (1877-1878)
HE WASN'T SOME PRE-CHRISTIAN GOD, NOR WAS HE AN ANGEL.
PERSONALLY, I FIND HIM TO BE SIMILAR TO LOKI, THE SCANDINAVIAN TRICKSTER GOD.
SHREWD, CALCULATING, AND YET FOOLISH AT TIMES.
I RECOMMEND READING THE NORSE MYTHS, AS THEY'RE QUITE FASCINATING, REALLY.
HAVING SAID THAT, I LOVE THE DAYTIME SOAP, SEX-AND-DEATH STYLE OF JAPANESE MYTHOLOGY, TOO!

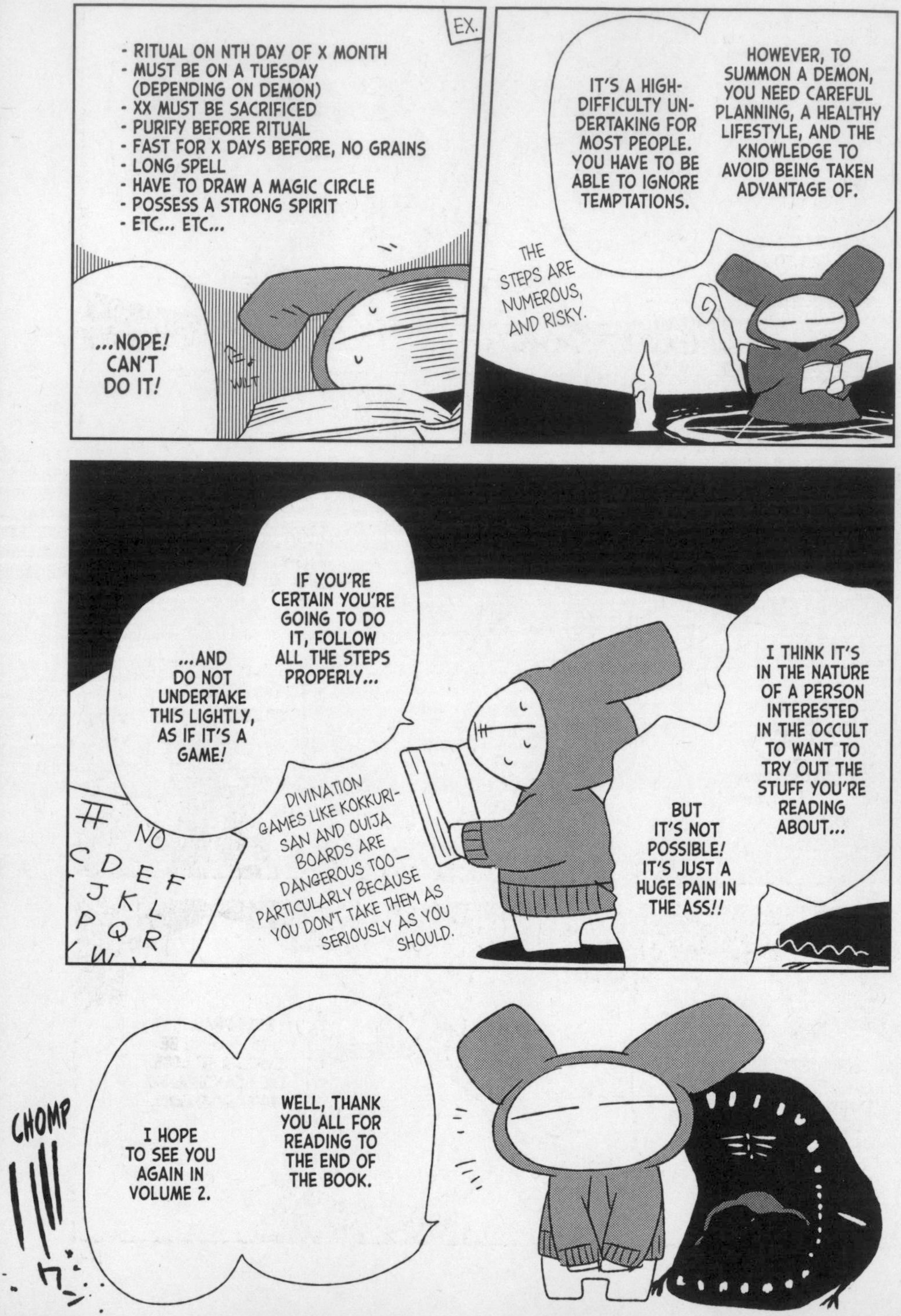
HOWEVER, TO SUMMON A DEMON, YOU NEED CAREFUL PLANNING, A HEALTHY LIFESTYLE, AND THE KNOWLEDGE TO AVOID BEING TAKEN ADVANTAGE OF.
IT'S A HIGH-DIFFICULTY UNDERTAKING FOR MOST PEOPLE. YOU HAVE TO BE ABLE TO IGNORE TEMPTATIONS.
THE STEPS ARE NUMEROUS, AND RISKY.
EX.
- RITUAL ON NTH DAY OF X MONTH
- MUST BE ON A TUESDAY (DEPENDING ON DEMON)
- XX MUST BE SACRIFICED
- PURIFY BEFORE RITUAL
- FAST FOR X DAYS BEFORE, NO GRAINS
- LONG SPELL
- HAVE TO DRAW A MAGIC CIRCLE
- POSSESS A STRONG SPIRIT
- ETC... ETC...
WILT
...NOPE! CAN'T DO IT!
I THINK IT'S IN THE NATURE OF A PERSON INTERESTED IN THE OCCULT TO WANT TO TRY OUT THE STUFF YOU'RE READING ABOUT...
BUT IT'S NOT POSSIBLE! IT'S JUST A HUGE PAIN IN THE ASS!!
IF YOU'RE CERTAIN YOU'RE GOING TO DO IT, FOLLOW ALL THE STEPS PROPERLY...
...AND DO NOT UNDERTAKE THIS LIGHTLY, AS IF IT'S A GAME!
DIVINATION GAMES LIKE KOKKURI-SAN AND OUIJA BOARDS ARE DANGEROUS TOO—PARTICULARLY BECAUSE YOU DON'T TAKE THEM AS SERIOUSLY AS YOU SHOULD.
NO
WELL, THANK YOU ALL FOR READING TO THE END OF THE BOOK.
I HOPE TO SEE YOU AGAIN IN VOLUME 2.
CHOMP

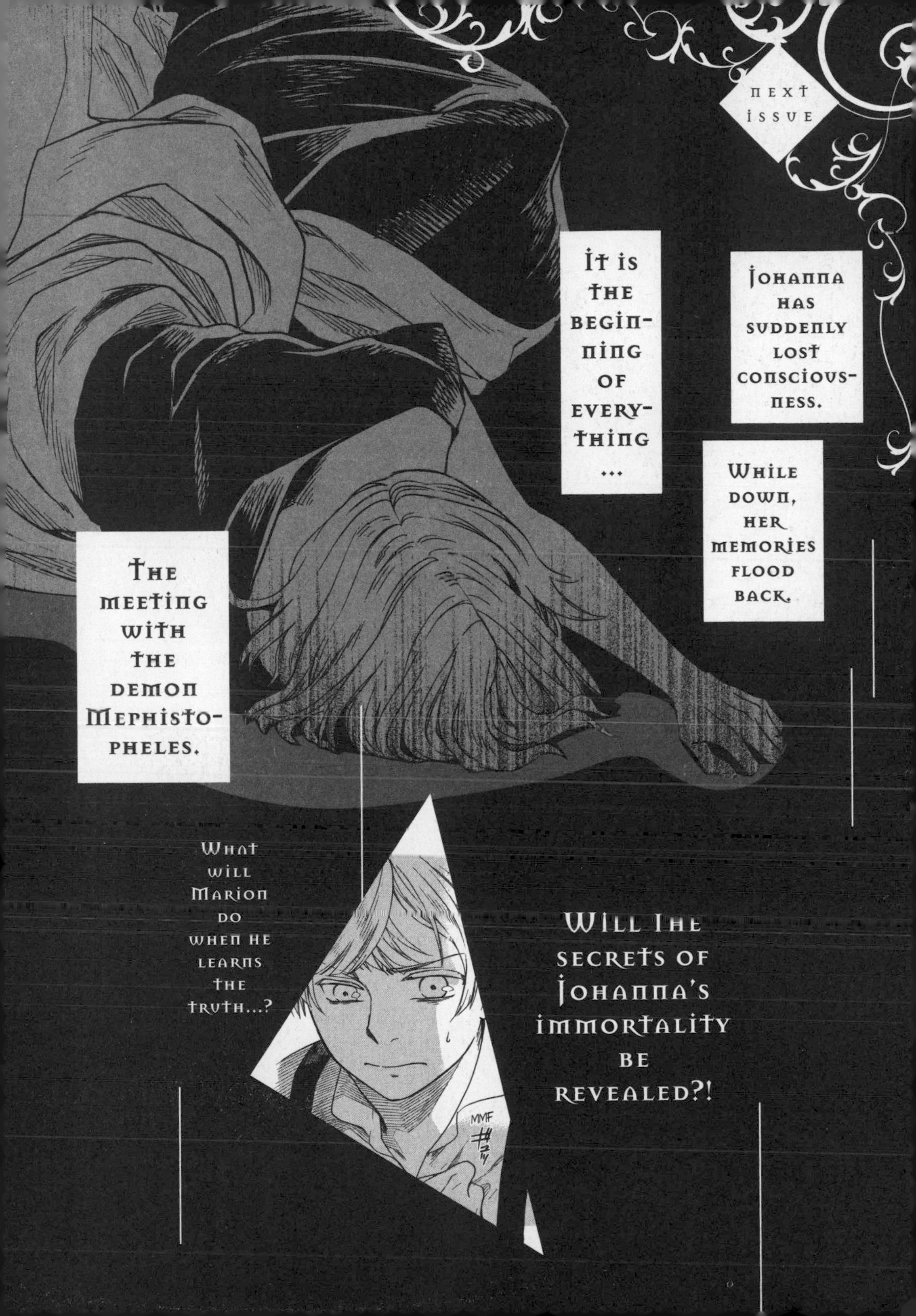
NEXT ISSUE
Johanna has suddenly lost consciousness.
While down, her memories flood back.
It is the begin-ning of every-thing...
The meeting with the demon Mephisto-pheles.
Will the secrets of Johanna's immortality be revealed?!
What will Marion do when he learns the truth...?

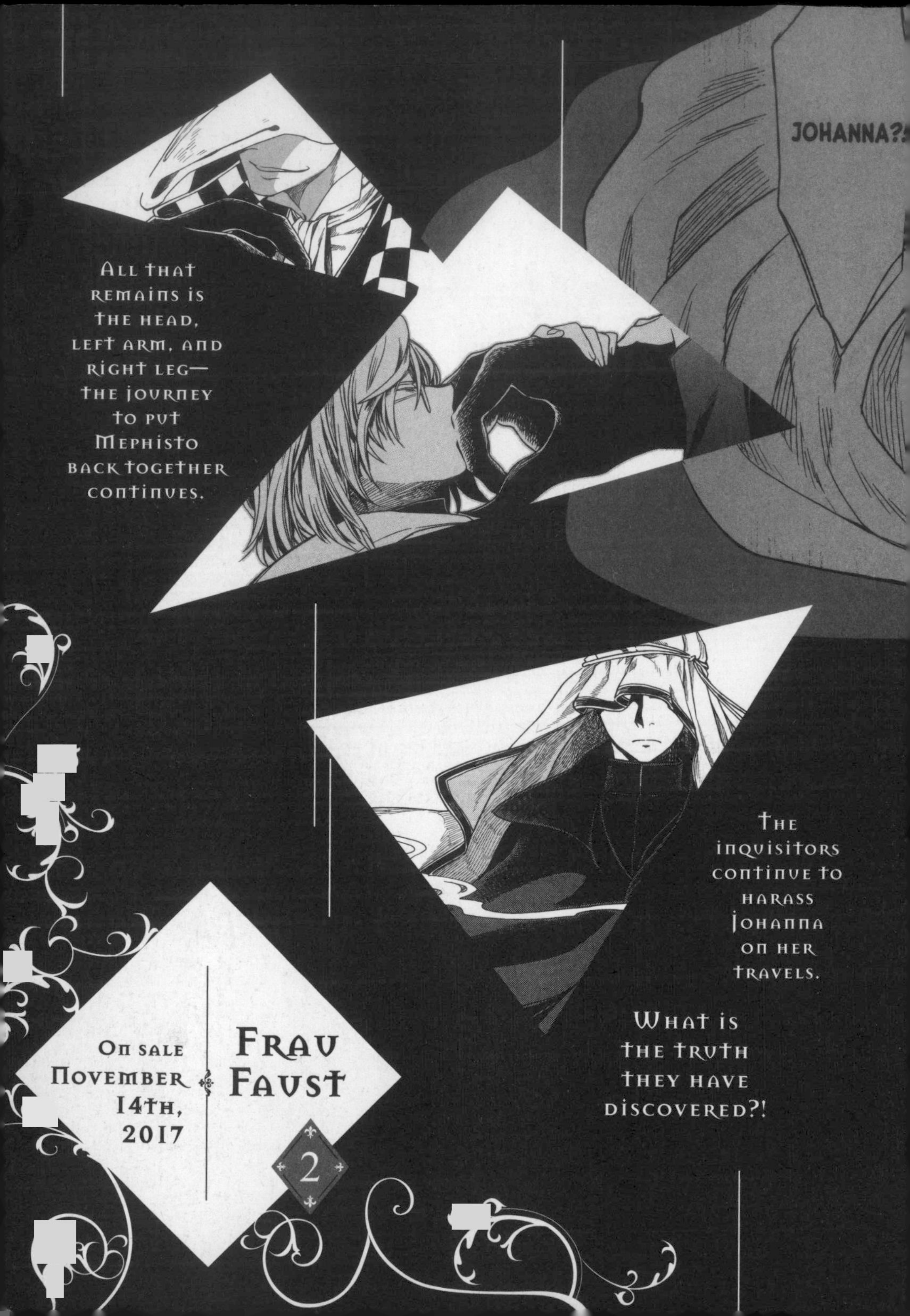
JOHANNA?!
All that remains is the head, left arm, and right leg—the journey to put Mephisto back together continues.
The inquisitors continue to harass Johanna on her travels.
What is the truth they have discovered?!
On sale November 14th, 2017
Frau Faust
2

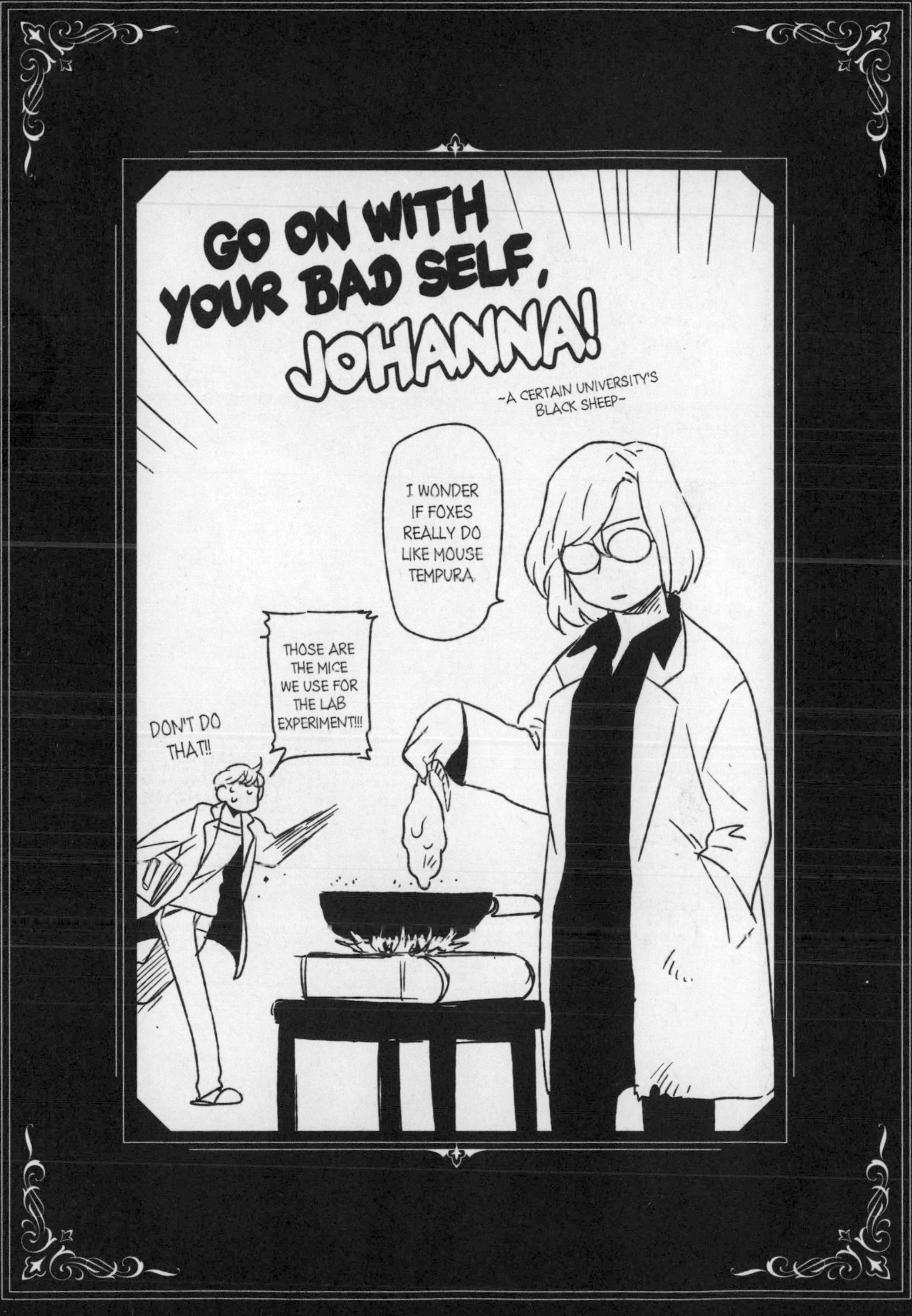
GO ON WITH YOUR BAD SELF, JOHANNA!
~A CERTAIN UNIVERSITY'S BLACK SHEEP~
I WONDER IF FOXES REALLY DO LIKE MOUSE TEMPURA.
THOSE ARE THE MICE WE USE FOR THE LAB EXPERIMENT!!!
DON'T DO THAT!!

GO ON WITH YOUR BAD SELF, JOHANNA!
~A CERTAIN UNIVERSITY'S BLACK SHEEP~
THERE SHE GOES, WORKING ALL NIGHT AGAIN...
WHERE DID THE CATS COME FROM?

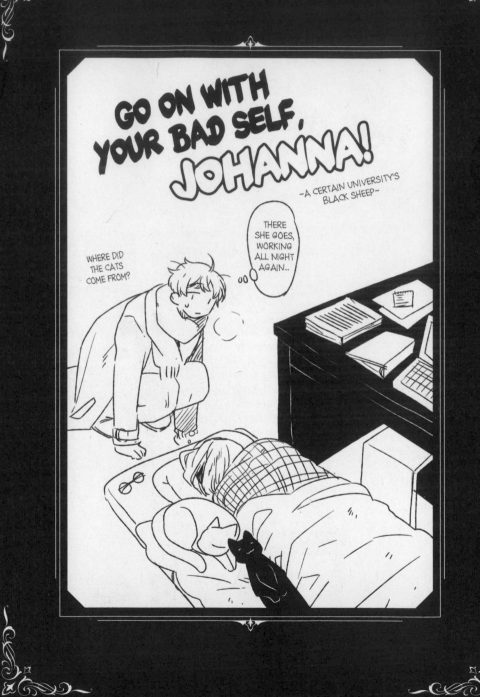

KORE
YAMAZAKI

This is Volume 1
of *Frau Faust*.
Johanna's been
bouncing around in
my head ever since
I was a student,
and now that
vague idea finally
has a solid form.
I hope that you
enjoy it.

TRANSLATION NOTES

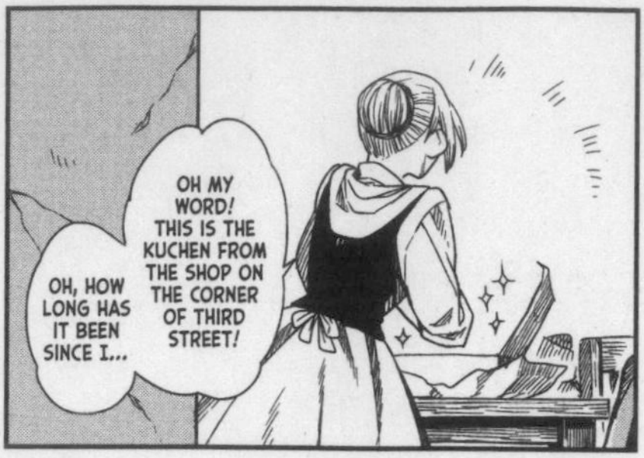
OH MY WORD! THIS IS THE KUCHEN FROM THE SHOP ON THE CORNER OF THIRD STREET!
OH, HOW LONG HAS IT BEEN SINCE I...

Kuchen, page 12
The German word for "cake" or "pastry." It is pronounced koo-hen.

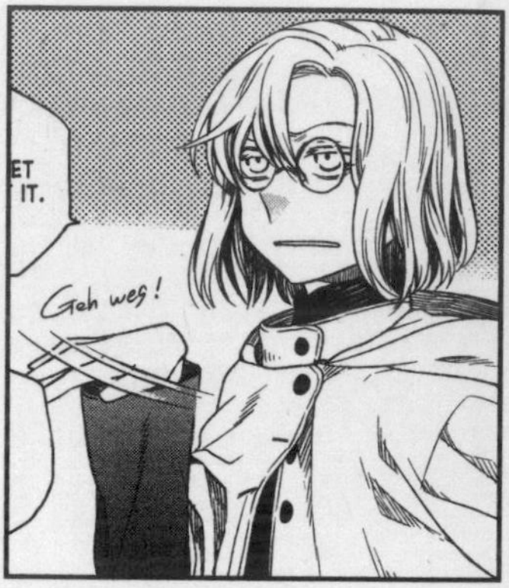
ET IT.
Geh weg!

Geh weg!, page 44
The German phrase for "go away" or "get lost," in case the hand-shooing motion didn't make it clear already.

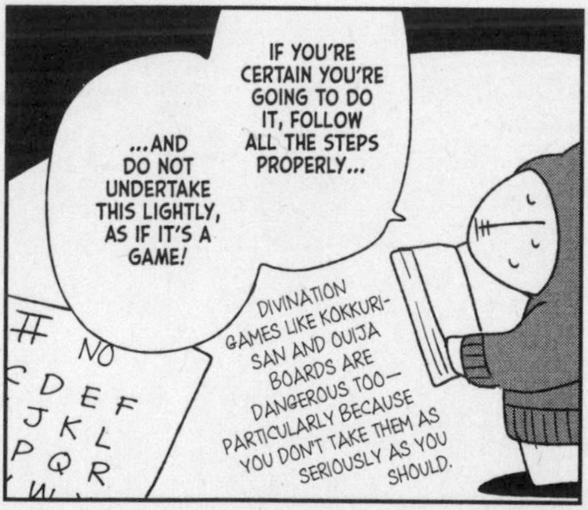
IF YOU'RE CERTAIN YOU'RE GOING TO DO IT, FOLLOW ALL THE STEPS PROPERLY...
...AND DO NOT UNDERTAKE THIS LIGHTLY, AS IF IT'S A GAME!
DIVINATION GAMES LIKE KOKKURI-SAN AND OUIJA BOARDS ARE DANGEROUS TOO—PARTICULARLY BECAUSE YOU DON'T TAKE THEM AS SERIOUSLY AS YOU SHOULD.
NO
D E F
J K L
P Q R

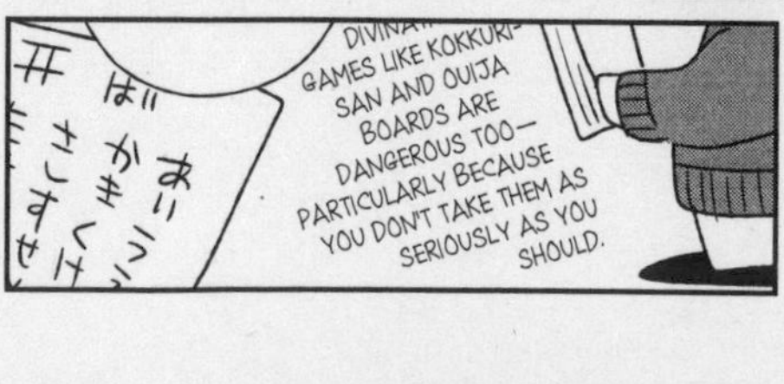
GAMES LIKE KOKKURI-SAN AND OUIJA BOARDS ARE DANGEROUS TOO—PARTICULARLY BECAUSE YOU DON'T TAKE THEM AS SERIOUSLY AS YOU SHOULD.

Kokkuri-san, page 165
Kokkuri-san is a divination game that is very similar to the Western Ouija board. The differences include using a 10-yen coin instead of a spade-shaped finder, using hiragana instead of alphabet letters, and the inclusion of a Japanese style gate (*torii*) in between the YES and NO sections of the board. Outside of those differences, the game is fairly similar in that all participants touch the main game piece, ask questions, and let forces from beyond guide the game piece in response. For quick comprehension, the example image shown in this volume was changed to the English equivalent, but the Japanese version can be seen in the image on this page.

The Black Museum The Ghost and the Lady

By Kazuhiro Fujita

Deep in Scotland Yard in London sits an evidence room dedicated to the greatest mysteries of British history. In this "Black Museum" sits a misshapen hunk of lead—two bullets fused together—the key to a wartime encounter between Florence Nightingale, the mother of modern nursing, and a supernatural Man in Grey. This story is unknown to most scholars of history, but a special guest of the museum will tell the tale of The Ghost and the Lady...

Praise for Kazuhiro Fujita's *Ushio and Tora*

"A charming revival that combines a classic look with modern depth and pacing... **Essential viewing both for curmudgeons and new fans alike.**" — Anime News Network

"**GREAT!** The first episode of Ushio and Tora captures the essence of '90s anime." — IGN

HAPPINESS

——ハピネス——

By Shuzo Oshimi

From the creator of *The Flowers of Evil*

Nothing interesting is happening in Makoto Ozaki's first year of high school. His life is a series of quiet humiliations: low-grade bullies, unreliable friends, and the constant frustration of his adolescent lust. But one night, a pale, thin girl knocks him to the ground in an alley and offers him a choice. Now everything is different. Daylight is searingly bright. Food tastes awful. And worse than anything is the terrible, consuming thirst...

Praise for Shuzo Oshimi's *The Flowers of Evil*

"A shockingly readable story that vividly—one might even say queasily—evokes the fear and confusion of discovering one's own sexuality. Recommended." —The Manga Critic

"A page-turning tale of sordid middle school blackmail." —Otaku USA Magazine

"A stunning new horror manga." —Third Eye Comics

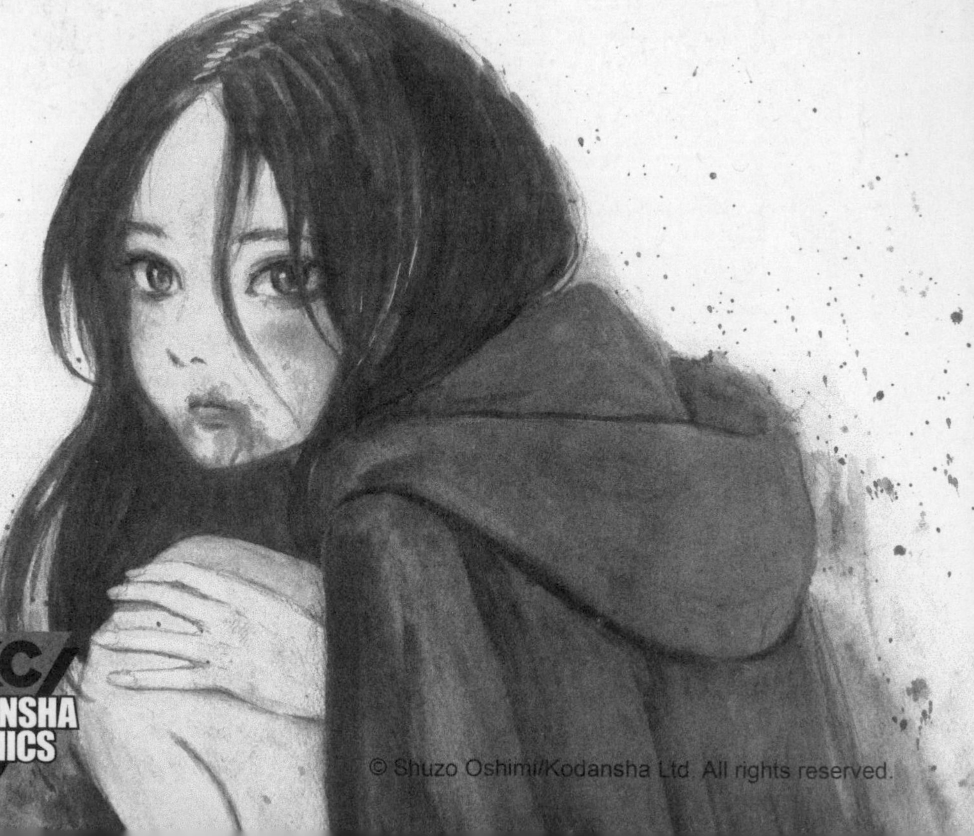

KC KODANSHA COMICS

Japan's most powerful spirit medium delves into the ghost world's greatest mysteries!

Story by Kyo Shirodaira, famed author of mystery fiction and creator of *Spiral*, *Blast of Tempest*, and *The Record of a Fallen Vampire*.

Both touched by spirits called yôkai, Kotoko and Kurô have gained unique superhuman powers. But to gain her powers Kotoko has given up an eye and a leg, and Kurô's personal life is in shambles. So when Kotoko suggests they team up to deal with renegades from the spirit world, Kurô doesn't have many other choices, but Kotoko might just have a few ulterior motives...

IN/SPECTRE

STORY BY KYO SHIRODAIRA
ART BY CHASHIBA KATASE

"An emotional and artistic tour de force! We see incredible triumph, and crushing defeat... each panel [is] a thrill!"
—Anitay

"A journey that's instantly compelling."
—Anime News Network

WELCOME TO THE BALLROOM

By Tomo Takeuchi

Feckless high school student Tatara Fujita wants to be good at something—anything. Unfortunately, he's about as average as a slouchy teen can be. The local bullies know this, and make it a habit to hit him up for cash, but all that changes when the debonair Kaname Sengoku sends them packing. Sengoku's not the neighborhood watch, though. He's a professional ballroom dancer. And once Tatara Fujita gets pulled into the world of ballroom, his life will never be the same.

KC
KODANSHA COMICS

A Kodansha Comics Trade Paperback Original.

Frau Faust volume 1 copyright © 2015 Kore Yamazaki
English translation copyright © 2017 Kore Yamazaki

Published in the United States by Kodansha Comics, an imprint of Kodansha USA Publishing, LLC, New York.

Publication rights for this English edition arranged through Kodansha Ltd., Tokyo.

First published in Japan in 2015 by Kodansha Ltd., Tokyo, as *Frau Faust* volume 1.

ISBN 978-1-63236-480-7

Printed in the United States of America.

www.kodanshacomics.com

9 8 7 6 5 4 3 2 1

Translation: Stephen Paul
Lettering: Lys Blakeslee
Editing: Ajani Oloye
Kodansha Comics edition cover design: Phil Balsman

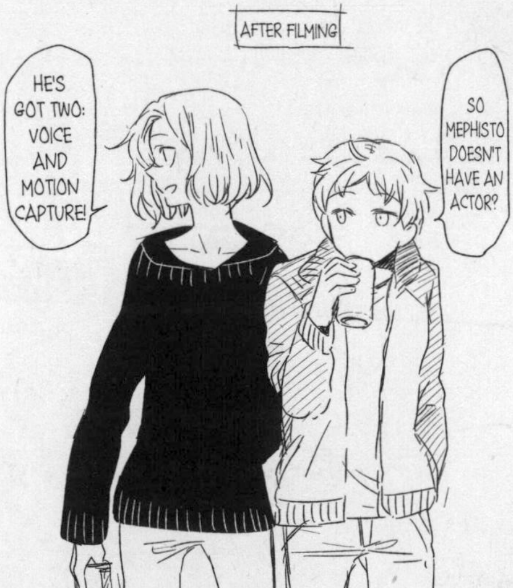
AFTER FILMING
SO MEPHISTO DOESN'T HAVE AN ACTOR?
HE'S GOT TWO: VOICE AND MOTION CAPTURE!

ON CALL

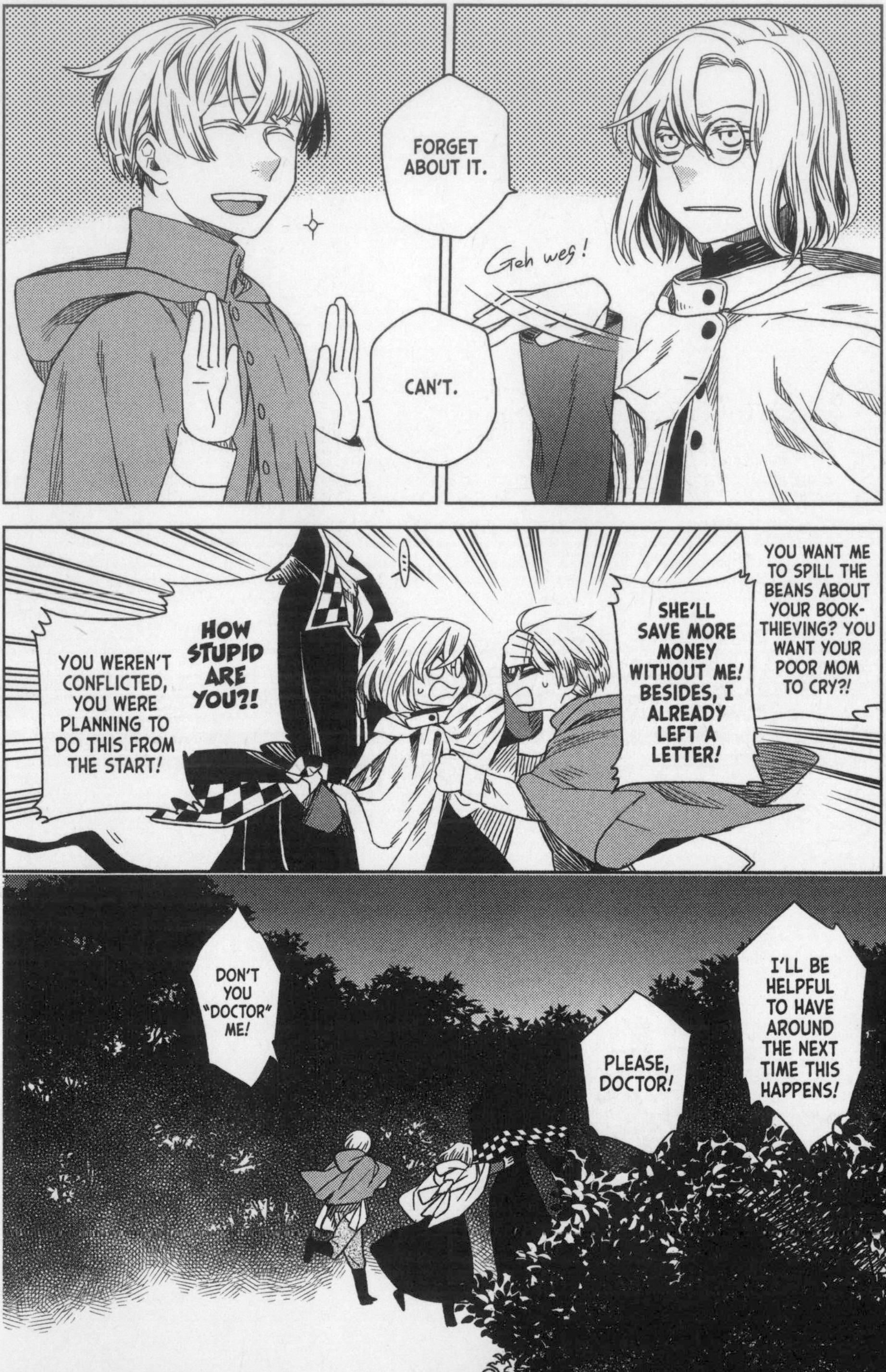
FORGET ABOUT IT.
Geh weg!
CAN'T.
YOU WANT ME TO SPILL THE BEANS ABOUT YOUR BOOK-THIEVING? YOU WANT YOUR POOR MOM TO CRY?!
SHE'LL SAVE MORE MONEY WITHOUT ME! BESIDES, I ALREADY LEFT A LETTER!
...
HOW STUPID ARE YOU?!
YOU WEREN'T CONFLICTED, YOU WERE PLANNING TO DO THIS FROM THE START!
I'LL BE HELPFUL TO HAVE AROUND THE NEXT TIME THIS HAPPENS!
PLEASE, DOCTOR!
DON'T YOU "DOCTOR" ME!

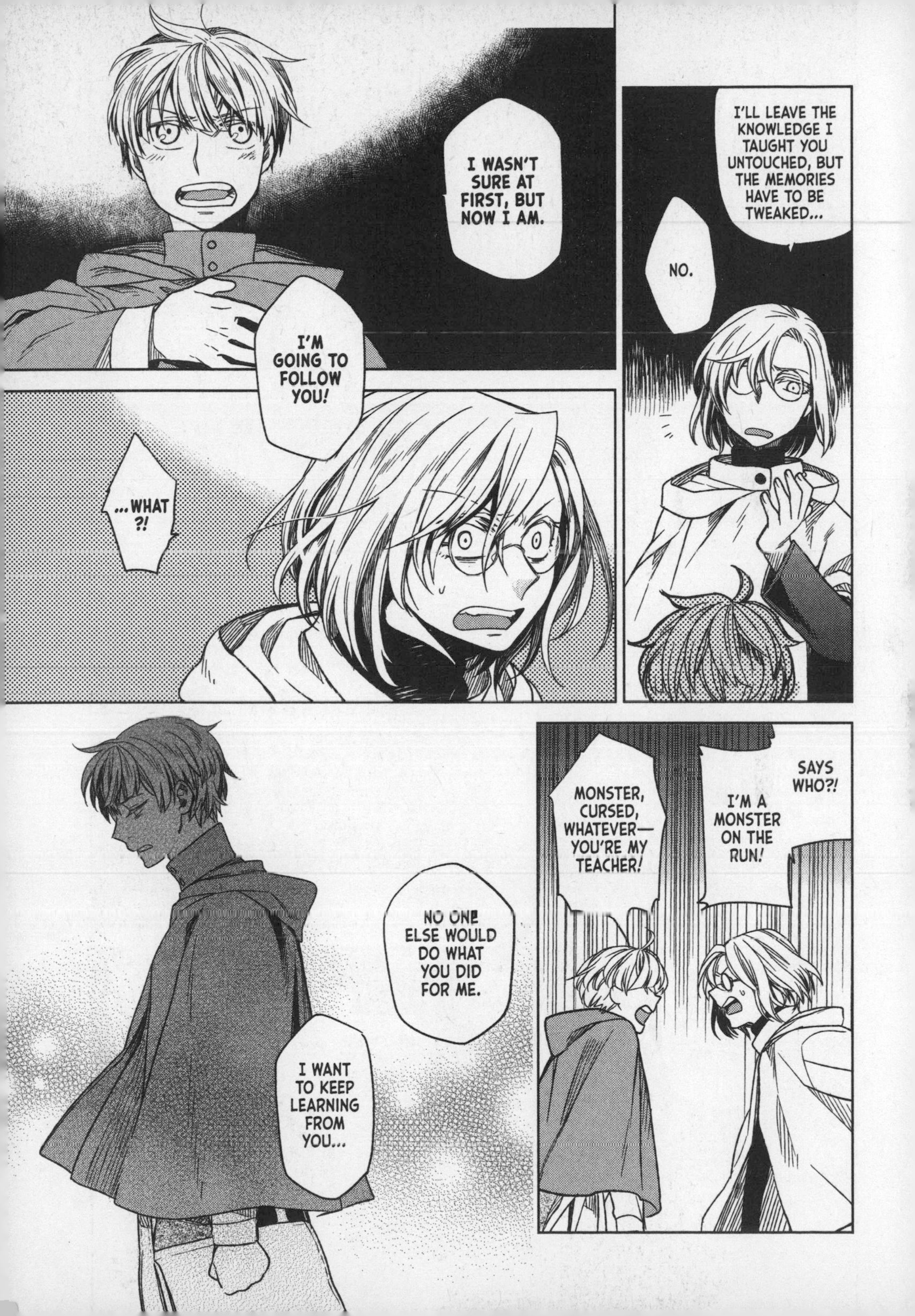
I'LL LEAVE THE KNOWLEDGE I TAUGHT YOU UNTOUCHED, BUT THE MEMORIES HAVE TO BE TWEAKED...
NO.
I WASN'T SURE AT FIRST, BUT NOW I AM.
I'M GOING TO FOLLOW YOU!
...WHAT?!
SAYS WHO?!
I'M A MONSTER ON THE RUN!
MONSTER, CURSED, WHATEVER— YOU'RE MY TEACHER!
NO ONE ELSE WOULD DO WHAT YOU DID FOR ME.
I WANT TO KEEP LEARNING FROM YOU...

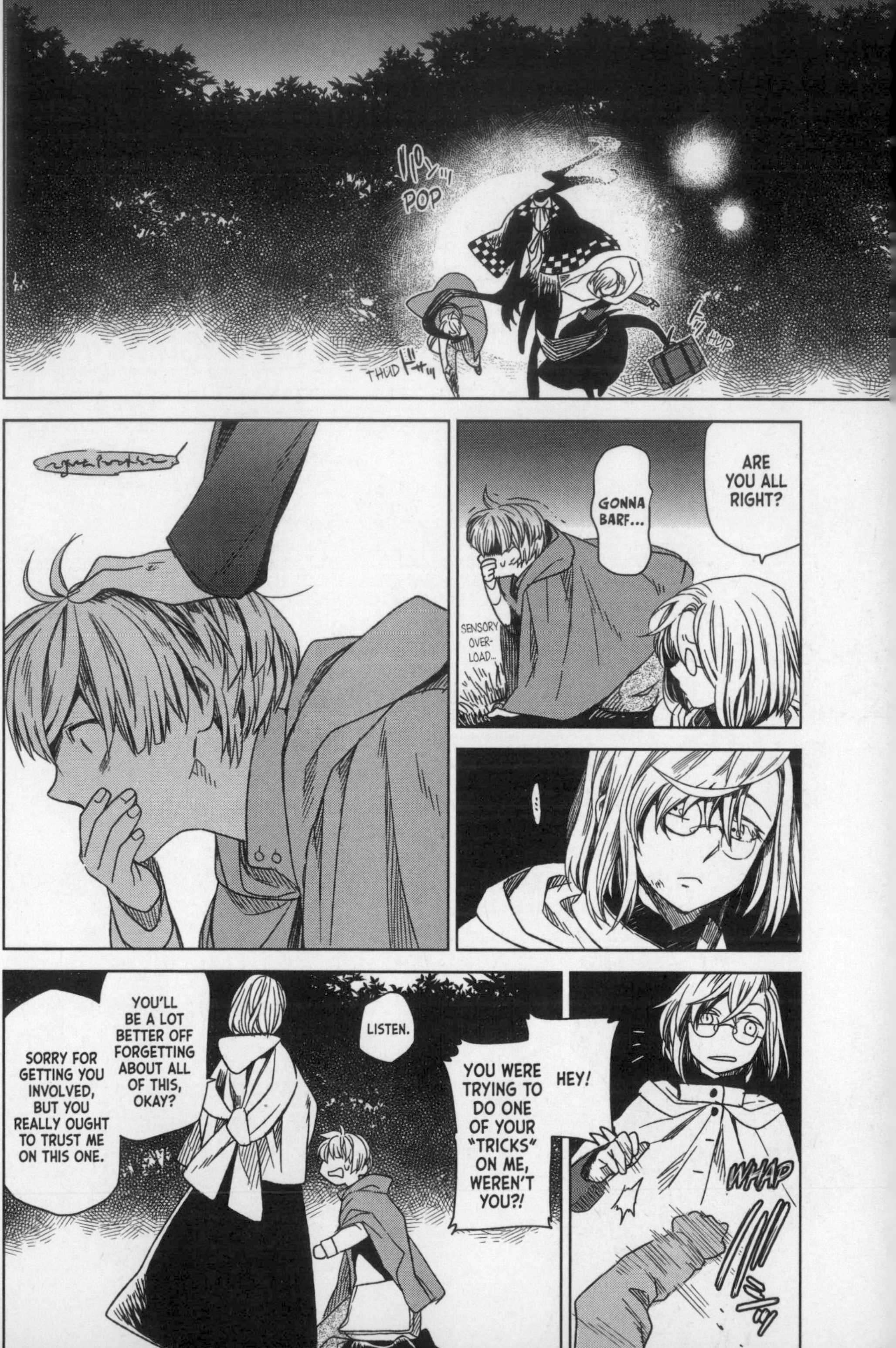
HUP
POP
THUD
ARE YOU ALL RIGHT?
GONNA BARF...
SENSORY OVER-LOAD...
...
HEY!
YOU WERE TRYING TO DO ONE OF YOUR "TRICKS" ON ME, WEREN'T YOU?!
WHAP
LISTEN.
YOU'LL BE A LOT BETTER OFF FORGETTING ABOUT ALL OF THIS, OKAY?
SORRY FOR GETTING YOU INVOLVED, BUT YOU REALLY OUGHT TO TRUST ME ON THIS ONE.